STUDIES OF THE EAST ASIAN INSTITUTE

THE EAST ASIAN INSTITUTE
OF COLUMBIA UNIVERSITY

The East Asian Institute of Columbia University was established in 1949 to prepare graduate students for careers dealing with East Asia, and to aid research and publication on East Asia during the modern period. The faculty of the Institute are grateful to the Ford Foundation and the Rockefeller Foundation for their financial assistance.

The Studies of the East Asian Institute were inaugurated in 1962 to bring to a wider public the results of significant new research on modern and contemporary East Asia.

Embassy at War

HAROLD JOYCE NOBLE

Edited with an Introduction by Frank Baldwin

UNIVERSITY OF WASHINGTON PRESS

Seattle & London

Library of Congress Cataloging in Publication Data

Noble, Harold Joyce, 1903-1953.
  Embassy at war.
  (Studies of the East Asian Institute)
  Includes bibliographical references and index.
  1. Korean War, 1950-1953—United States. 2. United
States—Foreign relations—Korea. 3. Korea—Foreign
realtions—United States. I. Baldwin, Frank, ed.
II. Title. III. Series: Columbia University. East
Asian Institute. Studies.
DS919.N6   1975   951.9'042   74-23645
ISBN 0-295-95341-1

Editor's Introduction

The Man

AROLD JOYCE NOBLE was tempered by the soil,
the winds and the shifting fortunes of twentieth century
Korea and Northeast Asia. He lived through and participated in the metamorphosis of modern Korea: from monarchy
to protectorate to colony of Japan to abortive freedom in 1945 to par-
tition into two Koreas, one north and one south of the artificial dividing line, the 38th parallel. He assisted at the birth of the Republic of
Korea in 1948 and saw the peninsula set aflame by civil war in 1950.
His death in 1953, five months after the armistice agreement returned
Korea to the status quo ante bellum, prematurely ended a close association with the country and its people across a tumultuous half
century.

Harold Noble was born in P'yŏngyang, Korea, on January 10,
1903, in the last years of the Yi dynasty, one year before the Russo-
Japanese War swirled around Korea. His parents were Presbyterian missionaries, Dr. William Arthur Noble and Mattie Wilcox
Noble, who had gone to Korea in the 1890s. Harold was four when
Emperor Kojong was forced to abdicate in favor of his son Sunjong
by the Japanese resident general in 1907. He was in elementary
school in P'yŏngyang when Korea lost its national existence through
annexation into the Japanese empire in 1910.

Noble returned to the United States for secondary school and
college, missing the nationwide nationalistic uprising for independence in 1919 and the adjustments in Japanese colonial policy of
the early 1920s. After receiving his A.B. from Ohio Wesleyan in
1924 and an M.A. from Ohio State the following year, he returned

to Korea to teach at Ehwa College in Seoul, a missionary-operated school for Korean women, from 1926 to 1928. In 1929, with rare personal knowledge of Japan and Korea, he entered the University of California at Berkeley to study for a doctorate in history and Oriental studies. He was a teaching fellow, wrote his dissertation on *Korea and Her Relations with the United States before 1895,* and received his Ph.D. in 1931.

In the same year he was appointed assistant professor of Far Eastern history at the University of Oregon at Eugene. Promotions to associate professor in 1934 and full professor in 1945 were to follow. Noble published seven scholarly articles on Korea between 1928 and 1941, wrote several book reviews, and served as an associate editor of the *Far Eastern Quarterly.* He later was a member of the editorial board of the *Pacific Historical Review* and chairman of a committee on awards in Pacific history of the American Historical Association. He returned to Japan as a professor at the Third College in Kyoto in 1939-40, on the eve of World War II, an experience that determined his subsequent military assignments.

Harold Noble served in the U.S. Marine Corps from 1942 to 1944, attaining the rank of major, as a combat intelligence and Japanese language officer. His duties included periods as company commander and division headquarters commandant in the 3rd Marine Division. He served in New Zealand, New Caledonia, and the Solomon Islands, receiving a navy commendation ribbon for an act of "outstanding bravery and devotion to duty" in November 1943 on Bougainville.

Harold Noble started a second career, journalism, before World War II ended. He began writing about Japan and the Far East for the *Saturday Evening Post* in the spring of 1945. An article entitled "Give the Devils Their Due" (May 1945) emphasized the skill and dedication of Japanese military forces, rejecting the popular wartime view that Japanese soldiers were subhuman fanatics. A second article in the *Post* in September 1945, "What It Takes to Rule Japan," became a theme of Noble's work for two years. The two *Post* articles were published as a book, *What It Takes to Rule Japan,* in 1946. He went to Japan in 1946 as a *Saturday Evening Post* correspondent and published five major articles on the U.S. occupation of Japan. The articles, averaging

4,100 words in length, appeared from July 1946 to April 1947. Noble wrote of reforms in Japanese education, the postwar role of Emperor Hirohito, Japanese disenchantment with former military leaders and soldiers, and the rise of the Left in Japan. He was consistently sympathetic to General MacArthur's command and apprehensive of Communist gains in Japan.

During 1946-47 Noble branched out to write lengthy single pieces for the *Post* on Australia, China, and Korea. "Australia Wakes Up a Pacific Power" (March 1947) explained Australia's vindictive policy toward defeated Japan and took exception to the White Australia policy. Noble wrote that "today, with the rise of China and India, with the development of a free Philippines and with a nascent Indonesian Republic, this racial creed will have heavy going as a cornerstone of Australian Pacific policy."

The articles on China and Korea were especially interesting. Writing from Tsingtao, Noble asked "Should We Pull Out of China?" (September 1946). After describing the activities of U.S. Marines in China and the successes of the Communist forces, Noble advocated extensive U.S. military support for the Nationalists. With the forcefulness and hard-line anticommunism that marks much of his writing on policy and political questions, he urged that "instead of transports being San Diego-bound filled with returning reservists and other long-service men, while returning nearly empty to north China, the transport-loading plan ought to be reversed."

Noble predicted a certain Communist victory if the Nationalists were not shored up by U.S. troops. He warned, however, that it would require massive U.S. military support to defeat the Communists and stated that if such a U.S. troop commitment could not be made, "we should cut our losses, shut our eyes to the future and bring the boys home."

The Korea article was prophetically entitled "Our Most Dangerous Boundary" (August 1946). Writing of the 38th parallel, Noble noted that "not many Americans are yet aware of the significance of this line through the middle of the Korean peninsula." He described the breakdown of U.S.-Soviet negotiations in Korea in 1946 and argued that "once our troops are gone from Korea there will be no way to stop the Russians from controlling the whole country." Noble attributed all responsibility to the Russians for the negotiations' failure. He also minimized the role of indigenous Korean Communists in the north, regarding North Korea as a creature of the Soviet Union. In a follow-up article, almost 10,000 words in length, in *The New Leader* in May 1947, Noble dissected North Korea's claims to democracy and praised the "nascent democratic society" in the south. He did not quarrel with the need to reform in Korea but opposed Communist methods. He wrote: "There are many abuses needing correction in Korea, exorbitant interest rates, extensive absentee landlordism, fantastic rents and horrible industrial working conditions. But only a Communist would claim that these evils can be corrected solely by Communist authoritarianism."

Opposition to North Korean communism and staunch support for the south were hallmarks of Harold Noble's views on Korea.

Harold Noble shifted to government service with the U.S. occupations of Japan and Korea in 1947. He was chief of the Publications Branch, Civil Intelligence Section, General Headquarters, Far East Command, Tokyo, in 1947-48. In 1948 he moved to Korea as chief of the Political Liaison Office, Headquarters, U.S. Army Forces in Korea and political adviser to the commanding general, Lt. Gen. John R. Hodge. The spring and summer of 1948 was a difficult and precarious transition period: a serious uprising on Cheju island was suppressed with great ferocity, and elections were held in May for a national assembly, which subsequently drafted and promulgated a constitution and elected Syngman Rhee as president. American military government ended and the Republic of Korea came into existence on August 15, 1948.

The locus of U.S. efforts to obtain international support and legitimization for the new Republic of Korea shifted to the United Nations. Harold Noble was appointed an adviser to the U.S. delegation to the United Nations General Assembly meeting in Paris, September–December 1948. He worked closely with the South Korean delegation and with John Foster Dulles to obtain U.N. sanction for the Republic.

Noble's deep involvement in Korean affairs in 1948 led the new American ambassador to the Republic of Korea, John J. Muccio, to request that he join the embassy as first secretary. It was a natural arrangement for both parties. The uncertain embassy needed a person of Harold Noble's stature to help with relations with the new South Korean government. Noble's long acquaintance with Syngman Rhee, his family's career in Korea, and his personal identification with the viability of the Republic gave him special access to President Rhee and other senior ROK officials. Robert T. Oliver, Syngman Rhee's official biographer, has described the first contact and enduring relationship between the Noble family and Syngman Rhee.

Syngman Rhee's first teacher at Pai Jai [a Methodist school in Seoul] was Dr. W. A. Noble. The first English sentence which Noble taught to the boys in the class Syngman joined was, "His father told him to go to Pai Jai and study chemistry." Years later, in 1912, while Rhee was attending an international Methodist convention in Minneapolis, he asked Noble why he ever thought the boys could profit by starting their study of English in such an unusual way. Noble laughed and replied, "I was just starting a course in chemistry and wanted to get some students!" From Noble, Rhee learned the English alphabet, and to Noble's gentleness, patience, and strength of character he has never ceased to pay tribute. Dr. Noble's son Harold was to have a considerable influence in the later life of Syngman Rhee and a part in the tangled diplomacy which eventuated in the establishment in 1948 of the Republic of Korea.[1]

For Harold Noble the opportunity to serve in Korea again, to shape history in a period of uncertainty and danger, was a great challenge. Personal letters written in the summer of 1949 show his impatience to return to the center of events in Korea.

While awaiting the completion of administrative procedures for his appointment, Noble continued to write about Korea and U.S. Far Eastern policy. He published two articles on Korea in *The New Leader* in May and June 1949. In the first Noble attacked North Korea as a puppet of the USSR where "people's democracy" was a façade for Communist authoritarianism. The second article, "Korea Must Stay Half Free," was part exhortation, part jeremiad. Noble described the genesis of the Republic of Korea and American responsibility for its formation and future existence. He argued against U.S. troop withdrawal (completed that month) and for military and economic aid to South Korea. Congress was then considering a recommendation for $150 million in aid to the Republic. He concluded with a speculative warning about the dangers of war in Korea and wondered what the American response would be.

The test of South Korean capacity to stand alone may begin within the next few months if our troops pull out. The communists' "People Army" has but one mission, the conquest of South Korea. Thousands of their troops already have been battle tested in Manchuria, and all their senior officers have had years of combat experience in the Russian or Chinese communist armies. Do miracles still occur? Can free Korea hope to last through the bitter winter which lies ahead? When spring comes will the patriots of Korea be but a memory of heroism to be pitied and then forgotten?

There were no hostilities that winter, but Harold Noble's fears were amply realized in June 1950. His personal role in those events is the subject of this book.

Harold Noble's final article before his appointment as a Foreign Service reserve officer and assignment to Korea was a strong dissent from State Department policy and advocacy of a bold new effort to forge a Pacific pact to contain communism in Asia. Writing in the *Saturday Evening Post* for July 9, 1949, in an article entitled "We Must Risk a New Policy in China," he found the reason for Communist success in China to lie in American policy errors and urged renewed support for the Chinese Nationalists. He lamented that "many of the same men who during the last five years so strongly advocated a Communist coalition in China are today the very advisers who tell us it was always too late—that it is far too late now, and nothing can be done." Convinced that there was still time to salvage U.S. interests and retard Communist advances, Noble promoted the formation of a "Pacific Periphery Alliance for joint defense." It was to be a "strong, precise, military alliance." A second aspect of the plan was an "Asiatic-Pacific pact" which would be a "multilateral agreement providing for regular consultation of all the Pacific powers which are determined to stop the spread of Communist aggression in Asia."

These ideas of containment and anticommunism were a call for the application to Asia of the United States' foreign policy tenets in force in Europe. Many of Harold Noble's suggestions were to become American Far Eastern policy immediately after the Korean War began. And the formation of multilateral security arrangements, such as the Southeast Asia Treaty Organization and various bilateral military treaties, were a salient feature of the 1950s.

Noble's analysis emphasized traditional American antipathy to colonialism and Wilsonian self-determination as compatible with the emerging forces in Asia. Thus he wrote:

> Over-all policy for the Pacific must have well-recognized spiritual elements as well as concrete machinery to express them. Spiritually, the United States supports the sovereignty and independence of every state in Asia. Every genuine movement for national independence has the sympathy of the American people. No objective Asiatic must be left in any doubt that the United States still follows its century-old policy of support to Asiatic freedom. Nehru's declaration for India, "Our foreign policy is that no foreign power shall rule over any Asiatic country," is an Asiatic Monroe Doctrine which should have wide sympathy in this country. We may recall that for many years British naval power made possible the enforcement of our doctrine for the Americas. We should expect to be of the same assistance to the Nehru declaration that the British were to Monroe's.

Foreign domination—imperialism as a general category—was condemned and Asian nationalism applauded. But what of nationalist movements consanguineous with communism? Were they to be approved because they were nationalist struggles to end foreign domination, or were they to be condemned and thwarted because they were Communist and added incrementally to the power of the Soviet Union? Harold Noble's thoughts adumbrated the American liberals' efforts to find a third direction on a two-way policy street.

> The problem of support to colonial peoples who have not yet achieved their independence is difficult. The nationalistic movement in Indo-China, for instance, is genuine. Yet, as in China, it is perverted by communist leadership for interests which are not local. Similarly, despite the Japanese origins of the Republic of Indonesia and of communist efforts to exploit this region, the nationalist ambitions of the people of Java are genuine. In both areas United States policy must be on a month-to-month basis. In neither area can the United States back the restoration of the prewar colonial empire, or yet support a movement to bring communists into power in Southeast Asia.

Harold Noble's *gestalt* concerning communism and Asian nationalism, in particular his support for Syngman Rhee and the Republic of Korea, are explained in the following: "We prefer democratic states, but our test should be whether the government concerned is determined to maintain its own independence, whether it is friendly toward us and whether it is willing to co-operate with other Asian states with similar views on foreign affairs."

To Harold Noble in 1949 communism appeared monolithic and all Communist movements and successes related to the Soviet Union. A counter-grouping of states into "Free World" and support for "free governments in Asia" became a moral imperative. The internal performance of such allies, their commitment to democracy or preference for fascism, was relatively unimportant compared to their resistance to communism.

The eighteen months as first secretary of the U.S. embassy in Korea, from August 1949 to January 1951, began with Cold War tensions and ended in hot war and disorderly retreat. Noble made the long trek—Seoul to Pusan to P'yŏngyang in 1950—and then flew from a burning Kimp'o airfield on January 4, 1951, hours before the second loss of Seoul. The months were crowded with action and pressure: he was the embassy's chief liaison officer to President Rhee, a demanding and exasperating assignment. His service was recognized by the State Department in October 1952 in an award bestowed "For superior service, loyalty, and devotion to duty, beyond that normally expected in the Foreign Service of the United States. His courage and fortitude, . . . notwithstanding danger to his own person, have been an inspiration to his colleagues."

In June 1951 Harold Noble returned to calmer waters. He joined the Committee for a Free Asia, serving in various positions including deputy president and acting president. He was director of plans when he resigned in November 1953. Noble hoped to write a book about Korea and had arranged to contribute articles to *The New Leader*. Two of his articles appeared in *The New Leader* in September and October 1953, the result of a fall trip to Korea. On December 22, 1953, Harold Noble died of a heart attack on a plane en route from Tokyo to Honolulu, while on his way home to join his family for the Christmas holidays.

The Manuscript

Harold Noble completed *Embassy at War* in July 1952. Several publishers were interested in the book but finally decided against publication, apparently because its commercial prospects seemed poor. By 1952 the Korean War had become a bitter political issue in the United States, an important factor in the presidential election, and a great bore to a weary American public that wanted to see the war ended, not to read about it. Noble made no effort to publish the manuscript after the fall of 1952, probably hoping that a shift of public mood in a few years might make publication feasible. The manuscript was in the possession of his widow, Bell Noble, after his death in 1953.

The *Embassy at War* manuscript was originally 575 double-spaced, typewritten pages. It was in need of extensive editing, stylistic and substantive, which Harold Noble himself would have done if he had lived to see the manuscript through to publication. Two kinds of material have been deleted on stylistic grounds. The first was primarily ancedotal in nature: vignettes of friends or individuals known in Korea, or mention of mundane or unimportant matters. For example, there was a lengthy account of the experiences of Major Dean Hess, a U.S. Air Force officer training South Korean pilots. Since Major Hess subsequently wrote his own biographical account of the summer of 1950, Harold Noble's remarks could safely be omitted. A second kind of stylistic deletion has been made to avoid repetition and prolixity.

One stylistic change requires special mention. In the original manuscript the words "North Koreans" or "North Korea" appeared only two or three times. In their place Noble used the words "Communists," "the enemy," or, occasionally, "Commies." That choice of words reflected Noble's unwillingness to regard North Korea as a separate, autonomous, legal state or its soldiers as Koreans. Rather, the pejorative and dehumanizing political term "Communists" was used. Nowhere in the original manuscript or in Noble's extensive writings did he ever view Koreans or Japanese in racist terms. The words "gook" and "chink," which appear with embarrassing frequency in early works on the Korean War, were anathema to him. But "Communists" and "communism" were in a separate category. It must be recalled that Noble was writing during the middle of the Korean War. He was engagé in that war, a supporter of South Korea, and an uncompromising opponent of North Korea and communism. The scholar's quest for balance and objectivity grappled with the government official-journalist's inclinations toward the partisan and the polemical. In very great measure the former, the academic discipline, prevailed. Otherwise, the narrative would be biased and too dated to be of value. Nevertheless, the reader should be aware that an occasional stridency due to terminology has been muted in the present text. It is to be hoped that this has not been done at the expense of Harold Noble's values and commitments.

A more substantive variation from the original manuscript was the omission of two chapters on the North Korean occupation of Seoul. While carefully written, apparently from what refugee information was available, the accounts could not be satisfactorily verified, either by Harold Noble at the time, because of his duties and the military reverses of late 1950, or by this writer. Furthermore, the two chapters did not directly concern Harold Noble's duties or the embassy's peregrinations in the summer of 1950. They thus intruded into the flow of the account without compensatory value as reliable history.

A similar concern to maintain the chronological sequence and narrative flow of Noble's account required that Chapter 5 in the original manuscript be placed in a separate appendix.

Embassy at War has one definite limitation as an historical account of the early stages of the Korean War. Harold Noble was writing in 1951-52 as a former government official still bound legally and morally not to reveal classified information concerning his official duties. The Korean War was in midstream, many of his former colleagues in the embassy were still in Korea, and his Korean friends and associates, including President Syngman Rhee, were in a desperate fight to retain political power in South Korea. These considerations, plus Harold Noble's own identification with the success of the Republic of Korea and a strong U.S. policy of "containing communism" or even "rolling it back," governed his selection of material, his emphasis, and his overall point of view. This is most evident in the avoidance of topics or incidents that would portray South Korea or the U.S. effort in a critical light.

The reader hoping for spectacular disclosures or volatile, inside information will be disappointed. If Harold Noble had lived to revise the manuscript five or ten years after the 1953 armistice in Korea, a different book would have evolved. That book would have been crowded with details of policy formation and balanced by more objectivity on U.S. actions in Korea and the performance of the Syngman Rhee government. Harold Noble's early death deprived us of a fuller record of the events of 1949-51.

The notes following the text are intended as supplementary information. They are generally complementary to lacunae in the original manuscript; occasionally an emendation has been necessary. It was hoped that Department of State records could be fully utilized and included in the notes. However, the records for 1950 are closed to researchers and will not be available until 1980, according to present regulations. A few Seoul embassy reports of 1950 were obtained; most of these have been included in their entirety. The same practice was adopted with letters by E. F. Drumright, counselor in the embassy, during the summer of 1950. In this way primary materials, which might not otherwise be published, are available to the reader.

A singular merit of the Noble manuscript is its uniqueness. No other member of the Seoul embassy has written of these events. Neither of Harold Noble's superiors, Ambassador John J. Muccio or Counselor Everett F. Drumright, has plans (as of November 1971) to publish such an account. *Embassy at War* is the first description by a direct participant from the vantage point of the U.S. embassy.

The Noble account is of special interest concerning the origin and first weeks of the Korean War. As one of the senior embassy officials, Harold Noble has reconstructed the events with a measure of chagrin, a tinge of *mea culpa*. His explanation of why the embassy was caught off guard on June 25 is in a sense an apologia, but, to this writer, it is also a persuasive and credible acccount. The Noble version of developments in June 1950 and during the first week of the war reinforces the view that North Korea initiated the war. Noble's description of uncertainty and confusion in the South Korean government rebuts the contention that Syngman Rhee stoically gambled on U.S. assistance by provoking a North Korean attack. The documentation of Rhee's doubts about the

U.S. commitment to Korea, even after U.S. troops had arrived, hardly suggests that he counted upon American support prior to June 25, 1950.

The manuscript does not, however, place the start of the war in the larger context of the political situation in Korea after 1945. The war was the culmination of a basic struggle between left and right that began with Korea's liberation in August 1945 (or perhaps back in the 1920s with the formation of the Korean Communist party). In addition, while the war challenged the U.S. policy of containing communism, to most Koreans it was a civil war to unify the peninsula which had been arbitrarily divided and occupied by the United States and the U.S.S.R. These fundamental issues, central to an understanding of the political context of the conflict, must also be carefully considered in assessing the origins of the war.

Embassy at War offers a rare glimpse of the U.S. relationship with Syngman Rhee. Noble's comments on President Rhee, guarded and circumspect though they are, portray a tempestuous marriage of convenience. The embassy wanted the president out of the way during the summer of 1950 to prevent any political interference with the war effort. President Rhee accepted a subordinate status temporarily and grudgingly. A blend of passionate Korean nationalism and apocalyptic anticommunism made Rhee a formidable foe—or friend. Rhee was determined to defend South Korean interests and his own power regardless of American advice or wishes. A capacious suspicion of American motives in Korea, a product of fifty years of unsuccessful appeals to the American government, made Rhee a mercurial quantity to the embassy. The candid remarks of E. F. Drumright, included in his letters in the notes, display U.S. doubts and frustrations with President Rhee. The uncertainties of a mutual dependency often marked by conflicting national interests are apparent in *Embassy at War.*

The Noble account of the origin of the war, the description of Syngman Rhee in 1950, and other issues touched upon in the book make *Embassy at War* a useful primary source for future research, although the manuscript is far from an exhaustive treatment of the summer of 1950. Such empirical research remains to be done, hopefully receiving a stimulus from *Embassy at War,* if we are to have a fuller understanding of the American record in Korea.

I would like to thank individually Mrs. Harold J. Noble, James L. Stewart, Everett F. Drumright, and Gregory Henderson for providing personal correspondence and other materials and assistance. The many individuals who kindly replied to inquiries are acknowledged in the Notes. My particular appreciation goes to Gregory Henderson and Bruce Cumings who, reading the manuscript from different perspectives, made critical comments and suggestions of similar value.

I wish to express my thanks to the staff of the East Asian Institute, Columbia University. Professor Herschel Webb, chairman, and other members of the institute's publication committee were a source of moral and material support. Lillian Lent typed the manuscript with a critical verve beyond the call of duty. Dale Anderson Finlayson's invaluable editorial assistance guided my fledgling steps along the slippery path of manuscript preparation. The institute provided a travel grant for me to visit the MacArthur Memorial, Norfolk, Virginia, and generous support for publication.

I am grateful to Alfred A. Knopf, Inc., for permission to quote from Courtney Whitney, *MacArthur: His Rendezvous with History* (New York, 1964), and to the Curtis Publishing Company for permission to use "The Reds Made Suckers of Us All" by Harold J. Noble from the *Saturday Evening Post,* August 9, 1952. A revised version of this article appears in the Appendix.

Author's Preface

THIS IS my story of the American embassy in Korea from the day war began on June 25, 1950, until we returned to Seoul on September 29. It is not a history of the war nor precisely a history of the embassy. It is my account of what I know and remember of those exciting if exhausting days.

There are many interesting events which involved the embassy staff in Korea that I have not mentioned. Any other member of the small embassy group who went down the dusty road to Suwŏn and beyond that Tuesday, June 27, 1950, would have another story to tell. Perhaps some might be more interesting, but this one is mine.

The American embassy in Korea profoundly affected the course of the war. I believe that without the embassy, in the shock of the surprise invasion and the early devastating defeat, the South Korean government might have collapsed and the ROK Army might have disintegrated.[1] The history of those few American civilians living together in the midst of a dreadful war, during which, despite danger and retreat after retreat, they always appeared certain of victory and so kept South Korean hope alive, is an untold drama of how a few men helped to sustain an ROK government and army for the United Nations to support against aggression.

We kept few official records in those moving days, although I kept notes throughout the period and have a detailed log covering the first most critical week. During those many months when we lived so closely together, we naturally told each other about our actions and "exploits" time and again, often interminably and tediously. I also wrote of events regularly to my wife; she kept the

letters, which have been very useful in supplying an elusive date
or even hours. Several friends who were also in Korea have lent me
copies of similar correspondence. I have corresponded with many
who fled Seoul that dreadful day in June two years ago, getting
their answers to questions regarding their own actions, especially
what they know and did at specific times. I recently made a trip to
Washington to check such records as are there, and especially to
talk with key officers of the United States Military Advisory Group
to the Republic of Korea (KMAG) now stationed in Washington.[2]

Naturally, these notes, logs, letters, and records have been clothed
in more detail by my memory of events. Fortunately, it is quite
good. I long ago learned the art of interviewing a man for hours
at a time without taking a note and then later reproducing a full
account of the conversation with dates, names, and figures. I would
not pretend, however, that I have remembered everything with
precision, nor that everyone who was there that summer would
agree to all my interpretations of events.

Since I am writing a true story as nearly as I can remember it,
I have to write of living people. This account is no happy flight
of fancy in which all the men on our side are sweet and beautiful.
Any adult knows that life cannot be like that, and that the best men
have weaknesses that war sometimes exaggerates. Inevitably, among
the Koreans and Americans of prominence in Korea during this
period we had a mixture of good and bad, wise and stupid, courageous and sometimes cowardly. I am happy to say, though, that
no man in our small embassy group ever showed any sign of cowardice. Naturally, a man would show up well in one spot and quite
badly in another, or differently on different days. But an honest
account must tell how key figures acted in times of crisis, and they
did not deserve medals every day.

As far as the embassy's responsibilities were concerned, during
the three summer months I probably was closer to the persons affected than anyone excepting the ambassador. Both my duties and
my prejudices brought me closer to Korean civilian officials and
United Nations officials than any other embassy officer, whether
to the president, to the chairman of the National Assembly, or to
the members of the United Nations Commission on Korea.[3] I also
knew at least casually most of the ranking officers in the ROK

Army, Navy, and Air Force, and especially well the chief of staff, Lt. Gen. Chŏng Il-gwŏn.

During those wearing but stirring days I was first secretary of the embassy, the third-ranking political officer. From that vantage point I followed the war through the summer of 1950.

Contents

Illustrations

EMBASSY AT WAR

CHAPTER ONE

Embassy Seoul

S U N D A Y , J U N E 25, dawned overcast and drizzly. It was a good morning to sleep in, a typical Korean rainy-season Sunday. Normally the embassy, located in the former Bando Hotel building in mid-city, would have remained nearly lifeless all day. Although there always was some activity, the embassy was officially closed on Sundays. A code clerk broke whatever messages had come in during the night, and a duty officer and a girl secretary sat in the ambassador's outer office until noon, just in case. The messages were usually routine and could go over till Monday, but sometimes they required immediate action. Because of the time difference between Washington and Seoul, an important instruction telegraphed from the department on their Friday night was received by us on our Sunday morning.[1] The ambassador usually dropped in about eleven o'clock on Sundays to read any telegrams that might come in. But on Sundays most offices were vacant and there was little to do.

The American ambassador to the Republic of Korea was John J. Muccio from Providence, Rhode Island. Muccio was born in Italy but brought to the United States by his parents when he was an infant. He grew up in Rhode Island, just outside of Providence, and went to college at Brown. Physically, he is not very big but he is large-boned and so gives the impression of being large. He has a huge head on broad shoulders. He was fifty years old then but his black hair scarcely showed a streak of gray. Although he was very conscious of his position as ambassador, he was relaxed and outwardly easygoing. He always dressed well and neatly whatever the

3

occasion, even during the most difficult days of the retreat. He usually wore a gay, factory-tied bow tie and was rarely to be found with a four-in-hand.

Either by temperament or from his more than twenty years in the diplomatic service, Muccio had learned the wisdom of the indirect approach, the wisdom of avoiding clashes between friendly governments. He had learned that many problems disappear of themselves if they are ignored and not put on paper. He was ideal as American ambassador to the new Republic of Korea. The South Korean government was so new and Koreans had had so little experience in government that inevitably they made errors, some of them most exasperating to an American. Time and again Muccio would be urged by some staff officer to take a drastic stand or to say harsh things to the foreign minister or the president. Usually those so urging were in the Economic Cooperation Administration mission (ECA), but sometimes they were our own third secretaries. Muccio would listen, ask a few questions, and say he would think about it. If the situation seemed to demand action of some sort, he would usually have me, unofficially, approach President Rhee, the foreign minister, or some other official to discuss the problem in a friendly way. It was very rare that this indirect approach did not reach a friendly and satisfactory solution without the exchange of harsh words. If anyone said anything harsh, it was I, and Muccio was left free to soothe irritated and ruffled feelings. No inflexible demands, no unrecallable words were written or said. Instead everyone's goodwill and "face" were retained unimpaired.

While I would not call Muccio a great man, I doubt that any other American was quite so suited to represent the United States government in Seoul at that particular time in history. The Republic of Korea was so new, it had so much to learn, it was bound to make so many mistakes, and its officials were so thin-skinned in their personal and national pride that Muccio's relaxed calmness and sympathy were ideal. He genuinely liked Koreans and most Koreans genuinely admired, liked, and respected him. He could go to a very official, very stuffy party where everyone sat on the floor to eat at little tables out of innumerable unappetizing dishes and in no time, by some magic of his personality, make everyone down the line

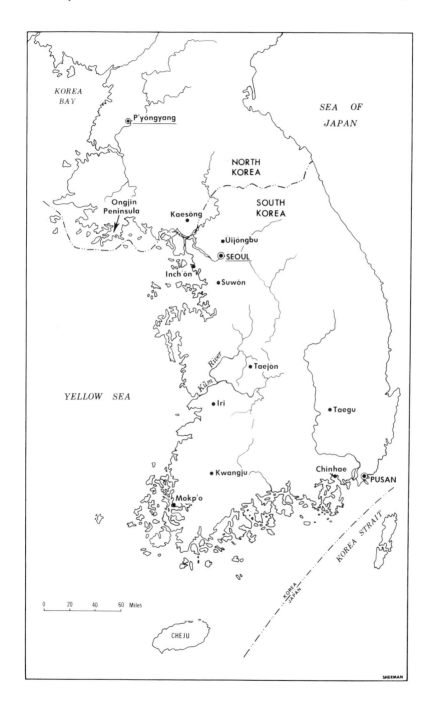

to the lowest ranking man present feel at ease and comfortable.
There was nothing stuffy about him.

Muccio had served all over the world, but his longest service
was in China. I think he had most enjoyed service in Latin America, and he loved to tell of his days in Panama. He had never tried
to learn Chinese, but his Spanish was fluent. Probably he had enjoyed the Latin ladies; I knew he enjoyed singing Spanish love
songs, which he was often asked to sing at private parties. His
service in Germany after the end of World War II had interested
him as a duty, but clearly it had not been a duty of personal pleasure.

Muccio had gone through all the grades and performed all the
duties common to the career of a Foreign Service officer. When I met
him in August 1948, he was an ambassador and had determined how
to run a chancery his way. He never wrote a telegram or a dispatch
if he could help it; I do not think he ever wrote a dispatch in the
time I knew him. He delegated responsibility for the paper work
to the counselor, Everett F. Drumright, and his other subordinates.
In fact, the few times that Muccio did write a telegram himself,
I thought he would have been better off if he had left the job to us.
He was very quick, however, to spot and have changed the parts
of our reporting that were defective or contrary to his thinking, but
he just was not good at composition himself. Perhaps he had forgotten how, or perhaps writing had never been his strong point. In
any case, he had the excellent judgment to delegate authority and
kept himself free to meet people, to think in terms of the overall
picture, and to make policy decisions. He had very great faith in
Drumright. Drumright had the privilege of sending telegrams and
dispatches to Washington without previously showing them to
Muccio. The great majority of our reports went out that way, a
folder of the previous day's communications being placed on
Muccio's desk every morning. If anything seemed to impinge on
policy, however, Drumright always showed the documents to the
ambassador before sending them out.

Drumright was a very different type from Muccio. Where Muccio was easygoing and relaxed, Drumright was hard-driving, energetic, and dogmatic. Where Muccio always had a smooth phrase
for a lady, Drumright seemed ill at ease with women. Both men

were bachelors. I do not think I have ever known a man who drove himself harder than Drumright did, and few who worked as hard. The amount of work he could turn out in a day was astonishing. In a mission the size of ours in Seoul, which with the various attached elements must have numbered about one thousand people, not a report or telegram or document went to or came from Washington that Drumright did not see.[2] If they had even small importance he read them carefully and understood them. Anything happening in the mission had to have his full knowledge and usually his approval, whether it had to do with expansion of coal mining facilities by ECA, changes at the motor pool, the height of the ambassador's compound wall, appeals for airplanes for the ROK Air Force, or reports and telegrams to the department on political affairs. In many of my own activities I reported directly to the ambassador, about conversations with the president or foreign minister or with some member of the U.N. Commission, but I always kept Drumright closely informed. I never knew when a corollary problem might arise on which he would have to take action. Besides, I liked Drumright very much and was far more in accord with his general views of the world than with those of the ambassador. I think Drumright and I both respected each other and understood each other. We did not aways understand the ambassador.

Drumright was about six feet tall and in his early forties. His hair was light brown, his face wide, lined, and very determined looking. He had been a career officer in the China service until it had become inundated by persons whose political views on the handling of the Communist problem in China were anathema to him. He got himself transferred, serving in London and Tokyo before coming to Korea. He spoke fluent Chinese, which helped him a lot in Seoul since so many government officials had been exiles in China during the Japanese occupation and spoke Chinese.

The language barrier was not too serious for us at Embassy Seoul. Of course, we had our staff of interpreters and translators but a very large percentage of educated Koreans could speak English. We had three third secretaries who spoke Korean rather well. Before their assignment to Seoul in 1948, the State Department had sent them to the University of California for an academic year

of concentrated study of Korean language, history, and culture.
Their fluency in Korean had improved with tutors. The head of
the United States Information Service (USIS), James L. Stewart,
could speak Japanese so well that he could and did on occasion
make public, extemporaneous addresses in Japanese to friendly
Koreans. The head of ECA, Arthur C. Bunce, spoke very fluent
Korean. He had lived in Korea for ten years before the war. Although ungrammatical, my own Japanese was fluent.

The U.S. embassy in Korea was unique. It was the only American embassy in the world where all American activities were the
ambassador's responsibility, where every representative of every
element of the American government located there was required
to report to the ambassador and for the most part act under his
direction. In this regard, Korea was an experiment and a most
successful one.

No report, telegram, or dispatch relating to policy could be sent
from Seoul to any U.S. government department or agency without
his approval. ECA, KMAG, USIS, and the Joint Administration
Services (JAS) for the whole mission were subordinate and responsible to the ambassador.[3]

Aside from its comparably very great size, which completely
dwarfed the other missions in Korea, the basic reason for the
prominence and influence of the American embassy in Seoul was
that American troops had occupied Korea for three years and, aside
from the Soviet Union, of the great powers the United States was
the only one with a major interest there. At the embassy most of
us felt the United States had a definite moral obligation toward
Korea. The United States and the Soviet Union had divided the
country at the 38th parallel, both an artificial division geographic-
ally and a monstrous one humanly, dividing families and resources
and even villages. Even the Japanese had never done anything like
this to Korea. The United States had attempted to atone for its
error by supporting the United Nations–supervised elections for a
free Korean government in the south. Now, we believed, the
United States was morally obligated to give this government sufficient moral and other support during its first few years so that it
could develop enough muscle to protect itself. American Embassy
Seoul was the formal expression of that obligation and that support.

We had undertaken a fair-sized ECA program for Korea, and we were assisting the Koreans in training their army and navy. Since the United States had taken the leadership in helping Koreans toward freedom and independence, which in time they would be able to defend by their own efforts, and since the United States had shown very clearly that there was no American governmental interest in territory or financial gain in Korea, most Koreans were very friendly to us, and most officials at one time or another turned to the American embassy for advice and even guidance. As representative of the United States government and with the power embodied in the monies of ECA and the military advice of KMAG the American mission in Korea had great influence for good or evil. We usually had to make our decisions and give our replies in a hurry, while always remembering that our advice once tendered would profoundly affect decisions and events in the Republic of Korea whether or not our views were accepted.

I think most members of the mission were aware of this responsibility to some degree. Many, however, were not sufficiently mature of mind to realize we had to create an atmosphere of trust in which our advice would be sought, and that for us to proffer it constantly on every subject without invitation inevitably would lead to controversy, ill will, and antagonism, which would defeat our purposes. Others, similarly from political immaturity, just could not adjust to being in Korea instead of, say, Oregon, and to the fact that there were many evils of life and government which only time, experience, and education could overcome. Idealism animated the activities and decisions of most of the mission staff, but in some cases this idealism was not tempered by understanding of the rough, nonideal world around us, especially a world in which a hostile army poised for invasion thirty miles away profoundly affected every decision of government.[4]

CHAPTER TWO

Invasion

WAR FLASHED all along the 38th parallel just before light. In minutes hundreds of South Korean soldiers lay bloody and dead in the screening posts at the border. The war reached Embassy Seoul more slowly, and more gently, by telephone.

In the American mission, KMAG was the first to hear of the attack. KMAG headquarters was alongside ROK Army headquarters in Seoul, not far from the Han River, and KMAG officers were on training duty with most of the ROK units under assault. As rapidly as possible, they reported the North Korean attack to KMAG headquarters. Since there had been so many border attacks before, and no man could see anything but his own front and that most imperfectly, the first reports were fragmentary and piecemeal. It is unlikely that any officer making the first battle reports suspected that this was an all-out invasion.

The first action reports coming into KMAG headquarters were probably filed by sleepy duty officers for report to their superiors at a more reasonable time. The scale of the North Korean assault was not evident for some time. Even after the reports continued and the picture grew alarming, both the ROK Army and KMAG were reluctant to accept them as evidence of full-scale invasion. The assault had been expected for so long that it could not quite be believed when it actually came.[1]

KMAG was troubled by a critical internal problem that Sunday morning: confusion over who was in command. The commanding officer, Brig. Gen. William L. Roberts, was in mid-Pacific on his way to the United States for a new assignment. The chief of staff and acting commander, Col. Sterling Wright, was in Japan on a brief holiday.² Most fortunately, Wright caught the naval attaché's plane at Itazuke and flew into Kimp'o early on Monday morning. This not only solved the command problem but gave KMAG determined, vigorous, and optimistic leadership. As the ROK Army was beaten back slowly from valley to bloody valley, only Sterling Wright remained hopeful that somehow victory would emerge from disaster. All his headquarters staff officers gave up the battle by Monday night, but Wright stood firm against them.

When the first reports of fighting reached KMAG, no immediate report was made to the embassy. As battle reports poured in, however, more and more officers were awakened and ordered to their posts. ROK Army orders began going out to move troops forward, to get supplies rolling, and to alert the reserves in Seoul and to the south. Loudspeakers were put in jeeps, and Korean officers and men already wearing leaves and branches in the nets over their helmets, dashed up and down the streets, summoning everyone back from leave to his post.

The defense plan against North Korean invasion did not contemplate fighting in force at the 38th parallel. The main line of resistance for the ROK Army was well south of the parallel, with only a screen out in front to give warning and to delay the enemy. I had been to the demarcation line, up the Ŭijŏngbu corridor due north of Seoul, just a week before the invasion and talked to Brig. Gen. Yu Chae-hŭng. General Yu, a short, stocky, good-looking man with an air of thorough competence, had outlined his problems in case of invasion. He commanded the 7th Division and guarded the closest and easiest invasion route to Seoul, a distance from the parallel along this route of just over thirty miles. He planned to establish his main line of resistance a few miles north of Ŭijŏngbu, about half way between Seoul and the parallel. He had a screen just below the parallel, but some elements of his division were back as far as Seoul. If he had adequate warning and the trains were ready to roll, General Yu said, he could get into position in about two hours. But if he could not move his troops by train and had to depend on his few trucks to move his supplies, his men would have to march. Then General Yu would need closer to twelve hours, and he gravely doubted the enemy would give him twelve hours. If they did not, and he had to join battle before he could bring up and deploy his reserves, he would be fighting practically in the outskirts of Seoul.

A week had passed since my conversation with General Yu. He had had no warning. No trains were ready to roll. Yet he did better, very much better than his estimates. Battle showed General Yu to have the skill at improvisation which is the mark of the really gifted soldier everywhere but which cannot be tested and discovered for certain before actual combat. Forty-eight hours passed after this surprise attack before General Yu was pushed back to the outskirts of Seoul, and then only after another division sent to support him, the 2nd, had collapsed.

Just before seven o'clock on Sunday morning someone at KMAG telephoned the embassy's military attaché, Lt. Col. Bob Edwards, at his house and gave the alarm. Edwards promptly called Drumright and then telephoned his assistant, Warrant Officer Bill Lynch, to get down to the office in a hurry. Edwards quickly dressed and drove to the embassy. Edwards' original call to Drumright had not contained enough information to establish that this was a general invasion, and Drumright held off taking action until he knew more.

Jack James of the United Press had been out on a late party and by all reasonable standards should have been snoozing until noon. But he woke early and went down to the embassy on the remote chance he could pick up some news. He arrived about eight o'clock and immediately ran into the bustle in the military and naval attachés' offices. Commander Jack Seifert, the naval attaché, had also come in early to work on a routine report for which he had a deadline and was told the surprising news by Bob Edwards. Seifert telephoned his staff to come in.

Jack James closely followed the reports flowing into the military attaché's office from KMAG and Korean sources. He saw no good reason to interrupt the sleep of the Associated Press man, who had been with him at that late party and was still sound asleep. But he did telephone somewhat cryptically to Jim Stewart, the USIS chief, suggesting he might want to come down to read the transcripts of P'yŏngyang radio that morning. Stewart, a very alert and intelligent man, caught on that something peculiar was going on and promptly drove to the embassy.

At eight o'clock Lieutenant Colonel Edwards again telephoned Drumright with more extensive information indicating a general invasion, but not with enough evidence to be positive.[4] Jack James kept watching the reports as they came in and checking with Stewart and Warrant Officer Lynch. If this were a full-scale Communist invasion, he wanted to say so in his first story. No one else was awake to compete with him, and he would have a beat all reporters dream of but few achieve. But if the attack were to prove limited, he ought to file what he knew now and later build up his story as more facts came in. Jack was an honest and conscientious man and despised the flamboyant type of journalism practiced on occasion by others. He had lived for some time in China, spoke Chinese, and had been a naval aviator in World War II. Jack was intensely loyal to the United States and intensely hostile to the Communists. As the war was to prove, he was not the kind of man who scared easily and gave up.

By 8:30 Jack James decided he must act very soon. He discussed the battle news with Drumright, getting Drum's reaction to it. While Drumright thought it was the long-expected general assault, he urged caution in handling the news until more facts were known. Jack hesitated but thought he had held back too long already. He sat down and wrote it as a story of general invasion, but held up his copy until more information came in to make his story positive. Then he filed it at 9:50 A.M. He had a beat of at least two hours on all other agencies.[5] The poor AP man was mortified when he woke up to receive a telegram. It was a rocket from his agency.[6]

Jack James's only immediate competitor was Walter Simmons of the *Chicago Tribune*. Walt came down to the embassy late in the morning, picked up the story, and filed at once. Walt was visiting Korea on a week-end assignment this time, but he had been in Korea from his Tokyo base perhaps fifteen times since the end of the last war and probably knew more about Korea than any other correspondent not regularly stationed in Seoul.

By nine o'clock it was clear that this was no border foray but an all-out invasion. Bob Edwards had gone down to KMAG headquarters to be closer to the picture, and just before nine o'clock he telephoned Drumright with the latest news from the front.[7]

Muccio sent a telegram reporting the invasion to the State De-

partment about 10:00 A.M. He had delayed until after Jack James
filed, knowing that James's story would serve as an initial warning.[8]
Muccio did not want to send his report until there could be no
possible doubt about the facts. Muccio's telegram, marked "Night
Action," stated that the North Koreans were making a general, all-
out invasion of the Republic of Korea.[9] The NIACT designation
was for emergency use only, and this clearly was the type of emergency for which it was intended. A NIACT required the State Department code room to give it immediate precedence and further
required its immediate delivery to the responsible official. There
have been many accounts of Dean Rusk, assistant secretary of state
for Far Eastern affairs, receiving the telegram at a Saturday night
dinner party in Washington.

Drumright promptly began getting key people into their offices.
He directed all the officers of the embassy proper to come in immediately, placing most of the calls himself. The girls and clerks
who worked in the chancery were summoned. Jim Stewart had
already sent for his secretary, while both the military and naval
attachés' offices now were manned, as were the code room and the
file room. There was no reason to bring in others, such as ECA
and a wide range of USIS people, however, and most of the offices
below the fifth floor were vacant throughout the day. Stewart did
call in one of his men who ran the embassy radio station, WVTP,
and had him standing by in case the ambassador should want to
send a message to the American community.[10]

Sunday morning passed very slowly at the embassy. YAK fighters crisscrossed the city and one group bombed the railway station.
Lieutenant Colonel Edwards went to KMAG again and came back
with more information. The telephones rang constantly with calls
from all over town, from members of the mission anxiously sitting
in their houses listening to the anti-aircraft fire, and from Koreans,
both private citizens and government officials, who wanted to know
the facts and just what the American embassy thought about them.
Probably the hardest thing the embassy officers did that first day
of war was to take those incessant calls and, with little knowledge
themselves of what was happening to the north, courteously say
encouraging things.

One embassy role emerged in those first few hours: it became the duty of the embassy to keep up morale, the morale of everyone, Korean officials and army officers, private citizens, diplomats from other countries, newspaper correspondents, and at times even high-ranking U.S. Army officers. No one foresaw this as an embassy responsibility that would last through the early months of the war. Every embassy officer simply knew that his phone rang constantly, with callers who needed to be reassured about the war and their personal safety.

There was one very bewildered group of people in Seoul that Sunday, teachers from Illinois Tech who had arrived the previous day by the regular Northwest plane. They had been brought out by ECA to teach a variety of useful trades in a newly established technological training institute that had not yet opened its doors. These unfortunate men got off a plane and walked into a war instead of a classroom. Arthur C. Bunce, chief of the ECA mission, had invited a very large number of guests to a cocktail party at his house on Sunday afternoon in honor of the visiting teachers. Bunce had a large house and a larger lawn and could easily entertain a hundred guests at cocktails. But at noon the war news had become so grave that Muccio advised Bunce to call off his party, which he did. Those poor men from Illinois never got a free drink in Seoul. They flew in on Saturday to take up a new and challenging assignment and then flew out on Tuesday under U.S. Air Force fighter escort. Very few had traveled so far for so little.

Knowing what we now do of the power, plans, and material superiority of the North Koreans, it is difficult to recall the optimism in Seoul during the first hours of war. But actually it was almost universal. Naturally, there must have been people who were terrified to realize that a vicious enemy was assaulting only a few miles north of the city. Yet almost everyone had great hope. Everyone had great confidence in the combat spirit and capacity of the ROK Army, and although no one doubted that severe battles were ahead, no one understood how vastly superior the North Koreans were in certain decisive weapons, especially tanks. All the first reports, while telling of severe fighting, indicated that the ROK Army, despite being surprised, was holding its own.

At the time the Communists attacked, the ROK Army had four of its eight divisions more or less in position a few miles south of the parallel. The 1st Division held the Kaesŏng-Munsan area, made world-famous by the truce talks. One regiment of the Capital Division, the 17th under Colonel Paek In-yŏp, was in the Ongjin peninsula, completely cut off from either support or retreat except by sea. A wide valley led from Kaesŏng down to Seoul with no natural barrier except the Imjin River near Munsan. Thus the Imjin River was the main line of resistance for the 1st Division. A series of mountains and high ridges separated the Kaesŏng corridor from the Ŭijŏngbu corridor to the east, which was held by the aforementioned General Yu's 7th Division. The next corridor leading easily into Seoul was much farther to the east, again separated by high and rugged mountains, the Ch'unch'ŏn corridor, which was blocked by the 6th Division. Even farther to the east, holding a line as far as the coastal road on the east coast, the 8th Division held positions in very rugged country. Available for reinforcements were the Capital Division, based in Seoul, less the 17th Regiment on the Ongjin peninsula, and the 2nd Division at Taejŏn. That left two more divisions, understrength and underarmed, the 5th at Kwangju and the 3rd. The latter had headquarters at Taegu but responsibility for the entire area south to Pusan. Within the first twenty-four hours of the war all these divisions had been committed to battle, mostly piecemeal.

Only the day before the attack, on Saturday, June 24, two Australian officers, Squadron Leader Ron Rankin of the RAAF and Major Stirling Peach, an army man, who were in Korea as observers for the U.N. Commission on Korea, had returned from a two-week inspection tour of all ROK Army units and dispositions in the general area of the 38th parallel. They had made a brief report, which they elaborated the following day. The essence of the report was that the ROK Army was so disposed, so equipped, and its supply dumps so arranged that it could fight only as a defensive force. It could not possibly be preparing to take the offensive. This report, which was adopted officially by the U.N. Commission on Monday, June 26, and cabled to Lake Success, had a profound effect on the decisions of the Security Council to halt aggression in Korea. The United Nations did not need to rely on American or Korean reports. It had the reports of its own commission in Korea, of which the United States was not a member.[11]

By noon on Saturday, June 25, some very disturbing news was filtering down the Ũijŏngbu corridor from where the boom of guns could now be clearly heard in Seoul. The rain lifted slightly, and North Korean planes flew over the city, strafing here and there without any apparent plan. Reports from the front said that bazookas just bounced off enemy tanks no matter how close the soldiers approached before they fired. The tanks rolled over the helpless bazooka men and kept coming south. The same story was told of the antitank guns which the ROK Army prized so much. Officers reported the shells would not penetrate. Only when the South Koreans could bring their 105-mm howitzers to bear on the tanks did they get results. And their plans to blow up the tanks with land mines on the narrow roads were being frustrated by the flow of the tanks right through the "impassable" paddy fields where tanks were supposed to be mired in mud.[12]

No one in KMAG or the embassy believed these tales. They were taken for panic stories to explain away retreat. ROK Army headquarters equally discounted such reports, but they sent staff officers forward to check on them. When they came back, they made identical reports, but I do not think anyone on the American side believed them.

Soon after noon it was clear, whatever the cause, that the North Koreans were driving slowly down the Ũijŏngbu corridor and if they kept up their momentum, they would soon be in Seoul. In retrospect I am amazed the North Koreans did not reach Seoul that night. That they were delayed for forty-eight hours is evidence of the ROK Army's courage and willingness to die rather than surrender.

South Korean infantry and artillery men fought heroically just above Seoul, willingly giving their lives to slow down the enemy attack. The North Korean tank commanders lacked the courage to sweep ahead of their infantry support and paced their advance to the slow movement of their infantry. The fight in that narrow Ũijŏngbu corridor must have been one of the greatest hells of modern warfare. How General Yu and his men held up the North Koreans, who had superior artillery, and planes and tanks which the ROK Army did not, is a drama of courage and devoted partiotism. Only very much later, after American troops, who did have

artillery able to outrange the North Koreans and whose planes commanded the air, had been driven steadily southwards, by this same
enemy, did the heroism of the ROK Army near Ŭijŏngbu, below
Ch'unch'ŏn, and at the Imjin River become clear. But by that time
few outsiders cared about the ROK Army, and to this day its honor
is besmirched by the misconceptions of those first few days of
battle.[13]

The NKPA storming down those corridors to Seoul that Sunday
was already largely a veteran army, while the ROK Army, although
well trained and with good morale, was green. Many thousands of
the men in the "People's Army" had served in the Chinese Communist Army until as late as the autumn of 1949, when they were
sent into Korea, changed their uniforms, and were given new unit
designations.

While the war raged north of the city, senior ROK government
officials quickly assembled in their offices, but no cabinet meeting
was called.[14] Most ministers saw each other, and most of them
saw President Rhee but not on a formal basis. Exactly what happened that afternoon at the president's residence, Kyŏngmudae,
I do not precisely know, but there was great coming and going
of officials, military officers, and private citizens to report, to confer,
and to seek advice.[15] The president was deeply shocked by the
attack and the reports of steady enemy advances. A strafing by
YAKs just behind his house particularly upset him and others of
his household. He was an old man, and he had never before heard
a hostile gun.

It is fairly clear that by late afternoon someone frightened President Rhee into believing Seoul would fall that night and he had
better get out if he wished to keep himself and the government
alive. Probably several people were to blame. I cannot pick out
any one person or a few individuals. Certainly some members of
the cabinet and of Dr. Rhee's official household were terrified and
infected him with their fear.[16]

I had known President and Mrs. Rhee since 1938 and was especially closely associated with them during the first six months of
the war. Before the outbreak of war, as the ambassador's representative but by invitation of the president, I called either on him

or on his wife every afternoon. Mrs. Rhee served in effect as chief of his secretariat as well as confidant. I have observed President and Mrs. Rhee closely in good times and bad. It is my considered opinion that Dr. Rhee is profoundly, even fanatically, devoted to the welfare of Korea and of Koreans, and that Mrs. Rhee in being devoted to the welfare of her husband is also devoted to the welfare of Korea. Mrs. Rhee is an Austrian by birth and upbringing, American by naturalization, and Korean by marriage and registry.[17] I consider President Rhee a man of honor and personal courage. Later I found it very hard to persuade him to leave dangerous places. He was always delighted to go to the front to visit the troops, often under fire. But I am inclined to think he did panic that Sunday afternoon, under pressures which I do not quite understand. Of course, he was an old man, past seventy, and had never personally experienced a war before. He knew that he was the primary target of the Communists, but he also knew that, if they captured him and his government in Seoul on the first day of the war, it would end his life's hope and dream, the Republic of Korea. He was aware that as long as the president survived, a new government could be formed.[18]

The Kyŏngmudae, like many presidential establishments, was a world of its own. Ministers, generals, and private citizens came and went, but there was always a secretarial staff and a special police force with its own intelligence section in regular attendance. Later in the war I found these police were reporting some of the blackest posssible information to the president, based on Japanese broadcasts. Even though the minister of defense or the chief of staff was available to give the facts on the military situation, often the president seemed to place more reliance on the reports of his police guard. Too often they were based on rumors, rumormongers, and the newscast of one particular Japanese radio station that later inquiry showed was controlled by Communists.

This probably explains part of the panic at Kyŏngmudae that Sunday afternoon. I have an idea too that the home minister, Paek Sŏng-uk,[19] a retired Buddhist monk, a combination of fatalist and military pessimist, who is said to have made most of his decisions from the early morning horoscopes cast especially for him by his mistress of younger days, had a gloomy effect on the president that afternoon. Later the president had to ask for Paek's resignation because of his dangerous defeatism.

Some of the blame probably lies with Defense Minister and Acting Prime Minister Sin Sŏng-mo.[20] Captain Sin was a man of the greatest personal courage, indefatigable in the face of danger. But he was always gravely apprehensive when the president was anywhere near a battle. Sin was concerned for the continuity of government, and partly, I think, he liked to be free to carry out his duties without having the president always breathing down his neck, asking questions, and issuing orders that showed he did not grasp the meaning of military affairs. I feel sure that this first Sunday afternoon of the war Sin Sŏng-mo was one of those who urged the president to get out of town, quickly.

In addition to Captain Sin and others, two former cabinet ministers called on the president late on Sunday afternoon—the former prime minister, General Yi Pŏm-sŏk,[22] and former Home Minister Cho Pyŏng-ok. General Yi, who had fought a lot of battles in his day, in Manchuria and in China proper, counseled cautious optimism. Dr. Cho was direct and forthright in his opinion. He insisted no one could yet know how the battle would go and said the president and government must stand fast. Later Cho attended a special meeting called by the president at nine o'clock in the evening. He was shocked to find that Rhee was advocating the removal of the government from Seoul. Cho argued very strongly against such a move, insisting that at the very least no such decision should be made without advising Muccio.

At Cho's insistence President Rhee finally agreed to ask Muccio to come over.[23] Muccio called on the president about 9:30 P.M. and found that Rhee wanted the government to leave the city. President Rhee also urged Muccio to get the American women and children out. Muccio used much the same arguments that Cho had used previously against the government's leaving, but because of his position was more persuasive. He pointed out that the outcome of the battle was still in doubt, that the divisions from the south were only just arriving in the battle area and would not be effective until the next day, while the abandonment of Seoul that night by the president and the government would so undermine civilian and military morale at a critical time that the whole war effort might collapse.

Rhee finally agreed with Muccio and decided he would remain in Seoul that night. Distressed and privately somewhat angered, Muccio got into his long Chrysler limousine and was driven back to the embassy. Through the strength of his character and the trust and confidence that almost all Korean officials had in his words, he had managed to surmount the first of many crises.[24]

Muccio returned to the embassy and was quickly briefed on the latest war news. He had to make the hardest decision of his life: to weigh the war news and the effect on Korean morale of anything that might be construed as panic at the American embassy against the security and the lives of the people for whom he was personally responsible. He was impressed by Rhee's urging that he at least evacuate the women and children. Although the situation was not hopeless, it was so desperate that Muccio felt he could no longer delay the evacuation of the women and children.[25]

The embassy had prepared an evacuation plan almost a year earlier.[26] A small committee with representatives of the chancery, KMAG, ECA, and JAS met monthly to go over the plan in the light of changing circumstances. On every such occasion weaknesses were found and changes were made. The plan contemplated that in the worst emergency everyone in the mission would be evacuated to Japan by plane from Kimp'o, and so it was coordinated with General Headquarters, Far East Command, and the Far East Air Force headquarters in Tokyo. The flash of a code word from Seoul was supposed to start the transport planes moving from Japan. That sounds simple, but how would all these people get to Kimp'o? What if the bridge were blown up? What if Kimp'o was being bombed?

The evacuation plan tried to provide for all such contingencies and combined evacuation by air from Kimp'o with alternative use of the Suwŏn airstrip, the use of ships in Inch'ŏn harbor, the railway, and the highways to Pusan. It provided for the removal of every American man, woman, and child in Korea, all British subjects, all French citizens, all members of the U.N. Commission and its secretariat, and the staff of the Chinese embassy. Since only the American embassy had the capacity to get great numbers out in a hurry, it also took the responsibility of looking after other foreign nationals in an emergency.

The American consul was supposed to keep adequate personnel records, to know where everyone lived and how he could be reached. Although everyone in the American mission and the other foreign missions had official telephones, the Christian missionaries did not, and in case of crisis they would have to be notified by messenger. Most of them, however, were expected to tune in WVTP if there was trouble and to follow instructions from that station. Early that Sunday afternoon WVTP began announcements urging everyone to keep tuned to the station all night.

The evacuation plan was marked "Top Secret," and few knew its content. A great many people, of course, did not even know there was a plan. When the crisis arose and evacuation was essential, many variations from the plan occurred. But the long work on it was well justified in that machinery had been prepared in advance, various key men knew their assignments, and arrangements had been made with the 5th Air Force for planes if they were needed.

Early on Sunday afternoon Maj. James D. Holland, who represented KMAG on the evacuation plan, came to the embassy and set up shop in a conference room near the ambassador's office. Thereafter, although all policy decisions regarding evacuation were made by Muccio and Drumright, Major Holland actually ran the evacuation. He showed himself to be a very capable and unassuming young man.

Jack Seifert had checked on available ships in Inch'ŏn and Pusan by telephone. He found a Norwegian and a Chinese freighter in Inch'ŏn harbor and more ships available at Pusan. Someone was sent to Inch'ŏn to ask the two skippers if they would be willing to take refugees out on their ships. Both said they would.

Alert notices were sent out to the married women over the embassy radio from midnight on.[27] Some were called by telephone. Messengers were sent to the missionaries. By this time the Korean girls had been sent home from the switchboard and American girls had taken over. American girls ran the switchboard until they too were evacuated early on Tuesday morning. Muccio announced that any woman could go, whether she was a dependent or a mission employee, but not one secretary or female clerk accepted the offer. Many of the girls insisted they would stay in Seoul as long as any man did.

The actual evacuation notice for the women and children was made about 2:00 A.M., Monday morning, June 26. Meeting places were designated near the major living areas where the refugees were to be picked up at 3:00 A.M. No one was to take more than she could carry herself. Each woman was advised to take a blanket. At 3:00 A.M. the buses and cars began picking up the women and children at the scattered residential areas. The refugees were driven to an assembly point at a place commonly called "Ascom City," more than halfway to Inch'ŏn. Each bus discharged its cargo and returned to Seoul for more. There was very little panic. A few women had tried to build up their courage from convenient bottles and were something of a problem. One married couple broke down and had to be carried out in improvised strait-jackets. But everyone else, whatever her fear for herself or for a husband left behind, went quietly down the road in the dark. Altogether about seven hundred women and children were driven to Ascom City during the night.[28]

CHAPTER THREE

Evacuation

EVERYONE WHO HAD a job to do came to the embassy sometime on Sunday and stayed until ordered to leave the city two days later. A few of those on duty were lucky enough to visit their houses or apartments at least once, but most never got home again after Sunday night.

A few men, not embassy officers who were all extremely busy, but some who had nothing to do, sat around drinking, listening to war stories, and exchanging frightening rumors. Not everyone could take the clamorous advance of a hostile army. The roaring guns reverberated steadily through the city now. Enemy planes frequently flashed from the sky to strafe some unseen target. When Muccio finally gave the orders to leave Seoul, some of these poor fellows were too drunk to walk steadily and had to be assisted into cars. They were very few out of the large number of men who went calmly and soberly down to Kimp'o and waited in a double line all day long for the rescue planes. But the few were enough to be quite conspicuous. A very, very few of the women were the same way.

Muccio felt reprieved after he got the women and children away early Monday morning. His most grievous personal responsibility had been met, although he still had about nine hundred men and women to look after, not counting the KMAG officers and men who were Colonel Wright's responsibility.

In the first hours of the attack six unfortunate American Methodist missionaries were captured in the border city of Kaesŏng. Since nothing had been heard from them at the embassy by Monday,

they had to be considered lost. A KMAG officer stationed in Kaesŏng had escaped with part of the ROK screening forces in the
city. The most that could be done now for these poor, lost people
was to pray that they were prisoners and had not been killed in the
early, fierce fighting.[1]

When the women were sent to Inch'ŏn it had been intended to
divide them between a Norwegian fertilizer ship, the *Reinholt,* and
a Chinese freighter, both lying several miles out from the mudbanks
of Inch'ŏn's inner harbor. Tides rise so high at Inch'ŏn, over twenty-
eight feet, that half the day there are many miles of exposed mud
flats with only a shallow stream for small craft. Ships must lie far
out or be stranded. Just after dawn on Monday morning the buses
began their relay runs on the short trip from Ascom City to the
Inch'ŏn piers, where a few ships' boats took over the relay. The
women were so terrified at the thought of boarding a Chinese ship,
which to their tortured minds might take them any place except
to safety, especially as they approached the vessel and saw the
curious Chinese crew peering down at them from high above, that
every single one of them refused to go aboard. They had had so
much terror back in Seoul, and they now recalled half-forgotten
tales of Chinese bandit vessels. There was no embassy officer with
sufficient authority at Inch'ŏn to make them go aboard. Actually,
they would have been far more comfortable had they taken the
hospitality of the Chinese captain, but they were not in a state of
calm reasonableness. They all crowded aboard the Norwegian ship,
almost seven hundred women and children on a vessel built to
accommodate six passengers. The heavy odor of the cargo, chemi-
cal fertilizers for the fields of Korea, seemed further to weigh down
both ship and passengers, everyone of whom thought fearfully of a
husband back in Seoul with North Korean forces steadily advancing and enemy planes flashing overhead.[2]

The three-day voyage to safety in Japan on this crowded, unprepared Norwegian vessel was a nightmare. Some of the women
were so shocked by the invasion and their frightening removal from
Seoul in the dead of night that this disagreeable, crowded, nearly
foodless voyage, fetid with the heavy smell of fertilizers, was more
than they could take. Some developed varying degrees of hysteria.
They became suspicious and hostile toward one another and every-

thing connected with the invasion and the evacuation. Even today
one can hear heated charges as to who took what, who was allowed
to bring out dozens of pieces of her choicest luggage, or who received
other special favors. This hysteria of a few obscured the good sense
and level judgment of the vast majority. Later inspectors had to
be sent out from Washington to investigate the various charges.
All were found baseless.[3]

Back at the embassy that Monday morning, however, everyone
was much relieved that the married women and children were safely
on their way to Japan. What difference did the type of ship or a
little crowding make? The lives and the freedom of this precious
cargo aboard the *Reinholt* were all that mattered to the embassy
officers and the husbands in Seoul.

Monday morning had dawned clear and hot after Sunday's
rains. Two more ROK divisions were moving into the battle areas,
which now were dreadfully close to Seoul. The Capital Division was
being fed into the battle piecemeal, as was the 5th Division later
when it arrived from the south. The 2nd Division was now moving
up to the Ŭijŏngbu corrido.. Hope began to spread throughout
the city despite the increased flights of enemy planes and the steady
sound of pounding guns in the north.

The 2nd Division, as its elements arrived, pushed up the Ŭijŏngbu
corridor to reinforce the 7th Division and take part in a general
counterattack. The 2nd was responsible for the east side of the
Ŭijŏngbu corridor and the 7th for the west. Until then the 7th Division had been fighting the whole battle. Unfortunately, the 2nd
Division was strung out for over a hundred miles, and when H-
hour arrived had only two battalions in position. Each division had
its outer flank anchored in high hills and mountains. Its inner flank
was the juncture with the other division down the center of the
valley where the North Koreans were attacking. The two divisions
were to jump off together in the afternoon, switching from the defensive to the offensive, driving back the enemy and rolling him
up. At H-hour the 7th Division under General Yu attacked on
schedule, but the 2nd, under General Yi Hyŏng-gŭn, did not move.
General Yi refused to attack with two battalions when he had been
ordered to attack with his whole division.[4] The North Korean
commander, sensing indecision and weakness in the 2nd Division,

concentrated upon it, drove it back, and then began rolling up the 7th Division's exposed left flank, forcing the 7th to retreat. By darkness on Monday evening what had started out to be the beginning of the successful counterattack of the ROK Army had ended in the rout of the 2nd Division elements and the retreat of the 7th Division from critical positions. Only the incredible efforts of General Yu and his men kept the North Koreans from just walking into Seoul. Panic gripped the city. Now there was no question of holding the enemy north of Seoul. How soon would the Communists force their way in?

Near Kaesŏng the 1st Division also fought stubbornly, without tanks or planes or long-range guns against an enemy who had them all. In the 1st Division, too, they found that bazookas and anti-tank shells bounced off those dreadful enemy monsters slowly grinding southwards. The only effective way to stop a tank was to swarm aboard regardless of losses, force upon the turret, and drop in hand grenades. Or to dash up in the face of a tank's chattering machine guns and plant mines right under the treads. Most of these South Korean suicide assaults were just that, suicide, but many a tank was stopped, and the North Koreans did not dare shove their armored force ahead of their slowly advancing infantry. When the enemy forced a crossing of the Imjin River and pushed tanks across, the 1st Division was forced to fall back from Munsan, but they still barred the way to Seoul. They were still fighting a very brave, roving mobile warfare days after everyone on our side had given them up as annihilated.[5]

The ROK government shared Monday morning's general optimism. The flurry of panic of the previous night died down. At ten o'clock the chief of staff, Maj. Gen. Ch'ae Pyŏng-dŏk,[6] a monstrous man weighing not very far short of three hundred pounds, appeared before the cabinet. Privately, everyone called the general "Fat" Ch'ae. I think he knew this and did not mind. He explained the military situation in detail. He said although his forces had been taken by surprise, they were giving a good account of themselves and were now being strengthened with reinforcements. He was bringing the 5th Division, and soon would bring the 3rd Division, from the south to protect Seoul, and he expected ultimately to commit both of them north of the city in a counteroffensive which

would drive the invader north across the parallel in disastrous retreat. Ch'ae obviously was under great strain but he answered questions clearly and concisely. The cabinet felt very much reassured.[7]
General Ch'ae was so fat he didn't walk, he waddled. His face
was crinkled into folds with rolls that almost hid his eyes. He always seemed in good humor and was lots of fun to know. He
was a professional soldier, having gone to various Japanese military
schools and risen to the rank of major in the Japanese Army in
World War II. He was an ordnance man and at one time held a
major command at the big arsenal in Osaka. After the war he
joined the Korean constabulary, predecessor to the ROK Army.
Whatever his girth, he had no fat in his head and he had risen
rapidly. Most of the ranking officers in the army had been professionals, either in the Japanese or Chinese armies. These were the
general officers of the ROK Army in 1950. Generally, the Japa-
nese-trained officers seemed to have a much sounder military education than those trained in China. "Fat" Ch'ae's deputy chief of
staff, a brilliant young officer in his early thirties, Chŏng Il-gwŏn,
was also a graduate of the Japanese Military Academy. Unfortunately, when war broke out he was just completing a military inspection trip in the United States and could not get back to Korea until
well after the loss of Seoul.

It seems to me most unlikely, however, that any other officer, no
matter how brilliant, could have fought a better battle for the
defense of Seoul than General Ch'ae did. The greatest military
genius could not have offset the North Korean artillery, tanks, and
planes. Without weapons to meet the enemy's great material
superiority, all the courage and infantry know-how in the ROK
Army could serve only to delay the fall of Seoul. The ROK Army
lost over 40,000 men, killed, wounded, and missing in three days,
out of a total strength of 98,000. No army could possibly have continued this rate of loss and still won the war. Whether "Fat" Ch'ae
was simply a good ordnance officer or an outstanding military tactician, I doubt that any other officer of any other nationality could
have done better against the odds which he faced.

Radio Seoul, Station HLKA, was taken over by the army on
Monday morning.[8] Although the same staff continued on duty,
only army-approved programs and messages were allowed on the

air. The army wanted the citizens to keep calm, and it especially did not want the roads and railroads blocked by panicky refugees when they were needed so badly for the movement of troops and supplies.

Long after the defeat at Ūijŏngbu was generally known, HLKA continued to put out happy bulletins. Several times they repeated a message from Muccio which he had delivered Monday morning when the picture was still bright. Among other things he had said:

We have been through a stirring twenty-four hours; we have endured a long, bitter night . . . the armed forces of the Republic of Korea have acquitted themselves well . . . their position at dawn today is stronger than the tenuous position they held at twilight yesterday. . . . Through the darkness of the night they fought bravely; they counterattacked and threw back opposing forces . . . with cool courage they withstood some of the most savage blows that a tricky enemy could hurl. . . . I am confident that the righteous cause of the liberty-loving Korean citizens of the independent Republic of Korea will prevail. . . .

By nine o'clock on Monday night messages from KMAG and the ROK Army, as well as the independent assessment of the military attaché, had convinced Muccio he could not delay much longer in evacuating most of the embassy staff. He telephoned Maj. Gen. Edward M. Almond, General MacArthur's chief of staff, at midnight and asked for enough transport planes at Kimp'o at dawn to fly two hundred personnel out of Korea. The individuals who were to leave were notified. Some went back to their rooms, but many already had the few things permitted with them at the embassy. Soon after midnight buses and embassy cars began to take them to Kimp'o airport. By two in the morning Embassy Seoul had a wholly male staff. Fortunately, a few of the secretaries were men, but not very many.

At first, even after he had decided he must send out most of the mission staff, Muccio thought he should keep about a hundred and twenty men in Korea, even though Seoul might have to be abandoned. But throughout the night, as the war news grew steadily worse, his estimates of the numbers he wanted with him decreased. By midnight he had decided to send out most of the men, but he could not start them moving until all the women were safely out.

All men now in Seoul were telephoned at their homes and told to come to the embassy and stand by.[9] Probably by three o'clock all the men were there, standing or sitting around and awaiting orders. It speaks very well for the general calm, orderliness, and friendliness of the citizens of Seoul that, despite the sounds of heavy fighting just north of the city and widespread fear, no ruffian or brigand or fanatic made the slightest move to harm a single one of these Americans moving through the blacked-out streets that night.

At dawn June 27, transport planes of the 5th Air Force, under fighter escort of F80 jets, picked up the personnel at Kimp'o and flew them to safety at Itazuke Air Base in Japan.[10] When YAKs tried to interfere, F80s swooped in and made the first air kills of the war. The United States was not in the war, but American airmen were fighting in it. No American plane was hit.[11]

As the night hours slowly passed and the battle reports grew more ominous, panicky rumors began to fly around the embassy. No one knows where they started. Perhaps too many men with nothing to do were sitting around in fear. Sometime during the night word spread through the embassy that the North Koreans had crossed the Han and now held Yŏngdŭngp'o, an industrial suburb just across the river, and Kimp'o airport as well. Drumright, however, just listened to the tale, picked up the telephone, and called Kimp'o. No, said the other end, there were no North Koreans there; Kimp'o was all right. That ended that rumor, but a small party was sent out in a jeep to test the road. They reached Kimp'o and telephoned back: all quiet.

The same grim news kept pouring in to the Kyŏngmudae and to other offices of the South Korean government. I am not sure when the president decided to leave, but he seems to have had his mind made up before midnight. Captain Sin Sŏng-mo made the travel arrangements and ordered a train to stand by. An emergency cabinet meeting was summoned to meet at the Kyŏngmudae at 2:00 A.M. (June 27), although the president did not attend. Defense Minister Sin had invited Yi Pŏm-sŏk, the former prime minister, to talk to the cabinet.[12] Because of his long military experience many people had more confidence in Yi's views than in the officers actually commanding in the ROK Army. Yi urged the government to go south of the Han River, where they would retain freedom of movement and would not be caught in the battle for the city. He described plans for the battle for Seoul, which would be defended house by house. He suggested that after the government had crossed the river, the Han bridges should be blown up, not only to deny the enemy an easy crossing but to make the Korean troops in the city feel they might as well stand and fight since there was no easy retreat possible for them. No vote was taken, but the cabinet generally seems to have agreed to these proposals. In addition to the cabinet, the chairman and one of the two vice-chairmen of the National Assembly attended this cabinet session. Following Yi Pŏm-sŏk's advice, the cabinet decided to evacuate government officials and their families from Seoul in two special trains, the ministers and bureau chiefs to go at 7:00 A.M. and those of lower rank at 8:00 A.M., although individual ministers were free to leave by motor car at will. The transportation minister undertook to provide the trains. Assembly Speaker Sin Ik-hŭi[13] was invited to tell the National Assembly of these plans, with the promise that the assemblymen and their families also would have space on the evacuation trains. Sin said he could not commit the Assembly to such a plan without consulting them, and he left to call the Assembly into emergency session.

Most of the assemblymen were awaiting a call, and a quorum had gathered for emergency session at four o'clock that Tuesday morning. Speaker Sin told the assemblymen what he had learned of the military situation at the cabinet meeting and of the government's plan to flee southwards. A bitter argument broke out, in which the government was accused of deserting and abandoning the people to save itself. Some spoke more moderately, pointing out that if Seoul did fall to the Communists and the government officials and assemblymen were captured, that would be the end of the Republic and the end of the war; but if they went south, they could continue to resist. To many of them, though, the capital was the Republic and its fall meant the end of the Republic. After an hour of angry debate a vote was taken. The majority decided that regardless of what the government did, the Assembly would not leave Seoul but would remain there with the people. Nevertheless, by nightfall the majority of the assemblymen had crossed the Han, very fortunately for the ultimate welfare of South Korea. About thirty-eight, however, hesitated. They remembered the vote and stayed behind. Most of them were captured by the Communists.

When the emergency cabinet meeting ended shortly before 4:00 A.M., several ministers went to see President Rhee. He and his staff were packed and ready to leave. The presidential party of secretaries and special policemen drove through the dark streets to the main railway station where a train was waiting. While the members of the National Assembly were still debating whether to remain in Seoul, the president's special train steamed off for the south. In a very few minutes it had crossed the Han River.[14]

After the cabinet meeting broke up, Foreign Minister Ben C. Limb,[15] Home Minister Paek Sŏng-uk, and the director of public information, Dr. Clarence Ryee, drove to the American embassy and called on Muccio. They found all the women gone, and the suitcases and other gear cluttering the halls were evidence that the embassy was about to decamp. A big fire was burning brightly in a parking lot beside the embassy, fed with the masses of classified documents from the embassy file rooms and individual safes. The burning had been going on all night, starting with the more bulky but less important documents, but by now including everything that mattered.

The three Korean officials had not been satisfied with the cabinet's decision and were concerned at the president's departure. They asked Muccio's advice. Naturally, they wanted some definite statement, but as usual Muccio talked in general terms. He was positive on only one point, so they said later: no matter what happened, he himself would not leave Seoul. There was some talk of American planes and American military assistance, but it is improbable that it was more than talk, although one of the Koreans present remembered Muccio saying he was urging his government to give Korea direct military assistance. Perhaps they misunderstood his remarks about the evacuation planes and their fighter escorts.

Muccio had a very hard time deciding what to do. If he let his people be caught, he was wrong, but if he sent them out prematurely he was also wrong. And if he did send them out, should he not keep the embassy alive in Seoul, at least in his own person?

He kept reducing the list of those who were to remain in the event of general evacuation until for a while it was down to only himself and a few others. Jim Stewart, who had been allowed two men on the stripped-down list, was finally told even he could not stay. He had to argue vigorously that the head of USIS must not leave Korea no matter what happened in Seoul before Muccio finally relented.

Muccio was in touch by telephone with the British Minister, Vyvyan Holt, the French chargé, Georges Perruche, and the Chinese ambassador, Shao Yu-lin. Holt and Perruche insisted they would not leave Seoul no matter what anyone else did, but Shao was more realistic. He knew that whatever restraint the Communists might show toward Holt, they would kill him if they caught him. He intended to leave if the American embassy did. Muccio was dean of the diplomatic corps; however, he did not call his colleagues together but communicated with them individually.

Muccio seems to have been much impressed by the arguments of Holt and Perruche, and during the night sent a cable to the department worded in such a way that it was interpreted as an offer to remain in Seoul with a small staff even if the North Koreans captured the city.[16] Today Muccio considers this a misinterpretation. He was thinking of the recent Chinese Communist conquest of China, when American diplomatic and consular establishments initially remained behind and did not leave with the retreating Nationalist government. Drumright, however, strongly opposed any such idea and insisted that if the government went south, the American embassy, which was accredited to that government, should do the same.

Had any part of the American embassy, especially the ambassador, remained in Seoul, the result would have been disastrous for the individuals and for American prestige. Actually, Muccio did not want to stay in Seoul and get caught by the Communists, but I think he became somewhat confused during that night as to where his duty lay. He was much relieved, however, when early in the morning a telegram arrived from Acheson expressing appreciation for Muccio's willingness to remain in Seoul but saying it was not advisable for him or any member of his staff to become voluntary hostages and therefore, unless there were compelling reasons not known in Washington, Muccio should leave Seoul to follow the government.[17]

Before Acheson's telegram arrived Muccio had considered what he would do if he remained and who would stay with him. If he remained, he planned to leave the embassy building and stay in his official residence when the North Koreans occupied the city, just as British Minister Holt actually did do. Donald Macdonald, a third secretary, was prepared to stay with Muccio, but Drumright was not. Drumright insisted it was the ambassador's duty to follow the government, not to be a martyr in his house. There was an exchange of words, and the rumor spread even to Kimp'o that Muccio would not leave Seoul whatever happened. Few heard of Acheson's telegram.

About 5:00 A.M. Muccio decided to get the rest of the mission staff off to Japan by plane and to keep with him the barest skeleton of a staff. The first "caravan" of men left the embassy for Kimp'o by bus and car about 6:00 A.M., and the last between 10:00 and 11:00 A.M. Muccio knew that Syngman Rhee had left, but he had not been told where the president intended to stop. Nor had Muccio received formal notice that the government was being transferred from Seoul, although Foreign Minister Limb believed he had given sufficient notice when he called to ask advice at four o'clock that morning.

Foreign Minister Limb did go around to the Chinese embassy and the legations and announce that the government was leaving Seoul. Then, driving his own car with some of his senior staff as passengers, he attached himself to the U.N. Commission on Korea, which was meeting at the Chosun Hotel. The commission, delegates and secretariat, was in a great turmoil. There were almost as many different ideas of what should be done as there were people. Limb kept them informed as far as he had information himself, which was not very much at the time. The commission members finally agreed to drive southward and make a decision after they had crossed the Han River. Limb escorted them as far as Suwŏn airstrip, where a nearly empty plane was waiting to take out some KMAG supernumeraries, and they were offered a ride to Japan. The temptation was too great, and after a hasty meeting on the concrete of the airstrip, the U.N. Commission climbed aboard the plane and flew away. The foreign minister waved them out of sight and then drove back north again toward Seoul.

The marines had broken out their M-1s, carbines, pistols, and plenty of ammunition on Sunday and had maintained a vigilant security watch ever since. Most of them remained at the embassy with Bob Heavey, the security officer, until he had finished his work, but some were sent on ahead to Kimp'o to give some sort of protection to the refugees gathering there and to keep order if need be. One of Heavey's last jobs was to destroy the coding machines. He used two thorium bombs and the machines burned up with a roar and swoosh. Everyone was much impressed. Precisely at ten o'clock Heavey smashed the essential parts of the telephone exchange with a sledge hammer. Muccio was still on the phone, talking to Tokyo, but the phone suddenly went dead and that was that. Heavey reported in but was told to take off. The last group from the embassy bound for Kimp'o and Japan left at eleven that morning. In this group were Bob Heavey, the consul, John Stone, and the second secretary, Tom Cory. For one reason or another Muccio brought them excess baggage for the trip he saw ahead of him.

Muccio and Drumright had drawn up a final list of those who were to stay behind in Korea. With the army crumbling, the government gone to some unknown place, and the future completely uncertain, Muccio wanted to have as few men as possible with him and selected only those for whom he could imagine specific duties and who had special qualities to execute them even in disaster and retreat. He saw no role for ECA and sent all ECA men to Japan. The small body of men remaining in Korea was split in two groups—a larger one with Drumright to find the ROK government and stay with it, and a handful to remain with Muccio while he decided what to do and where to stop.

In his search for the government, Drumright took with him Jim Stewart, Lt. Col. Bob Edwards, and Master Sergeant Davis from the military attaché's office, Commander Jack Seifert and Rodgers from the naval attaché's office, Third Secretary Curtis Prendergast, and Ioo D. Fattegatti, a code clerk. Later two JAS men, Carlin Wilson in charge of maintenance and Bob Smith in charge of the motor pool, joined this group. They were supposed to go to Japan but preferred to remain in Korea. Their special skills made them very valuable additions.

Drumright's party rendezvoused about 1:00 P.M. on Tuesday, June 27, in Yŏngdŭngp'o, across the Han River to the south of Seoul, having twice taken to ditches, once for enemy and once for friendly planes. They rode in three jeeps and Drumright's Buick, of which he was very proud and took the greatest care. They were soon on the main road to the south, the road that goes through Suwŏn, Taejŏn, Taegu, and ends at Pusan, a road they were to know so well. They proceeded uneventfully to Taejŏn, arriving about five o'clock, and found that President Rhee had already established himself in the provincial governor's residence.

Back in Seoul, Muccio kept with him Donald Macdonald, Marine Sgt. Jack Edwards, and Sam Berry, chief code clerk of the embassy. Muccio went to his house, packed some things into his private car, and drove to ROK Army headquarters, where he stayed for several hours. KMAG headquarters was in the same complex of buildings, which were strafed several times while Muccio was there. Muccio ate lunch out of cans with some KMAG officers, but Macdonald drove back across the city to his house, where he had a leisurely lunch prepared by his servants. The firing was now very heavy just over the hills to the northeast, and there were rumors that enemy tanks had already entered the city. But Macdonald took a perverse pleasure in eating a pleasant lunch at home. After lunch and farewells to his servants, Macdonald went to the capitol, a short distance away and went through the offices. The only officials he found in that large building were Home Minister Paek, Director of Public Information Ryee, and Vice-President Yi Si-yŏng, an aged and gnarled little man.[18] Then Macdonald drove to ROK Army headquarters and joined Muccio. A message had arrived that Brig. Gen. John H. Church and fourteen other officers representing MacArthur's GHQ would arrive at Suwŏn airfield at 6:00 P.M. Both for this reason and because of the steady accumulation of grim battle reports, Muccio decided to get moving and about two o'clock he started for Suwŏn.[19] Macdonald, Edwards, and Berry were with him. Later the assistant army attaché, Warrant Officer Bill Lynch, came down to Suwŏn on his own and joined the party in his usual very self-effacing way.

Soon after Muccio left, Col. Sterling Wright cut his staff to the fewest necessary and ordered all surplus KMAG officers to go to Suwŏn to await evacuation by air to Japan. These orders did not affect the KMAG officers and men in the field, who remained with the Korean units in battle.

Meanwhile, Chief of Staff Ch'ae, with part of his staff, had left Seoul, crossed the Han River, and set up a new headquarters about five miles south of the Infantry School. Colonel Wright considered this removal of headquarters not yet warranted. He drove down to the Infantry School and persuaded General Ch'ae to return to Seoul.

While the Americans were moving out of Seoul in orderly fashion, Korean officials and Korean private citizens were having a desperate time. They lacked transportation and knowledge of the battle situation. The seven o'clock train left as scheduled that morning, so jammed that many people were even riding on the roofs, but few of the ranking officials were aboard. They dallied too long at their houses or had trouble hurrying wives who did not want to abandon all their things. All cabinet members and some others, of course, had motor cars, but the great majority of officials did not. So they had difficulty just getting to the station. Most of those who had missed the seven o'clock train were there in time to board the eight o'clock, but there was no eight o'clock train. The station master said he had no orders to dispatch a special train, and no one could locate the transportation minister. As the morning passed, more and more people crowded into the waiting rooms and began packing the outer concourse. Finally, the station master gave in and dispatched a very long, special train to the south just at noon. Not everyone could get aboard, and many had already started walking so they could at least get across the Han River three miles away. This was the last train from Seoul.

After Muccio left the embassy, the great iron shutters were pulled down over the high doors and windows of the first two floors, giving the place a forbidding appearance. No one had raised the flag that morning, so none was lowered. The embassy seal was left over the center doorway and months later it was still there untouched. All the bustle and confusion around the embassy building of the past three days was now replaced by ominous silence. Hundreds of Koreans came by that day to observe the Americans, hoping to get a clue about the real war situation. They did not trust their radios or their newspapers. Depressingly, however, at the American embassy they found only closed iron shutters and silence. Some went back home, but others immediately started walking south.

Clarence Ryee, the information official, was still in Seoul. He spent part of the morning at ROK Army headquarters and returned to the capitol about noon. He too stopped en route at the American embassy and was appalled at the signs of total evacuation. Ryee had nominal responsibility for public morale and for radio station HLKA, but since the army had taken over the station and the issuing of war bulletins, he was at a loss what to do. He had been impressed by the activity at army headquarters and encouraging statements by General Ch'ae and Defense Minister Sin Sŏng-mo.

The chief of the Army Information Section, a Colonel Lee, came to see Ryee at his office in the capitol, and together they put out an encouraging newscast telling the people to keep calm, urging that everyone remain at home and keep off the roads, and reassuring them that the government was still functioning in Seoul. At 6:00 A.M. the radio had broadcast that the government was moving south to Suwŏn, but this 10:00 A.M. broadcast denied the earlier report.

Many people were relieved by the HLKA broadcast and relaxed a bit. Many who were about to start off on the long refugee trek decided to wait a little longer. They did not know where they would go anyway.

At eleven o'clock HLKA corrected the most misleading part of of the ten o'clock broadcast, saying that part of the government had left for Suwŏn but "a part of it is still in the capital," implying that the movement to Suwŏn was merely precautionary and the situation was not desperate. In a narrow sense this eleven o'clock broadcast was true, but in the broad sense it was completely false. The minister of defense was at army headquarters, and the home minister and vice-president were still at the capitol. Most of the assemblymen were still in the city. Yet the government as such was no longer in Seoul and the decision to leave had been made before four o'clock that same morning.

This misleading broadcast is still a subject of bitter controversy among the citizens of Seoul, and properly so. Many thousands who might be free today, who might be alive today, listened to it, were assured by it, and decided to wait at least until the next day. The next day was too late. Even Clarence Ryee thought Seoul was still safe for two or three days as he sat anxiously in his office at the capitol. He was still sitting there when Macdonald stuck his head in the door and told him that, aside from the vice-president and the home minister, he was the only man left in that big, doomed building.[20]

Ryee got a phone call from General Ch'ae about 2:20 P.M. Ch'ae told him the situation was now hopeless and Ryee had better get out of Seoul immediately because he intended to blow up the bridges across the Han River.

Ryee talked with Home Minister Paek, who insisted he would not leave Seoul no matter what happened. But Ryee knew Paek for a rather queer type; Paek reminded him of a Buddhist monk sitting alone in that quiet office. Ryee decided Paek's advice was useless, got in his car, and crossed the bridge about 3:00 P.M. The driver stopped the car so everyone could take cover from strafing YAK planes, but they got to Suwŏn safely in the late afternoon.

In the past Muccio had been diplomatically correct with the Chinese ambassador, Shao, but he was not friendly. Muccio's hostility to Chiang Kai-shek and his government carried over to Shao. In the excitement and confusion of the early morning Muccio forgot to be wholly correct. He did send word to Shao that the American men were being evacuated by air, with an offer to take out Shao's staff. Shao thought Muccio himself was going, and after sending his military attaché and a third secretary down the road to Pusan in a jeep, he went out to Kimp'o with the rest of his staff and joined the long queues of men waiting for the evacuation planes. There were 15,000 Chinese citizens living in Seoul and Inch'ŏn, and obviously there was nothing Ambassador Shao could do for so huge a number. They would have to look after themselves and take their chances with the Communists.

British Minister Holt was flatly determined that no North Koreans would scare him away from his post. He had both diplomatic and consular functions, and he insisted that in his consular guise he must remain to protect British citizens. Holt was a bachelor, a former army officer who had served with Lawrence of Arabia and whose diplomatic experience before he came to Korea in 1948 had been in the Middle and Near East. He spoke Arabic, Persian, Turkish, and several other languages and had acquired a beginner's knowledge of Korean. He was a man of honor, determined conscience, and a kind friend. He attended services daily at the Anglican cathedral just beyond his legation gate.

Holt's first secretary and consul, Sydney Faithful, argued urgently with his superior that if anyone should stay behind it should be he, Faithful, not the minister. Holt was unyielding, however, and finally gave Faithful categorical orders to go to Kimp'o and fly out with the Americans. Holt would remain behind with a vice-consul and a clerk to protect British interests. If the worst came, Faithful would be able to inform London of what had happened and to maintain continuity for the British mission. Reluctantly, Faithful drove to Kimp'o to wait for those rescue planes.[21]

The situation at the French legation was similar to the British. Georges Perruche, the chargé d'affaires, had sent out his wife and children when the American women were evacuated. He kept with him a vice-consular clerk. As soon as the military collapse seemed imminent, he telegraphed Paris for instructions, but no reply came. In addition to being chargé d'affaires, Perruche was consul general, and there were numerous French citizens in Korea, primarily Catholic priests who refused to leave. Weighing his two responsibilities, the diplomatic in which he should follow the government and the consular in which he should stay to try to protect French citizens, he decided he should follow his consular responsibility. Perruche doubted that the North Koreans would bother him very much. The Chinese Communists had inconvenienced French consulates in China during their conquest there, but still the consulates had always had considerable freedom and ultimately the consuls had been permitted to leave.

A French correspondent, Maurice-Georges Chanteloup, who had been in Korea a short time covering various stories for Agence France Presse, was with the French consular officials. He had haunted the American embassy during those first nerve-wracking days and nights, getting information and filing stories, and shuttling back and forth to the French legation to inform Perruche and get the French slant. At first he could not make up his mind whether to leave or to stay. O. H. P. King, the Associated Press man, whose wife had been evacuated with the other wives on Monday, went out to Kimp'o with the other refugees. Jack James of United Press, a bachelor, remained at KMAG headquarters for a time but finally decided to drive south in his jeep to Taejŏn, where he could file his story. Walter Simmons of the *Chicago Tribune* went with him. Chanteloup eventually decided he would stay with the French legation and cover the Communist occupation of Seoul from the inside. When the Communists arrived the next morning and arrested Perruche, they took Chanteloup along too, and as I write, two years later, they still have him.[22]

The apostolic delegate in Korea, Bishop Patrick Byrne, did not have to worry about making a decision, since he had made his long before. A very shrewd and likeable Irish-American, Bishop Byrne had sat out World War II in Japan, and he hoped it would not be too hard to sit out the war in a Communist-occupied Korea. He knew, though, that there were plenty of signs it might be. The previous year the government had arrested all Catholic priests and nuns in North Korea, most of the Westerners being German Benedictines, and had either imprisoned them or sentenced them to hard labor in the mines or elsewhere. The German bishop had already died. Bishop Byrne never concealed his contempt for Communists, his belief they were enemies of religion, civilization, and all human decency.

Once, many months before, we had had a long talk about what would happen if the Communists managed to capture Seoul. He remarked that I would get out with the American embassy because we were accredited to the South Korean government, but his position was different. He was accredited to the whole Korean nation, not to the government, and whatever happened in Korea it was his duty to remain.

When the crisis came Bishop Byrne kept in touch with the war news and with the American embassy, but only for information. When the embassy withdrew, he and his secretary remained quietly in their house until the North Koreans came and took them away.[23] All the other Catholic priests in and near Seoul refused the chance to get out, following the bishop's example. They too thought it was their duty to stay, but I doubt that if they had known of the many who would be killed, tortured, and imprisoned, they would have seen their duty in quite that light. With the exception of the six Methodists captured at Kaesŏng, all the Protestant missionaries in Seoul packed up when advised to by the embassy. The women left on Monday with the embassy wives, and the remaining mission-ary men were in the long lines at Kimp'o on Tuesday morning. None of their missionary societies believed that their men would do Korea any noticeable good by sitting in jail.

By early afternoon on Tuesday, June 27, government officials and private citizens in uncounted thousands were pouring down the road towards Suwŏn and on south. Few had much money with them and fewer had food or possessions. The first great movement of refugees was on. Most were on foot but some were in cars, even American mission cars which they had found abandoned and very sensibly rescued for their personal use. Seoul was being prepared for a battlefield; it no longer was a seat of government. ROK Army headquarters was still in Seoul, receiving an increasingly confusing series of messages from the front by radio, by messenger, and from staff officers who had been sent forward and were reporting in. Headquarters was repeatedly staffed by YAKs and while it seemed as though the anti-aircraft guns fired incessantly, no significant damage was done by either side.

There was no longer an American embassy in Seoul. The Ameri-can mission in Korea now consisted of that long, patient, double line of men standing on the concrete apron of Kimp'o airport, waiting interminably for the transport planes; of the KMAG group scattered out en route to Suwŏn and in-between; of the small group of men with Drumright now well on their way to Taejŏn; and the persons in Muccio's car.

CHAPTER FOUR

Caught by Surprise

I WOKE UP very late on Sunday, June 25, 1950, wonderfully at ease and relaxed. This was my first Sunday, in fact my first day, in nearly a year when I did not have to go to the embassy. I had been working very hard, seven days a week and most evenings. But not this Sunday. I was not even in Korea! Two days earlier the naval attaché's small airplane was flown to Tokyo for overhaul. I had been offered a seat, the ambassador had given me leave, and here I was lying in bed very late on a fine Sunday morning in Tokyo.

The attaché's plane was at Tachikawa Air Base, about twenty miles from the city. The pilot was Chief Petty Officer Curtis R. Allen, accompanied by CPO Albert P. Emsley, radio specialist, and CPO Walt Coe, mechanic, all from our naval attaché's office in the embassy. Allen arranged at Tachikawa for a general overhaul of the plane, which would require several days.

Soon after I arrived at the home of some old friends I telephoned Northwest Airlines and reserved a seat on the regular plane to Seoul on the following Tuesday. I remember now I have not yet canceled that reservation, but I don't think Northwest will mind. They did not fly to Korea that Tuesday, nor for a long time afterwards.

I got up leisurely on Sunday morning and had eggs and coffee with my hostess. I think my host was still in bed. We talked a little and casually read the morning's *Stars and Stripes* and *Nippon Times*. About 11:30 I left for what I intended to be a series of calls on old friends. I had lived in Tokyo for several years previously, both before and after the war, and knew a great many people

whom I had not seen for a long time. Walter Simmons, a close
friend, was in Seoul for a few days to cover the opening of a newly
elected National Assembly, but his wife very kindly lent me their
Ford to use during my stay. My conscience hurt me to take the car,
but my need for it was stronger than my conscience.

My first call was on Dick Hughes, a huge and kindly Australian
representing the Kemsley Press. He has a combination of clarity
and subtle humor in his writing that I have always admired and
envied. He was living then in a small apartment but had just been
told by the GHQ[1] housing authorities he would have to get out,
since his wife had recently died and as a bachelor he had no right
to an apartment. Dick and I expressed many views we shared in
common about various aspects of GHQ, not confining our remarks to the housing authorities. I recall we even mentioned Maj.
Gen. Charles A. Willoughby, the tall, handsome chief intelligence
officer of GHQ. It was just idle chitchat, but we had both been
around GHQ for a long time, and we doubted very much that in
a showdown Willoughby's assessments would be very reliable. Dick
asked about Korea. Maybe there was something he could use in a
story? No, I said, just the usual things: border raids, a few murders
here and there, Communist spies, violent radio propaganda from the
north. Just the same old story.

My next two calls were on Japanese, the first a medical doctor
whom I had not seen for years but who once had been very helpful to me on a story when I was a foreign correspondent in Tokyo.
He seemed quite glad to see me, and we tried to cover the passed
years in a few minutes of talk while his wife served tea. When I told
him I was first secretary of the American embassy in Korea, he
began to talk of the dreadful news from over there, of how awful it
was for the Communist Army to be invading the peaceful south. He
was surprised that I did not seem particularly concerned. I pooh-
poohed his fears, saying there were border raids and forays at the
38th parallel nearly every night. I had become so used to them
that they no longer worried me. No, said the doctor, this time it
is different; this is war! The radio news had been full of it. We
were talking in Japanese, and he used a phrase I had never heard
before but which he insisted a radio announcer had used. He got

out a small dictionary and we looked it up. He had been saying the North Koreans had declared war on the Republic of Korea. That I could not believe. I knew that whatever they might do, the Communists would not declare war. They would send their army to "liberate their down-trodden brothers in the south." So I completely discounted the rest of the tale. I had heard so many exaggerated accounts of events in Korea during the past several years that I assured him this must be just another, the exaggeration of a border incident far out of proportion. The doctor was polite: he said I ought to know, but obviously he was still concerned. I soon said goodby and drove on to my next stop.

This call was only partly social. Several years back when I had lived in Tokyo I had gone regularly to a nearly blind Japanese masseur who lived in Ueno ward. He was a remarkable fellow. Not only is he the best masseur I have ever known, but he is a keen business man. He managed to parlay a small amount of capital in the ruins of postwar Tokyo into a fair fortune, while sitting in his home and continuing to give massages. Rumor said he had started his financial rise with a corner on bicycle tires at the height of the transportation shortage after the war. Later he bought into and expanded a perfume and face powder manufacturing firm, marrying his daughter to his partner's son to be certain of continuity. When he found time for these business schemes I never knew, because he always seemed busy at his profession, now and then giving radio lectures or writing magazine articles on the best techniques. He was especially proud one day to tell me of a series of demonstrations he had given at a school for brides so the young women could relax their tired husbands.

My calls on him had early settled into a semi-social pattern. I was received as a distinguished family guest and shown into a small, Western-style sitting room. His wife and daughter served me tea and fruit as we sat and talked of a thousand things. My friend hated the Communists and saw no solution for the Soviet threat except an immediate American attack, supported by Japan, on the USSR. Near blindness and national defeat had not destroyed his martial ardor. His gentle wife, though, thought quite differently. The memories of a bombed and burning Tokyo were still vivid for her. She thought Japan had had enough of wars for a century, and she wanted whatever policy would keep Japan at peace. In due course we finished our tea and the amenities and retired to another room where my friend would give me a first-class workout, talking all the time. I responded only enough to be courteous.

This Sunday, as soon as I had entered and said the appropriate greetings, not having seen them for some years, my host said, "Isn't it terrible! What will happen now? What's the United States going to do? The American Army had better move in and destroy those Communists!"

I did not know what he was talking about until he explained that the radio had flashed several bulletins describing the Communist invasion of South Korea. Like the doctor, he said the North Koreans had declared war and severe fighting was in progress.

Well, I thought, this sounds like last summer all over again; the Communists must have started some pretty big drives across the border. We kept on talking and I began getting more and more uneasy, but somehow on that pleasant, relaxed Sunday in Tokyo it just did not seem possible that the war in Korea, which I had been predicting ever since 1946, had suddenly burst upon us.

We went through the courtesies and then proceeded to the massage couch. My friend worked while he talked, and again I mostly listened. Aside from a few polite words he speaks no English. The radio was playing Japanese music. Suddenly the music was interrupted and an announcer, speaking in Japanese, said that he was sorry to break in but he had an important announcement. He gave a brief bulletin of heavy fighting in Korea, and then music came back on.

Having heard the announcement myself I began to believe the startling news. Still, I thought, it was possible that some news agency was playing up a border battle into a major war, or that with my limited Japanese I had not correctly understood the announcer. But I got up, dressed hastily, and drove a few blocks to the home of another Japanese friend who had a shortwave radio. I was inside his house just before three o'clock, told him what I had heard and asked if he could catch the three o'clock broadcast from the Armed Forces Radio in Los Angeles. He too had heard some of the Japanese radio accounts but was not sure of the facts. He had his short wave receiver tuned to Los Angeles just as the announcer came on the air. The first words left no question that the war, which I had expected so long that I had scarcely come to credit its reality, had now burst furiously upon us.

I was appalled to find myself in peaceful Tokyo when my post was in Korea. So many times I had written and spoken of the inevitability of a Communist attempt to conquer free Korea that I was shocked to find myself on my only vacation exactly at the time when the North Koreans struck. Later I tried to sort out the reasons for my miscalculations, but at the moment I had just one urgent determination: to get back to Embassy Seoul to assume whatever duties the war should place upon me. Could will have overcome space, I would have been in Seoul the next instant. But there were over twelve hundred miles between me and Seoul, and my immediate need was to catch a plane.

I did not wait for the newscast to finish. Hastily excusing myself, I rushed out and drove at top speed to the SCAP Diplomatic Section in the Mitsui Bank building in center city. I found a young duty officer; on Sunday afternoon no one else was there. I told him I must get on a Korea-bound plane immediately. Foolishly I dismissed any thought of the little plane I had flown over in, since I thought it would have been stripped down so far by then that it could not fly again without many hours of work. The duty officer quickly got on the telphone. In no time he told me there would be a C-54 transport plane ready to take off for Seoul from Haneda airport at four o'clock. If I could get there on time, I could go on it. He gave me a Diplomatic Section car and driver so I would not be stopped for speeding. I gave him the keys to the Simmons' Ford parked outside. He said he would telephone Mrs. Simmons and my hostess for me.

Protected by the diplomatic license plates, I went through Tokyo at sixty miles an hour. I stopped briefly at my host's house just off the route to the airfield. All my things had already been packed in my suitcase and briefbag. I had no idea what was ahead of me in Korea, whether I would be working normally in Seoul or whether I would be on the run, and I did not dare risk being weighted down. I suppose I had a premonition of disaster. I quickly dumped out everything, repacked the briefbag with a few essentials, and took off again in a rush, with everyone, host and hostess and all the Japanese maids, calling farewells and good wishes from the gateway of their charming Japanese garden. Not until I had been in two retreats from Seoul, not until the next year, did I see my suitcase again.

I reached the airport and was ready to board the plane just after four o'clock. Only a little more than an hour had passed since I had heard that Los Angeles broadcast confirming the outbreak of war in Korea. The plane was in the air by five o'clock, and we thought we were off to the war.

About a dozen foreign correspondents, most of whom I knew well, were the other passengers. Most had covered the last war in the Pacific, a few had fought in it. Some of these men were soon to die in unknown Korean fields, but no one was thinking of death then, only of war. As we flew along most of the correspondents, including the one woman aboard, gathered around me where I sat on a canvas "bucket seat" and fired question after question. They asked about the opposing armies and every aspect of Korea they might conceivably be able to use either as background or for a quick estimate in their first stories, which they intended to file in Seoul that night. My voice finally became a hoarse croak trying to shout my answers loud enough to be heard by everyone over the roar of the motors.[2]

After some time the pilot came back and told us he had been ordered to fly in circles and not to continue toward Korea without further orders. If he knew why, he would not say. We flew and we flew, but we didn't get anywhere. Mostly we were over the ocean. Finally, the pilot came back again and told us we were returning to Haneda, and about eight o'clock we landed back where we had started from. Only after we were on the ground did we learn the reason. YAK fighters had been strafing Kimp'o airfield while we were flying those circles. The air force had decided not to risk any transport planes into Kimp'o that night.

I was bitterly disappointed and so were the correspondents. Several of them promptly telephoned stories to their offices in town, pegging them on me: "Harold J. Noble, first secretary of the American embassy in Korea, while flying back to his post this evening, was turned back by YAK fighters strafing the Kimp'o airfield." Several people at the embassy in Seoul heard this story on the radio that night and knew at least I was trying. Back in the States, somehow my wife missed it, but friends told her of it later.

As soon as I got back to my host's house, I telephoned a very senior colonel at GHQ G-2,[3] under whom I had served several years before, told him my troubles, and asked him to help me get back to Seoul right away. He said there was nothing he could do for me that night, but he would try first thing in the morning.

Back at my host's house I had a second severe disappointment. Just after I had left for Haneda airfield, Chief Petty Officer Allen had started telephoning me from Tachikawa airfield and had kept up for about an hour. He and the others had been out at Tachikawa all day putting the plane together. They intended to fly back to Seoul during the night and Allen thought I would want to go with them. But by the time I got back from my aborted flight, Allen had taken off for western Japan. There, at Itazuke Air Base, where they stopped to refuel and to get the latest information, Allen ran into Col. Sterling Wright of KMAG who, like me, had been caught vacationing in Tokyo. He, however, had heard of the outbreak of war earlier than I and had managed to get as far as Itazuke before the air force ordered that no planes fly to Kimp'o that night. But Allen's little plane was not under air force orders; it came from Embassy Seoul, and Allen got clearance to return to his home base. He picked up Colonel Wright and flew him into Kimp'o, landing Monday morning and giving KMAG a commander. Allen, Emsley, and Coe went on into the city and reported to Commander Seifert. Seifert ordered Allen and Coe to fly the plane back to Itazuke before dawn to save it from expected YAK attacks on Kimp'o in the morning. He kept Emsley with him at the embassy. Allen and Emsley were married, but their families had already left for evacuation to Japan before the two men reached the embassy. They did not meet.

In the morning I again telephoned my friend, the G-2 colonel. He spoke sharply and harshly. "Mr. Noble, General MacArthur has

ordered that there will be no American planes over the land mass
of Korea today. There is nothing whatsoever that we can do for
you." Then he hung up.

I was under great emotional tension. I absolutely had to get back
to my post in Korea. I could not walk there. I was certain someone
at GHQ could figure out a way. Someone finally did, but I did
not ask for help from G-2 again.

CHAPTER FIVE

I Find the War

I N TOKYO on Monday I spent a very long, nerve-racking day trying to get back to Seoul. The decision that "there will be no American planes over the land mass of Korea today," announced so harshly to me by an erstwhile friend, seemed to assure that I would not be in Seoul on Monday. There was no possible way to get back there except by airplane.

I spent all Monday in an office at the GHQ Diplomatic Section, not daring to leave even for lunch for fear a message might come in. I knew most of the ranking officers of GHQ, although none in Far East Air Force (FEAF), but whether I knew him or not, I telephoned and explained my predicament to any officer I thought might be able to help: the chief of staff, the secretary of the general staff, the GHQ operations officer, the chief intelligence officer at FEAF, the A-2, and others. Everyone was courteous, everyone wanted to help, everyone agreed that I must be in Seoul and promised he would do what he could to get me there, but each reiterated that orders were that no American planes should fly over Korea that day. Each officer in turn guaranteed that I would be on any plane going into Kimp'o if there were any change.

The FEAF A-2 was especially cordial, even though no one at FEAF had ever heard of me before. He was anxious to help, but he was even more anxious for United States planes to fly over Korea knocking YAKs out of the sky. Despite their promises to call me back, I kept telephoning these officers about once an hour. I am sure these very busy men that uncertain day were annoyed by my persistence, since for many hours there was nothing they could do

to help me, but they never showed it. The A-2 even told me I
could help the air force. He said their planes were ready and standing by if they only could get orders to go in. He urged me to try to
get the hold-back orders removed. Early in the afternoon he had a
semi-serious suggestion. He said if I was willing to parachute in,
he would have me dropped over Kimp'o. I thought that over a
bit. I had learned the general principles of the jump early in World
War II, but only in theory. I had never jumped and doubted
that this was the time to begin. I was still hoping someone in an
airplane would land me gently on the concrete. I declined with
thanks but said if nothing turned up by the next day, I would accept
his offer and jump in. I am glad I was never put to that test.

At midmorning I got Drumright on the phone. He told me the
battle picture was better, reinforcements were going forward, and
he hoped a decisive and victorious battle would be fought near
Ŭijŏngbu in the afternoon. I told Drumright of my difficulties; he
told me to get back as fast as possible but had no suggestions how
I could do so.

In the early afternoon I called Drumright again, but he was
busy and Macdonald talked with me. The situation was inconclu-
sive, and Macdonald did not seem nearly as hopeful as Drumright had been. A couple of hours later I again telephoned Drumright. He said things definitely were not going well, and he urged
that I get over immediately. I suggested that Muccio telegraph
MacArthur stressing his need for my services and asking that I be
given emergency air transportation. Drumright said he would do
this, and in the early evening a long and very flattering telegram
from Muccio addressed to MacArthur was on nearly every desk in
GHQ urging that I be sent posthaste back to Seoul. I had served
previously in GHQ and knew that such a telegram would be widely
reproduced and circulated. I counted on its having an effect where
it was needed most, whether or not MacArthur did anything about
it. But before the telegram arrived, I was already set to go.

Drumright had suggested that I get to Itazuke at the far western
tip of Japan just across from Korea, where the naval attaché's plane
was being held for safety. He said he would instruct Chief Petty
Officer Allen to fly me into Kimp'o during the night, just as he
had flown in Colonel Wright early that morning. I said I would

get on to this right away, although of course I would have to wangle
a plane ride from Tokyo to Itazuke first.

It was about 4:00 P.M. when I called Brig. Gen. Edwin R.
Wright, the G-3, who had been about to call me. The prohibition
against flying over Korea had just been lifted and a C-54 transport plane was to go into Kimp'o in the early morning. It would
leave Haneda airport at 4:00 A.M., pick up fighter cover at Itazuke,
and have me at Kimp'o by 8:00 A.M. I told Wright of Drum's
suggestion about flying in during the night on the naval attaché's
plane. General Wright advised against this. He said the C-54
would fly nonstop from Tokyo to Kimp'o and be protected by
fighter cover. The little unarmed navy plane would be strictly on
its own. If any enemy were in the air near Kimp'o, we would either
be shot down or forced to land at Pusan, where I would be
scarcely better off than if I never left Tokyo. Besides, he said, he
did not feel justified in setting up a plane just to carry me from
Tokyo to Itazuke.

When I hung up, the FEAF A-2 was on the line. The orders
against flying over Korea had been canceled, there would be a
C-54 going directly to Kimp'o from Haneda leaving at 4:00 A.M.,
and I was on the passenger list. I asked his views on Drumright's
suggestion and told him what General Wright had said. The A-2
either had more imagination or was more frank with me than General Wright had been. He said it would not be a bad idea at all to
go to Itazuke and fly in during the night on the little naval
attaché's plane, and he would be glad to set up a special plane to
get me to Itazuke. He said that no matter how I left Tokyo, my
actual departure would be from Itazuke, not from Haneda, since
Itazuke was the base for operations into Korea. It might be a good
idea to be there to take advantage of whatever plane came along
instead of being tied to only one scheduled flight out of Tokyo. In
my ignorance, however, I decided to be guided by General Wright,
not knowing that the Ŭijŏngbu battle already had been lost and
everything would be very different in Seoul that night. I liked what
Wright had said about being covered by a fighter escort. That's
the way I preferred to fly.

I was at Haneda about 3:30 A.M. (Tuesday, June 27) and
gave my name to a lieutenant colonel from GHQ. He had me on

his list. A lieutenant colonel from FEAF came along, the pilot of
the plane. He had me on his own, separate list. The GHQ colonel
said he had orders to get me to Kimp'o. The FEAF colonel said
he had orders to get me to Kimp'o. It looked as though I would get
to Kimp'o.

Promptly at 4:00 A.M. the big plane took off and I thought, "At
last we are on the way to Korea." This was my second departure
from Haneda by C-54 since the war had begun on Sunday.

The primary passengers were a group of thirteen officers and two
enlisted men from GHQ, led by Brig. Gen. John Church, a division
commander in Europe in World War II with a fine record; they
were going to Seoul as a survey party.[1] They were to report back
to MacArthur's headquarters on how the war was going and what
the ROK Army needed to defend itself. Aside from one colonel
whom I knew slightly from a very recent visit he had made to Seoul,
the officers were mostly all lieutenant colonels in staff positions.
Through the colonel I quickly became acquainted in a casual way
with the whole group.

To my disappointment, we landed when we reached Itazuke.
General Church said he wanted to have breakfast. We waited at
Operations for some time, but finally cars arrived and we were
driven all the way around the field to the officers' club, where we
very leisurely ate a full meal. This was not quite the fast trip into
Kimp'o I had visualized.

As we finished breakfast, two girls from Embassy Seoul came
into the club. They had just arrived on a rescue plane from
Kimp'o. Fifth Air Force transport planes had been taking our girls
out since dawn. I was told that my secretary was in the next plane
to come in, but I never saw her. I was too busy following General
Church around for fear I would be left behind. Jet fighters, which
had flown cover for the rescue planes, flashed and roared in and
out of the sun, swooping down onto the field in a steady stream.
I listened to some of the pilots talking. A group was laughing and
shouting around a young kid who had just landed. He had shot
down the first YAK of the war when it tried to interfere with
one of the C-54s with all those girls aboard.[2]

General Church said he had to telephone Tokyo for orders. Quite
shamelessly I stood beside him at the counter while he called GHQ.

He was told to stand by for later orders. I was unaware, of course, but back in Tokyo they knew Embassy Seoul was evacuating and were trying to decide what to do about Church and his party.

We went back to Operations and waited. Hour after hour crawled by. The dispatcher assured me there was no question of our plane not going to Kimp'o. But it would take at least two hours to refuel the jet fighter escort, and until they were ready the C-54s would be held. Out on the field I thought I could count a dozen C-54s lined up and ready to go.

Finally, there was a telephone call for General Church. Again I hugged the counter beside him. Church was told that his mission was canceled and he should return to Tokyo. I cannot put into words my agony when I heard Church tell the officer in charge at Operations that he wanted his C-54 to take his party back to Tokyo immediately. I had come so far and yet was still so far from Seoul! I did not know what was happening in Seoul but I suspected the worst. Now it appeared that I had lost my one chance to fly in.

The air force officer in charge at Operations was only a major, and a brigadier general was telling him to get his plane in the air. But the major protested and finally refused. He told Church that this C-54 was one of the rescue planes set up to go to Kimp'o to bring out American men who were waiting there, and he could not give it to Church to carry him back to Tokyo. Church was equally insistent that the plane had been assigned to him, that he was ordered to return to Tokyo and the plane was going to take him. The major got a lieutenant colonel who backed him up, but Church got on the telephone to GHQ. The major called FEAF. Each was told from the other end that the issue would be decided in Tokyo.

I thought Church's indifference to the rescue of those men at Kimp'o was appalling, and a couple of his staff to whom I talked quietly thoroughly agreed with me. I located the air force lieutenant colonel who had flown us to Itazuke. He told me not to worry. He still had orders to get me to Kimp'o. He was going to get me to Kimp'o, and by God, general or no general, Church wasn't going to fly off with a rescue plane! I felt reprieved but did not stop worrying until finally we were airborne and Korea-bound.

At last the telephone calls came from Tokyo. Church was told to release the plane for the airlift and to make other arrangements to get back to Tokyo. I shook hands and said farewell to several officers in Church's party, and they wished me luck. The pilot of our plane waved at me. I ran for the plane, swarmed up the ladder, and we were moving down the runway. We were the first C-54 off the ground in a group of four flying to Kimp'o to rescue the men patiently waiting there. I had been told that because of the great difference in speed, the F-80s would not take off until we were nearing Kimp'o, and in fact we did not see a plane until we were coming in to land. Each transport plane must have flown a separate course, because although we were first in the air, we were third to land and the two planes ahead of us were already loaded with their passengers. I think we touched down at Kimp'o about 2:00 P.M.

As we came in, I could see the familiar landing strips, the big concrete administration building, and beyond it the hangar. A double line of waiting men wound along the strip. I peered out the small, round porthole and recognized many faces. My brother's was not among them; he had already boarded the plane ahead.[3]

We came to a stop, the great motors were finally throttled off with their last gasping roars, and silence and peace seemed to have settled over Kimp'o airport. The doors were unlocked and a long ladder thrust out. I picked up my briefbag and stepped to the head of the ladder.

"Harold, get back, get back inside," someone shouted.

I looked down, and close to the ladder were Tom Cory, the second secretary who worked under my direction, Bob Heavey, security officer, and John Stone, consul. It was Tom who was urging me back into the plane. I had not made all that effort to fly over to Kimp'o just to stay aboard the plane, and I began climbing down the ladder while Tom kept telling me to get back, all was lost, I would lose my seat and perhaps be left behind.

I will never forget that scene. Although two planes already had been filled, there were close to two hundred men still waiting. Locker trunks and open suitcases were strewn everywhere. The marines, who apparently had not shaved since the first shot of the war and all looked like pirates wearing the most variegated headgear, had M-1s and carbines slung over their shoulders and pistols at their belts. They were checking on baggage and requiring those men who had expected to bring out all their things to cut down to hand luggage. Some men were opening trunks to pick out items of special value. When they had rearranged their hand baggage, they did not bother to close the trunks and suitcases strewn on the tarmac. The men knew they would never see them again.

When I reached the concrete, I asked Cory what was up. Very much, everything was up. The North Koreans had captured Seoul and had already crossed the Han River. They had entered Yŏng-dŭngp'o, south of the river, and were scarcely twelve miles away. Tom kept insisting that I must get back in the plane and return to Japan if I wanted to stay alive. I was very much disturbed.

"Where is Muccio?" I asked. "I must join him."

"You can't," said Tom. "He's lost, he's disappeared, and no one knows what's happened to him."

"Well, then, where's Drumright, I'll join Drum," I replied.

"No, the guerrillas must have him by now. He was last seen driving south in the mountains and that's the end of Drumright."

"Well, that leaves me with a greater responsibility. I'll join the ROK government and stay with them until I can get instructions. Where's the government?"

"There isn't any government. It's collapsed, disappeared, there's no government for you to join!"

I was stubborn, but I must say I was shaken. I had come all the way from Tokyo after what seemed enormous difficulties, and I did not want to return ignominiously. But I had not come over only to be shot uselessly. I asked Cory how he knew the enemy was in Yŏngdŭngp'o, and he answered that everyone knew it. I turned to Bob Heavey and asked him about Muccio. "Oh," said Bob, "you can find Muccio if you want. He's holed up in his house, and if you want to be a prisoner you can go and join him. There are plenty of abandoned cars around here for you to pick from."

"What about the North Koreans in Yŏngdŭngp'o?" I asked. Heavey doubted it but was not sure. John Stone kept silent; he never opened his mouth.

I turned away from Cory and walked past the fourth rescue plane to talk to the marines. I thought they were more likely to know about the North Koreans than Tom. They were a relaxed, happy, carefree lot, and they did wonders for my morale. I remained deeply concerned but now felt that there was still a chance I could find someone to go with me. At that moment CPO Al Emsley, with whom I had flown over to Tokyo the previous Thursday, drove up in a jeep with a small trailer crammed with suitcases and other gear. Emsley wore navy dungarees and had his chief's hat cocked over one eye. He said he was going to drive down to Pusan, where he could catch a ship. None of this air evacuation for him. He wouldn't abandon his gear, Christ, no!

I asked the marines where KMAG was. Someone said he had heard KMAG was to rendezvous at Suwŏn. Emsley asked whether I wanted to ride with him to Pusan. I asked him what he thought of the North Koreans at Yŏngdŭngp'o, which we would have to pass through to get on the road to Suwŏn and Pusan. He said he didn't know but he would take the chance. I agreed to go with him as far as Suwŏn and look for KMAG. Maybe someone there could tell me where the ambassador or the government was. If not, then I too would drive with him down to Pusan and out that way.

The marines gave me a carbine, a .45, and some extra clips. Emsley was armed the same way, and we spread extra ammunition loose on the floor of the jeep, ready for a fast refill. We expected to be taken under fire at Yŏngdŭngp'o, but we hoped the enemy was not yet there in force and that with luck we could successfully fight our way through to the main southbound road.

We had made arrangements and I was still talking with the marines when Cory came and again urged me to leave for Japan. He was positive everything was hopeless, that there was nothing I could do to help, and that I must get out before it was too late. His intentions were good, but he was rattled. His positiveness, however, unsettled me again. I asked myself whether I was foolishly and obstinately driving to Suwŏn to be killed for no purpose at all. I had been shot at many times, but I never looked for a suicide bullet. Fortunately, a pilot of one of the rescue planes was standing nearby. Disturbed as I was, I turned to him for advice. I outlined my position and my problem. He spoke very abruptly. My duty, he said, was to find the ambassador and stay with him. I have never seen that man again and would not recognize him if I did, but I have always been grateful for his simple, uncomplicated view, which cut through the fog of my uncertainty. I thanked him and stepped in beside Emsley, who had just driven up again. We drove up the strip, past the waving marines and the silent lines of waiting men. As we drove away Cory shouted, "Harold, don't do it! You're finished! Harold, you're just asking for it!"[4]

Before we drove off the strip, Emsley stopped the jeep beside one of the open, abandoned suitcases. I helped myself to a new plastic raincoat and several bars of soap. Emsley found other things equally useful. Later I wished we had taken the time to go through all that scattered gear. We needed so much and had so little.

We drove up the road toward Yŏngdŭngp'o wondering where we would meet the first North Korean fire. It occurred to me that if I were killed or captured, the calling cards of Korean friends in my wallet might be used against them by the Communists. As Emsley drove along, I methodically tore each card into small pieces and dropped them on the road.

At the outskirts of Yŏngdŭngp'o I guided Emsley to a road which, while it entered Seoul, nearly skirted it to the south. I hoped that the North Koreans might not have come so far or that only patrols would be in the town. I had my pistol cocked with the safety on and I held the carbine ready to fire. The jeep had no top, and we could have answered fire from any direction. Emsley was less free to fire, since he was driving, but his weapons were equally ready. We drove swiftly into Yŏngdŭngp'o. No one appeared on the streets, and the silence seemed ominous. I kept my trigger finger ready to squeeze. We drove silently along, waiting, waiting, waiting, but nothing happened. No shot, no rifle fire, no hostile movement. In a few minutes we were through town and safely on the road to Suwŏn.

I did not know it then, of course, but the ROK Army was still fighting just north of Seoul and did not abandon the city until late that night. There were no North Korean forces in Yŏngdŭngp'o. Rumors and panic had gripped many men at Kimp'o, and I had almost become their victim.

As we approached Suwŏn, about twenty miles south of Seoul, I asked Emsley to drive out to the airport to look for the KMAG detachment. I wanted to ask about Ambassador Muccio and the

ROK government. If I found any semblance of government left anywhere, I would try to join it; otherwise, I intended to continue south with Emsley.

Neither of us had ever been to the Suwŏn airfield, and I had to ask directions from various policemen and others on the crowded streets of the city. As it turned out, the airfield was a short distance off the main road just south of town. We were southward bound to the airfield when I saw a familiar blue Mercury sedan rapidly approaching from the opposite direction. As we passed, I saw that Muccio was driving and recognized Macdonald beside him. Emsley and I waved frantically, and both cars stopped some distance from each other. I got out and ran eagerly over to the Mercury, while Macdonald got out and ran to greet me. We shook hands, and I looked happily in the car door at Muccio.

"Where the hell do you think you're going," barked Muccio, "Japan?"

I suppose he was half kidding, but after all I had done to get there, I was startled.

"No," I said, "I'm reporting for duty."

"Oh," said Muccio in a much friendlier tone, "get in." I climbed in beside him. Macdonald got in the back seat with Sam Berry, and Emsley turned his jeep around to follow us. Muccio explained to me that he was meeting a General Church and other officers from GHQ at 6:00 P.M. at Suwŏn airport. They were coming to set up an advance command post for GHQ. In the meantime, he was looking for the defense minister, who was said to be somewhere around Suwŏn. I was startled at his remarks about Church and told him that Church had been ordered back to Tokyo. Muccio was equally surprised at my comments and told me that Church very definitely was on his way to set up an advance command for GHQ. Each of us thought the other was a bit balmy. I did not know that MacArthur had reversed his decision on Church, had changed his mission from survey to one of command, and after my departure from Itazuke had ordered Church to take the same party to Suwŏn to set up a headquarters.[5] Muccio did not know of my experiences with Church, thought I knew nothing about the general, and could not comprehend my comments. At the beginning of the retreat, therefore, we started out on the wrong foot. We worked very closely for the next three months, but it was not until we were back in Seoul in the fall that Muccio relaxed with me again.

We drove to the railway station in Suwŏn. The square was packed with refugees seeking trains for the south. Standing near the station, talking to the minister of agriculture and forestry, was the minister of education, Dr. George L. Paik. As usual, Paik talked to us calmly and pleasantly, asking about the war situation. He said he had heard that the president was setting up the government at Taejŏn about a hundred miles farther south and he planned to go on down. Muccio spoke encouragingly and urged Paik to tell the president and everyone he met that if the Koreans would just hold together and not despair, they would win out despite the early defeats. They must not give up hope; the worse the situation, the more they should pull together. This was Muccio's war song. He had to repeat it nearly to exhaustion.

Paik said the defense minister was inside the station, so we went in. Captain Sin sat in a small room eating a bowl of *kuksu*, a delicious form of Korean vermicelli with meat. This was Sin's first meal for a long time. Muccio and Macdonald were hungry too and called for bowls of *kuksu*. I was not hungry, but I went out to Muccio's car and with his keys opened the trunk. There lay several bottles of scotch, the greatest treasure of the war. I brought one in for the long delayed meal. We all drank a little and soon felt much better.

Muccio told Captain Sin of the impending arrival of General Church as ADCOM commanding general. They decided that for the moment Captain Sin would tell General Ch'ae to set up ROK Army headquarters in the same place if he were forced out of Seoul. There was an agricultural experiment station and an agricultural college about two miles west of Suwŏn. Attached to the station were three small Japanese-style Western houses. One of them had been occupied before the war by an agricultural adviser who had been evacuated. Madonald was sent to get the houses in shape.

Muccio and I went out to Suwŏn airfield in the softly falling rain to wait for General Church. I was still puzzled about Church's mission, since I had heard him ordered back to Tokyo, and Muccio was still annoyed with me for thinking I knew anything about Church. The Suwŏn field has only one short landing strip, but it later turned out to be big enough for C-54s. Church, however, was flying in a C-47. Some KMAG officers were gathered around the vehicles at the side of the airstrip, waiting to be evacuated to Japan. The rain came down harder, and many who had been walking restlessly back and forth got back into their cars. Muccio and I wandered around aimlessly talking to different officers. Suddenly a message crackled into a receiver on a radio truck. It was from Colonel Wright at ROK Army headquarters in Seoul. Wright ordered his officers and men waiting at Suwŏn airstrip to saddle up and get back to Seoul. I have never seen a sadder, more dispirited bunch of men than that KMAG group as they started north to Seoul again. They were almost sure that the battle was lost and they were being ordered to a duty which would bring them death or imprisonment. But they were good soldiers and they obeyed. Soon Muccio and I were left alone at the field.

At about 6:00 p.m. a C-47 came sliding out of the west, touched down, and pulled to a stop in front of us. Out climbed General Church and the other officers I had left behind for good at Itazuke that morning. Some of the KMAG vehicles had been left for their use and we all piled in to drive to the agricultural college.

We went to the small house Macdonald had picked out for the embassy party and ate a supper Macdonald had had prepared by the servants who were still there. It was a delicious prototype of all subsequent meals at Suwŏn. Well-seasoned cabbage soup with a soupçon of meat, and coffee on the side. During the few days we were in Suwŏn, one thing or another kept me from eating more than one meal a day, and I can honestly say I have never tasted anything finer than that daily cabbage soup à la Macdonald.

After the meal I went up to the buildings of the experiment station with General Church's G-1 and talked to the director. He was a small, sad man who spoke a little English. I explained our needs, said that we would have to take over all the main buildings for our headquarters, and asked his permission to inspect it. Poor fellow! As he led us through room after room, he kept repeating, "I am so sorry you are here, I am so sorry you are here."

We selected the director's room for General Church's office, with a general duty room just outside. The whole structure, an old wooden building, was very shabby and had little furniture, and such as it had was not intended for a military headquarters. I deliberately did not select a separate office for the embassy. I felt the army officers, despite their eagerness to help, were so ignorant of Korea and the problems they would face in dealing with Koreans that we had to be close by to assist them at all times. The only way we could do so was to be in their offices, not separated somewhere else in the building. Like Muccio, I made a practice of entering General Church's office at will, and so did Drumright. We welcomed the army very much, but we knew they needed help and doubted they were aware how much they needed it.

At the very beginning, therefore, circumstances made us recognize our fundamental role as liaison between the U.S. Army and the ROK Army and government.

Church kept saying that he must go up to Seoul and look over the situation, but Muccio argued there was not much to do in the dark. At best he might get lost, and at worst he might get killed or captured. Muccio suggested that they go into Suwŏn, telephone Col. Sterling Wright from there, and follow his advice as to whether Church should go immediately to Seoul or wait for morning. While they were talking, Ben Limb, the foreign minister, drove up. He said there was a Tokyo phone call for Muccio in Suwŏn. Muccio and Church drove off, and Limb followed them. For reasons I do not recall, several of us decided that we too should go to Suwŏn. We took a sedan and I drove. Because of the YAKs we drove without lights in a very black, rainy night. A few hundred yards from our headquarters the front wheels started gently sliding off the dirt road into a deep ditch. I could do nothing but stop the car, leaving it hanging almost on its side. I remember that, surprisingly, I was not worried about the loss of a sedan. I had seen several hundred abandoned cars that afternoon at Kimp'o, and one more lost sedan did not strike me as important. That shows my frame of mind that first night. Later, I strongly condemned myself for not having driven one of those excellent abandoned cars south from Kimp'o instead of riding with Emsley in his jeep. That night, fortunately, someone got a jeep and pulled the sedan out of the ditch and drove it back to our headquarters. Whatever it was that we needed to do in Suwŏn, we did not do it.

When Muccio picked up the telephone at Suwŏn police headquarters, he was on a line to Tokyo by way of Seoul. A female voice with an American accent cried, "God damn it, they've all run off and left me." It was the chief operator of the international telephone exchange in Seoul, a Korean woman who had lived most of her life in Hawaii. In the last confusing hours Muccio had told her she could be evacuated with the Americans but had had too much on his mind to remember her or do anything about it. He did not think of her again until she despairingly cried out to him over the long distance telephone.

Church talked with Sterling Wright and decided to wait for morning before going to Seoul. When morning came, Wright was searching for a way out of the capital. By that time Church very definitely did not want to visit a city occupied by the North Koreans.

CHAPTER SIX

Suwŏn Interlude

AT EARLY LIGHT on Wednesday, June 28, a sergeant from KMAG headquarters in Seoul hurried up the stairs to the loft where we were sleeping and awakened us. I listened to his bad news and fell asleep again, but Muccio got up and went out to learn more.

The sergeant's story could not have been more disturbing. The North Koreans had steadily pounded their way into the northeastern part of Seoul from Ŭijŏngbu, and at midnight reports reached ROK Army headquarters in Seoul that tanks were cautiously nosing into the center of the city. The 7th and 2nd divisions, or what was left of them, with broken units from other divisions, were still fighting, but army headquarters decided all hope of defending Seoul was gone.

General Ch'ae quietly informed his staff that he was moving his main headquarters south of the Han River, and one by one Korean staff officers slipped away and drove south across the bridge. A headquarters rear echelon staff, headed by the acting deputy chief of staff, remained behind in Seoul until the end to control the fighting from there and to command the considerable ROK forces still engaged in the city.

In the confusion, the American officers did not notice that the headquarters had thinned out. Suddenly the deputy chief of staff came to the senior American officer on duty with a message to Colonel Wright from General Ch'ae, who had just crossed the river. The message was that KMAG should move south at once; the bridges would be blown up in ten minutes. Wright was hurriedly summoned from his nearby house, where he had gone for a brief nap. Forty-eight KMAG vehicles were quickly lined up in a convoy ready to start for the Han. But before they could get moving, at 2:15 A.M., the reverberating roar of the explosions at the bridges rolled back into the city. No warning was given to anyone at the bridges. Several hundred refugees and soldiers are said to have been killed on the vehicular bridge, and some American correspondents who had almost reached the other side were injured slightly.[1]

The remnants of the divisions fighting in Seoul on the road to Ŭijŏngbu were now cut off from retreat, as was the rear echelon of ROK Army headquarters and KMAG. No KMAG officers or men were on the bridge when the long central span fell into the river with a gigantic roar. The railway bridge nearest to the vehicular bridge also was destroyed, but a second railroad bridge merely buckled, and the charges on the third railway span did not explode. The North Koreans still had a bridge to cross the river on if they could fight their way across. About the same time that these lower bridges were being blown up, other engineers very thoroughly destroyed the long bridge several miles farther upstream.

The sergeant who awakened us had swum across the river to an island in midstream and then had made a shorter swim to the southern bank. Despite the great confusion on the road, he managed to pick up rides and was in Suwŏn at our cottage by 5:00 A.M. He gave us the essential facts, and from then on a steady stream of American and Korean soldiers began reaching us at Suwŏn, filling in the gaps in the story. But even that early in the morning we knew that Seoul was lost, that the divisions north of the river were trapped, and that Colonel Wright was still in Seoul.

About 7:00 A.M. I suddenly reawakened and realized I was sleeping alone in that attic room. Muccio and Macdonald were gone. I jumped up hastily, fearful I had missed out on some important development. Downstairs I found Macdonald directing the servants in the kitchen. Without taking time to shave or eat, I hurried up the hill to the experiment station ,where ADCOM headquarters was located. Muccio was with Church, and I joined them. We sat listening as report after report tumbled in on the collapse of Seoul. It appeared that almost everyone in KMAG was safe except Colonel Wright; of him no one had any word.

I was bursting with eagerness to go to the Han River to see for myself, but of course I could not leave without permission. I talked to two GHQ officers, lieutenant colonels, who were with ADCOM as operations officers. I suggested that with the collapse of Seoul, ROK Army headquarters was likely to have been established at the Infantry School just south of Yŏngdŭngp'o and that undoubtedly they would want to go up there to get an estimate of the situation for General Church. They promptly agreed, and I offered myself as guide. Then I told Muccio of their prospective trip and asked whether he objected to my going to guide them. He was not enthusiastic but did not say no.

As we drove north in a jeep, we often had to nearly force our way through a tremendous stream of refugees. Men, women, children, even children carrying children, and nearly everyone seemed to carry a bundle as big as he was, were walking steadily south, filling the road from side to side. Mixed in with this stream were many, many thousands of South Korean soldiers. Beaten and exhausted though they were, most of them waved and many cheered as we went by. We were greatly impressed that almost every soldier was carrying his weapons, and often tied to the muzzle of a rifle or carbine was a small Korean flag. Rifles, carbines, pistols, even BARs, were coming down the road in the hands of their trained users. They were a defeated army, but not a panicked army. They were retreating, but not stampeding. All they needed was someone to round them up, give them orders and a meal, and they would be a fighting army again. Civilians, too, as our jeep passed with the two American uniformed officers aboard, cheered and clapped their hands. Our whole drive northward was accompanied by this steady sound of cheering and clapping. These pitiful refugees still had hope and believed that we symbolized ultimate victory for their country and a peaceful return to their homes.

At the Infantry School we found four or five thousand soldiers standing and sitting in orderly rows on the parade ground, officers and NCOs moving among them, giving them orders and instructions, creating new formations. There was no point in our counting the numbers, since a constant stream of soldiers kept coming through

the compound gate, guided by MPs, officers, and special patrols who
had found them walking aimlessly on the highway and guided them
in.

Maj. Gen. Kim Hong-il,[2] commandant of the Military Academy,
on his own initiative had started to reform the broken army. General
Kim, one of the handsomest men I have ever seen, had fine features
crinkled with smile wrinkles, set off by a striking head of silvery
gray that would have drawn attention to him anywhere in the
world. He had been a general in the Chinese Army in World War
II, and there was some thought that he lacked the fundamental
military know-how necessary for his rank and position. Before the
war there had even been some talk of easing him gently out of the
army into retirement as soon as more competent younger men
came along. But at this crisis it was a wonderful thing for the
Republic of Korea that this loyal, patriotic soldier was on active
duty with two stars on his shoulders.

General Kim inspired everyone he met during those days of defeat, and he met just about every soldier who was led into the
parade ground of the Infantry School on that black Wednesday.
General Kim would not consider defeat. Aided by a group of
very determined younger officers, he reformed and, as far as he
could, rearmed the ROK Army from the broken remnants of the
fleeing divisions from the north—the 2nd, Capital, 5th, and 7th.
The 1st Division had been cut off and had not been heard from,
while the 6th and 8th Divisions were still fighting well in the east.

Soldiers who in the morning were walking south aimlessly in
dejected defeat marched back to fight again before night fell. I
doubt that many generals in history have shown better the true
qualities of leadership and skill at impromptu organization in the
midst of military disaster than did General Kim that somber day.

We were much encouraged when we looked over this force as it
was being reorganized. Luckily, most of the men still had their
rifles, but not a single piece of artillery had been brought across the
Han River and very few antitank guns or machine guns. We
counted six machine guns being stripped and oiled. We were led
around in a quick inspection tour by several courageous Korean
officers who had flatly refused to accept defeat and were working
swiftly to get a new force into shape so they could go back and fight

again. They organized these soldiers into provisional battalions without regard to their original regiments or divisions.

I asked what the situation was at the Han River. Quiet, they thought, but they did not seem entirely sure. They knew that General Yu was up there somewhere trying to hold the crossing. I suggested to the U.S. officers that we continue up to the river and see for ourselves. I assured them that if the North Koreans had not yet crossed the Han we would be safe enough, since the railway embankment on the south side of the river was very high, towering above the street like a great fortified wall; if we could get there without being spotted, we would be safe enough from enemy observation or fire. The two officers quickly agreed, and again we drove north.

When we reached the outskirts of Yŏngdŭngp'o, we came over a small rise and could see all Seoul spread out before us across the river, with the high mountains beyond. Everything seemed quiet and peaceful. We could hear a few distant guns, but not enough to disturb the uninformed. If I had not known better, I would have thought Seoul was as safe a place for us to visit as it always had been.

We quickly drove down that rise, apparently not spotted by the distant enemy, and were soon under the protection of the high railway embankment that cut us off from hostile view completely but also cut us off from sight of the river. Only once, when we passed a small bridge, could we see or could we have been seen. There was not a soul moving on what normally was a very busy street. We turned and drove very slowly toward the southern approaches to the Han bridges, where we would no longer be protected by the embankment. My heart was a bit in my mouth as I wondered whether the North Koreans might have pushed a patrol across and whether that frightening silence might soon be blasted by gunfire.

Suddenly an armored car came rapidly toward us, a huge South Korean flag streaming out behind. I started waving. We stopped and the armored car stopped beside us. I asked the lieutenant in command about the situation ahead. He was conducting a reconnaissance along the south side of the river and had only recently been out to Kimp'o airport. He denied the rumor that Kimp'o was in

enemy hands but said he'd been fired on about five miles northwest
of Kimp'o and so assumed the North Koreans had crossed near
the mouth of the river and were moving slowly along the south bank
toward the airport. The lieutenant said no North Koreans were
across the river near the bridges, where we were then standing, but
of course he did not know when they might try.

I asked the lieutenant where General Yu was. He did not know;
he had been so busy scouting the enemy, he did not know the disposition of friendly troops. He did know that some South Korean
soldiers were in the little railway station just at the end of the un-
damaged railway bridge, and possibly that was where General Yu
had set up his command post. I thanked the lieutenant and wished
him luck. He climbed back into his armored car and went dashing
down the road with the big flag whipping behind in the breeze.
He was a very trim and alert young man—"sharp" would be the
word. I wonder what happened to him.

We got out of the jeep and told our driver to put it in an alley out
of sight and stay with it. The three of us continued on foot. The
railway station was completely exposed to sight and fire from the
other side of the river. We approached very cautiously, myself in
the lead since I knew the way, hoping no one on the other side
would spot us. No Korean soldiers were visible. As we stepped
around to the front entrance facing the river and started to enter
the door, we were sharply challenged by a sentry. I saw a familiar
figure sitting at a desk in the rear of the small room in semi-dark-
ness. Hastily getting up from his chair was one of the most fatigued
men I have ever seen, a gray exhaustion over his face, and yet
vital and cheerful. It was General Yu.

I introduced the two U.S. Army officers, and Yu obviously was
delighted to meet officers who had just come to Korea from General
MacArthur's staff. After all his disasters of the past three days, he
now had a symbol of hope.

General Yu apologized for not offering us anything to eat or
drink and for the absence of most of his small staff. He said they
had not managed to bring anything with them, and since most of
them had not had a meal for several days, he had sent the others
out to find something to eat in nearby houses. He was waiting for

them to return and hoped he could get something himself.

We asked General Yu his estimate of the situation. He was holding the crossing of the Han River and the North Koreans were holding the city. He had about four hundred men to cover two thousand yards, but he considered the bridge in front of him the most critical. He had no explosives with which to destroy it, and he begged us to send him some when we returned to Suwŏn. Meanwhile, he intended to deny that bridge to the enemy. He had one antitank gun and one machine gun trained on the bridge. Otherwise he had nothing but rifles and carbines for his men, who did not even have entrenching tools. He expected reinforcements to be sent from the Infantry School before dark and was determined to hold the Han crossing to the maximum of his ability.

As we talked, a few casual shells whined across near the head of the bridge where the antitank gun was mounted, but they did no damage. There was no general barrage, and as far as we could see on the other side, no preparations were being made for an immediate attempt to force a crossing. General Yu remarked that the North Koreans had such a tremendous superiority in equipment that it was going to be hard to keep them from forcing a crossing somewhere, but he and his men would do their best. He urged that American planes be sent to bomb and strafe the north banks to keep the enemy from building up for a crossing.

I was very much heartened when we drove south to Suwŏn again. Not at the thought of Yu with only four hundred men holding off the whole Communist Army, but at his determination and cheerfulness and the willingness of those four hundred to try showed that the ROK Army had passed the greatest test that war can force on any army. The attitude on the river bank and at the Infantry School was inspiring. These, of course, were the officers and men of the prewar ROK regular army; they were not the ten-day trainees who later often made a bad impression on American soldiers.

As we drove south, we passed truck after truck northward bound, filled with South Korean soldiers who cheered and waved flags at our jeep. These were the same retreating soldiers who had passed us on foot that morning away from the battle. They had been

assembled, reorganized, and turned around. Yu had his reinforcements that night, and they beat off several attempts to
force a crossing.

Events of considerable importance also occurred a hundred miles
south of Suwŏn at Taejŏn. They should be described here, and to
do so it is necessary to go back to Tuesday, June 27, to pick up the
thread of the narrative. It should be remembered that I have described developments in Seoul and Suwŏn to the afternoon of the
twenty-eighth; otherwise, the following description might seem
chronologically confused.

President Rhee and his party left Seoul early on Tuesday morning, bound for Pusan and the naval base at Chinhae, where the
president had a summer cottage. The president had the train stopped at Taegu for a time while he obtained news from Seoul by
telephone and on the radio. Dr. Rhee began to think he had been
too hasty in leaving the capital and started talking of returning to
Seoul. His staff, however, was opposed to going back yet. Finally
Rhee decided he would go back as far as Taejŏn and stop there
until he had a clearer understanding of the military situation.

When Drumright and his small party reached Taejŏn about
five o'clock that Tuesday afternoon, they found that President Rhee
had just established himself in the provincial government offices.
Drumright and Stewart set themselves up in one of the empty
KMAG houses in Taejŏn and went immediately to call on the
president.[3]

Rhee was in a nasty mood and still in something of a state of
shock. He was sarcastic with Drumright about the lack of American military support. He claimed the United States had always
promised support in case of invasion, that KMAG was an outward
expression of that interest, and only a week earlier Ambassador
John Foster Dulles in a speech before the National Assembly had
declared that the United States would never abandon Korea.
But where, asked Rhee, were the American troops? He was sardonic
in blaming the whole defeat on unfulfilled American promises of
aid. He was quite unfair, but it was perhaps understandable.
Drumright listened but made little attempt to reply to the tirade.
When he finally was able to speak, Drumright said he was at the

Harold Noble standing at the thirty-eighth parallel marker, Korea, before the 1950 conflict.

Gen. Douglas MacArthur (third from left), Harold Noble (third from right), staff members, and Korean Army officers discuss the situation after the Communist invasion of South Korea. U.S. Army photograph.

president's service for whatever he could do, and then he and Stewart left.

Other members of Drumright's group had been working hard to restore the telephone exchange at the temporary chancery. When the KMAG officers had received their withdrawal orders by radio earlier that day, they had smashed the switchboard. Someone managed to patch it together, and by seven o'clock Drumright was able to get through to Seoul by phone. He had a very encouraging conversation with Colonel Wright, who was still at ROK Army headquarters and told Drumright that Muccio and Church were at Suwŏn. The connection was bad, and Drumright understood Wright to say that there had been effective U.S. plane activity north of Seoul that day. Wright was probably talking of the jet fighter cover for the transport planes. In any case, Drumright was delighted and hurried back to give President Rhee the news. Stewart again accompanied him.

This time President and Mrs. Rhee were in the home of the provincial governor, the president seemed to be in good spirits, and the conversation was quite friendly. Drum gave Rhee a message from MacArthur: "Be of good cheer." Rhee was happy that MacArthur was thinking of him and of Korea and hoped the brief message was a portent of substantial assistance.[4]

Rhee kept repeating to Drumright, "I want to go back to Seoul, I want to go back to Seoul," but Drumright did not encourage the idea.[5] By this time many civilian government leaders had reached Taejŏn, and many were at the provincial governor's house milling around, shaking hands, and exchanging gossip. Drumright told Rhee of the ADCOM headquarters at Suwŏn, saying Muccio and Church were there. He said Truman had ordered MacArthur to give air and naval aid to the Republic of Korea south of the 38th parallel, and United States planes already had knocked out enemy tanks and transportation north of Seoul that day. This information seems to have been based on that telephone conversation with Colonel Wright, but it was premature. Drumright, however, believed it to be true and the president was delighted and greatly moved. He clasped his hands in front of him in an attitude of prayer and said he wanted to go on the radio to encour-

age the Korean people. Stewart arranged this, and in short time
the president was speaking over Taejŏn radio to the Korean people
throughout the south. This was the first time President Rhee had
been heard since the war began.

The next morning, Wednesday, June 28, Drumright and Stewart
made an early visit to President Rhee. The purpose of this call was
to hand President Rhee the text of President Truman's statement
of the commitment of U.S. air and naval forces in support of the
Republic of Korea.[6] The text of the statement had been copied during the night from a shortwave broadcast received on a portable
radio set Drumright had brought from Seoul. On the way they met
Defense Minister Sin. He said he had been in direct communication at 7:00 A.M. with General Yu, who commanded the eastern
defenses of Seoul. Yu had reported that unless American planes
bombed the enemy outside the east gate, Seoul was lost. When
Drumright and Stewart reached the governor's residence, they found
everything in great confusion. The president was terribly alarmed
again. Mrs. Rhee told Drumright that Sin Sŏng-mo had called
his previous day's report a lie.

Drumright showed the message to Rhee, who was tremendously
relieved, especially by one short sentence which said, "In these
circumstances I have ordered United States air and sea forces to
give the Korean government troops cover and support."[7] Soon
Truman's statement was on the radio and being passed out on the
streets in handbills.

Drumright and Stewart were back at their quarters again by
10:00 A.M. and tried to get through by telephone to Seoul to find
out what had happened up north. But the telephones were dead in
every direction, whether to Seoul, Suwŏn, Pusan, or Tokyo. Drumright's Korean houseboy, Johnny, worked steadily at them. As occasion demanded, he talked in English, Korean, Japanese, or Chinese—
whatever came from the other end. For a long time nothing came
in, not even a buzz.

Captain Sin called at their house about eleven o'clock. He seemed
exhausted and beaten. About 11:30 Mrs. Rhee herself arrived,
almost in a panic. The vice-minister of defense and the home
minister had both arrived from Seoul, and they were telling some
very scary stories. The home minister would not tell anyone how

he had gotten out of the city, but he said he had remained there until the very end. The president was said to be terrified, to want to get a pistol and start out personally shooting Communists.

Muccio arrived from Suwŏn about 2:15 P.M., muddy and bedraggled but radiating confidence. He had been at the Suwŏn airstrip, just ready to get into his light plane, when YAKs strafed the field. He took cover in a hurry. When the strafing was over and he returned to the miraculously untouched observation plane, he found himself covered with mud and one trouser leg torn and bloodied. As he told me later, Muccio thought he must be the first American ambassador in history to call on the head of state to whom he was accredited with his clothes in tatters and covered with mud.

Muccio went directly to call on the president and was joined there by Drumright and Stewart. That afternoon Muccio did the most superb job of his career, speaking first to the president, then to the cabinet, and finally to the National Assembly, infusing into these naturally frightened, weary, uncertain but patriotic men a conviction that they must and could fight to victory. They began to believe that a battle had been lost but not the war, and that help was coming.

Muccio risked his career and stuck his neck out a mile in saying what he did. The only instructions he had received from the State Department had been, "Act boldly."[8] He did so.

Muccio hoped intensely that the United States would decide to help Korea, but he did not know what the decision would be. Yet he did know that unless he could persuade the South Korean leaders that substantial American help was on the way, their shock and fear would overwhelm them, they would cease to be leaders, the war would be lost, and the free Republic would die. He was sure that if given time, the United States government would decide it must stop aggression in Korea. But what if before a decision was made the government of the Republic of Korea should collapse? Then there would be no one for the United States to assist against the aggressor, for the aggressor would have succeeded in his conquest.

Muccio threw himself into a battle that afternoon, the battle of saving the Republic from the fears of its leaders. To each group

Muccio said much the same thing. He spoke very informally, still
in his mud-stained clothes. He told of Suwŏn and of his flight down.
He remarked that Taejŏn was off the normal air route from Japan
to Korea, and therefore people at Taejŏn could not see the great
increase in American planes flying northward. If they were at Suwŏn, however, they would be much heartened by the constant
flights of jet planes and the YAKs being shot from the skies. As
for Seoul, even though the enemy held the city, the situation of the
Republic was not desperate. Most of South Korea remained free.
Korea had great resources and great resilience, ability, intelligence,
courage, and patriotism — enough to successfully meet this dreadful trial.

Muccio continued. Yesterday the United States had decided to
go all out to help South Korea. Hereafter, the enemy would not be
able to bring any more supplies south to the 38th parallel because
American naval and air forces would stop them. General Mac-
Arthur had an advance command post at Suwŏn under a very able
general, Church, and ROK Army headquarters under General
Ch'ae was also being redeployed near it. The ROK Army was still
fighting with superb heroism, but they must be given a chance to
reorganize. Adequate supplies to rearm them were being rushed
over from the U.S. Far East Command in Japan. Only today
American planes had knocked out a whole train of Communist
troops coming down to Seoul from North Korea.

Muccio hammered away on the fundamental necessity of keeping a government and an army in being. The conduct of the war
must be left to the military professionals, with a minimum of civilian
interference. The cabinet and the assembly should establish themselves in some place where they could conduct their affairs without
getting in the way of the military. It was essential that all police
and youth corps activities should be coordinated with the army,
and that the chief of staff should command all paramilitary
organizations as well as the army. There must be only one chain
of command through the minister of defense to the chief of staff.
The railroads should also come under army control.

Muccio went on to say that this was a joint Korean-American
effort. Certain things could be done superbly by the Koreans, much
better than the Americans did them, but certain other things could

be done better by the Americans. "We must unite and coordinate so that we can get the best total effort from them both," Muccio said. The ambassador continued:

"I know you have been forced to leave your dear ones behind in many cases, and you are often confused and deeply worried. Everything is very difficult for you now. I won't try to minimize the difficulties before you. But I and the government I represent are convinced that the Korean people have the determination and the will to see this through. If I didn't have this confidence I wouldn't be here, and United States forces wouldn't be in Korea."

What Muccio said was simple enough, but coming from him at that time to these frightened, worried men, it was one of the most important speeches ever made. When Muccio sat down, the speaker of the National Assembly, Sin Ik-hŭi, spoke of Muccio as "our most beloved ambassador who is showing us his confidence and giving his life to stay with us. When we recover and our situation begins to improve, we shall never forget his aid to us."

Muccio's reply hit exactly the right note. He said, "This aid reflects the determination of the American people through their government to do all they can to support the people of Korea in this crisis to their liberty. I am only the symbol of the determination of the American people."

In those critical days it was touch and go whether the ROK government would survive. More than any other man Muccio prevented the government from crumbling before the crushing thrusts of the Communist Army. He did it through his enthusiasm, his optimism, and his hints of aid to come. Of course, the South Korean leaders neither wanted to nor planned to dissolve the government, but if Muccio had not supplied them with this cement of unity and hope, I think that in a few days the government of the Republic of Korea probably would have disappeared in the fear and fright of those shocked and defeated men.[9]

When the meetings were over, Muccio talked again, briefly, with President Rhee, giving him further hope. Muccio had a very secret message from MacArthur which he urged Rhee to keep secret from even his ministers. MacArthur would be in Suwŏn the next morning to observe the situation personally, to determine what needed to be done to turn the war against the Communists, and he had asked the president to meet him there. To President Rhee this was something far more tangible than Muccio's words of hope, and nothing could have kept him away from Suwŏn.[10]

Muccio then went to the temporary embassy, and Drumright flew to Suwŏn to replace him. Drum had persuaded the ambassador that he must take a rest and, at least for a night, get away from the war.

About the same time Defense Minister Sin also flew up to the new military headquarters. He was in a small L-5 observation plane piloted by the U.S. naval attaché. About halfway between Taejŏn and Suwŏn, Commander Seifert noticed two planes flashing in the air high overhead apparently diving on his tail. He asked Sin's instructions. "Carry on," said the ex-British commodore, and Seifert took the plane into long, crazy dives through deep valleys, close to the floor, and shook off his followers. They finally landed safely at Suwŏn.

While these events were taking place in Taejŏn, I had returned to Suwŏn from my trip to the Han River and for several hours was the senior embassy officer. General Ch'ae arrived and set up his headquarters in another wing from that of General Church, but only a few steps away. Colonel Wright also arrived and established a small KMAG office near General Ch'ae's office.[11]

I must make some comment on General Church and his decisions at Suwŏn. I do not know what went through his mind during those hectic days, but he was a confused man who did not do justice to himself. Later he commanded the 24th Division with skill and aggressiveness after the loss of Maj. Gen. William F. Dean and showed outstanding leadership. In that command he had many thousands of Korean soldiers integrated with his American troops, and he came to recognize their good qualities and to wish he had more of them. That autumn when I saw him not far from the Yalu River, despite the bitter cold that kept most men bundled to the ears, he walked around vigorously in just a winter shirt with a bright parachute silk scarf around his neck, cheerful, optimistic and gay. But there at the beginning at Suwŏn, he seemed wholly lost within himself. He was in a completely strange country with very strange ways. He was suddenly given responsibility in a war that was rapidly distintegrating around him. He knew nothing of the

ROK Army or the qualities of its commanders, and he did not trust them. He remarked to me one day that he would rather have one hundred New York policemen than the whole Korean Army. He had not yet learned for himself of the tremendous offensive power of the North Korean Army, and he attributed the South Korean defeat, which had catapulted him into his unwanted position of leadership, to a combination of military incompetence and cowardice. He had thirteen staff officers and a few enlisted men, but no combat troops to command. The very air around him was thick with rumors, each one more discouraging than the last. Most of them, but not all by any means, came from the Koreans, and he did not know what to believe. For reasons I have never fathomed, he did not seriously turn to KMAG for advice and information.

In his position at Suwŏn, I would have expected General Church to try to learn all he could about past actions in the war, the ROK Army, the enemy, and the enemy situation, and military possibilities through long conversations with General Ch'ae and Colonel Wright. But he distrusted Ch'ae and ignored Wright. He talked to his staff and to me, but that was inadequate briefing in the perilous situation then prevailing.[12]

I was much disturbed by all this and took it upon myself to serve as liaison between General Church and General Ch'ae. I did what I could to bridge the gap between their offices. It was small in distance, but since that distance was never covered by request of General Church, it might as well have been many miles. Ch'ae had come to Suwŏn to set up his headquarters next to the American commander. Otherwise, for convenience of communication a command post up at the Infantry School would have been better. Ch'ae sat in his office, getting reports and issuing orders, and eagerly waiting to be consulted. He did not dare to force himself on the distinguished American general. Even though he outranked Church by one star he waited to be summoned, but no invitation came. I did manage once to get Ch'ae to Church's outer office, at Ch'ae's urgent request, so that he could transmit some military intelligence. Church was very abrupt and after a few words turned away to enter his private office, clearly indicating his lack of confidence in any information which Ch'ae might bring.

Since ADCOM had not brought any codes with them and KMAG had had to destroy theirs, for a few days the only available codes at Suwŏn were the State Department's, which Sam Berry had brought with him. During the next few days I wrote most of the coded messages from Suwŏn, whether diplomatic or military, while Drumright wrote the rest. A KMAG radio truck stood under a tree near the front door of the building, ready to transmit.

When YAKs strafed the airfield, destroyed American planes, and wounded American flyers, I wrote the reporting telegrams. When we had ROK Army accounts of the military situation, I wrote those messages too. And, of course, I wrote several diplomatic telegrams also. I showed the military telegrams to General Church for his concurrence before sending them off.

For this reporting we lacked even the barest essentials except the codes themselves. We did not have the proper writing paper or pads, but we managed to find some brown wrapping paper and used that. I composed messages on the wrapping and gave them to Sam Berry. Sam worked swiftly with his code book, put the message into some gibberish, and took it out to the radio truck. Since our codes could only be broken at the State Department, we had to address to Washington even the military messages for Gen. MacArthur's command. There they were decoded, re-encoded, and transmitted to GHQ in Tokyo. I have heard there was much anguish at Tokyo headquarters during those first few days when strictly military telegrams originating in Suwŏn—for example, a message containing the name, rank, serial number, and physical condition of an air force pilot who had been shot down, or the statements of a YAK pilot who had parachuted into our hands— were received from Washington, signed Acheson.

I was so disturbed about the way American airpower was being used that I wrote a telegram to the department on my own responsibility, of course signing it "Muccio," as all our telegrams were signed. When Drumright arrived in Suwŏn on Wednesday night, he also was so concerned that, despite my earlier telegram, he sent one of his own only a few hours later. We had been told that at 11:00 A.M., that day, June 28, U.S. planes would start attacking the North Koreans. We considered such support for the ROK Army not only vitally necessary militarily, but equally necessary for its morale and psychological effect on the ROK Army and people. If the Korean people and the few remaining ROK soldiers holding the Han River could see the American jets and bombers flashing over them, if they could see the billowing smoke of their bombs and hear the crackling roar of their rockets, they would be tremendously uplifted. The South Koreans badly needed concrete evidence of American military support, not just rumors that it was coming.[13]

Unfortunately, that Wednesday most of our planes flew so high that no one saw or heard them, and whatever destruction they inflicted on the enemy north of the river, no one was aware of it down our way. After being buoyed by the report that American planes were coming to their aid, the Koreans became further discouraged by the suspicion that the promise had not been kept. In our separate telegrams both Drumright and I explained the situation and urged the department to take what steps it could to persuade the air force to send its sorties in low so that they could be seen in front of Seoul. Whether because of our telegrams or because of an independent change of tactics, the next day the American planes, fighters and bombers, strafed and bombed the long, wide strip of sand on the river bank where the North Koreans were setting up guns and assemblying men to force a crossing of the Han. The planes and the explosions of their bombs could be seen, heard, and even felt by the ROK Army on the south bank of the river, and they had a splendid effect.

Drumright got to Suwŏn from Taejŏn that Wednesday night just before dark. He, Colonel Wright, and I soon got into a prolonged argument with Captain Sin and General Ch'ae on future strategy and tactics. Quite separately Wright, Drum, and I had reached the identical conclusion: despite every odd, the ROK Army must hold out on the Han River or the war was lost. Perhaps they could not hold out very long, but the longer they did, the more chance there was to reorganize troops in the south and the stragglers coming down from the north, to get new equipment from Japan, and perhaps to bring in American ground troops. But if the Han line should be surrendered, there was no other place where the ROK Army could make a stand. There were not sufficient forces available to make a line any other place between the Han River and Pusan. The ROK Army was still disorganized, it had lost all its artillery and most of its equipment, and American policy had not yet been determined.

Separately, we began talking to Captain Sin and General Ch'ae. We found them both convinced they could not defend the Han and must immediately order withdrawal farther south. Soon all five of us were gathered around a small schoolroom table, debating, arguing, and insisting. According to the book, Ch'ae's position was correct. He did not have sufficient force to hold the Han. The North Koreans could turn either flank at will and come in behind, slashing his communications and rolling up his small force. By standing at the Han River, he risked losing what remained of his battered army. Far better, he argued, to move south quickly to take up positions which he could hold and where he could wait for new troops, new equipment, and the Americans. Sin supported General Ch'ae without reservation.

But, we said, where is this new line? Don't you risk far more by retreating now without plans, with no newly designated defensive position, and with two divisions still out on the frontier in the northeast, than by standing to fight now? Sure, you may be outflanked, but if so, you can still withdraw before you are surrounded. But if you retreat now, the war is over. This is the time for utter boldness.

The debate waged. No member of Church's staff had any part in it or was aware of it.[14]

It was obvious that both Ch'ae and Sin were weary to exhaustion. I do not suppose either man had slept since the first alarm on Sunday morning. Ch'ae, with his mountain of flesh, had trouble keeping awake even when he was talking. But we were determined that even their obvious weariness should not permit them to make that disastrous decision. They wanted to put out the retreat orders that night.

Finally, reluctantly, Sin and Ch'ae began to give in. They said they saw our point and were just about to agree when a young KMAG major who had been listening came over and joined in without asking Wright's permission. He flatly associated himself with Ch'ae and Sin's position. He said it was impossible to hold the Han; it was suicide to try to do it. Wright intervened and sent the major from the room, but for the moment the harm had been done. Sin and Ch'ae were again all for retreat.

I suggested that the decision be put off at least until morning, that the Han position was not so desperate that action had to be taken that night, and that, besides, no sensible retreat order could be issued since no one had decided where the retreat was to go. Both Ch'ae and Sin agreed to this compromise. I then urged them both to come and sleep at our quarters, pressing them to leave their offices at once to get some rest. Drumright strongly supported me in this. Wright had already left the room and later was very surprised to find a huge figure snoring in his bed.

Drumright and I thought that if these two exhausted men could get one full night's sleep, they might have an entirely fresh approach to the question of fighting for the Han. Both Sin and Ch'ae took a lot of persuading, but finally they consented—largely, I think, because I would not leave them alone—and I guided them down the lane in the dark. By that time we had several cots in our attic room, all allocated. I put Ch'ae and Sin in the best ones, next to Muccio's, and the foreign minister and his vice-minister, who happened along just as I was issuing this invitation, into two others. I knew some of our people who would come in late at night feeling their way in the dark to their beds were going to be very unhappy, but that did not count. I hoped by this simple maneuver to bring about the defense of the Han River.

I was busy at the cottage for a few minutes after I put the defense minister and the chief of staff to bed and then went back to headquarters. For some unknown reason I wandered into General Ch'ae's office; Captain Sin was back working at a desk. I remonstrated with him, insisting he was supposed to be in bed and asleep. He became rather annoyed with me but finally gave up and let me lead him back to his bed, where he went to sleep and slept soundly. I went back to headquarters and there was "Fat" Ch'ae, half asleep but nevertheless ponderously trying to work at his desk. I am afraid I talked more sharply than a major general and army commander is accustomed to hearing. Ch'ae gave up and came along meekly and apologetically. This time when I put him to bed, I stayed in a neighboring cot. In seconds General Ch'ae was deeply asleep, but with plenty of sound. All night long I kept awakening intermittently to feel his snores shaking the slight structure. He and Sin exhaustedly slept through until morning.

In the morning Wright, Drumright, and I again approached Sin and Ch'ae about the fight for the Han. They had already sent their orders forward. The ROK Army would defend the Han River.

CHAPTER SEVEN

Runout at Suwŏn

G ENERAL MacARTHUR flew over on Thursday morning, June 29, giving everyone, both Koreans and Americans, extravagant hope. Thirty hours later most of the Americans were running for their lives, from a terrifying rumor.

MacArthur's visit was Thursday's big event. Word first got around that a distinguished VIP was coming, but very soon it was obvious that it was MacArthur himself. MacArthur was to be briefed on the military situation and then go north for a personal inspection.

Those of us who did not go down to the airstrip could see Mac-Arthur's *Bataan* swoop in from where we stood on the hill at the experiment station. The *Bataan* was well protected by jet fighters, as it should have been. In about fifteen minutes cars and jeeps swept up the hill and out stalked MacArthur, wearing his famous cap and smoking his customary corncob pipe, followed by most of the senior officers of his GHQ staff. Rhee and Muccio had also gone to the airfield to meet MacArthur, following their earlier arrival from Taejŏn, and they soon drove up.[1] Among the visitors were Lt. Gen. George E. Stratemeyer, commanding the Far East Air Force; Maj. Gen. Edward M. Almond, chief of staff; Maj. Gen. Edwin K. Wright, G-3; Maj. Gen. Charles A. Willoughby, G-2; Maj. Gen. Courtney Whitney, head of the SCAP Government Section and MacArthur's personal confidant; and many others.

We soon gathered in Church's office, where chairs had been arranged and maps hung. MacArthur sat at the side of the front row with Rhee and Muccio nearby. Aside from Church, various AD-COM officers made brief statements on the military situation as seen from their specialties: personnel, intelligence, operations,

85

supply, and the air force. From time to time MacArthur, pointing the stem of his corncob pipe for emphasis, asked a question; at other times General Almond questioned the speaker.

The American officers finished and General Ch'ae was invited to speak. Ch'ae had not originally been scheduled to participate. When I asked General Church earlier who would attend the briefing, I was surprised to find that Church did not plan to invite any Korean officers, although President Rhee would be there. Not to have General Ch'ae, the commander of the ROK Army take part in the briefing seemed to me to be bad militarily, and also to be very bad public relations. For the commander-in-chief, Far East, to come to Korea to see a war that was being fought entirely by Korean ground forces and not be briefed by at least one Korean officer did not make sense to me. The Koreans, of course, would feel the slight keenly, although they would be unlikely to say anything.

When Muccio arrived from Taejŏn I told him of my concern and he agreed. We strongly urged Church to invite General Ch'ae to speak at the briefing, and he did so. But aside from Ch'ae and his interpreter, no other Korean officer was in the room to help inform MacArthur on the military situation.

General Ch'ae's English was limited and he spoke through a Korean officer interpreter. He stood over at the side of the room, and his huge bulk and fat, sleepy face did not impress a stranger as the proper casing for a warrior. The breaks for interpretation slowed down what he had to say, and after the extensive and in general fluent briefing of the American officers, his broken sentences gave the impression of a lack of clarity and precision. Ch'ae did not talk very long and so could not give a thorough briefing from the point of view of the ROK Army, covering all phases of operations and areas of responsibility. It did not seem to me at the time that Ch'ae was listened to very carefully, and that impression was strengthened when I read General MacArthur's testimony to a Senate committee in Washington in 1951.[2] MacArthur stated that when he visited Suwŏn, he found the Korean Army completely beaten and in rout. That was largely the impression left by the briefing of the American officers, but it was not the fact.

The situation of the ROK Army that morning was as follows. In the east, the 6th Division had recaptured Ch'unch'ŏn and had radioed for permission to continue across the 38th parallel. The 8th Division, farther to the east, had driven off all attacks and also wanted permission to cross the parallel to the north.[3] The 1st Division, which had been presumed destroyed, had only been cut off. It had counterattacked and recaptured Munsan the previous day, thereby cutting the main enemy supply and communication road from Kaesŏng to Seoul. Unfortunately, since we had no word of this, when the U.S. planes made their first bombing attacks they assumed Munsan to be in enemy hands and bombed it so heavily that the 1st Division suffered severe casualties and had to withdraw southward. While MacArthur was being briefed, the 1st Division, which had fought its way south to the Han River, was crossing to the south bank to continue the war.[4] The remnants of the Capital, 2nd, 5th, and 7th divisions had been reformed into a task force with provisional battalions disposed along the Han River to prevent a crossing and in reserve south of the Han. Part of the 3rd Division was still at Taegu. The 17th Regiment of the Capital Division, which had been stationed in the isolated Ongjin Peninsula, following the North Korean attack had driven forward into the Communist-held city of Haeju in North Korea and then had withdrawn in good order. The regiment thereupon embarked in a great variety of seized boats and sailed down to a west coast port in the south. They had landed, intact minus their casualties, with high morale, outstanding leadership, and a victory under their belts while we were having that briefing in Suwŏn.[5]

It would be foolish to pretend that after their defeat above Seoul this army could have won the war without help. Very definitely it could not. But it was a good army, an intact army, numbering about 48,000 men still in organized units and with another 30,000 stragglers steadily coming in to rejoin these units. The ROK Army critically needed two things: to be re-equipped and to be reinforced. Nevertheless, it was a good combat infantry force for its size. Only reinforcements from U.S. troops in Japan, however, could arrive in time to turn the war. It would have taken too long to train new Korean soldiers, and above all new Korean officers, even if adequate equipment were available, which it was not.[6]

It was an account like this, plus the reasons for the defeat north of Seoul, that General Ch'ae tried to give General MacArthur that morning. But he was a defeated and so a discredited general, and not much attention was paid to what he said. After seeing his huge bulk and his fat, sleepy-looking face, MacArthur told Rhee and Captain Sin they must get a new chief of staff who would inspire confidence both in the ROK Army and in the Americans. Mac-Arthur was promised a change would be made promptly. The deputy chief of staff, Brig. Gen. Chŏng Il-gwŏn, a very able officer only about thirty-four years old whose English would make communication much easier, was to arrive in Taejŏn by air from the United States the next day. He would be appointed to relieve Ch'ae.[7]

Naturally, Ch'ae did not know of his impending removal while he was speaking his piece for the supreme commander, but he probably expected that the ax was out. I felt sorry for the big, fat, sleepy-looking, good-humored man. He had shown considerable moral courage the previous afternoon when he had assembled the KMAG officers, told them the blowing of the bridge had been mishandled and a mistake, took the blame for not giving them adequate warning, and apologized for the danger and discomfort they had suffered.

My only participation in the briefing was a curious one. During the G-4 part, General Almond asked how many locomotives had been saved from Seoul and what was the total number of locomotives available in South Korea. No one knew the answer, and of course a great deal of military planning rested on the question of how many trains could be moved. Muccio turned to me and told me to go and find out. I had not the slightest idea where the answer lay, but by a series of lucky meetings with people who had been studying this vital question, to my very great surprise I discovered the answer.

Within fifteen minutes I was back in the room. As I entered the door MacArthur noticed me for the first time and waved his corncob pipe in greeting. By then the subject was far away from locomotives, but I wrote my information on a paper and passed it to Almond.

One other point still intrigues me about that briefing. When General Wright was describing the situation at the Han River, he mentioned that one of the railway bridges was still intact, while another was only buckled and could still be crossed by foot soldiers. MacArthur turned to Stratemeyer and with a wave of his hand said, "Take them out." Not knowing much about the precision bombing of bridges, I assumed that ended that and by tomorrow the bridges would be gone. I was much relieved. If the North Koreans had to force a crossing with boats, they would have a much rougher time. But all summer long I attended air force briefings, and all summer long reports were made of the repeated attempts to bomb those bridges. Different types of attempts were made, and they all failed. Now and then I would see an aerial photograph of the Han with the two bridges still intact. Finally, about the time of the Inch'ŏn landing, they were destroyed, but I never knew whether by our bombing or because the enemy blew them up.[8]

After the briefing and separate, private talks with Rhee and Muccio, MacArthur set out to see the Han for himself. A somewhat ancient Ford sedan was provided for him, and the rest of the party went by jeep. MacArthur was unarmed as usual. I had been talking with Willoughby and Whitney, whom I had known for some years, and with General Wright and offered to be their guide, an offer which they accepted. With a GI driver and the three generals the jeep was rather crowded. I sat on the metal tool case on the left.

During the ride up we pressed forward through a never-ending stream of refugees who cheered and clapped as we passed, just as others had done the previous morning. This time we were quite a caravan, however, including the GHQ officers, ADCOM officers, a few from KMAG, some Korean officers, and a great number of foreign correspondents who seemed to be swarming in every available space.

During the drive I answered many questions and was told of activities at GHQ which I had not heard of at Suwŏn. Willoughby confided to me that MacArthur had already issued the orders to the air force to fight in North Korea. He said that during the flight over MacArthur had consulted with his staff on various problems

related to the war in Korea. General Stratemeyer had very forcefully insisted that air operations limited by the 38th parallel were
impractical. Such a limitation enabled the North Korean planes to
escape to a sanctuary across an imaginary line. Stratemeyer urged
that the air force be free to follow enemy planes into North Korea
and to bomb and destroy their bases there. MacArthur had listened
carefully and then had told Stratemeyer to operate north of the
parallel as the tactical and strategical situation warranted. This
permission was radioed back to Tokyo from the plane. According
to Willoughby and the other generals, it would not be until the
following day that the air force could readjust its schedule and actually begin operating in North Korea. I was impressed that Mac-
Arthur had made this decision on his own responsibility as field
commander. I understood it was not until the next day that he
received similar orders from Washington.[9]

We reached the suburbs of Yŏngdŭngp'o. The car and jeeps
were parked behind a cut and we walked forward into the open,
to high ground about four hundred yards from the Han River.
We could see the river well and across into Seoul, but we were too
far away to see any North Korean emplacements or troop movements, even with field glasses. The North Koreans were firing in a
desultory way across the river, much more so than the previous day,
but still rather haphazardly. There was no response from our side,
of course, since the ROK Army had no guns. Nothing was falling
anywhere near where we stood.

MacArthur looked over the scene and asked questions of Colonel
Wright, of a Korean colonel responsible for that sector, and of members of his staff. Reporters and camera men massed in front of
MacArthur snapping his picture from every angle. I was standing
beside him for a time. One picture seems to have been run in most
newspapers back in the United States. It shows MacArthur, Wright,
the Korean colonel, and myself. Whoever sent it off failed to identify
the subjects and in a few papers at home, aside from MacArthur,
identification was faked. The sun was shining brightly on my hat-
less forehead, so that in the photograph my forehead appeared very
white. One New York newspaper in its early edition put a band-
age around my head and identified me as a "Department of the
Army civilian artillery expert." The same paper put glasses and a

moustache on Wright and identified him as Major General Almond, MacArthur's chief of staff. They did not know what to do with the Korean colonel. I am told that the *New York Times,* which had a man on the desk who knew both Wright and myself, identified us correctly without any fancy bandages or other props.

Almost everyone wanted to go closer to the river, and some correspondents urged MacArthur to do so. He told them he wanted very much to go, and if he were there with a small staff he would do so. But with such a large party, including practically all the foreign correspondents then stationed in Tokyo, he had to think of their safety. He said such a large group would probably be noticed, and if he went forward they would draw shell fire and someone would be hurt. He knew he could not keep the correspondents from going down with him just by telling them to stay behind, so in the interests of the many he would not go to the river. I thought it was a pity that the eagerness of the press to get a story kept MacArthur from a closer view of the scene of action and from meeting General Yu, who was holding the crossing down below us.[10]

On the return trip to Suwŏn a jeep filled with correspondents sped along the line to warn everyone that they had sighted YAKs coming our way. MacArthur had his sedan driven under some trees but did not get out. The rest of us jumped out in a hurry and stood under the trees, looking around for ditches for protection against strafing. Fortunately, there was a very deep ditch just over the crest of a small ridge running alongside the road. I stood at the top of the ditch with several others ready to jump in if the planes began to dive. The YAKs were very pretty, silvery in the bright blue sky. They flew around in our general area for about half an hour, while our caravan of jeeps waited under the trees. All this time MacArthur sat alone in his old Ford sedan and the rest of us poised on the edge of ditches. Finally we heard some American jets flying up fast from the south, and the YAKs dipped and flew away. We started south again.[11]

MacArthur had further conferences at Suwŏn and then left for Tokyo.[12] With the *Bataan* went also the jet fighters that had been flying cover for the airfield.

As soon as MacArthur left, Muccio and Rhee were to fly to

Taejŏn in a small plane. They were already in the plane when YAKs dove out of the sun and strafed the field. The pilot tried to take off but instead spun the plane around in a half circle. Someone tore open the door, helped Rhee and Muccio out, and taking the president's hand, helped him run for a nearby rice field where he took cover with the rest. The raid was soon over, although several American planes were shot up on the ground, including one big C-54 transport which had just landed with supplies.

When the planes flew away, Rhee got up dirtied but grinning. It was his first strafing, Muccio's second. Muccio suggested that if the YAKs were that plentiful and our planes that unprotected, it might be better to drive to Taejŏn, and Rhee promptly agreed. They walked back to Muccio's car and with Sergeant Edwards and Chief Petty Officer Emsley in the back seat, Muccio made a very fast one-hundred-mile drive to Taejŏn.

Friday morning, June 30, was quiet enough. Little information came in and there was not much to do. Muccio was still down at Taejŏn. I drifted back and forth between Ch'ae's and Church's offices and talked about the war with various people. Around noon I suggested to Drumright that I go up to the Han River again to get the feel of the situation for our own reporting. Drumright and I both held the same opinion on the necessity of embassy officers being closely in touch with the battle situation. While it was not the embassy's job to report combat developments, we thought it was essential for some embassy officers to make as many personal reconnaissances as possible to get the proper background for nonmilitary reporting. We also believed that there were several borderline areas between military reporting and political reporting which were the embassy's responsibility and for which we had to make our own observations and estimates. Muccio disagreed, on the grounds that we should not risk our lives since we were not soldiers and had other duties. Consequently he had been reluctant to let me go to the front lines. Later he stopped me from doing so. He tried to prohibit Drumright later also, but Drumright would not be stopped.

I arranged for a jeep and a Korean driver and was just about to start off north again when YAKs began strafing the airfield once more. Enemy air intelligence was excellent. They seemed to know when the jet fighters flying cover pulled away sooner than we did. In no time YAKs would be diving on the field and too often would be safely away before our jets came back. Sometimes they were not so lucky, though, and several times our side picked up valuable prisoners who described the organization and operational plans of the North Korean Air Force.

In this instance the U.S. fighters pulled away just as two C-54 transports were coming in to land. One was on the field and the other just preparing to set down when the YAKs attacked. The C-54 on the field was hit and burned, but the other one put on a burst of speed, got into the air again, and began climbing as near straight up as a C-54 can, with two YAKs close on its tail pouring in tracers.

Like most of the others at headquarters, I was sitting under a tree up on the hill with a nearly perfect view of the battle. It seemed impossible that the unarmed C-54 could escape as it sluggishly disappeared into a cloud with the YAKs close behind. When I radioed an account of this action to GHQ, via Mr. Acheson, I reported the plane as probably lost but was delighted to learn the following day that it had returned safely to Japan, albeit with some unplanned ventilation.

The air show in front of us was so interesting that many would forget and edge into the open to get a better look. Then someone would yell harshly at the culprits and they would sneak back under the trees. The North Korean pilots did not know where our headquarters was and never approached closely or strafed it. Naturally, we wanted to keep things that way.

Before I left for the Han that afternoon I talked with Lt. Col. John McGinn of the air force, a member of the ADCOM staff. McGinn had been operating the Suwŏn airstrip since his arrival, placing anti-aircraft guns and advising Church on air problems. He told me that the air force was badly in need of targets and was hounding him to get some. So little was known of the location of the North Korean forces that it was difficult for our airmen to operate. They did not want to waste bombs on nonmilitary targets, nor did they wish to hurt civilians unnecessarily. So McGinn asked me to get a list of targets from the Korean officers up forward.[13]

I went first to the Infantry School and called on the senior officer present. I told of the air force need for targets and was promptly
given a map on which the location of North Korean units near
Seoul had just been entered. It was the only complete map and
I hesitated to take it, but the Korean officer insisted.

Two KMAG captains were at the headquarters and decided to
go up to the Han River with me. They had not seen the Han for
several days. Both drove their own jeeps for greater security. I rode
with one and and left my jeep with the Korean driver at the Infantry School, with many admonitions to be there when I got back.

As we approached Yŏngdŭngp'o and the Han, we heard heavy
firing from the general area of Seoul, but before we could round
the bend on the road into Yŏngdŭngp'o, a jeep followed by a
truck filled with South Korean soldiers came south toward us.
At that point the road was on a high hill but sunken behind a much
higher hill that cut us off from sight of the Han and Seoul.

In the jeep was General Yu. We all stopped and got out.
Yu seemed much refreshed since I had seen him in the railway
station two days before. He told us that the North Koreans had
finally succeeded in forcing the Han River just above the bridge,
and had thrown a bridgehead across. His men had repelled repeated
crossing attempts and had wiped out one bridgehead, but during
the night the North Koreans had landed in strength again. Yu
had been forced to pull his line back from the river at that point,
although he held the river banks up and down from the bridgehead
and was trying to contain the bridgehead with forces entrenched
on the forward slope of the hill in front of us. His command post
was just up the hill in a half-hidden building which we could see.

As we stood there talking, a devastating thunder clap roared over
us. Frankly, my first reaction was fright. I could see some of our
planes racing across the sky on their bombing runs. The air force
was plastering the wide sands on the north bank of the Han River
where the North Koreans had artillery and tanks dug in as artillery.
We were trying to prevent them from assembling troops to exploit
their bridgehead. When I saw the cause of the devastating noise I
relaxed a bit, but the explosions were so continuous and the rever-
berations so great, I remained a little uneasy. From where we
stood on the road the planes seemed to go into their dives or drop

their bomb loads just beyond the hill in front of us, and I think we all were secretly afraid they might forget which side of the hill the enemy was on.

I asked General Yu about targets for the air force and got out my map. I was standing on the upper side of the road, and Yu and the two KMAG officers on the lower side, on opposite sides of the large map spread out on the road. Yu went over the map carefully and made suggestions, which I marked down. While we were concentrating on this, a shell roared over the hill and burst nearby. Exactly where it hit I do not know because I became very busy, but it was close. Everyone jumped for cover down the grassy embankment on the other side of the road, which gave perfect protection against anything but a direct hit. Being close to the outside edge of the road, General Yu and the two KMAG captains only had to step over and roll down for safety. But I ran from the far side of the road and dove head first over the grassy embankment.

Amusingly, my Homburg hat was not fazed by this undiplomatic conduct and stayed securely on my head. Perhaps I was dressed somewhat oddly for a war. When I went to Tokyo for that brief vacation, I had worn my Homburg, which even then was somewhat worn, and it was my only hat when I came back to Korea. It remained my badge of office until winter, when I replaced it with a beautiful captured Russian fur hat. I wore civilian clothes. In the embassy we considered it improper to dress otherwise. We represented the civil branch of our government no matter how much of a war was going on, and since nearly everyone else, including civilians, was in uniform, our civilian clothes became a diplomatic uniform. On this occasion, I wore a Homburg, an open shirt, trousers from a washable summer suit, and low shoes. My .45 pistol was in a holster fastened to my belt. During the subsequent months my Homburg became more beaten, more dirty, more creased, but a Homburg still. It seemed most appropriate.

The shelling stopped as suddenly as it had begun, and we returned to the road. I gathered up my map and was talking to General Yu when the two KMAG captains called that we should get the hell out of there in a hurry. They were not going to risk their jeeps in any more shelling. Before I realized what they were doing, they jumped in their vehicles and the first started off. The second,

with whom I had been riding, called that he intended to get his
jeep out of range fast, and I could catch up to him by running
across the rice field down below the embankment. The road at this
point made a wide half circle, and a direct line through the paddy
fields would take me across the diameter line. He gunned his jeep
and took off.

I was astonished! There was nothing I could do but run down
the side of that grassy embankment and start through the wet rice
fields, running on the ridges between the paddies but often slipping
into the muck. I felt thoroughly ashamed and disgusted to have
General Yu see me running like that, but if I didn't want to be
marooned there I had to catch that captain with his jeep. I kept
plunging through the soggy fields. As I came across the diameter
of the circle the jeep drove up the road, stopped and I got in.
Just as we started on, several planes in column swept over us.
We couldn't tell if they were friendly or enemy, so we stopped and
knelt in the ditch nearby until we were sure. The planes soon
disappeared, and we drove on without incident to the Infantry
School. I was thoroughly annoyed with the captain, but saw no
point in making an issue of my near abandonment, and we drove
south in silence. At the Infantry School I found my Korean driver
still waiting, and we set off for Suwŏn.

We must have left General Yu around 6:30 P.M. and reached
Suwŏn just about sunset. I went to our cottage, had a satisfying
supper of cabbage soup, and walked up to headquarters.

I ran into an old friend, a KMAG officer who had a "liberated"
sedan he had picked up in the evacuation from Seoul. He offered
to leave it with me for the night if I would drive him to his billet,
about two miles away at the agricultural college, and promise that
if anything went wrong I would come and get him. Several KMAG
officers were billeted there but they had no telephone. He said there
were disturbing rumors going around that night. I drove him to his
quarters with the firm promise that if anything did go wrong, I
wouldn't leave Suwŏn without him.

Early darkness was setting when I got back to headquarters.
I found Drumright and Jack Seifert standing by the main doorway, somewhat at loose ends; the whole ADCOM staff was in a
conference in General Church's office. Neither Drumright nor

Seifert knew exactly what was up, but they did not like the signs. I told them of my experience at the Han River and of the enemy bridgehead. I intended to turn my map over to the G-3 and Lieutenant Colonel McGinn. It seems now that a long time passed while we were talking there. Soon it was completely dark. Now and then a red or green flare went up from the airfield, presumably as signals to planes overhead.

Suddenly, the staff meeting ended and the officers poured out. One of the lieutenant colonels whom I had guided up to the Han on Wednesday slapped me on the shoulder and said, "Better get going, Noble, enemy tanks are just behind those hills. See the red flares going up from the airfield? We're going down to the airstrip immediately to wait for a plane to take us to Japan."

By this time everyone was rushing helter-skelter in the dark. A slight rain had begun to fall. I hurried down the lane to our cottage, climbed the stairs, and in the dark packed what I could find of my few things in my briefbag and trotted back up the hill to headquarters. Later I discovered I had overlooked two shirts of the four I owned but had partly made up for the loss by picking up a woolen brown shirt belonging to the former occupant of the house. It was too small for me and the buttons bulged dangerously across my chest, but it was first class for jeep riding and never seemed to show the dirt.

There was a hasty, confused rush to the cars and jeeps in the dark parking area outside headquarters. I found "my" Ford and climbed in, seemingly cruelly refusing rides to several people. I had to drive quickly over to the agricultural college, alert the KMAG officers there, and pick up some of them. At the gate an officer was acting as a checker and at first would not let me out because I had no passengers. I explained where I was going and he waved me through.

About a half mile from the college I pushed the horn and held it down the rest of the drive. The KMAG officers were thoroughly alerted by the time I arrived. They had one station wagon, but without "my" sedan they could not all have ridden out. I suppose we spent about half an hour while they packed their gear and got ready to leave. They had two Korean interpreters with them; one got in my sedan and the other in the station wagon. As soon as

we were loaded, with Jack and an interpreter in the front seat and
the back seat full, I took off without waiting for the station wagon,
which was not quite ready.

When we got back to the main road, not a soul or a car was
visible. We thought we were the last men out. I learned later that
a few men had not yet left the headquarters but did so within a few
minutes. The dark and the rain hid everything. After we had gone
down the road a few miles, we were surprised to see flames suddenly roaring upward from the headquarters. Someone had walked
into the signal room and, believing enemy tanks were just a few
miles away around the next range of hills, had tossed in a thorium
bomb to destroy the codes and equipment, which had only arrived
and been set up that day. They made a beautiful, roaring
blaze, but the sight sickened me. I had had a part in securing these
buildings for our use, and I remembered the sad little director
saying over and over, "I am so sorry you are here." Poor man!
By morning he had no buildings left.

I drove as rapidly as I could in the pitch dark without headlights, my memory of a few nights before when I had gone into the
ditch under similar conditions fresh in my mind, and soon we
reached the entrance to the airstrip. There was a "Y" in the road
at that point, one fork pulling away from the main highway for a
short run to the airstrip. A group of officers were standing in
the clear space between the arms of the Y. Drumright was among
them, talking loudly, but not loudly enough for me to hear. I already
had thoughts of not going to Japan, so I didn't stop the car but
drove right on to the concrete entrance to the strip.

We stood around the field for some fifteen minutes, questioning
senior officers about what was to happen. The best picture we
could get was that the whole party would be evacuated to Japan
as soon as a plane could be brought in, which might be about
dawn. In the meantime, a perimeter defense would be set up for
the airfield, and if necessary the enemy would be fought off until
the planes came. The field had to be defended regardless of losses
or no planes could land and there would be no escape for anyone.
The enemy tanks were reportedly behind the nearest hills just east
of Suwŏn, and they might arrive at any time.

Jack, my KMAG officer friend, and I talked this over and so did others quite independently. We saw no reason to escape to Japan just because North Korean tanks were approaching Suwŏn. I had expected them to get that far sooner or later, but there was a lot of Korea left. Jack and I agreed that we should drive down to Taejŏn where the ambassador was, not go kiting off to another country. Moreover, militarily an attempt to defend that airstrip against tanks was downright foolish. The field, of course, was flat and quite in the open with no defensive terrain features nearby. We had a few machine guns, actually light anti-aircraft guns, some rifles and carbines, and plenty of pistols. To fire them we had perhaps fifty officers and men of the U.S. Army, and a few civilians from the embassy. A fine fight such a group could put up against enemy tanks! The whole scheme seemed fantastic to me that night and it still does. If those people wanted to fly away happily to Japan, there was no reason why they couldn't drive down to Taejŏn or Taegu and peacefully catch rescue planes there. As for myself, I intended to remain in Korea as long as there was an embassy and a Korean government.

Jack and I agreed we were not leaving Korea that night. We climbed back in the car, this time with Jack at the wheel. Our other passengers joined us and we shoved off. At the Y in the road I again saw Drumright talking with some officers. I wrongly assumed that he was prepared to leave for Japan with ADCOM and so avoided him to keep from receiving an order to go along too. We stopped the car some distance down the road and I had Jack walk back to tell Drumright that I was on my way to Taejŏn. Then we began the hundred-mile drive.

Before describing events in Taejŏn, I must recount what I found out later about those North Korean tanks and our flight from Suwŏn.

Earlier that evening, while I was driving unconcernedly down the main road on my way back from the Han River, a frightening rumor reached the ADCOM chief of staff that enemy tanks were proceeding down a parallel road and would soon be outside Suwŏn. General Church was away at a town called Osan, about ten miles to the south, where he could telephone Tokyo. With the fall of Seoul, the normal telephone route from Suwŏn via Seoul to Tokyo was closed to us.[11]

There were plenty of South Korean officers and soldiers in Suwŏn from whom reconnaissance patrols could have been formed. There were plenty of KMAG officers, including Colonel Wright, available to arrange for such a reconnaissance. But no attempt of any kind was made to verify the rumor. The senior colonel, the only full colonel of the Tokyo group, called a meeting of the ADCOM staff and discussed what should be done. The whole discussion was based on rumor and emotion and not on an assessment of the facts, which should govern decisions in war. Panic was the result. The colonel made the decision, but he had extensive support from his staff, who wanted to get away fast from so perilous a position. They decided that with North Korean tanks so near, the situation was hopeless and they must get out immediately. A radio call was made to Itazuke for rescue planes, and the meeting broke up with a rush for the cars and the airstrip.

Colonel Wright decided he and his staff would not leave Suwŏn that night. He had numerous officers up forward with the divisions in the east, which were being withdrawn southward, and with the task forces straight ahead. He had already called in many of them to rendezvous in Suwŏn. He could not run out and let his men fall into a trap. He had to stay long enough to be convinced it was a trap and, if it was, to order a new rendezvous point farther south. Wright and his immediate staff remained near Suwŏn all night, except for some officers who were already posted to Korean units to the south. He, too, was amazed at the rapidity of the run out and at the fear engendered in many minds at the sight of flares and rockets going up from the airfield. The burning of the experiment station also hurt him because it was so unnecessary.

In the morning Wright and his group were still in Suwŏn and so was the ROK Army, which was still holding most of the crossings of the Han. There were no tanks just behind that dark hill. The ROK Army was still holding Suwŏn when the first elements of the U.S. 24th Division reached Korea to reinforce them. Then there were tanks behind that hill and behind many other hills below the Han. But not on the night of June 30.[15]

I also discovered I had been most unfair to Drumright in thinking he was prepared to accept the ADCOM decision to fly away to

Japan. He was standing at that fork in the road arguing fiercely that no one should go to Japan, that so far there was inadequate evidence to support even a withdrawal farther south, that if AD-COM must leave they should drive down to Taejŏn, not leave the country. Sterling Wright added his voice to Drumright's, but neither of them was able to make any impression, neither then nor later in the evening to General Church when he returned.[16]

I had had a long day, including as it did that visit to the area near the Han River under shell fire. The hundred-mile drive to Taejŏn seemed to pass very slowly. As soon as we were well away from Suwŏn, we turned on our lights and driving was much easier, but the dirt and gravel road did not allow any speed. Now and then we were stopped by sentries who quickly examined us and passed us on. At one point the road was blockaded and the officer in charge told us he was under strict orders not to pass anyone, whoever he might be, unless he held a pass from ROK Army headquarters. I suppose this was to catch the less easily indentifiable type of straggler. I explained my position at the embassy and its location at Taejŏn and, after some consultation with others, the officer decided we were an exception to his orders and waved us on.

All this time the rain was falling harder. It seemed that more headlights were illuminating the road behind us. About halfway down we stopped, and every car behind stopped too. We had become a convoy of six vehicles. I walked down the line and peered into each one to see who else had decided not to fly away to Japan. In the second one back were Bill Lynch and Jack James of United Press, the man who had filed the first story of the war only six days before. It seemed six months ago.

At last we reached the outskirts of Taejŏn. It was now almost 2:30 in the morning (July 1), pitch black, and pouring rain. I had never been in Taejŏn before and expected difficulty finding Muccio. As we came slowly down a main street, we saw a jeep parked at an angle almost across it. A man standing in front of the headlights began blinking a flashlight. It was Curt Prendergast, embassy third secretary, who had left Seoul with Drumright's party on Tuesday. Muccio had heard of the debacle at Suwŏn and had sent Curt out to guide the stragglers in. In a few minutes we were in the former KMAG compound and someone directed me to Muccio's house.

I walked over to the small wooden house which was now both chancery and residence. There was a pleasant, fairly large living room, now filled with us "refugees." I do not recall any special greetings. Muccio was on a couch at one end, nursing a scotch, and nearby sat Jim Stewart with another. Johnny, Drumright's versatile Korean houseboy, was sitting at a table by several telephones. Several other men were scattered around the room. One was Walter Simmons of the *Chicago Tribune,* who always treated what he saw and heard that night as privileged, since he was present as a guest.

I joined Muccio on the couch. He told me he had received orders to go south and was trying to figure out the route from a large map in his hands.[17] He said he thought the main road up from Taegu should be left open for military movements and we should take a different route. He seemed weary, depressed, and irritable. I asked for a drink myself, and Stewart poured me a big slug. Then I went over routes with the ambassador, although he was not in a mood to consider suggestions. Fortunately, the phone rang. President Rhee was on the line and wanted to talk to the ambassador.

Muccio talked with Rhee for a short time, telling him that the news from the north did not sound too good but there was still hope. Then he added, "Mr. Noble has just come in from Suwŏn and I'll send him over. There are some things I want him to tell you I'd rather not discuss over the telephone."

Piecing together what I learned that night and later, I found out that until about eleven o'clock no one in Taejŏn had any premonitions of disaster at Suwŏn. It was raining hard and seemed to be a good night to sleep. The 17th Regiment, which had fought so well in the Ongjin peninsula, was now in Taejŏn, and orders came from the north to send it up. Army Attaché Bob Edwards had a part in these arrangements, and the regiment was entraining at the station when the disastrous news of the ADCOM abandonment of Suwŏn, with all the undertones of collapse, reached Muccio about 11:30 P.M. Muccio told me he had received instructions via Tokyo to leave

Taejŏn, but I am not sure he didn't confuse the message from Suwŏn with messages from Tokyo which did not come. General Church telephoned him at 11:30 that the whole party had left Suwŏn, that the situation was hopeless, and that Church himself was coming down with a message as fast as he could get there.[18]

I was not aware of these calls when I arrived, only of a tense and confused atmosphere. Muccio told me he would wait for Church to arrive and then evacuate the embassy group by road through the southwestern provinces. But he considered it most important to persuade President Rhee to leave Taejŏn, for Rhee's own safety, to maintain the continuity of the government, and also as a magnet to lead others away. He thought that many ministers and assemblymen would be glad to go if the president set the example, but they would stay if he stayed. Additionally, there was a large group of politicians and influential private citizens hanging around the government offices and the president in Taejŏn, getting in the way of the war effort. They were spreading ugly rumors, agitating against responsible officials, and making a dangerous nuisance of themselves. Certainly, they would leave town if the president did. And of course, since Muccio in the past few days had made such a point of everyone sticking at his post and had said many extravagant things to boost morale, it would look very bad for the American embassy to leave while the ROK government remained in Taejŏn. He believed only four or five ministers acting as a war cabinet, including the defense and home ministers, should stay in Taejŏn with the army command.

At 3:20 A.M July 1, I started out in a jeep for the provincial governor's house to find President Rhee and persuade him to go south. It was still very dark and raining.

CHAPTER EIGHT

Following the President

I DROVE AWAY in the darkness expecting only a brief talk with President Rhee. I never imagined that I was on the first leg of a very long, difficult, and frustrating trip. It would lead me over strange and dangerous roads by night and by day. I would even spend twenty-one hours at sea. After a period of dreadful frustration in that rumor monger's paradise, Pusan, I would joyfully begin a swift return by rail to the war front at Taejŏn. That return would end one hundred miles short, at Taegu, because a surprisingly swift and bloody North Korean advance forced a hurried retreat on both United States and ROK forces.

The night was too dark to see much of the provincial governor's residence despite a few pale lights. I could tell it was a large two-story, semi-Japanese semi-Western building with a fine Japanese garden. I was quickly ushered into a large parlor where President and Mrs. Rhee were anxiously waiting for me. They were worn and tired by their past experiences and by the new, bad news from Suwŏn. Their weariness had been greatly increased by the lateness of the hour, up to which they had had no sleep.

I briefly described the situation at Suwŏn and the Han River, as far as I knew it, and gave Muccio's recommendation that the president and Mrs. Rhee leave for the south as quickly as possible. I said that Muccio and his staff would follow as soon as General Church arrived to tell Muccio of the military situation, and that we planned to drive down through the western provinces, the Chŏllas, leaving the main road between Pusan and Taegu free for military traffic.

General MacArthur leads the recitation of the Lord's Prayer at ceremonies held in the capitol building, Seoul, on September 29, 1950, restoring the capital of the Republic of Korea to its president, Syngman Rhee. U.S. Army photograph.

At the ceremonies were, left to right, President Syngman Rhee, Maj. Gen. Doyle Hickey, Gen. Douglas MacArthur, Ambassador John Muccio, and Maj. Gen. Edward Almond. U.S. Army photograph.

Dr. Rhee was angrily determined he would not leave Taejŏn, and Mrs. Rhee supported him vigorously. Rhee saw no further hope for victory. If North Korean tanks had reached as far as Suwŏn, the small South Korean forces still fighting could not stop them anywhere. American air and naval power appeared to have had no effect in even slowing the North Koreans down. Soon the Communists would reach Taejŏn, and if they caught him and killed him there, so be it. He preferred to die in Taejŏn rather than humiliate himself by further flight. Mrs. Rhee said she too would remain in Taejŏn, where she would die with her husband. At least the Korean people would remember that the president and she, facing the enemy without fear, had been killed rather than desert their people, just as the soldiers and so many civilians already had died and many more would die. Perhaps in some future and happier day the memory of their death would help Koreans to fight to recover their liberties and to establish a peaceful and independent nation.

Naturally, our conversation consisted of short sentences, with arguments back and forth. No one made speeches. But this is the essence of what the president and his wife said.

I argued strongly against such acceptance of defeat, against such a fatalistic invitation to death. I reminded the president that he was not an individual but the chief of state, and he had no right to follow solely his individual preference. He might personally prefer to wait for the Communists to come and kill him, but his duty was to the people of Korea, to the citizens of the Republic of Korea. If he died, the Republic died. In the midst of battles and defeat, there would be no opportunity for the National Assembly to meet and elect his successor. Instead of waiting to be killed, he must leave Taejŏn and go farther south. He must maintain the continuity of government; he owed that to his people through whose votes he held his high office. Furthermore, if he left Taejŏn, most of the other members of the government would also leave, as would the National Assembly; but if he persisted in remaining out of perverse pride, the others also would feel they must remain. Then they too would be captured and killed.

We talked and argued back and forth for nearly an hour. At first I was discouraged, but little by little I felt that my arguments were having an effect and the president was weakening in his determination. Mrs. Rhee became ready to accept my views earlier than the president did. At this final stage, Defense Minister Sin Sŏng-mo and the newly designated chief of staff, General Chŏng Il-gwŏn, just arrived from his trip to the United States, came in and joined the discussion.

Both Sin and Chŏng supported me strongly. In order to keep Mrs. Rhee in the conversation, they both spoke mostly in English, which of course helped me too. With their aid, the president finally agreed to my arguments, but not before I had enlisted Mrs. Rhee on my side. While the two Korean officials were talking to the president, I made a separate appeal to Mrs. Rhee, basing my whole argument on the president, the need for him in Korea and his role in future history. I said he would go down as a far greater president if he led his people forward despite disaster than if he remained in Taejŏn to be killed like an animal. I made no appeal to her own fear of death but based my request solely on her husband's proper decision. She finally agreed and joined me in urging the president to leave.

Dr. Rhee insisted he would not leave Taejŏn while Muccio and the American embassy remained behind to face the danger. I promised him, categorically, that Muccio would leave as soon as he had had a chance to talk to Church and that if the president's party drove down the road through the Chŏllas, we probably would catch up with him.

The determination of the Rhees to stand and meet a cruel death at the hands of a vicious enemy, instead of running away for safety, does credit to the courage and patriotism of both. Rhee said he would not go abroad to lead a government in exile again; he preferred to die on the soil of his native land. Mrs. Rhee wholly identified herself with her husband and her husband's country. That they had not considered the political implications of their deaths at that time, and that it took my arguments and persuasion supported by the minister of defense and the new chief of staff, to make them see that their greater duty was to live, only re-emphasizes their determination to stay and meet the worst in Taejŏn.

Few persons knew at that time of my early-morning session with the president, and the few who did soon forgot that as far as Rhee or I knew, American troops had not been committed to action in Korea. Nor, outside of the embassy, was anyone aware that a condition Rhee laid down in agreeing to leave was that the American embassy follow him promptly out of Taejŏn. Consequently, most foreign correspondents, knowing nothing of the facts, assumed that the president had run away from danger to save himself. Even when they did not write that, their later reporting on Syngman Rhee was colored by this misconception. I am glad to have the chance to give the facts here.

That was a thoroughly exhausting hour. It was now nearly 4:30 A.M. I had had a hard day ever since I first rose the previous morning about seven. My chief thought, as I drove back to report to Muccio, was to get some sleep before I was routed out to accompany the embassy farther south.

When I got back to Muccio, General Church had just arrived. He had electrifying news, and everyone who was still up was excited and overwhelmed with happiness. Church had been told in that telephone call from Osan to Tokyo that President Truman had ordered United States ground troops into Korea to support the ROK Army, and that the first elements of the 24th Division would be flown to Taejŏn in a few days.

I well remember the naïveté of my relief at the news. I thought then that just one United States division would knock those North Koreans back on their heels. Now we would really see something! In a few days the enemy would be a beaten and retreating army.

Muccio was equally delighted, but when I reported on my success in persuading Rhee to leave town, he realized that someone must immediately tell Rhee of the changed situation. There was no reason now for the embassy to leave Taejŏn, nor any reason for Rhee to leave either. Muccio did feel it would be better if the president went down to Pusan for a short while. That would get the political camp followers out of the way of the army, but the government, with the president still officially at its head, could very safely remain in Taejŏn now that the American Army was coming to the rescue.

First Muccio told me to go back and tell Rhee; then he changed his mind and decided to go himself. I had demurred a little. After my strong arguments, which had led to some sharp words on both sides, I was embarrassed to say it was all a mistake.

Muccio drove off quickly, and I began looking for a place to sleep. The few bedrooms were all filled, as well as the additional cots that had been put up. Most everyone was sound asleep. I found a sleeping bag, put it on the living room floor, and was just crawling in when Muccio returned.

President Rhee's party had already left for the south by motor car. The president had left word that he would drive through the Chŏlla provinces where I had told him the American embassy party also would go. Muccio was very upset.

There was nothing I could do at the moment despite my flat promise to Rhee that the American embassy, including Muccio, would be following him in the morning. I turned over in my sleeping bag and was asleep instantly. I woke up at nine o'clock to find that people had been moving around and talking in the living room for hours without disturbing my deep, weary sleep. Some joker had stolen my pistol, which I did not find till afternoon, hidden behind cushions of the couch.

I ate breakfast and went to the provincial government offices, which now housed not only the provincial government and the national government, but also the headquarters of the ROK Army and of ADCOM GHQ. I talked with General Church for a while. I had the map which I had been given the previous afternoon at the Infantry School near Yŏngdŭngp'o, with the information General Yu had added on enemy installations and concentrations. In the excitement of fleeing Suwŏn I had not turned it over to anyone. In fact, there was no one to turn it over to. By the time I found any officers who could use it, they were rushing madly for the airstrip and a flight to Japan. It seemed a very long time since I had received the map and discussed it with General Yu, but it was only the previous evening. So much had happened, and I had traveled so far and done so much, that the previous day seemed weeks away. I explained the map to Church and his operations officer and left it with him. I hope it helped.

Several people who came down from Suwŏn after me told me more of that peculiar session at the Suwŏn airstrip. As I have noted, Drumright and Colonel Wright were unable to budge the ADCOM staff from their decision to fly to Japan. But soon after I left, General

Church came back from Osan with the good news that United States ground forces were being committed to action in Korea. That made Drumright believe even more strongly that ADCOM should not leave Suwŏn, and he argued vigorously with Church against running out. But Church would not be convinced. He canceled the orders to defend the airstrip and fly to Japan but ordered the party to drive down to Taejŏn instead, where they would meet the first American troops to arrive.

I left General Church and went looking around. In the office next to Church sat Generals Ch'ae and Chŏng Il-gwŏn. They wanted to talk with Church to discuss the military situation, in the light of the commitment of American troops, and arrange common plans. But they did not know how to reach him even though he was in the next office.

General Church had not changed a bit. I opened the door that joined the two rooms and told Church that the Korean generals wanted to talk with him. He invited them in, and I soon left them in conference. It was extraordinary at this stage of the war that the ranking American officer in Korea constantly had to be nudged into even talking with the men who were running the ROK Army. Fortunately, there was none of that difficulty when General Dean arrived, or subsequently with General Walker.

Muccio told me in the early afternoon that I would have to go after President Rhee and stay with him. The news of the changed situation, of course, would soon reach Rhee, and he would probably start back at once for Taejŏn. Muccio thought Rhee's early return would be unfortunate, because not enough time would have elapsed to get the scheming out-of-office politicians out of town and the National Assembly established in some nearby city. Taejŏn was not big enough for all these activities and an army command besides. Many politicians were using the crisis to try to promote their political fortunes and were spreading the most malicious gossip about able men in office. These vicious stories implied that almost every minister and high ranking officer was secretly a Communist spy. Others, equally intent on getting into power, had their own strategy, their own tactics to peddle around. Since high appointments came from the president, if these men wanted positions they would have to go with the president. I was to persuade the

president to stay away from Taejŏn for several days, thereby at-
tracting the hordes of office seekers to him and relieving the pressure, political and psychological, on the government and army in
Taejŏn. I was also to explain that I had spoken in good faith when
I promised Rhee that if he left Taejŏn the embassy would soon follow and to make him understand that at that time neither Muccio
nor I knew U.S. ground troops had been committed to action in
Korea. I was to use what persuasive powers I had to keep President Rhee away from Taejŏn until Muccio considered his return
desirable. Muccio thought that should be in four or five days,
when U.S. troops would have entered the battle and the war would
be going in our favor.

Since we did not know how far the president had gone nor how
far I would have to go to catch him, Muccio sent Curt Prendergast with me. We also took the senior embassy interpreter, a Mr.
Sin, to help us out of difficulties. While both Curt and I knew a little
Korean, Mr. Sin had a very thorough command of English. He
was a gaunt man in his fifties with a long, drawn face. He had
dignity and I think had widespread political connections despite
his employment by us. He seemed to be respected and well known
to Korean officials.

We started off with two cars, a sedan which I drove and a jeep
driven by a Korean driver. The jeep was for an emergency. There
was always the possibility of a breakdown, and we could not afford
to be stalled for several days in some village far from a garage and
spare parts.

We tried to get out of town on a direct road to the west, but a
bridge was down and the rainy season stream was too deep for the
sedan. A water-stalled Buick promptly convinced me of that.
We turned back and drove north toward Suwŏn about twenty-five
miles before we found a good road leading over to the Chŏlla
provinces in the west. This was an area entirely foreign to me.
I had been over the central valleys numberless times by train, but
I had never been in the Chŏllas. I knew the names of many of the
towns and cities and even knew people who lived in them, but each
was quite strange to me as we drove up.[3]

Korean roads, even good roads, are very badly marked, and unless a driver knows his way, he has to stop constantly to ask direc-

tions. Frequently these directions are highly misleading, since the "director" has never ridden along the road himself. We must have gotten on the wrong road. If we were on the right road, the authorities should be impeached. I was at the wheel and found myself driving for several miles in slimy, deep mud. The sedan often would slither back and forth across the road; even the jeep had trouble. Twice I thought we were stuck, wheels turned sidewise in the goo, but each time we managed to get going again, once with help from the jeep. At one place in that sea of mud, almost at its end before we entered the city of Iri, we passed a fine, new Packard, hopelessly mired down. It was Mrs. Rhee's personal car. We were on the right track.

It was about 6:00 P.M. when we drove into Iri. We had great hopes of ending our quest there. Iri is a pleasant city of fairly wide streets and shade trees on the west coast railroad. Oddly, I had not known of Iri before this trip. I heard a good deal of it sometime later when, in one of their first operations in Korea, the Australian Air Force (RAAF) mistook Iri for a city farther north in Communist hands and bombed it. I had to do a lot of explaining about this Australian mistake to President Rhee, drawing on my experiences in the last war when our planes had bombed our own troops. It still was not a very satisfactory explanation.

I drove first to police headquarters to talk to the chief of police, thinking he would be the best source of information on the president's whereabouts. Curt, Sin, and I went in and found the police chief in his office with some other police officers. I asked him whether President Rhee was in Iri. The chief seemed uneasy and promptly asked why I wanted to know. When I explained I was from the American embassy and had a message for the president from the ambassador, he asked for credentials. I produced my diplomatic passport, which satisfied him, and he led us into another room where he talked in whispers.

The chief said only he knew where President Rhee had gone; most of his officers didn't even know the president had been in Iri. It was vital for the president's safety that the information should not get around. His party had arrived from Taejŏn in the late morning and driven directly to the railroad station. The president's secretary found the station master and asked for a special train to

Mokp'o, a port at the southwestern tip of Korea, over very high mountains, about two hundred miles away. The station master had not believed the secretary, thinking he was pulling a fast one for some rich refugees from Seoul. But when he saw the president with his own eyes, he invited him into his office and sent for the chief of police. The station master put a special train together, and in the early afternoon it had steamed off for Mokp'o. The chief had told none of his men who the passengers were, and the station master also had kept his own counsel.

There we were in Iri, two hundred miles away from a speeding train, Mokp'o, and the president, with a sedan, which was having engine trouble, and a jeep. I had quite a bit of Korean money with me but not enough to hire a train. I asked the chief about trains, though, and found that none ran at night and no regular passenger trains ran in the daytime because part of the route was guerrilla infested.[4] It was too dangerous. The president's special train had been heavily guarded, and it ran only in daylight. The chief did not see how we could get to Mokp'o, since there were no trains and the road was too dangerous for motor cars.

But Muccio had given me a mission with orders just about as direct as he ever gave. To carry it out I had to reach Mokp'o before Rhee boarded ship and went some place else. If we drove all night, we could be in Mokp'o by morning and perhaps catch up with the president there. As for the guerrillas, we would have to take our chances.

We stopped about an hour in Iri to have supper, rest up, and have some work done on the sedan at the garage. I have never cared for Korean food, especially their hot pickle, *kimch'i,* but Curt and Mr. Sin did and ate their supper very gustily as we sat on the mat floor of a fairly good restaurant.

About seven o'clock Curt, Mr. Sin, and I began our long, wearing drive. We still had about an hour before dark. I gave the Korean driver some money to pay for his hotel and left him with the sedan and orders to return to Taejŏn. We continued in the jeep, with Curt and I taking turns at the wheel while Mr. Sin sat in the back seat, jammed in uncomfortably with a duffle bag and other gear. The one of us not driving carried the carbine. We found that any firing would have to be through the windshield, since we were in an enclosed jeep and the square opening in the side door was so small, it was impossible to shove the carbine through and aim at anything. Mr. Sin was unarmed.

We could have taken a road to the coast and largely have missed the mountains, at least the guerrilla- and bandit-ridden mountain, but that would have added so much to our distance that we could not have hoped to catch up to Dr. Rhee before he boarded ship at Mokp'o. Our only chance was to take the shortest route—over the mountains.

We were able to keep on the right roads until dark, but after dark we repeatedly took the wrong turns. We stopped, found someone who knew the way, and tried over again. The later it got, the more difficult it was to find someone on the road to question. However, at every village we were challenged upon entering and leaving, and in the towns we were challenged several times on the streets as we drove along.

The local youth corps, augmented by police or other vigilant citizens, was on the watch for Communists in every village and town in South Korea, especially in the area through which we were driving, since we were steadily coming closer to guerrilla country. Most of the guards were armed with homemade spears, a knife on the end of a bamboo pole, or swords, but a few had firearms. All the police, of course, were armed, patrolmen with rifles, usually old Japanese rifles, and officers with pistols or revolvers. The sentries were often posted just off the road and we couldn't see them until their challenge rang out. I always slowed down at once and slid to a stop at the point where the guards were coming onto the road. Then I shined my flashlight on my face, while both Mr. Sin and I explained that we were from the American embassy. The flashlight made it obvious that Curt and I were Occidentals, and since no one suspected the Russians of having gotten that far down, our story was always accepted without further question. Sometimes we were asked where we were going, and we usually had questions to ask about directions.

At last we reached a small city, the last place on the plain before we began climbing straight up into the mountains. We looked for the police headquarters to ask for information and advice but got lost in a labyrinth of streets and alleys. After a half hour of searching we found the police building. It was almost midnight.

I went in and asked for the senior officer. This was a large police post, with many officers working at desks and others waiting around for emergency calls. I was led into a room where there were three or four officers and introduced to the night chief. He was a big, good-looking, obviously very fit man, courteous but dynamic. I told him we wanted to drive over the arm of the Chiri Mountains in front of us, down the other side, and on to Mokp'o on a special mission for the American ambassador. I asked his estimate of our chances of getting through.

The chief said the mountains seemed to be quiet that night and a police patrol had gone over in the early evening without trouble. But he would telephone to the first police station on the other side of the mountain, in the next province, and find out whether they had any other information. Someone cranked and cranked on a telephone, and the officer finally got his party. The police on the other side of the mountain also reported a quiet night. Still, it had been several hours since anyone had gone over, the danger increased with the depth of the night, and there was no certainty the guerrillas would not be out by the time we got up in the mountains. They were very few, but a one-man ambush might be enough.

He explained the police positions. His station, aside from an outpost, was the last police station in North Chŏlla Province and the last police station before the mountains began lifting skyward. It was too dangerous to keep any posts in the mountains. From his outpost there was a twenty-mile run, nearly straight up and then nearly straight down, through no man's country, and if we were attacked it would be up to us to defend ourselves. No police patrol would go out over the mountains until daylight.

That seemed to give the picture fairly clearly. I had left Curt in the jeep to guard our gear, so I had to make up my mind without asking his views. I asked the police officer for advice. Should we go on or should we wait till morning? "Well," he said, "I've never met you before, so I don't know you and don't know how you react. But if you ask me what I would do under your circumstances, I," he repeated, grinning oddly, "would go over the mountain now."

If he would, so would I! I thanked him and the others for their assistance and went out and told Curt we were going to start right away for the mountains, which we could see dimly looming up ahead of us in the dark. The night chief and other policemen came out and wished us luck. I took the wheel and started off.

As we drove along that night, Curt and I had time to talk of many things. I had known him at the embassy but not in a personal way. He was in his early thirties, blond, with a wide, pleasant face. After starting out as a reporter in California, he decided to try for the diplomatic service, passed the examinations, and was appointed to his first post in Embassy Seoul, arriving in August 1948. For about ten months before his arrival, he had studied at the University of California: Korean language, history, and social institutions.

Curt was a sensible man, but he had come to Korea with preconceptions, which he found difficult to change. He was basically solid and sensible but distressed by the imperfections of life in Korea compared with his home state of California. One of his deepest concerns was the South Korean National Police, who frequently used the third degree to extract confessions and build up evidence, who were not too careful about securing warrants for search and seizure, and who sometimes arrested the wrong people.[5]

I mention Curt, but he was only one of a great many who were disturbed by these things. I was too, but I could also see the police in another perspective. They were the organ of state security which maintained law and order in the face of the most violent threats and acts of Communist terrorists, arsonists, murderers, and guerrillas. Many of their families had been murdered by the Communists, and most had lost good friends among their fellow officers. Such experiences did not lead to kindness toward suspected Communists.

But this night we had driven along hour after hour in the greatest security. When we had trouble, we looked for a policeman, who took care of us. If we needed guidance, it was to the police that we turned. I asked Curt as we drove along early that Sunday morning whether he had changed any of his previous ideas about the police. He laughed and said he had just been thinking about the same subject. He said he had to admit that the night's experience had given him an entirely new perspective.

We began a gradual ascent toward the mountains. Just before the ascent became sharper, we saw ahead of us what appeared to

be a medieval castle. It was a large, concrete structure, with fire-
ports overhead. The road wound through its enfolding walls in
such a way that no vehicle could drive straight in or out, nor could
a man even walk in without being shot down from above if he
were hostile. This was the last police outpost before no man's land.

We were challenged before we could enter the winding entrance.
The police not only had rifles, but machine guns too. When we got
inside they told us that the night chief in the town had telephoned
we were coming and said to give us help. We also were told we
were not very wise to go over the mountain in the dark, but if we
wanted to that was our affair. They could not promise to rescue us,
although they would listen for firing and if it was near enough to
them perhaps they could do something. They bade us farewell.
I drove out the other end and we started to climb sharply.

Before I got on that narrow, winding mountain road, I thought
that with our two weapons and the speed of the jeep, we could
escape anything but an unlucky shot or a road block. As soon as we
began to climb I knew better. The road was so steep I had to go
in low gear almost the whole twenty miles. And it was so narrow—
too narrow for two jeeps to have passed at most points—that had
we been fired on, I could not possibly have taken my hand from
the wheel to fire back without risking going off the road in an abrupt
drop into the rocky canyons far below. The defense of the jeep
was up to Curt and his carbine, which he could not maneuver
out of his window and would have to shoot through the windshield. It did not seem likely that many guerrillas would stand in
the road in the direct line of fire. Mr. Sin sat quietly in the back
seat and said nothing while the jeep slowly labored up the mountain,
its bright lights flickering from rock to rock across the valleys. We
drove over the worst part of this shoulder of the Chiri Mountains
about 2:00 A.M.

We finally, and with a great sense of relief, reached the crest
and started the ten- or twelve-mile run down the other side. Somehow I felt safe now that we were going downhill. The best place for
an ambush would have been while the jeep was climbing up, not
crawling down. At the foot of the mountain we ran into another
police castle, where we were welcomed like old friends. They had

been waiting for us and promptly telephoned our safe arrival back across the mountains.

We drove along at about twenty-five miles an hour, swiftly and smoothly for us, and soon were in the city of Kwangju. It was now a little after 3:00 A.M. and of course all shops were shuttered, all doors were closed, and all streets were deserted. I drove along looking for the police station to ask directions for the main road to Mokp'o, but we were soon stopped by a police patrol. The whole south had been alerted since the outbreak of war, and especially since the defeats in the north. These particular policemen seemed to accept our story somewhat reluctantly and then questioned us about the whereabouts of various refugees from Seoul, of whom we knew nothing. They pointed out the road to Mokp'o but invited us to come to police headquarters first. I decided that, however hospitable their intent, there was no reason to waste time there and swung around on the Mokp'o road.

As soon as we had left town, Curt and I agreed we were both too tired to drive safely. We had begun nodding as we drove along, and a couple of times the jeep had started for the wrong side of the road before the driver awoke and caught himself. We pulled off the side of the road just outside a village and tried to sleep sitting up. It was now the gray period before daylight; as we restlessly tried to doze the dawn came bright upon us. The raucous crowing of roosters, the snorting of hogs, and the barking of dogs all joined the buzz of a swarm of lazy mosquitoes to make our sleep very fitful. I think I did sleep a little, and so did Mr. Sin; Curt said he never slept a wink. But at least we had an hour's rest, and we no longer nodded at the wheel during the rest of the drive. We got out to stretch before driving on and discovered one rear tire quite flat and somewhat torn. Curt changed the tire while I gave him advice and encouragement.

Finally, about nine o'clock, July 2, we saw the wonderful, great long bay of Mokp'o before us. I had heard of Mokp'o all my life but had never seen it before. It lies at the base of one of the finest harbors in the world, but the entrance from the sea is so long that other Korean ports are more economical to use.

We made our way to the office of the ROK Navy captain in

charge of the port. I told the captain who we were and asked him where President Rhee was, adding that I had an important message to deliver.

We had just missed him! President Rhee had come in by train the previous evening and spent the night in Mokp'o. But early that morning he had left by naval launch for Chinhae, the chief Korean naval base, where he had a summer cottage. The captain was distressed that we had come so far with so much difficulty only to miss the president. After thinking a bit, he said he would get a ship ready and have us taken to Chinhae, jeep and all. He needed a few hours, but he hoped we could leave about noon. Meanwhile, if we would care to go to his home we could wash up and have breakfast.

He was a very kind man, that captain, and I shall always be grateful to him. Before we left he asked us many questions about the war. He was disgusted with himself. He had been stationed in Mokp'o for three years, and now when his country's existence was in critical danger, all he could do was direct the shipping in and out of the port. He wanted a transfer and he wanted action. I learned later that he got both and distinguished himself repeatedly in battle against Communist forces. But that morning I saw him only as a kind host in naval uniform.

We were taken to the captain's house, where we washed up and sat in comfortable wicker chairs in a small sitting room to wait for breakfast. It must have been an hour later when I awoke; Curt and Mr. Sin were still sleeping. Sitting quietly in a chair beside us was a Korean woman whom I had known for years, the president of a Seoul women's college, whose escape route from Seoul had led her also to Mokp'o. She was staying temporarily with the captain's wife, and had come to tell us that breakfast was ready. She found us soundly asleep and just sat there until we awoke. We had a most satisfying breakfast, with the Korean lady serving us.

After breakfast I sent Muccio a radio message over ROK Navy communications. Since we had no codes and I did not want to pass out information to the enemy on the location of the president, I radioed, "Missed Princetonian proceeding Chinhae" and hoped Muccio would remember that Rhee had a Ph.D. from Princeton but the North Koreans would not.

About noon we went to the docks where a one-hundred-foot diesel vessel was tied up. Long boards were run down and Curt drove the jeep upon a hatch. It seemed a more dangerous drive to me than the one over the mountains the night before. The jeep was lashed down, and we were taken into a good-sized passenger room with mat flooring and four double-decker alcove bunks alongside. We had one fellow passenger, President Rhee's cook, who somehow had been lost and left behind.

The next twenty-four hours were a relaxing respite from the war, sailing along the beautiful South Korean coast.

We arrived at the Chinhae naval base about nine o'clock on Monday morning, July 3. Although none of us had been there before, from previous descriptions we could pick out the president's house high on a bluff overlooking the tranquil bay. Curt and I were delighted at this assignment, now that we were there. I had enjoyed my duties closer to the war, but since I had been ordered to this lovely place, I intended to make the most of it. Muccio had told me to try to keep the president away from Taejŏn for about a week, and neither Curt nor I could think of any pleasanter duty than spending a week in that beautiful spot, swimming, sunning, maybe even fishing. We were eager to get ashore.

The naval authorities were apparently surprised at a civilian vessel coming in to land in the inner harbor at a naval pier. A lieutenant commander was at the dock to question the skipper and tell him to shove off, but we explained who we were, and he allowed us to come in. Curt ran the jeep upon the dock and we asked to see the captain of the port. The commander would not answer our questions about President Rhee but had us driven immediately to naval headquarters.

At naval headquarters we met Capt. Kim Sŏng-sam, commander of the Chinhae naval base, a very senior officer in the ROK Navy. I had not met him before but quickly explained why we were there. Captain Kim had sad news for us. During his trip from Mokp'o to Chinhae the president had changed his mind and ordered his ship into Pusan. It had not even stopped at Chinhae. If I wanted to deliver a message to President Rhee, I would have to go on to Pusan.

What a letdown! No swimming, no sunning, no fishing, no rest. Pusan! That hole!

I told Captain Kim that one of our tires was useless and the other punctured and asked for assistance. He promptly gave an order and said that in an hour the puncture would be fixed and we would have a new tire as well. The chief U.S. Coast Guard adviser to the ROK Navy had been stationed in Chinhae before the war and had left a small cache of jeep tires. Captain Kim said he would not permit any Korean to use them, but since they were U.S. government property, we could have one.

We had a snack at naval headquarters and then, with a brand new tire and the punctured tire fixed, we started the twenty-five mile drive to Pusan. They were not like any twenty-five miles at home, more like fifty I would say, but still it was not long until we were in Pusan and looking for the American consulate. As we drove along, we were surprised and happy to see U.S. jeeps and trucks moving along the streets, American soldiers on the sidewalks, and even to find that the consulate building had been taken over by the U.S. Army as its headquarters.[6] We were directed a few blocks away to the United States Information Center, where the consulate had moved.

I was amazed at the transformation of Pusan in so short a time, short in fact but very, very long in experiences. It was now midafternoon of Monday, July 3. It had been only the previous Tuesday that I arrived at Kimp'o airport and was warned not to proceed because the ambassador was lost and the government had disappeared. Just the previous Friday night I had left Suwŏn for Taejŏn when ADCOM decided that all was lost and they must wing away to safety in Japan. On the previous Saturday morning I had my long argument with President Rhee to get him out of town, when he had wanted to remain and be killed because the cause was hopeless. In so short a time all had changed. The Americans had arrived!

I felt like a small boy seeing a cowboy picture, when at the end as the villain is about to kill the still-resisting hero, gallop, gallop, gallop come the good riders to kill the villain and save the girl. When I saw those American soldiers in Pusan that afternoon, I had no more doubt of a speedy and favorable end to the war than I had of my own name.

We drove to the USIS building, where we got directions and with hardly a wait, dusty, unshaved, and travel-stained, continued on to the president in the provincial governor's residence, a short ten minutes away.[7] All the president's guards knew me and welcomed me as I drove up to the gate. The chief of the guards, a Special Police Captain Kim, whom I had known for several years, came up grinning, shook hands, and asked about my trip down. He was much surprised when I told him I had been following him all the way.

I was led into a large room with a long table in the center. I suppose this had been the governor's formal dining room, but the president used it as his reception room for formal callers. Later he sometimes used to receive me in a small study, or even in the garden among the flowers which he loved so much.

President and Mrs. Rhee received me cordially. Rhee told me he had been very angry at me when he first learned that the Americans were coming in, the American embassy was not moving out of Taejŏn, and he alone was on the road. But he had had time to think it over and realized that I had acted in good faith and had been unaware of the commitment of U.S. troops. But now he wanted to go back. What would people think and say about him if he lived comfortably in Pusan while the government was near the battle front in Taejŏn?

I gave him Muccio's messages and emphasized very strongly the importance of getting the political camp followers out of Taejŏn and the role he could play as a magnet to draw them down to Pusan. The president did not seem to have been fully aware of the struggle for power among ambitious politicians. I named names to him and told him of specific things certain men had been doing which harmed the war effort. Rhee agreed it would be helpful to get these men out of Taejŏn. He was willing to wait in Pusan for a few days, but he must go back soon. After all, he said, he was the head of the government, and how could he make decisions and direct the government at such a distance? He was cut off from direct contact with his ministers, and even the telephone connections were so bad he could not talk to Taejŏn. While agreeing with him, I urged that he wait till I heard from Muccio and had a chance to give him Muccio's advice. Rhee accepted this for the time being.

I then had a private talk with Mrs. Rhee. She was all for staying in Pusan with occasional visits to Chinhae. The drive down had taken a lot out of her, and she was fed up with running around from place to place. She mourned her lost Packard in the mud above Iri. She hated living out of a few suitcases, and she felt that the president's health was not up to many more trips such as they had gone through. She hoped I would persuade him to remain in Pusan and promised to use her influence to that end.

I went back to the USIS center and finally got through to Muccio. I had radioed him from Mokp'o and again from Chinhae that I had just missed the "Princetonian." Now I was able to tell him I had caught up with the "Princetonian," had delivered his messages, and thought I could keep the president satisfied for a couple of days. After that I would need some stronger authority than my persuasiveness.

Muccio said that General Dean had arrived and wanted the military situation stabilized before Rhee returned to Taejŏn. Dean did not want the president in the middle of a fluid tactical situation, nor to have the president's safety on his mind in the midst of more pressing military problems. Muccio said that when it was safe he would let me know, and I should advise the president accordingly and come up to Taejŏn with him.[8]

CHAPTER NINE

Slowdown in Pusan

URING THE FIRST few days of the war the events of each passing half-hour differed sharply. One hour some- times seemed to stretch out into whole days of action. But today it is hard to realize that I was in Pusan on this trip only from Monday afternoon until Saturday morning, July 3 to July 8. Even at the time it seemed like weeks, and as time has passed those five days of frustration have taken on the quality of months.

I hated Pusan so! It was very far from the front and filled in- creasingly with rear area soldiers and refugees who gossiped the war away with dreadful rumors. I wanted so intensely to get back to Taejŏn that every hour of those five days dragged out interminably.

My impatience to get back north was matched only by Presi- dent Rhee's, but I had to keep persuading him he should not go until Muccio notified me. Later Muccio told me he couldn't tell whether Rhee really wanted to come back to the front, or whether I was only expressing my own desires when I telephoned daily and told him how impatient the president was with being delayed longer in Pusan. The ambassador suspected me of exaggerating the president's insistence on returning to Taejŏn and never realized how difficult it was to persuade him against his wishes that he should wait to hear from Muccio. The truth was that I did my level best to keep him contented in Pusan till I got the word myself. But how I loathed the place!

At the beginning of the war the ROK Army had taken over the railroads. They were actually run, and run extremely well, by the Transportation Ministry, but decisions on allocations of trains were

made by the army. When the Americans came they superimposed
their decisions regarding railway traffic movement on the ROK
Army and Transportation Ministry. This included issuance of
passes for private passenger travel between Pusan and Taejŏn.
In theory at least, the president of the Republic of Korea could not
board a train in Pusan and ride to Taejŏn without first getting a
pass from the transportation office at U.S. Army headquarters in
Pusan.

This situation naturally infuriated President Rhee, but I used it
to support my arguments that he should stay in Pusan for the
present. He asked, most reasonably and somewhat plaintively, what
the point of being president was if he could not decide for himself
when to ride on a Korean railway train. I had to agree with him
but urged him to respect General Dean's wishes, since Dean did
have military responsibility at the front and Muccio had assured me
that Dean would agree to the president's move as soon as the
military situation improved. Naturally, had Rhee insisted on his
prerogatives, he could have secured permission to ride the trains
to Taejŏn. Otherwise there would have been an ugly conflict between Americans and Koreans that would have hurt the war effort
far more than the presence of the president in a dangerous place.
It was part of my job to see that no such situation arose, and it did
not, due in large part, despite his fuming and occasional anger, to
the good sense and reasonableness of President Rhee.

I got through to Muccio every day, often after hours of trying,
to receive a new message or just a greeting. Armed with this I called
on the president to tell him what I knew. Rhee had such confidence
in Muccio that his messages and my use of his name enabled me
to persuade him to wait at least another day. But the one time I
could not reach Muccio I really had difficulty preventing President
Rhee from driving to the station and demanding transportation.

On the other side, I always told Muccio how impatient Rhee was
and urged that he be allowed to come back as soon as possible. I
said, entirely truthfully, that I was sure I could not keep him in
Pusan indefinitely and I would not be surprised if one day he simply
ordered a train and got aboard. Then we really would have a nasty
situation, because the 24th Division people in Pusan had little
understanding of Korea. They had just come from occupied Japan

and had difficulty realizing they were in a free and independent country. I was afraid some major would make a scene that would cause serious difficulties in our joint effort.

I tried to think of things that would be useful and arouse the president's interest during his exile in Pusan. I encouraged distinguished visitors and generals to call on him to pay their respects, going along as escort and protocol officer. When a representative of the International Red Cross arrived in Pusan that week, I took him to see the president and supported his proposal that the president sign the 1949 Geneva Prisoner-of-War Convention which he did without hesitation. It is noteworthy, I think, that Rhee issued a proclamation to the army and to civil officials implementing the convention before the United States government announced its formal adherence or General MacArthur issued his implementing order.[1] President Rhee was also busy writing telegrams to the heads of friendly states asking for assistance against aggression and to those who had already offered assistance, such as President Truman, expressing the undying gratitude of the ROK government and the Korean people. He also made several radio recordings for use both in Korea and abroad.

This activity by President Rhee led to an odd experience. The first day in Pusan, I established connections with the headquarters of the 24th Division. General Dean and a small staff were up forward in Taejŏn, so I called on his chief of staff. I explained my position and told him of the president's presence in Pusan. The colonel was very considerate and helpful and within the limits of his authority offered to do anything he could to assist me. He called in his signal officer and told him to transmit messages for me to Tokyo or for relay to Washington.

To be assured of adequate communications, the U.S. Army had taken over control of Korean telegraph and cable facilities. There was a commercial cable from Pusan to Tokyo, but no messages could be sent over it except by U.S. Army permission. Military traffic was so heavy that ordinary commercial traffic had to be dropped for the time being.

President Rhee's appeals to the heads of states were written, of course, in such a way that they could be released as an appeal to world opinion for support of the Republic of Korea. The problem was how to get them out. Rhee decided to telegraph them to his ambassador in Washington, who could then give copies to the various ambassadors and ministers stationed there for forwarding to their governments. I took the long message to 24th Division headquarters and went to see the signal officer, but he was out. The sergeant in charge of the office promised to send the message as soon as the traffic lightened, so I left it with him without a second thought.

I returned to the Signal Office the next day on another matter and discovered that the message had never been sent. I was astonished and asked why. A major informed me that the public information officer had chanced to see it and had killed it. He said parts of the message were contrary to command policy and the express orders of the 24th Division. The signal officer apologized but could do nothing.

I tried to see the chief of staff, but he was up north. Instead I talked to the G-2, who told me the 24th Division had explicit orders not to put out anything about or related to the USSR. In Rhee's telegram there was a statement that the North Koreans had attacked following the plans and orders of the Soviet Union. No amount of arguing with the G-2 that this was not a 24th Division message but a message of the president of the Republic of Korea, who could say what he liked, had any effect. We were at an impasse. The G-2 said the communication channels were the division's and therefore the order applied. If the president wanted to send the message, he would have to find another way. I insisted that the 24th Division had no responsibility whatsoever for what President Rhee said or did, and it did not assume such responsibility by transmitting his messages. The division had seized the Korean civil communications channels so there was no other way for Syngman Rhee to telegraph out of Korea.

The message developed a fantastic aspect that night. While I was having dinner at the mess, a major came up to me diffidently and asked if I were Mr. Noble. When I indicated I was, he asked to speak to me privately. We went to a quiet corner of the room, and he asked me to produce credentials. He was from G-2— Military Intelligence! I showed him my diplomatic passport with its entry regarding my assignment to the American embassy in Korea.

We talked some more, and it appeared I had passed his security check. After further talk the major apologized for bothering me and said the message would be sent out in the morning.

I went to headquarters in the morning, but the message had not been sent and the signal officer still had orders not to send it.

While I battled this out, I kept the facts from President Rhee. I knew he would blow his top if I told him an American PIO would not let him use this or that language in his own message as president of the Republic of Korea to the presidents or prime ministers of friendly states. It was two days before I got the message moving. Fortunately the second day, when I went to see the chief of staff, who was now back, I was told that General Dean was in the next room holding a staff conference. I quickly wrote a note telling Dean I was there and asking to see him before he left. In 1948, when Dean was military governor of Korea and I was political liaison officer for General Hodge, I had known him fairly well.

Dean came out as soon as he read my note and was his usual cordial, smiling, always pleasant self. I mentioned Rhee's being in Pusan, which he knew, and my assignment in that connection. I said I needed his help. What was it? I asked him to introduce me to his staff, tell them he knew me as a good citizen and ask them to do what they could to help me within reason. And I especially mentioned transmission of messages from Rhee or directly from myself. Dean at once called in the staff, made some brief, half-humorous, but very direct and flattering remarks about his acquaintance and knowledge of me, and told them to help me. He told the chief of staff to see to it that Rhee's cable was sent off, which he did. Dean then excused himself, saying he had a lot to do before he flew back to Taejŏn. I never saw this fine man again.

On Friday, July 7, the good word came from Muccio that General Dean was agreeable to the president and his party coming up the following day and was issuing the necessary orders to the transportation people.[2] I hurried over to tell the president, who was boyishly happy, and then went to U.S. Army headquarters to check on the transportation. They had received the order, and a train would be ready to leave for Taejŏn the next morning. The train was primarily a mail train, and the mail for the troops took precedence over baggage. The president's party was limited to about half his secretaries and guards, with the rest to come later. No one possessed very much baggage, so the transportation people actually had nothing to worry about there.

We were all at the station and aboard the train in good time. Various transportation officers were around, with orders regarding the president and the size of his party. Before they were through, they had loaded so much extra gear on the train that the president's party was cut down to Dr. and Mrs. Rhee, his chief police officer and two guards, one secretary, and myself. He was hardly riding in state, but he was delighted to be going back again. Mrs. Rhee regretted being uprooted once more, but she made no complaint.

About noon we ran slowly into Taegu station and stopped a hundred miles south of Taejŏn. The station master told us he had been instructed from Taejŏn not to let the president's train go any farther north. A U.S. transportation officer repeated the same message. I tried to find where the order came from and was told that someone had received a telephone call from Ambassador Muccio to that effect. But none of the people I talked to had any direct information nor any new information about the battle above Taejŏn. I had known all week that things had not gone as we hoped and that our forces, committed piecemeal, had already suffered several defeats. However, in the previous days' telephone conversations with Muccio he had told me that conditions were much brighter now, and Dean thought it was all right for the president to come up.

While we were talking and speculating, Col. Bill Collier walked into the carriage, saluted and took his hat off his billiard ball bald head. He had just arrived in Taegu the day before to set up 8th Army headquarters for Gen. Walton H. Walker, who would come later,[3] and hearing that the president and Mrs. Rhee were passing through the station, he had come down to pay his respects. Bill Collier was another old friend. I first met him when he was Capt. Collier of the 15th Infantry, stationed in north China, in 1932. The next time I saw him he was deputy chief of staff to Gen. John R. Hodge in Seoul, in 1948. In the interim he had been a brigadier general under General Walker in Europe. Of course, he knew President Rhee, and it was a nice gesture on his part to come down to the station.[4]

But Collier did not know anything about Muccio's message or what might have changed the situation back at Taejŏn. I did my best to find out, through the railway station telephones, which were incredibly bad, through the police telephones from a police station across the square, and through a military circuit. After an hour of trying, I managed to reach Muccio indirectly. I got someone at headquarters in Taejŏn, and asked him to telephone a message to Muccio and then relay the reply. After a long wait the reply came back that the military situation had deteriorated so suddenly and so badly that it would be unwise for Rhee to continue, and that Muccio would fly down the next afternoon and explain in person to the president.[5]

Later Muccio gave me hell for not immediately disembarking upon receipt of his first message. I tried to explain that I had been unable to verify whether he had actually sent a message or whether I was only receiving rumors and had taken what I thought was the correct step in making a check. Muccio did not think this was a good explanation. He thought I was so eager to get back to the war that I would not stop unless I was batted down.

Rhee was impatient during this hour wait but accepted Muccio's "advice" to remain in Taegu. I think Muccio's promise to come down to see him the next day helped enormously.

The news spread that the president was on a siding at the railway station. The provincial governor, Cho Chae-chŏn,[6] the police chief, and other local dignitaries arrived. Cho at once invited the president to come to his house and sent for cars. I went along to see them settled, and the governor was kind enough to offer me a room at his house. But Colonel Collier had already offered to put me up in the guest house at the KMAG housing area which he was taking over for 8th Army. I saw there was nothing more I could do for the moment and left for my new quarters.

At the KMAG area, a short distance on the other side of the campus of a rather large school which was being taken over as headquarters for the 8th Army, I was assigned a comfortable house for myself. It had just been vacated by a KMAG officer who was off somewhere with Korean troops, but his servants and his furnishings were still there. His wife had left after the outbreak of war, going down to Pusan with the other wives from Taegu and the southern area generally, and then over to Japan. Many marks of her presence were still in the house, and her maid, whose English was fluent if ungrammatical, praised her to me at every opportunity.

After getting squared away at my cottage, I went to 3rd Division headquarters to see the KMAG advisers. I wanted to find out how the war was going, for my own information and to keep President Rhee informed. Headquarters was in a large, two-story stone and brick building almost downtown, with two long wings sweeping away from a central portion. I assumed this had been a Japanese Army headquarters before the liberation.

Lt. Col. Rollins S. Emmerich and his staff of advisers were in two small rooms on the second floor, keeping in touch with the local Korean command by walking down the hall and with the rest of South Korea by telephone. When the war broke out, the 3rd Division had only three thousand officers and men and no artillery. Until the ranks could be filled up and some artillery supplied, it could not fight as a division.

Emmerich was red-eyed and weary to the point of exhaustion, and his subordinates were not much better off, but I couldn't discover when Emmerich, at least, ever took time off to sleep. He had a thousand things to do to help the Korean general get that division into shape for combat. The more I saw of him, the more impressed I became. I was not surprised later, when the 3rd Division was committed to holding and advancing on the east coast, that it fought so heroically and so ably. Emmerich became one of the legends of the early part of the war.

One time a new Korean general came to take command and saw that the division was nearly cut off and retreat to a safer position almost impossible, while army orders were to attack. The general concluded attack was impossible and told Emmerich they must radio for landing craft to get them safely out to sea and down the coast. Emmerich insisted they were ordered to attack, not to retreat. The general, a prewar "hero" who had been relieved of command in 1949 for political activity, insisted that they must get the division out and that attack was impossible. He wanted to radio for help from the navy to save his division. Emmerich risked his career, and all future Korean cooperation, to carry out the attack orders to save a vital position. He grabbed a club and knocked the

general cold. Then he gave the order to attack. The division attacked brilliantly, the enemy was driven back from its attempted
encirclement, and our position on the vital east coast road was maintained. Instead of turning against Emmerich, the Korean staff supported him, as did the Korean chief of staff. The general who wanted to row away in a boat was promptly relieved of his command
and made a provost marshal in a distant rear area.[7]

When I called on Emmerich that first afternoon in Taegu, he
was far away from shot and shell and from thoughts of bludgeoning
a general. He welcomed me and told me to make myself at home
any time I dropped in. An officer got a line through to Muccio
for me, and I learned a bit of the deteriorating situation in front of
Taejŏn. But I learned much more from Emmerich's situation map,
which for the next week or so I took pains to examine about twice
a day.

I went back to see Rhee, who was now established in the ground
floor of Governor Cho's home. I told him what I knew of the
situation up north, emphasizing that the Americans had only been
in action piecemeal and saying, quite truthfully, that I was sure that
as soon as the 24th Division could close and bring the weight of its
main strength to bear, the results would be quite different. Rhee,
of course, had many other sources of information, including his
police guard and their Japanese radio gossip, and he was depressed.

There were two rooms in President Rhee's new, temporary quarters: a large parlor and a second reception room fitted up now as a
bedroom. There was also a low, brick back porch facing a very
pleasant garden. Since the compound was surrounded by a high
wall, was almost in the center of the city, and this was South
Korea in July, Dr. and Mrs. Rhee were unbearably hot. Sometimes
there was a slight breeze in the garden in the evening, but it bore
a horde of hungry mosquitoes. Little could be done to cool the room
despite the several electric fans. The heat was so weighty and op-
pressive it would have made anyone irritable, even if he had no
worries. But the president of Korea, hearing of the steady defeat
and retreat of the American rescuers, had plenty to worry about.

The next afternoon, Sunday, July 9, I drove out to the Taegu
airfield to meet Muccio. The airfield was six miles away across two
concrete bridges spanning two closely parallel streams. The road

was always very dusty, and generally a person who had been to the airfield could be spotted from the layers of dust on his sweaty face. One of the streams was always crowded with boys and men bathing naked and women pounding their laundry with wooden clubs on flat rocks or modestly bathing in the stream, apparently fully clothed. When I drove back and forth to the airfield at Taegu, I always looked hopefully for some daring, modern young women who would set a new style in public bathing, but I was always disappointed. Bare breasts, of course, did not count. They flapped openly throughout the Korean countryside during the summer months and, no matter how well formed, soon lost all elements of surprise or interest to anyone who would have been pleasantly startled at a similar display at home.

Muccio flew in in a light observation plane and I drove him to town for his call on President Rhee. Muccio said every encouraging thing he could think of. Rhee was delighted to see Muccio, but otherwise the meeting was uneventful.

Later Muccio told me privately that the situation was very grave: we had suffered repeated defeats, were still being driven back, and the outlook was very gloomy. He hoped, however, that the U.S. 24th Division and the ROK Army could stabilize the front and that other U.S. troops who had been alerted to come over would soon arrive and stop the North Korean advance. The two intact ROK divisions in the northeast, the 6th and the 8th, had been pulled south and were holding a line in the center. The other South Korean troops were at the right of the Americans, but the North Koreans were making their main thrust straight down the Suwŏn-Taejŏn road against the Americans.

Muccio said he would be down again on Tuesday and then, very gay and dapper in snappy, clean gray hat, bright bow tie, and well-pressed clothes, he stepped into the little plane and flew away. How he always was so well turned out I never knew.

One of Muccio's suggestions to President Rhee was that he call the whole cabinet to Taegu for a meeting and then keep all but the war cabinet there. With the battle approaching so close to Taejŏn, Muccio thought it unwise for not only the president to be in Taejŏn but the government and the assembly as well. If the government established itself at Taegu, it could function under much less pressure than in crowded Taejŏn. The next Tuesday (July 11) Muccio repeated his suggestion, which I had been working on in the meantime, and Rhee agreed. The president sent for his cabinet for a meeting the following day.

The cabinet guessed Rhee's intentions and only a few came as spokesmen. They argued very strongly with President Rhee that South Korean morale was badly shaken and it was the government's duty to remain in Taejŏn, regardless of inconvenience or inefficiency in communications, to retain public confidence. If they all came to Taegu it would be taken by the general public to presage a surrender of Taejŏn, and they asked the president to reconsider. They urged the president himself to remain in Taegu and direct the government from there. They would take turns in coming down to see him, to inform him, and to receive instructions, but the seat of the cabinet should remain at Taejŏn. Rhee agreed with them.

When I saw Muccio off after his visit with President Rhee on July 11, I dropped in to talk with Maj. Dean Hess, commanding officer of a U.S. Air Force training group based at the field. Hess had been in Japan when the war started and volunteered to train Korean pilots to fly F-51s. The desperate battle situation, however, forced Hess and his men to suspend training and fly combat missions themselves. I had first met Hess a few days before and we subsequently became good friends.[8]

On this day we talked casually, and I asked some questions about air combat. Finally, he started to say something but stopped, saying he couldn't. I urged him to continue, and finally he said he was wondering whether I would like to go with him on a combat air patrol in his F-51 the next day. He said, however, he shouldn't suggest it, since I had very responsible duties and could not afford to be lost. But I snapped up the idea and pressed him until he agreed to take me on an early patrol the next morning.

The night before the flight an old friend from New York walked in. He had just arrived in Korea to cover the war for a New York newspaper. He knew Korea well, having served for years as a correspondent in the Far East, and seemed admirably suited for the assignment. We had a few drinks and talked over old and new times. I drove him down to the railway station where he could catch a train of some sort for Taejŏn. It was about eight o'clock.

I set my alarm for 5:00 A.M. to allow just enough time to dress and get out to the airfield by six o'clock. I awoke to a heavy pounding on the door. I looked at my watch; it was only 4:00 A.M. It was my friend from New York again, with a stranger, another correspondent. He told me he had reached Taejŏn all right but had stayed in the station area. He quickly got a full appreciation of the battle picture and learned from other correspondents that there were long delays in getting stories back to Tokyo. He decided his story was so pressing he should come out immediately and fly back to Tokyo to file it. Eight hours had passed from the time he left my house, rode a hundred miles to Taejŏn, fully covered the war, and came back another hundred miles to fly to Japan. I confess I was somewhat disappointed in him, perhaps because he had cost me an hour's sleep.

Hess was ready when I reached the Operations shack. I was fitted with a parachute, and with Hess carrying a sponge rubber cushion, we walked out to his plane. He planned to put the cushion on my lap and then sit on it, flying the plane from there. I climbed into the seat, put the cushion in place, and Hess climbed in and sat down. I was not as fat then as I am now, but I seemed pretty big for that small cockpit. Hess tried one way after the other, but he couldn't find enough room for the two of us under the closed canopy to leave space for his hands on the controls. He finally decided that while he could fly the plane, he couldn't fight it sitting up so high off the seat. Reluctantly he told me he would have to cancel. I was intensely disappointed.

Hess said as the next best thing he would send me up in an observation plane, an AT-6. There would be no bombing, rocketing, and machine gunning for me to watch, since the AT-6s were unarmed, but I could at least see the country and look for the enemy. He promised his squadron would keep an eye on us in case any YAKs appeared. He asked if it made any difference to me whether I had an American pilot or a Korean. I mumbled something about not caring, when of course I cared very much; I wanted an American pilot. Hess said that made it easier for him because no American pilots were alerted for the AT-6s, whereas the Korean pilots were standing by. That closed the subject as far as I was concerned, but quite unfairly I remembered those South Korean pilots who had flown their planes into the ground during the first days of the war.

We walked over to the ROK Air Force headquarters building to meet Brig. Gen. Kim Chŏng-yŏl.⁹ I had known him for some time and had always liked the cheerful, stocky, youthful general. He had a good combat record in the Japanese Air Force during World War II, flying fighters in the southwest Pacific. He seemed horrified at the idea of my going on a reconnaissance flight over enemy-held territory and protested vigorously to Hess and to me. He insisted that there was too much danger, that I was too valuable in my work with the embassy and with the president to be risked. But I insisted and Hess supported me. Finally, General Kim gave in and ordered his best pilot, a full colonel, to take me up. I heard him tell the colonel not to fly below four thousand feet, and for the most part the colonel obeyed, but now and then he came down pretty close to the ground.

Hess was late for his sortie, so he hurried over to his plane and soon was roaring off the runway. I never saw any F-51s, however, during the two hours I was north of the enemy's lines, but then I didn't see any YAKs either.

The North Koreans had pushed the Americans and South Koreans almost to the Kŭm River, which flows in front of Taejŏn, so we had a very short flight to reach the front lines. We flew north about fifty miles, and east and west for about the same distance, for at least two hours over enemy territory, constantly searching for the North Koreans. We could not see any. There were no soldiers on the roads and none in bivouacs or assembly areas. I could see a few scattered vehicles on the roads, but not more than three which might possibly have been tanks parked here and there in villages. They were so camouflaged that I couldn't be sure. If I had not known the invisible North Koreans were there, I would have believed that our forces could have advanced unopposed for at least fifty miles. I saw our troops in light force north of the Kŭm River, with artillery firing here and there on unseen targets.

From this experience I learned never fully to trust reports of visual aerial reconnaissance. Precisely the next day the North Koreans attacked with wave after wave of infantry, with tanks and artillery, in such great force that they drove us across the Kŭm River and into the outskirts of Taejŏn! Yet the day before the enemy had so successfully hidden his forces that despite our careful search we hadn't seen a thing!

It was an exciting flight, but I did not plan to try my luck again. When Muccio heard of it he was very angry, and I don't think he forgave me until some time after we returned to Seoul. Quite properly, he felt that I had no business flying around over enemy territory risking my life capriciously. It was my job to execute embassy business, not to go kiting around with the air force. Objectively, of course, I shared his view, but I wanted that ride, made it, and no harm had resulted. I understood his anger but could not appreciate his staying angry. I paid plenty for that little plane ride.

Out at the KMAG compound, the 8th Army, in the person of Col. Bill Collier, firmly seized control. On four hours' notice the KMAG officers were ordered to vacate their houses and not to take with them any article of furniture, including their own rugs. The houses were now for high-ranking 8th Army staff officers. In principle Collier was right, but in fact much of the furnishings in those houses was the personal property of the KMAG officers. They were also ordered not to appear again at the mess, which now became the senior 8th Army mess. The first day or so the dispossessed KMAG officers ate in the kitchen until they could set up elsewhere. The crowning high handedness was to forbid them to take away any mess supplies, all the luxury items of which they had paid for with their own money. They couldn't even take anything out of the deep freeze. This was an order and they obeyed it, but with bitterness. The deep freeze was filled with venison and other game meat which they had shot themselves. I felt very sorry for these officers, but of course there was nothing I could do to help them. They were no longer even attached to the mission but were under the 8th Army now.[10]

For a few days I was left undisturbed in my cottage. Then one day Collier said he had something to talk over with me and asked me to come to his office when it was convenient. I made it convenient immediately and he explained. General Walker was about to arrive, with numerous officers of his staff. My house was reserved as a guest house, and many army dignitaries were expected to use it. Collier wanted my house. He did not want to hurry me, and I could take my time as long as I was out by the next day.

Collier suggested that I might want to take over several vacant homes of the Southern Presbyterian mission in Taegu. He said the air force had already taken two, for Maj. Gen. Earl Partridge, commander of the 5th Air Force, and his deputy, who were soon to arrive. There were three others in tolerably good shape, one more still occupied by some missionary men, and a couple in bad repair. I could have any house that was left. He said that the best of the three vacant houses had been taken by the ousted KMAG officers, but I could have that too. I only had to say the word and he would have them thrown out.

I told him I would go out at once to look, but I would not disturb the KMAG officers who I thought had gone through enough. Collier said that was a soft attitude. They were soldiers and could sleep any place.

I must remark here that Collier proved himself a first class operations officer. He was deputy chief of staff for operations for the 8th Army under General Walker, and whenever there was an advance operations base for 8th Army headquarters, Collier commanded it. He was tireless, and as rough on himself as he was on others. I think he prided himself on getting things done without regard for other people's feelings. I know that in the embassy we owed him a great deal for his consideration, forethought, and friendship in a very trying time. But he was a tough cookie, and it would be silly to pretend otherwise.

I looked over the three missionary houses, including the one where the KMAG officers were. Two or three officers were there unpacking their locker trunks and they seemed disturbed to see me, wondering whether I was going to have them put out of their new haven. I assured them I would not. But I did decide that I would take title, as it were, to three houses: theirs, a smaller one next to it, and a third, very large house down the lane. I had no instructions of any kind from Muccio to prepare a place for the embassy, but it seemed to me from the battle reports and Muccio's insistence that the president should stay in Taegu that sooner or later the peripatetic American embassy would be established in Taegu. So, too, would the British legation, the U.N. Commission on Korea, and the Chinese embassy.

I returned to see Collier and asked for the three houses. Collier again urged me to let him kick the KMAG officers out of the big corner house, but I again refused. I wanted to take title to it for the embassy, but unless we got pressed for space, I thought we could make out in the very large building which, originally built for a group of single female missionaries, had numerous separate bedrooms. I asked Collier for blankets and rations, and that evening everything was delivered at the house. I also hired several servants, starting with Bessie, a woman past sixty, a remarkable character, who had been working as a cook for various missionaries for forty years.

That night I called Muccio, who said the situation was fast deteriorating, the enemy was very close to Taejŏn, and if it got much worse he would have to move the embassy to Taegu. I was glad to be able to tell him I had anticipated this move and had a place for us. That was a Thursday night, I think, and on Saturday the embassy staff began driving up to the new house. Drumright and Stewart did not come in until the next day, Stewart being the last man in, after we had all begun to be seriously concerned about him. He drove blithely in just before dark in his fancy, gadget-covered, enclosed gray jeep.[11]

When we sat down to table, we found we had eighteen people. The staff had been expanding, with men being called back from Japan. The table could seat sixteen, but usually two were away somewhere at mealtime. Muccio still had some scotch left, and before that first meal in Embassy Taegu we all had a drink. Bessie, the lifetime cook for missionaries, was horrified. She had never seen Americans drink before. She managed to adjust to our bad habits, however, and served us loyally thereafter.

CHAPTER TEN

Embassy Taegu

WE STOPPED in Taegu longer than any other place that summer. Although our basic responsibilities remained the same, the situation was so different that Taegu marked a unique period for us all. The rapid decline in our fortunes ever since the first day of the war now changed to a much slower rate of retreat. The high hopes and great chances we took at Suwŏn were no more. The certainty of early victory which swept through the small embassy group at Taejŏn when the first American soldiers arrived had been followed by tragic defeat after tragic defeat. Taegu became a very different chapter in our lives.[1]

I was in Taegu from July 8 until August 18. Throughout that period, the North Koreans made an almost continuous, if slow, advance against American and South Korean forces. If we checked them at one point of the perimeter, they pushed through at another. We had no real reserves; our "reserves" General Walker had removed from the line in a terrific gamble to keep a fire brigade of troops in readiness to rush to every seriously threatened sector. This fire brigade was part American, part Korean.

Throughout those hot summer days the North Koreans were greatly superior in numbers and in understanding of the tactical use of the terrain.[2] Only the ROK troops and the U.S. Marines could match them. But no one could match them in their use of masses of half-trained soldiers and even pitiful refugees who were driven ahead of the main forces into our lines to confuse and overwhelm us.[3]

It was deplorable that so many lessons of the war in the Pacific, learned at such cost, had been forgotten or were unknown to most of the American officers in Korea. Naturally, most of these officers and NCOs had fought in Europe, where the pattern was very different, and they had not learned what the Japanese had taught us the hard way. Infiltration, "banzai" charges, using the high ground, the need to establish a perimeter defense by early evening, and not to be panicked when the enemy slipped past in the dark but to wait calmly for mop-up squads to take care of him in the morning were lessons learned by both the army and the marines in the Pacific War. Yet up to the second loss of Seoul in January 1951, they had not been mastered by the American troops in Korea, except the marines. And only the marines made a habit of keeping out of towns and cities unless they had to fight for them. Our army took to cities and valley roads like law-abiding citizens.

In Taegu the American embassy's greatest contribution to the war was to maintain and always express intelligent optimism. Personally, I never doubted at any time, no matter how badly the battles went against us, that ultimately we would win. I imagine that the optimism of the others similarly was based on real faith. But whatever its basis, during this grim period we were the one group in Taegu, not excepting the U.S. Army, which was always cheerful, which always expressed conviction of ultimate victory, and from whom others could draw strength when cumulative disasters so shook them that they were overcome by despair. We lived a quiet and as nearly normal life as we could, considering that we were in the midst of a losing war and that the enemy at times fired into the city over our heads from five or six miles away. I think that many visitors, correspondents, South Korean government officials and civilians, and U.S. armed forces officers found the relaxation of our place and our confident optimism a source of renewed strength. I cannot speak for the troops in the field just north and west of us or down the perimeter along the Naktong River to Masan and the sea, since I did not talk to them, but I believe that of the 8th Army staff only General Walker had the same consistent inner assurance that defeat would not overwhelm us. There came a time when despair ran through nearly the whole top 8th Army staff. Walker talked of it to Muccio and me. I like to believe that that great and courageous soldier drew some strength from us during his worst hours.

My days in Taegu evolved into a familiar routine. In the morning I accompanied Muccio on two calls: on General Walker and on President Rhee. After a long lunch I made a series of calls, which usually included a second call on President and Mrs. Rhee. Late every afternoon Muccio and I attended the 5th Air Force briefing for General Partridge. The briefing covered both past and projected air and ground operations. It was much easier to reach the air force briefing at six o'clock in the evening than the army briefing at 8:00 A.M.

After an eight o'clock breakfast Muccio, Drumright, and I went to our other house to read telegrams and prepare replies. Unlike in Seoul, Muccio paid much closer attention to the queries and the replies before they went out, but in comparison to Seoul we had little traffic. Very early in the war we had asked that nothing be sent us unless vital to our own operations. The second day at Suwŏn two mail sacks filled with classified documents for the embassy arrived from Tokyo. They consisted entirely of tedious material prepared by the State Department on developments all over the world, printed for the information of interested Foreign Service officers. They told us of developments in Finland or South Africa, but not a thing about what we were supposed to do in the middle of a war in Korea.

I looked the stuff over and had it burned. It was all classified and we had no safe place to put it, let alone time or inclination to read it. I sent a telegram to Washington asking that nothing further be sent to us not related to our duties or informing us on developments that would affect our responsibilities. Thereafter we did not have much official reading matter to examine after breakfast. We only originated telegrams on urgent matters. We did not transmit the customary written reports on general political and economic developments or on embassy activities. The future historian will not be able to find the records of events in Korea for the first three months of the Korean War preserved in any extensive degree in the State Department.

Every morning shortly before ten o'clock Muccio and I, with Sergeant Edwards as armed guard, drove to 8th Army headquarters.

At first we had a little difficulty with the sentries in trying to drive up to the front entrance, a drive limited to full colonels and above. Most—but not all—sentries were impressed when Muccio told them he was the American ambassador. Finally, Muccio got from Tokyo the proper bunting for his car: two standards riding on the front bumper, one with the American flag and the other a blue jack with forty-eight white stars. I had kiddingly asked him how many stars he intended to display, since Walker flew three stars and other generals a lesser number. "Forty-eight," said Muccio. "I represent the whole United States." And of course he did. After that we had no trouble with sentries.

If General Walker was free, Muccio and I were shown in. As we got to know Walker better, we just walked in. Always during these morning calls Muccio and I wore coats and ties, I with a pistol in a shoulder holster under my coat to give Muccio protection in addition to that provided by Sgt. Jack Edwards when we drove through the streets.

At our first meeting I was taken with Walker, and the better I knew him the more I came to respect and downright like him. He was short, stocky, almost squat. His face was crisscrossed with smile wrinkles, and he spoke softly with a slight southern drawl. His mind was clear and incisive, and he was a model of courage and military leadership. I firmly believe that if he had been allowed to make his own decisions on troop dispositions and retreat in Korea, he would have gotten very different results in that dreadful period in the autumn when the U.S. Army retreated so fast that for weeks it was out of contact with the enemy. Walker had earned his nickname of "Bulldog." He hung on in Taegu when nearly everyone told him he must get out.[4]

These calls on Walker never lasted very long. He told us about the battle picture and his future plans; we told him about the South Korean political situation. Walker was greatly interested in developing a first-class ROK Army, and he asked questions and listened carefully to suggestions. Being civilians but close both to the American and the Korean military scene, and also close to the ROK government, Muccio and I were able to bring Walker information and a point of view which his staff could not.

A mark of the great change from ADCOM days was the welcome

extended by Walker to Sin Sŏng-mo and Gen. Chŏng Il-gwŏn, the new chief of staff, and to the new home minister, Cho Pyŏng-ok. Walker was always available, within reason, and they often called on him. His war room was open to them, and at critical times they were asked to come for special briefings there. They were invited to attend the daily 8th Army briefing for General Walker and his staff.

At our first call on Walker, Muccio said he thought Rhee's morale would be helped a lot if Walker would visit him, which the general agreed to do. A few days later he went with us, riding in Muccio's sedan but having his own jeep trail behind to take him home. Walker was strictly a field general. He would not allow a sedan at his headquarters. His own jeep was famous all over South Korea. It was always kept well painted, the cushions were custom made, and three stars hung in front. Walker sat beside his driver; his aide and a machine gunner with a .50 calibre gun sat in back. Whenever the jeep entered a combat area, which was nearly every day, the machine gunner stood up behind the gun, with the belt in place ready to pour it on. It was in this jeep that Walker was killed the following December, a very tragic Saturday for all of us in Seoul, but no premonitions of such a tragedy touched us when Muccio and I escorted Walker to call on Rhee.

Walker made a tremendous hit with the president at his very first call. It was not that Walker said anything so striking during this brief conversation. It was his character, his obvious sincerity and determination, the impression he gave of solid professional competence, his conviction that we would win, which Rhee gathered from his short exchange of words with Walker.

I came back and saw Rhee after Walker and Muccio had left. Both he and Mrs. Rhee were really uplifted. At last they had hope again. Here was a man! Whenever Rhee got hopelessly low in spirits, we took Walker to call with us again. It always worked.

Walker was a remarkable man in many ways. Often he and Partridge, commanding the 5th Air Force, went on personal reconnaissance flights together. They took a light observation plane, an L-5 or an AT-6, with Major General Partridge as pilot and Lieutenant General Walker as observer. They flew all over the front, repeatedly on the enemy side of the line, to get a personal appreciation of the terrain and of the general situation. This was the damnedest flying combination I have ever heard of.

The embassy helped General Walker in a political way by advocating the appointment of a new home minister. The former Buddhist monk, Home Minister Paek Sŏng-uk, had become a serious menace to the successful prosecution of the war. He was so pessimistic that he even infected high police officers with his defeatism. Walker asked Muccio what could be done, and that same day Muccio and I called on the president and told him what the home minister had been up to. When Rhee discussed the problem of a replacement, Muccio and I suggested Cho Pyŏng-ok.

At first Rhee did not want to appoint Cho, and I could understand why. Dr. Cho was a man of determined character who respected the president but who in a crisis insisted on presenting his own point of view and working to accomplish it. But these were qualities that made him very well suited to be home minister in that dangerous time. Dr. Cho had the character, decisiveness, and know-how to brace up the National Police. He had once been director of the National Police, and he had also once been home minister. I raised the subject of Paek's relief and Cho's appointment with Dr. Rhee every day for several days, and very obviously he did not want to appoint Cho. But in the end he did. There was no one else so capable of filling the post.[5]

Our morning calls on President Rhee were often a trying ritual. Muccio would tell the president what optimistic news he had of the war or talk of interesting events or opinions in the United States and minimize the gloomy side of the picture. Dr. Rhee was good-humored and highly irascible by turns. The hot, muggy weather was against him. He was cooped up and inactive, and the war left him little latitude for decisions. The American defeats were a terrible shock. Like us he had thought our troops well-nigh invincible. When they lost battle after battle to the Communists, and when he learned that some of them had fought badly and even run away, so much so that a major general had felt it necessary to fight in the streets to give his men an example, Rhee's ardent hopes for victory and Korean independence, and his confidence in American support and will to fight, sank very low. I found him exceedingly difficult to talk with those days.

Every day he begged for arms, saying there were innumerable thousands of trained Koreans eager but unable to fight because they had no guns. At first there was a great shortage of equipment in Korea, but in fairness to Rhee I must say that as it began to come over from Japan and ultimately from the United States, the great mass of it flowed disproportionately into the hands of the U.S. Army, with only a trickle for the ROK Army. Often this was to the good, but too often it went into the hands of a U.S. quartermaster who was concerned only with building up a proper balance of supply for his unit and didn't give a damn about arming the ROK Army. KMAG had a very rough time those days trying to pry loose a proper share for the South Koreans, who held half the battle line.

I assured the president daily that everything was being done that could be done, but he was never satisfied that this was so. While there was a basic justice in his pleas for guns for the ROK Army, there was none in his pleas for the Korean Youth Corps. Rhee had never learned anything about how modern wars are fought, and he seems to have been too old to learn that summer. He knew about the Minutemen at Concord and appeared to think that modern war was like that. All that we needed, he truly believed, was guns. The Korean youth had the élan and the know-how to drive the enemy back to the Yalu River, if they had the guns![6]

The Youth Corps was composed of thousands of the most physically fit young men in South Korea, who rendered relatively small service to their country. They did a certain amount of auxiliary police work in villages and country districts, and played a part in enforcing the conscription law, but I always thought they showed an undue eagerness to remain in the Youth Corps instead of getting into the army. Probably this was unfair, since many thousands did join the army, but at the early stages in Taegu no rush to the colors from the Youth Corps seemed evident. My constant rejoinder to the president, when he extended his trembling hands and prayed for arms for the young men, was to urge that the Youth Corps be drafted into the army. Then they would get basic training and learn how to use a rifle. By the time they were trained, rifles would be available. But Rhee never got over his belief that these patriotic young men only needed American rifles to win the war, and that once they were armed the American flag could go home.

The president often asked my views on a formal letter or public statement he drafted for use abroad. We frequently had lively but always very friendly arguments when I disagreed with the form in which his ideas were couched. As an example, one day he wanted to issue a public statement attacking the government of India. Personally, I agreed with him that India was wrong in trying to settle the Korean conflict by appeasing the Communists and making proposals for a settlement without consideration of the ROK government or the wishes of the Korean people. But I also thought it most unwise for the president publicly to attack the head of the Indian government. After we argued over the point, President Rhee changed his draft to express his objection to any attempt to settle the Korea question without consultation with the Republic of Korea, a sound principle which did not lose value by being tied into an emotional questioning of the wisdom or unwisdom of Nehru's conduct.

My afternoon calls were informal and varied. I might visit the International Red Cross representative, the Chinese ambassador, the G-1 of 8th Army (where I often helped work out problems relating to the admittance of foreigners to South Korea), the chief of staff of the ROK Army, the ROK foreign or defense ministers, the National Police headquarters, or a theater where the National Assembly was meeting, where I would talk with the speaker, Sin Ik-hŭi, about the war and politics. I sometimes went out to the airfield or to a hospital to see friends, or to the press billet where old friends whom I had not seen for years had gathered from all over the world. After dinner I almost invariably dropped in next door on my friends of the U.N. commission and the British legation.

As the "owner" of the house, I found myself with incompatible co-tenants. I had been assured by U.N. commission people that only two representatives would be stationed in Taegu and understood that the British legation also would have only two people. There seemed to be enough space in the house for four, and I thought the four could eat at a common table. But several things were wrong in my calculations.

The U.N. commission kept the two representatives plus a varying number of the secretariat personnel, several military observers, and visitors in the house. They wanted much more space. The British legation had a staff of three. I had tried to do a favor for both groups by taking title to the house from 8th Army and letting them use it. I found myself saddled with unexpected responsibility for their welfare, whether getting other quarters, arranging for rations, cots, and blankets, or hiring servants. Try as I would, I could not find other satisfactory quarters. The U.N. people felt strongly that the British should move out to give them room. The British chargé felt very strongly that the U.N. people should move out to give the British legation adequate space. I was in the middle and wished that I had never allocated the house to either.

The situation was especially bad while the first British chargé was there. The British minister, Vyvyan Holt, had been captured by the Communists in the fall of Seoul. The British had then sent a consul general from Japan as chargé d'affaires. He was not a happy choice for the post. He hated Korea and Koreans, could not stand the somewhat primitive conditions under which we all lived, and as time passed he became more and more distressed. One day he just caught a plane and flew over to Tokyo, which was a good thing for British prestige. His superiors soon relieved him, and ultimately the Foreign Office sent as a replacement an admirable man who did great credit to his country in a wearisome and difficult post.[7]

The Chinese embassy was in the city in a Japanese-style house. It was a comfortable and pleasant place with a garden, although not as cool as our houses because we were on the highest ground in Taegu. I felt very sorry for Ambassador Shao Yu-lin, who lived there with his staff, because they had so little contact with the rest of us. Being Chinese, their military attaché did not have the freedom of movement at 8th Army headquarters that the British military attaché or our embassy staff did, and they did not like to bother us by coming out constantly to ask what was going on. Their solution was to send the counselor and the attaché to the daily 8th Army press briefings. Several ROK officials, notably the foreign minister, also used these press briefings as their way of keeping up with the military situation. Rumors were so constant and

so dire that even with some information being held back the press
briefings at 8th Army were a valuable source of information on the
progress of the war.

The Chinese embassy had their mail sent from Tokyo in our
care through U.S. Army channels. I always delivered these letters
personally. They gave me an excuse to call on Ambassador Shao or
the Chinese counselor. As far as I knew, no other foreigner ever
visited them, and I believe they appreciated such calls. Several
times I found they were inadequately informed and dispirited, but
with the additional information I could provide they cheered up.
As the situation got steadily worse and rumors spread daily that
the 8th Army would withdraw from Taegu, the Chinese began to
fear they might be forgotten and left behind. I promised them
that I would tell them of any dangerous developments and give
them plenty of warning of a withdrawal.

Through these calls I was of some help to various persons and
kept more closely in touch with Korean political activities than anyone else in Embassy Taegu. Since we were not writing despatches
to Washington in this period but only sending telegrams, most of
the information I gathered was kept in my head and reported to
Muccio as it seemed important. Now and then, however, a telegram
developed out of it.

After a time Muccio objected to my going to the press billet, so
I never saw my friends there except by chance. Occasionally, however, a correspondent would call on Muccio late in the afternoon
and be invited to dinner. Later in the evening, since he had no
transportation, I would offer to run the correspondent downtown
to his billet in my jeep. I then looked up particular friends and
perhaps had a beer before driving back home. It was on such
a night that I talked with three men who were killed the next
morning. Naturally, no one was thinking of death that night.

A group of men I knew especially well had taken over one room
in the billet and only permitted others of like mind or friendly habits
to put up their cots there. Among the newcomers in that room
were Ian Morrison and Christopher Buckley, two British correspondents whom I had met only that summer. I talked briefly with
them that night and then drove back to our house on the hill.
Muccio was away somewhere, so I walked down the lane and met

Col. M. K. Unni Nyar, Indian military observer for the U.N. commission. Nyar was an extraordinary fellow, a most unusual Indian. He was a superior soldier with a first-class, logical mind. He had fought in the desert in World War II, in Burma, and then back in Italy, and had ended the war in Burma again. Usually he was with tanks. I invited him to come to the embassy house for a drink. We sat and discussed the war, and he outlined his ideas of proper tank tactics for Korea.

Drumright came in, and I had Nyar begin over again. Here was a man with remarkably versatile experience in tank warfare, and he had developed what seemed to be sound tactical ideas for the use of tanks in the Korean terrain. Up to that time the American use of tanks in Korea had been poor, and Nyar did not think that even the North Koreans had fully understood their possibilities. We sat late that night listening and asking questions, and I resolved that the next day I would try to get someone at 8th Army G-3 to talk to Nyar and explore his ideas.

About the middle of the next morning word reached us that a jeep in the battle area had been blown up by a land mine. Killed instantly were an unknown Korean officer, Colonel Nyar, and Ian Morrison. Buckley died on the way to the hospital in Taegu. These were all unusually fine and able men.

Burial had to be soon in that scorching summer heat. Several British correspondents took an active part in arranging the funerals of Morrison and Buckley. The Indian alternate delegate to the U.N. commission, Mr. C. Kondapi, took charge of the funeral of Colonel Nyar. The British chargé d'affaires had official responsibility and dashed madly about making arrangements for the two British funerals.

Nyar's funeral was set for 2:00 P.M. and the Englishmen's for 5:00 P.M. Muccio delegated me to represent him at Nyar's ceremony, while he went to the burial of the two Englishmen in the little missionary cemetery in our front garden just across the lane. Kondapi, a very brave man with a strong sense of duty, arranged for a proper Hindu ceremony for Nyar, funeral pyre and all. I drove out into the country to the funeral site, where I found most of the cabinet ministers of the South Korean government had come to honor the memory of this fine Indian officer who had died in and

for Korea. The Chinese counselor of embassy was there, several
U.N. commission people, and a large delegation from the foreign
press corps, especially the British. But there was no representative
from the British legation at the funeral of a fine Commonwealth
officer who for a very long time had held the King's Commission
and had fought with great distinction under the British flag. The
British chargé was really an odd chap.

Kondapi had a funeral pyre built of faggots on the side of a hill
south of Taegu. He personally wet it down with kerosene. In
solemn procession Kondapi carried Nyar's body from the ambu-
lance on the road, up the hill, and deposited it on the faggots. Nyar
was covered with a U.S. Army blanket, but his army boots stuck out.
After the ceremony and before the ignition, Kondapi knelt down
and removed the boots so that the fire would burn better. Those
of us who were there as representatives of the ROK government
or the embassies stood in the front row and at indicated times
walked around the bier and dropped flowers on that still form.
After Kondapi lit the flame and it was burning brightly, most of us
came away and left Kondapi alone to finish the burning and to
select the ashes for mailing to India. Nyar never had a chance
to outline his concept of tank tactics to anyone at 8th Army.

Back at the house I could see a firing squad assembling for the
funeral of Morrison and Buckley, but I had had enough of burials
for one day and did not go down into the garden. Muccio and
Drumright and several others were there, however. After a time
I heard the volleys over the graves and the mourners came back
to the house, somberly. Everyone had a drink.

The most serious problems facing 8th Army, which early in our
stay in Taegu came to include the ROK Army by assignment of
command authority by President Rhee to General MacArthur,[8]
were a critical manpower shortage, green troops, lack of equipment,
and skillful, large-scale enemy infiltration. The South Korean
regulars were veterans by now, but their conscripts were very, very
green. They got just ten days of training from the time they were
called up until they were sent forward to a replacement center.
Muccio played a significant role in helping solve several of these
problems by bringing his knowledge of the Koreans to General

Walker and his staff and then softly banging away until they accepted his advice.

There was nothing we could do about the extreme greenness of our own troops except to wait for battle to turn them into veterans, and for replacements and reinforcements from the United States. There was no alternative to filling up the ROK Army with tens of thousands of thoroughly green troops, those ten-day trainees. The need for men was too desperate. It always surprised me that these pitifully trained soldiers did so well. Of course, the ROK Army tried to mix them in with veterans, but soon the raw levies greatly outnumbered the veterans.

All the arsenals and supply dumps in Japan were soon stripped of their equipment, which was distributed in Korea, chiefly to United States forces. Until more could come from the United States, there was nothing anyone could do except work for a more equitable distribution between the United States and the Korean troops. This was a major emergency and required emergency methods. It was far more important that Korean soldiers fighting at the front have rifles, machine guns, ammunition, and trucks than it was that rear area U.S. soldiers have them at such places as Pusan, regardless of what the book said. Muccio reiterated this point and Walker agreed, but it remained very difficult to translate Walker's orders all the way down the line to the many junior quartermaster officers in the rear and to the transportation officers along the lines. There were even cases in which arms assigned to Korean units at the front were highjacked by underequipped American units in rear areas. In such cases it was not too difficult to trace responsibility, and Walker always cracked down very hard on the responsible officers.

Fortunately, while the president remained suspicious of American intentions during this period, Minister of Defense Sin Sŏng-mo and Chief of Staff Chŏng Il-gwŏn did not. They understood the problems and worked very closely with the American command, not simply as subordinates of General Walker but as colleagues with good will.

It would be inaccurate to give Muccio entire credit for getting the U.S. Army to use Korean police and to integrate Korean soldiers into the American divisions, but I think it is true to say that he had more to do with effecting these decisions than any other man.

Muccio was inspired by the action of the Seoul police chief, Kim Tae-sŏn, in organizing a combat battalion from the Seoul metropolitan police and leading them into action alongside the Americans near Choch'iwon and elsewhere north of Taejŏn. They were an example of what could be done by Korean police to spot enemy infiltrators and agents in civilian clothes and to fight alongside the Americans in critical situations. Instead of being impressed with the work of the Korean police in these actions, many of the newly arrived American officers, who had never been in Korea and had never heard of the police combat training or combat activities, refused to have anything to do with them. General Dean, under whom Kim Tae-sŏn and his men fought, was lost and unable to testify. An astonishing amount of contempt for the ROK Army was expressed by newly arriving American officers. One general, a division commander, upon arrival in Korea informed a press conference that he did not intend to take the ROK Army into consideration at all in making his estimates and dispositions.[9] Of course, he soon found out he had to consider it, since the ROK Army formed his right flank and saved him from very severe maulings by an enemy he did not understand at first.

The same general's solution for the Communists' infiltration tactics was to force every Korean out of the division's area of responsibility, on the theory that once they were removed, any Korean caught in the area would be an enemy agent. His order included the Korean National Police, whom he sent back to Taegu.

This way of thinking, while superficially sensible, was actually absurd. Orders had already been issued that no farmers or townsmen were permitted to move south out of their home areas unless their safety was directly threatened. The refugee problem was acute, not only as regards food and shelter but also in clogging the roads so that military traffic was slowed down interminably. The general's order promptly swelled that problem geometrically. Furthermore, great numbers of farmers simply would not leave their land, even when shells fell close by. They belonged to the land and the land belonged to them, and no one was going to scare them out. Despite the order, thousands of men, women, and children remained in the division area, and they were not enemy agents.[10]

But the most ghastly error was in ordering the National Police to get out. The American division was newly arrived from Japan and knew about as much about detecting enemy agents and infiltrators among the Koreans as they would if they had suddenly landed in China. But the police could; that was part of their job. The dogmatic general, by one of his very first orders, took a long step toward destroying the security of his division.

I accompanied Muccio when we told General Walker of this monstrous error. Walker was embarrassed to force a major general to countermand his own order, although after talking with us he agreed a serious error had been made. Finally, he talked with the general and permitted him to save face by issuing his own change order without receiving anything in writing from army headquarters.

This incident, coupled with the exploits of Kim Tae-sŏn above Taejŏn, led Muccio to believe that all the American forces would be helped if the police were organized and trained as special combat battalions, in effect as light infantrymen, with the special mission of spotting infiltrators, plugging holes, and covering the rear against the enemy's favorite trick assault. Home Minister Cho Pyŏng-ok and Kim, who now had become director of the National Police, were both enthusiastic and went to work drawing up tables of organization. But the idea first had to be sold to General Walker.

Every day when Muccio and I called on Walker, Muccio raised the question of organizing special police battalions to serve with the American divisions; every day Walker put him off. As opportunity warranted, I put in a few words supporting Muccio. After we left Walker, we would go back and talk with the two chiefs of staff, Bill Collier and Col. Eugene M. Landrum, and make the same pitch. Collier was the easiest to convince, because of his longer experience in Korea, but we had to wait for Walker to agree.

Of course Walker had a thousand other things to think about and to preoccupy him. What made him accept the advice in the end I do not know, except that it was sound and logical. Perhaps he had been especially shocked by some inexcusable infiltration and attack upon an American position from the rear. At any rate, one morning he asked how soon the battalions could be formed and committed. We said that all the preliminary work had been done, and if the arms were provided, rifles and machine guns, Kim could supply every American division with a combat police battalion in a few days. Walker asked us to make the arrangements.

Muccio and I promptly drove to ROK Army headquarters and told Sin Sŏng-mo and Chŏng Il-gwŏn of the decision. They were delighted and said that they would get hold of Director Kim immediately and that the American divisions would have the police battalions in three or four days, assuming the arms and rations were available. I went to see Kim in his office at National Police headquarters, and he almost bounced with joy. Unfortunately, things did not move that fast. One of the KMAG officers took offense at the way the orders had been transmitted out of channels through Muccio and myself and held up action for a week until he and the channels had been satisfied. But soon the combat police battalions were with every American division. The South Korean divisions did not need them, since the Korean soldiers were quite capable of distinguishing friend from foe. It was noteworthy that the Korean forces were rarely infiltrated while, in this period at least, the American units were constantly.[11]

I considered this one of Muccio's major contributions to winning the war in Korea, and especially to saving American lives.

Muccio made another contribution which ultimately was even more important, in fact which was vital to the success of the U.S. Army in Korea until long after the fall of Seoul. The basic problem was the serious undermanning of all the American divisions except the marine brigade. Some divisions had only two regiments instead of three, or two battalions in a regiment instead of three. There just were not enough American soldiers to fill the gaps, and there was no pool of reserves at the time in the United States to call upon.[12]

Muccio's solution was to mix Korean soldiers in with American soldiers to bring every division up to strength. His proposal did not involve any change in the ROK Army, which also had to be built up in strength and equipment. The idea was that Korean conscripts should be assigned for duty with the U.S. Army. They would get their short basic training at American army camps in Japan and then be sent to join one of the American divisions in Korea or about to come to Korea. There, under the "buddy system," each young Korean would be assigned to an American soldier with more training and experience, who would help him learn his new profession. The officers would be American, the troops mixed, with Americans in the majority but in some divisions, if they were to be brought up to strength, not a significant majority.

At first the South Korean authorities did not like this idea. They were afraid both that soldier material would be kept from the ROK Army and that, with the Koreans limited solely to enlisted categories under American officers, they would be in an unfairly inferior position. But when they were convinced that this was an excellent way to get a large number of men trained quickly so that eventually, when the American divisions were filled up by replacements from the United States, the ROK Army would inherit the results, they became enthusiastic.

General Walker and his staff were opposed to the whole idea. Walker accepted the idea of police battalions as auxiliaries for special functions, but he could not believe that mixing Korean soldiers with American soldiers would work out to anyone's advantage. He was afraid the American soldiers might not accept the Koreans, and as a result there would be serious morale problems in every division, which would reduce instead of increase their combat efficiency. He had his doubts that the Korean soldiers, with their brief basic training, could learn enough to function as part of the American divisions. And he thought the language barrier would be almost insuperable, that in the heat of battle orders would be issued hastily but the Koreans would not understand them well enough to obey. Every morning Muccio presented the arguments for his plan of integration of the Koreans and the Americans. And every morning Walker said he did not think it would work.

The proposal finally reached MacArthur, however. MacArthur became greatly interested and ordered Walker to send a senior officer to his headquarters to discuss this and other problems. Walker sent Colonel Landrum to Tokyo with instructions to oppose the program, but Landrum returned with orders from MacArthur to Walker to accept it. Like the good soldier he was, Walker then worked hard to carry out his orders, and later he told us he had been wrong and the integration was almost the decisive element in giving adequate punch to those very understrength American divisions.[13]

It was not until late autumn that enough American replacements came in so that the Korean soldiers could be relieved and turned over to their own army. The experiment as a whole was an unqualified success. Some commanding generals accepted their unusual replacements more gingerly than others, but before the war had gone along very much longer, none would part with them.[14]

History will have to record that Muccio showed imagination, determination, and a capacity to translate his thoughts into action. He did more than any other man to save the Republic of Korea from being engulfed and destroyed by panic, as much as by enemy arms, in the early days of the war. His ideas and his persuasiveness in getting the U.S. Army to use the police against enemy infiltration and to fill up its ranks with Korean soldiers must also stand out as a tremendous contribution to the saving of American lives and to allied success.[15]

CHAPTER ELEVEN

We Must Leave Taegu

O UR ROUTINE at Taegu continued with little change. Compared to the soldiers fighting a few miles north and west of us, we lived in luxury, but compared to the top staff of the 8th Army, we lived an almost Spartan existence.

The Southern Presbyterian compound was a large area sprawling over a hill in the western part of town. Our houses were along a lane just at the ridge of the hill, which was high enough to give us an evening breeze. In addition to the missionary residences, there was a boys' school being used for an ROK Army officers training school, a dormitory used as quarters by the 5th Air Force, one vacant house in very bad repair, another house used as a nurses' residence, a large mission hospital, a couple of other schools, and an athletic field. In the garden just below our house was a small area cut off by a low hill: the missionary cemetery.

Except for the pressures of war, our life in Taegu would not have been unpleasant. The nights usually were cool enough up there on the ridge so we could sleep, and after we moved out of the big house, those of us living with Muccio had adequate space. Even though our menu did not change very often, we had plenty of well-cooked food. Good friends of the ambassador in Japan were constantly shipping him cases of scotch whiskey, which the rest of us shared with pleasure. I think he bought a lot of it himself. What our house lacked most was the warmth of generous conversation and the foolish banter of men who are relaxed and filled with good will. The pressures on the ambassador were so great that we usually ate our meals under a strain and talked about little other than official business.

By the time Muccio got to Taegu, the war had taken a very great deal out of him. During the first few days he had played way over his head. He had been decisive and precise, yet decisiveness and precision were foreign to his nature. He had literally worn himself out pouring enthusiasm and hope into the listless and fearful. Seoul, Suwŏn, Taejŏn—each city and each defeat was a great blow and took more out of him. I think Taejŏn was the worst, since he had hoped for so much and the disaster to American arms there was so complete. He knew little about the tactical side of war, but he knew we had taken a hell of a licking. By Taegu, Muccio had no strength left to inspire anyone inside the embassy. He had to reserve his strength for the Koreans, the U.S. Army, an occasional missionary, and the correspondents.

The crowding at Suwŏn and again at Taejŏn Muccio had put up with without complaint. But now that he was settled down for the long haul, he wanted space, quiet, and release from the constant presence of his fellows. He had never lived with anyone else since he had left college, thirty years before. He was unaccustomed to having anyone at his table whom he had not invited, and he was used to eating most of his meals alone. Our life at Embassy Taegu must have been torture for him.

I was pleased to have secured that large missionary residence for our use. After Suwŏn and Taejŏn it seemed spacious to me. Muccio had a bedroom to himself, Jim Stewart and I had one to ourselves, and so did Drumright and Bob Edwards. The others were more crowded, but not badly for a war. We used the large dining room as a living room, with comfortable easy chairs and an overstuffed couch. We even had a small office for the clerks. Yet I hadn't suspected how greatly this degree of crowding would depress Muccio. When he saw how comfortably generals lived, whether 8th Army or 5th Air Force, he was even more discontented. In protocol, as ambassador he ranked as a four-star general.

As a result, most unhappily for us all, our long, sixteen-place table was not a site for quiet conversation and comfortable dining.

At first I sat up near the head of the table and wondered why Jim Stewart, who from his rank should have been up there too, always chose to sit down at the foot. I later realized how wise Jim was and gradually made my way down the line until I was as far away from Muccio as I could get. The ambassador took violent exception to anyone commenting on the conduct of the war or even making remarks on military operations he had seen. He would shout, "If you know so much, why don't you join the army?" One day he said this rather harshly to Don Macdonald, who was seated halfway down the table and had made some casual remarks about the war. Macdonald took him up, saying, "Sir, I shall do so tomorrow." Being a reserve army officer, Macdonald's quiet answer was no idle threat. I don't know what was said later to smooth things over, but Macdonald did not join the army. Instead, he continued his valuable services as third secretary in the embassy.

I suppose everyone on his staff caught a bit of hell from the ambassador in those Taegu days except Jim Stewart and Alan Loren, the ECA representative, who had been called back from Japan. Jim had an extraordinary ability to keep his mouth shut and never argue, and in addition the ambassador was very fond of him. Al Loren, a man with a fine mind and a pleasant, agreeable character, somehow always expressed himself in such a way that no one took offense even though he disagreed with him.

Drumright was more likely to talk back to Muccio than anyone else, since he was the second-ranking man amongst us. His comments were based on grounds more fundamental than nearly equal rank. Drumright was a man of strong convictions and determined character. No one silenced him. He expressed his views at table and elsewhere. Muccio would get him into an argument by oblique means. The two men differed violently about Chiang Kai-shek and U.S. China policy, and meal after meal we sat through the same arguments repeated with increasing heat and obstinacy. Muccio regarded Drumright very highly and I think was genuinely fond of him, but he could not resist bringing out the China question and waving it at Drumright like a red flag. Then the two of them hammered away violently, while the rest of us sat silent. Regardless of our views, we saw no point in arguing socially with the ambassador on something he considered so important, especially since everything that could be said had been said ad nauseum by the two major debaters.

I had several strikes on me before we set up housekeeping at Taegu, and aside from Muccio's continuing quarrel with Drumright over China policy, I became his chief target. Among other things Muccio felt that I had needled him excessively to get Rhee back to Taejŏn and that I had wrongfully gone on that air reconnaissance. He blamed me for our inadequate housing. Besides, I did not take my rebukes quietly. I suppose my memory of that time is too severe, but it does seem that I could not make a remark at table, no matter how innocuous, without hearing Muccio roar, "What do you mean?" and then attack what I had said. If I thought it would rain, he thought it would shine; if I thought it would shine, he thought it would rain. Of course, these were our family manners. When we had visitors, we were always loving and sweet.

Muccio finally could not stand living in the crowded big house any longer and had the KMAG officers evicted from their house. I had title to the house for the embassy, so all Muccio had to do was to ask Colonel Collier to get them out. This Collier was glad to do. We left most of the embassy staff down at the big house, but Muccio, Drumright, Stewart, Loren, Sergeant Edwards, and I moved into the corner house, where we had much more room and only six regularly at the table.

Some of the pressures on Muccio seemed reduced in the smaller house. Little by little I learned to keep my mouth shut and to express few opinions. More and more our table conversations consisted of Muccio's long anecdotes about his service in different parts of the world, especially in Panama. Naturally, he repeated some of those Panamanian adventures time and time again, but no one told him so.

We dined early, and usually when the meal was through I started out in the twilight for a stroll down the lane. Almost invariably one or more of the servants from one of the houses would intercept me to ask about the war, to ask some personal advice about taking a new job farther south or the possibility of our looking after their relatives in case of disaster. Very few of the servants could speak Japanese and only one knew English. Consequently, I was the only one they seemed to talk with. Besides, I had hired most of them in the first place before the rest of the embassy had come down from Taejŏn, and they seemed to feel we had a special relationship. Possibly they also talked to Macdonald, who could speak Korean, but I never saw them do so.

Bessie, the cook in the big house, was the most forceful character among them. She had a sharp tongue and knew what she wanted. One of the servants who had come down from Seoul tried to boss her because of his previous employment and metropolitan experience, but Bessie put him in his place promptly.

I always tried to say something reassuring to these anxious servants, most of whom were middle-aged or elderly women. I told them they could see how we were living, that we had settled down, and they knew we were making no preparations to get out. They should know that we would not stay in Taegu if we thought the North Koreans were likely to invade the city, so they should just go about their work and stop worrying. This kind of remark worked for a while. After the North Koreans got closer and the guns boomed loudly every night to the northwest, with bright flares lighting up the hillsides for minutes at a time, they became frightened all over again. But we had our little talks again in the lane and they all, even Bessie, seemed relieved just to have someone to tell them not to worry.

Most evenings I dropped in at the U.N.-British legation house next door for an hour or longer. It was much gayer there than at our house, and I was more relaxed than when I had to defend my unimportant comments from the ambassador. Usually several of the U.N. military observers were present, as well as one or more of the U.N. delegates, some of their secretariat, and the small British legation staff. Even when the first British chargé was there, his generally sour outlook did not harm the high spirits of the others. After he disappeared, Sydney Faithful, who during the chargé's presence had carefully kept his mouth shut and his eyes very closely on a book, took part in the conversation and blossomed into a first-class wit.

Maj. Bob Turp, the British military attaché, was quite good on the piano.[1] Often we gathered round to turn out some of the most amazing disharmony of the Korean War. Or we sat around the

table and fought over every day's battle and argued out tactics for
the next move. We had a lot of fun and did no one any harm. I
suppose my contribution, if any, was to keep these people au courant
with general developments in South Korean politics. Naturally, anything I learned in confidence I kept to myself, but there was a great
deal going on which they needed to know to balance their own
judgments but for which they lacked the proper channels of information.

When the Communists captured Taejŏn, our house in Taegu was
about one hundred miles behind the front lines, and we expected
that approximate distance to be maintained. Just a few weeks later,
however, enemy shells were roaring overhead to burst in the railway
yards down in the city.

Just west of Taegu there is a great series of mountain ranges
along whose eastern base runs the Naktong River, flowing south
into the sea near Pusan. North of Taegu it is only a creek, but as
it nears Pusan it becomes a deep, swift, wide river. The Naktong
could be crossed, but it was still a barrier.

West of the mountains and in the mountains themselves we had
no troops, and we had no organized forces of any kind in the two
western Chŏlla provinces, except the police. We were completely
without the personnel to put up a defensive force in the Chŏllas ourselves. The best that General Walker could do was to build up a
defensive line along the Naktong River and hope for reinforcements.[2]

The North Koreans had two choices after they captured Taejŏn.
They could try to bang their way south through the American and
South Korean forces into Taegu and then down the road to Pusan.
Or they could merely put a holding force below Taejŏn and swing
their main effort to the west through the open Chŏlla provinces,
finally swinging almost directly east along the southern coastal
region and driving into Pusan. If North Korea had captured Pusan,
the war would have been over. We had no other supply port for
our constricted area. If Pusan was lost, with luck we might have
gotten our troops out to transports lying offshore from several small
harbors and beaches, but we could no longer have fought the war.

But the North Koreans hesitated! They thrust their main force
against our lines north and east of Taegu. They hit with such great

strength and skill that they pushed us back daily, despite our complete and absolute control of the air. The North Koreans seemed to prefer to win the war the hard way.[3] For many days not even patrols inched into the Chŏlla provinces, and several weeks passed before North Korean units began moving down that route in force. General Walker recognized that the main enemy thrust was coming at him right down the road to Taegu, and he refused to move troops out of the main defensive positions south to the Masan area, which blocked the road into Pusan, until the absolute last minute, regardless of the intelligence reports of an enemy buildup in the southern Chŏllas.

General Walker had set himself for a siege in the north, knowing he could expect no more reinforcements, but was prepared to make a fast backfield shift from one end of his line to the other. ROK Chief of Staff Chŏng Il-gwŏn, however, devised an offensive gamble in mid-July and begged Walker to try it. He planned, by stripping troops from several quiet sectors, to mass a strong South Korean striking force and to drive forward through an area north and east of Taegu held relatively lightly by the enemy. He then proposed to swiftly swing his forces in a wide arc to come behind the North Koreans above Taejŏn and the Kŭm River, cut their communication lines, destroy their supplies, and drive into the rear of their forces. The Americans would launch a general attack directly northward, catching the enemy in a pincers, and the combined attack would chop the North Korean forces to pieces and destroy them.

The plan was bold and might have worked, but despite General Chŏng's pleas, Walker had to reject it. Walker maintained that his margin of safety was too small already, and if the ROK Army attack failed, there would be a wide opening in the center of the line north of Taegu. I was present during the presentation of this plan in the 8th Army war room.

Aside from his own estimates, Walker had MacArthur's orders to stay on the defensive except for limited offensives for limited objectives. Chŏng was deeply disappointed, and President Rhee suspected the Americans of a lack of courage and aggressiveness. This suspicion angered Muccio, who told the president nobody was stopping the ROK Army from attacking what was in front of them.[4]

The unprotected Chŏlla provinces were an invitation to North Korean occupation, but also an opportunity for guerrilla operations by our side to disrupt the North Korean offensive. There were innumerable hills, mountains, and caves for hiding places and sally points. Small guerrilla units could have been supplied by a thousand routes over the mountains from the Naktong River or by sea. The population was overwhelmingly loyal to the Republic of Korea, and the National Police were well established and knew the area. A South Korean Marine unit was in the port of Kunsan, and thousands of members of the Korean Youth Corps, all supposedly clamoring for rifles, were available for the formation of guerrilla units. The North Koreans could not possibly have established more than tenuous control over the area. Their armored units would have been vulnerable either in bivouac or when moving across country.

When the Chŏllas were threatened, President Rhee sent for Yi Pŏm-sŏk, the former prime minister and defense minister, and offered to appoint him a general on the active list with the job of creating and directing a guerrilla organization in the Chŏllas. If it proved successful, the operation would be expanded northward.

Yi Pŏm-sŏk seemed ideally suited to organize a guerrilla defense of the Chŏllas. He was an energetic man of infectious enthusiasm who had successfully fought the Japanese for years in guerrilla warfare in Manchuria. He did not win all his hit-and-run battles, but he kept alive, kept his forces going, and did a lot of damage to the Japanese. In the summer of 1950 there was no one in South Korea so experienced in guerrilla warfare, and with his reputation he could very quickly have recruited thousands of volunteers to serve under him.

Since the outbreak of the war, Yi had been actively trying to get himself reappointed to his former position of prime minister or minister of defense or to a military command in the field. The many defeats of the ROK Army, and later of the American Army, seem to have further convinced him that his military leadership and tactics were essential to victory. Perhaps he was not entirely wrong. He was no military upstart. He was a gradaute of a Chinese military academy, and in addition to his guerrilla activity he had experience in political warfare from as far back as 1932, when he had served with the Chinese in Manchuria, down through World War II, when he held a general's command in the Chinese Army. But his political machinations at this particular time were harmful to the South Korean military effort.

Yi refused the guerrilla post. Muccio talked to him and told him something of the story from the American point of view, but still he refused. No argument could persuade him. It seemed clear he wanted a higher post, and his obvious ability to carry out this critical assignment did not affect him. Rhee was disappointed and a bit angered. He told me that if Yi had taken on the assignment and made good, no post in the ROK government would have been too high for him to aspire to. But now, Rhee said, he would not offer him anything, although a few months later he relented and sent Yi to Taipei as ambassador.[5]

Unfortunately, with Yi's refusal the nascent guerrilla program died aborning. No one else took it over, and one of the greatest opportunities of the war was lost. The North Koreans came slowly down the Chŏlla roads, and the police fought or ran as circumstances and their hearts directed them. Here and there young men attacked Communist soldiers at night, but not as part of any organized resistance.

About this time Drumright began going out on regular trips to the battle lines with Col. Bob Edwards, the military attaché. Drumright and Edwards were close friends, and Edwards liked to have company with him on his numerous trips to the front. Drumright found himself with little to do in Taegu and a consuming interest in the war. He also believed, as I have described earlier, that some embassy officer should see the war from close up, a belief which I shared but Muccio did not.

Once, after the North Koreans had moved down the Chŏllas and were getting into position near the Naktong River, Drumright and Edwards went off for a one-day visit to the front. We expected them back before night. The lines were quite fluid at the time, and we frequently had to drive through areas held by small North Korean units to reach American troops. Night came and no Drumright. The second day passed and no Drumright. Meanwhile, Muccio and I had been watching the battle story closely on the maps at 8th Army and we were disturbed. The third day, just before lunch, Edwards and Drumright drove in, dusty and tired, but

happy. They had had a wonderful time seeing the war, and Drumright had an eyewitness observer's report that greatly surpassed the
maps at 8th Army headquarters. After that, Drumright and Edwards were off to the front two or three times a week, and we
were kept far better informd.

One day I heard that a marine general was in town as advance
for the marine brigade. I hurried down to 8th Army headquarters
and located him sitting with some aides in a vacant room. He was
Brig. General Edward A. Craig, whom I had known fairly well
during World War II as a regimental commander in my own division. We went overseas on the same ship and served in one major
campaign together. He remembered me despite my civilian clothes,
and we had a long talk of old times and the new war. He asked
many questions about Korea, including about landing beaches.
I told him what I knew and got Sgt. Jack Edwards, who was an
amphibious tractor man in World War II. We talked about Inch'-
ŏn, and both Edwards and I thought the miles of deep mud and
the racing high tides made a landing there too hazardous. We were
thinking, of course, in terms of a beach defended as the Japanese
used to defend against us in the Pacific. I suggested two other
possible beaches in the general area without these defects, and I
imagine Craig had them studied. But Inch'ŏn was not defended
the way the Japanese defended beaches, and it is now a matter
of history that the marines made their surprise landing at this point
of wide mud flats and high racing tides.[5]

The North Koreans finally gathered sufficient force to put heavy
pressure on us above Taegu and along the Naktong to the south,
while at the same time moving down the Chŏllas to threaten Pusan
from the west. The heaviest blows were always thrown against the
American forces, who were steadily pushed back. The South
Koreans were not hit so hard in this period and consequently
usually retreated under orders to straighten out the lines rather than
from their own defeats. Often the South Koreans could not understand these tactics and deeply resented them. Many highly placed
Koreans seemed to think Americans liked to retreat, lacked aggressiveness, and enjoyed forcing the ROK Army to retreat. Suggestions
of this sort angered me, but afterwards I had to admit that they

were the reverse side of the coin whereby Americans irresponsibly criticized ROK troops and ROK leadership.

Reports came in daily of new North Korean advances down the Chŏllas. Nearly every day General Partridge took his little observation plane, with General Walker as observer, and swung out over the Chŏllas, looking for enemy movements, especially tanks. I attended 5th Air Force briefings every evening and often heard Partridge himself speak. We were always told that there were no tanks. I never believed this "evidence" because of my earlier experience above Taejŏn when I had not been able to locate a tank, yet the area had proved to be full of them the next day.

The North Koreans' capacity to hide their tanks away in the daytime was uncanny. They drove a tank through the wall of a Korean thatched roof, mud-walled house. As long as the tank sat there it kept the wall from falling and the roof from tumbling in. From the air the thatched roof of the house was perfect camouflage and the best camera could not detect a tank.

Day after day the North Koreans built up stronger forces on the approaches to Masan. South Korean and American outposts were forced back daily, but were able to keep a fairly good count of enemy strength. In one of the desperate efforts, Gen. Ch'ae Pyŏng-dŏk, now charged with recruitment and training, accompanied an American battalion into the mountains to block the North Korean advance. General Ch'ae was killed and the U.S. battalion routed.[7] Another disappointment came with the loss of the first U.S. medium tanks to reach Korea, in a battle in which AP correspondent Bill Moore was also killed. The surviving ROK and American troops rapidly retreated, and the three American tanks, of which we had such high hopes, were captured. We were all greatly depressed that day.[8]

There were almost no forces between the advancing North Koreans and Masan, and then their grand prize, Pusan. A few thousand newly trained South Korean troops, about the same number of police armed with rifles, and about a regiment of Americans—that was all! But still General Walker did not make a move. He faced not only this tremendous threat in the south, which if successful would end the 8th Army as a fighting unit, but also a strong enemy offensive in front of Taegu. Taegu was the hub of all our operations, just as Pusan was our port, and so was no less vital than Pusan.

The most critical time as I recall it was from a Friday until the next Thursday. Had the North Koreans attacked in force during those few days, there is little doubt that they would have burst through at Masan and could have almost strolled into Pusan. A brigade of U.S. Marines was on its way, closely followed by a U.S. infantry division fresh from the United States. The brigade had to arrive, disembark, unload and distribute its gear before it could deploy for battle. And Walker had to perform a major miracle by producing a division at Masan overnight, although he was heavily engaged above Taegu.

We just had the time. Miraculously, the 25th Division disengaged itself, being replaced by a South Korean division, and was brought to a railhead by truck. Overnight the division was moved from action north of Taegu to new positions in front of Masan. The marine brigade landed and got into position.[9]

On August 7 the 25th Division plus the marine brigade and the 5th Regimental Combat Team counterattacked against the North Korean forces converging on Masan. Even though limited, this was the first major American counterattack since the early days of the war. The battle raged fiercely for several days, ending in a stand-off, but at least the North Korean attack had been stalled.[10]

As soon as General Walker had effectively blunted the North Korean offensive thrust, he pulled the marines out of the line, to their great anguish. The average marine didn't realize that they were Walker's fire brigade and could not understand why they were not allowed to keep on going until they destroyed the enemy in the Chŏllas. Many of them suspected that their withdrawal over ground they had fought to win and where their dead still lay was an army plot to keep glory from the marine corps. They soon found out there was plenty of glory to go around, especially for the marine brigade, which was repeatedly called upon by the army command to save the day for wavering army forces.[11]

The war came steadily closer to us at Taegu. We lived for several weeks with the enemy as a close neighbor. Gunfire was clearly audible, and often at night our flares lit the landscape a brilliant white, making a very pretty sight but also making us uncertain and apprehensive. Near the end of our stay North Korean artillery and mortars roared over our ridge at night. It sounded as though the shells passed directly over our beds. I think we all were quite startled, the first time we were awakened in the middle of the night, to hear those shells rushing over the house to explode somewhere down in the dark city.

Those shells only emphasized a problem that had been troubling us. With the battle lines only five or six miles away, was it wise for the government, and was it wise for us and the other diplomatic missions to remain in Taegu? We were not organized for a sudden evacuation, and the way the North Koreans had been breaking through our lines in the past gave no guarantee we would not awaken some night to hear fighting in the streets. How would we get out? How would the government get out? Even if we did manage to escape, we would certainly be in the way of our troops during a critical battle.

On the other hand, if we and the government left Taegu prematurely, it would have a very bad effect on Korean morale. The high morale among the troops would soon be eroded by despair and defeatism among the populace in the rear. We and the ROK government had to do everything within reason to maintain the highest possible confidence in victory among the civil population and within the ROK Army. We were determined to remain in Taegu as long as possible.

About July 27, when the situation still seemed desperate near Masan and in front of us, so desperate that a reasonable man had to recognize that the North Koreans might break through at any time, General Walker privately advised Muccio to get out.[12] General MacArthur was gravely concerned at the continued presence of the ROK government and the foreign missions in Taegu because of the danger that the enemy might overrun the city. He told Walker to urge Muccio to persuade President Rhee to remove the government and leave himself

Muccio asked if Walker thought the North Koreans might break through at any moment. Walker thought he had them stopped and could keep them out. On the other hand, with the North Koreans so close and their past record of victories, no one could say that they could not break into the city. Then there would be all hell to pay. Muccio emphasized the morale aspect and explained to Walker the importance to Koreans of August 15, Liberation Day. It was the anniversary of the Japanese surrender in World War II and marked Korean liberation from Japanese rule. For that reason, it had been chosen as the day for founding the Republic of Korea in 1948. It made a great difference to Koreans to have their government in Taegu when they celebrated August 15, as a symbol of past liberation and the certainty of future victory and freedom. Muccio was very much afraid that if the government left now, popular morale would collapse. He urged that unless the military situation absolutely forced removal, the government and the diplomatic missions be permitted to remain in Taegu until August 15. Walker saw the point and said he would not press for their evacuation now. If the situation deteriorated, however, they would have to leave.

By this time North Korean forces were so close to town that 1st Cavalry Division headquarters were also in Taegu. Militarily, that was a strange situation. The headquarters of the division fighting five miles away was in the same city as the army headquarters responsible for every division, Korean and American, fighting anywhere.

The North Koreans had been stopped at Masan and they seemed stopped outside Taegu, although five miles is not much of a margin of safety. August 15 was celebrated in Taegu with formal ceremonies participated in by the president and his cabinet, the National Assembly, and the heads of the foreign diplomatic missions. The speeches expressed defiance, determination, and confidence—just what was needed for the home front.

The next day Walker again raised with Muccio the question of the removal of the government, the National Assembly, and the foreign diplomatic missions, including ours. General Walker explained that he himself was under similar pressure. MacArthur wanted him to move 8th Army headquarters to a safer place, and so did all his staff. In fact, Walker said he was the only member of his command who did not believe that 8th Army headquarters should be moved south. He agreed with his staff's tactical arguments, but for the same reasons of popular morale that concerned

Muccio, he believed he should take a chance and stay in the city. General Walker was afraid it would affect the Korean troops and civilians adversely if they learned that the top American commander had left Taegu.

Militarily, of course, the argument against the retention of 8th Army headquarters in Taegu was unanswerable. An army headquarters must always keep firm control of all the battles of the units under its command. If the North Koreans suddenly broke into Taegu, even if Walker and his staff could get out, several days would pass before they could re-establish communications, and in that period Walker might lose control of the battle and the war.

This was a gamble Walker decided to take. It was far more important, of course, that his headquarters should not be overrun and that he and his staff should remain alive and free to function than that the American embassy should be safe. But it was even more important that the ROK government should remain intact, free, and functioning. Without a government, there would be no Republic of Korea, no cohesive army, no organization for the refugees, the railways, the police, and a hundred other vital essentials. General Walker hoped that we would leave as fast as possible.

Muccio, Drumright, and I called on President Rhee. Muccio thought that the three of us might be needed to persuade the president to leave Taegu. Rhee had often told me he would not retreat again, that if necessary he would fight in the streets with one hundred loyal men he had with him. All he asked was that we give him one hundred rifles.

Always before, after the usual courtesies about health and the weather, Muccio had given the president the bright side of the picture and I had backed him up. Rhee, on the other hand, gave us the gloomy side, which we tried to refute. But this time Muccio said he had some very serious information to report. The military situation was no worse than it had been for some weeks, but at any moment it might collapse and both General Walker and General MacArthur wanted Rhee and his government to go south to a safer place immediately.

Rhee reacted very sharply. He would not leave Taegu. If other members of the government wanted to leave, very well, but he would stay regardless of danger. He again mentioned the one hundred men, his need for a hundred rifles for them, and his desire to die fighting in the streets rather than desert his people by fleeing to the south.

Muccio gave Rhee much the same arguments I had given him in Taejŏn. The need to maintain the continuity of the government and the impossibility of Rhee acting like an ordinary soldier in a street fight. Rhee said he would resign, someone else could be president, and he would then be free to stay and fight in Taegu if it came to that.

It is hard to know how much of this was genuine and how much was a grandstand play. I doubt that Rhee himself knew. I am convinced that in Taejŏn he was utterly sincere in preferring to stay and die; I suspect that in Taegu his emotions were somewhat mixed.

Muccio urged the president to call in his war cabinet and discuss the question with them. Muccio had already talked with Defense Minister Sin and Home Minister Cho, and they had talked to the other three. Rhee finally sent for them, and they came over promptly from their offices. Muccio explained the problem, stated the source of the advice, and added his own plea that the government, including the president, leave Taegu promptly. He advised that this be done gradually as far as the public was concerned, that no announcement be made for the time being so as not to frighten the people of Taegu into taking to the roads, and that the war cabinet alternate between Taegu and Pusan, the presumed new seat of government.

As for the president, Muccio urged that he fly to Pusan or Chinhae as suited him, and then fly back for brief visits from time to time, showing himself on the streets but not stopping overnight in Taegu. In this way, people would know that he was around and concerned with their welfare, and the worst effects of the removal of the government would be offset.

President Rhee strongly objected to the removal of the government, but said that if the others wanted to go, he would not stop them. However, he intended to stay in Taegu. The five members of the war cabinet spoke in turn around the table, and each one supported the proposal to remove the government to Pusan. The president attempted to argue, but Dr. Cho argued him down. Getting no support from anyone, he finally gave in and agreed to fly to Pusan the next day, with the government to follow him. Rhee emphasized that he intended to fly up to Taegu every now and then, and Muccio assured him that if no Korean planes were available, he would see that American planes were put at his disposal.[13]

The next day, August 17, the president, Mrs. Rhee, and several members of their household flew to Pusan in an American transport plane. The government prepared to leave the following day. I visited Ben Limb, the foreign minister, at his hotel room and reminded him to notify all foreign missions that the government was moving to Pusan. It had occurred to me it would be wise not to have any of the recriminations that followed the evacuation of Seoul.

Limb said he would call on everyone that evening. I urged him not to forget Muccio. "But," said Limb, "why tell Muccio? He already knows!" "Yes," I replied, "he knows unofficially, but he is the American ambassador as well as dean of the diplomatic corps, and it is only fitting that he be informed formally by the ROK foreign minister that the government is moving to Pusan."

Limb made his rounds that night and stopped in at our house to tell Muccio. We were saddened at the prospect of another retreat, but less sad later when several shells roared over the house and crashed in the distance.

Perhaps, we began to think, it would not be so bad to be farther away from the Communists.

CHAPTER TWELVE

Retreat from Taegu

BY THE TIME I awoke the next mornng, most of our neighbors, the U.N. Commission and the British, had left. Everyone was driving the longer but better paved road to Pusan, which made a southeasterly curve to the east coast and then continued down the coast to the port. No one planned to take the shorter road due south because of its poor condition, made worse by the heavy military truck traffic during the past six weeks.

I had suggested to Muccio that the embassy keep one officer in Taegu as long as General Walker remained and offered myself as that man. I believed Muccio had agreed and was very pleased. I intensely hated the thought of going to that crowded, rumor-ridden, rear area city of Pusan, which most writers even to this day confuse with Taegu as the heart of our defense. Properly, the defense arc should have been called the Taegu perimeter, not the Pusan perimeter. Pusan was merely the port of entry for troops and supplies; all military operations were based in Taegu.

When I asked Muccio for my special instructions, however, he told me with some asperity that Drumright, not I, was going to stay in Taegu. I was to drive down to the naval base at Chinhae and remain there, representing the ambassador to the president, as long as Dr. Rhee stayed at his summer house. I was very disappointed, possibly a little angry, because I had been sure he had agreed the previous night that I should stay behind in Taegu. But it was an order and there was nothing I could say. I learned later that Drumright had not known of my request to stay in Taegu and had made the same plea independently, which Muccio granted. Of course,

Drumright outranked me and was entitled to his choice.

By noon that August 18 everyone who was going had left, as far as I recall, except Muccio, Jim Stewart, and I. Perhaps Al Loren was there. We planned to eat a last lunch and then start driving. I had persuaded Jim Stewart to come with me on the rough, direct Taegu-Pusan road to keep me company, since I had to follow it to reach the Chinhae naval base. While we were waiting for lunch, someone brought us several handbills in Korean.

One was from the cabinet and one from Governor Cho Chae-chŏn. The cabinet statement announced the removal of the seat of government from Taegu to Pusan. While we had understood no such announcement would be made until after the event, actually it was not too bad. As some of the ministers explained later, they felt they had no moral right to hide this fact from the Korean people, especially from the citizens of Taegu. They had been severely criticized for not keeping the citizens of Seoul informed of their intentions back in June, and they did not intend to warrant such criticism again.

But the statement from the provincial governor was exceedingly harmful. It said that because of the increasing danger of a North Korean breakthrough into Taegu, the citizens should promptly evacuate the city. Flooding the roads with refugees was exactly what the military wanted to avoid, and we had understood that, far from urging the citizens to leave Taegu, the cabinet and the president would urge them to stay fast.

How this statement was put out I have never fully understood. I do not believe it was initiated by Governor Cho, although he did participate in it. Someone higher in the government was responsible, I am convinced, although I am not quite sure who that was.

The handbills were out by midmorning, and they terrified the people of Taegu. They had been living so close to the enemy lines for so long that they were used to the sound of guns and confident that our lines would hold. Their confidence and morale were fine when suddenly this broadside from their governor told them, in effect, to flee for all was lost. They quickly began packing the belongings they could carry. A few had cars or hopes of getting aboard trains, but the great mass, the many thousands upon thousands, started trudging down the road to Pusan.[1]

While we were still having lunch and cursing whoever had put out the frightening statement, the phone rang and I took it. It was a call from a U.S. officer at Taegu airfield. President Rhee had just arrived! We had gotten him out of the city the day before, the government was moving to Pusan, and just as we were about to leave town ourselves, here was the president back again. I asked if President Rhee could be kept at the airfield until we came out to talk to him. No, he was sorry, but Rhee being Rhee, they had promptly supplied him with a sedan and he had already driven off for Taegu!

Muccio was angry and in despair. He had persuaded Mac-Arthur and Walker not to insist upon evacuation of the government until after August 15. After Independence Day in Taegu he had persuaded President Rhee and his government that their only recourse was to leave for Pusan. He had gotten the president out of town. The U.N. commission, the British legation, the Chinese embassy had already left. The American embassy was all gone except the senior people, and they were to leave in a few minutes. The streets were filled with handbills telling everyone that the government was moving to Pusan that day. Now Rhee was back in town.

Muccio first suggested I go down to see Rhee, then changed his mind and went himself. He thought he would probably catch him at the provincial government building, where the cabinet was to meet before leaving for Pusan. Muccio rushed off saying he would either be back in an hour or would telephone so we could get started. It was not wise to drive alone at night in those days.

I did not see Muccio again for about ten days, but later he told me what happened. He found Rhee at the cabinet meeting giving his ministers hell. It seems that before the president flew to Pusan, he had left orders that no decision on removing the government to Pusan should be made until he came back to Taegu. This, of course, countermanded the instructions he had previously given the war cabinet when Muccio, Drumright, and I were present. We had not learned of Rhee's later orders. As president, Rhee had full authority to decide where he would stay and where he would place his government, but in view of the military situation he owed careful consideration to the urgent advice of General Walker.

After Rhee had left the day before, the cabinet met to discuss the situation, especially the advice from General Walker as relayed by Muccio. They decided unanimously to accept the advice; they were in a combat zone and should be guided by the judgment of the responsible military officers. But they felt their hands were tied by Rhee's orders to do nothing until he came back.

Home Minister Cho Pyŏng-ok took the lead in insisting that the cabinet must act immediately, regardless of Rhee's change of orders. Cho knew the whole story of MacArthur and Walker's desire for an early evacuation and the delay at Muccio's request. Defense Minister Sin Sŏng-mo supported Cho's insistence that with the president away, in a time of crisis, the cabinet could not refrain from action. Cho said that if the others were afraid to act, he would issue a public statement, on his own responsibility as home minister, that the government was moving. The others then agreed to a statement, but it is my understanding that the handbill announcing the removal of the government actually was put out on the signed orders of Dr. Cho. President Rhee never forgave his very able minister for this act of defiance.

Muccio found Rhee furious but impotent to change anything. The handbills already were on the streets. Muccio had quite a difficult time talking with the president, and I do not think their relations ever were genuinely cordial again. Rhee claimed to have been tricked into leaving town and said that the cabinet, or at least the home minister, had been insubordinate in deciding to move the government without his concurrence. Muccio reminded President Rhee that he had agreed with the war cabinet, in Muccio's presence, that the government should be moved.

I do not know what made the president vacillate. Perhaps he had drawn some new strength from a quiet night's sleep in Pusan and had changed his mind about moving south. Perhaps his pride was bruised that he, the president, was unable to take some dramatic part in the removal of the government.

Finally, however, Muccio persuaded Rhee that the deed was done, that it was desirable for him to leave town at once, and that this was General Walker's urgent wish. Muccio stayed with Rhee while he went to his house and then out to the airfield, where a special plane flew him to Chinhae.

We waited till two o'clock at the embassy house without word
from Muccio and no idea where he was. Jim Stewart and I
thought we had better get started if we were to reach our separate
destinations by dark. We said our hasty farewells to Drumright,
Bob Edwards, and the servants. Jim picked up a friend, Chang
Ki-bong, a newspaper reporter from Seoul who had often helped
him out. It was nearly three o'clock before we were able to move
our two jeeps through the refugee-jammed streets of Taegu and
reach the Pusan road, a road neither of us had ever traveled before.

The mass of refugees was so dense that we had to drive in low
gear, not faster than five miles an hour, with more horn than motor.
There were Korean MPs on a bridge just at the edge of town who
helped control traffic a little, but otherwise everyone was on his
own. Men, women, and children of all ages, and with every conceivable kind of box and bundle on their backs or their heads,
crowded around us. I was in the lead, but Jim's jeep was far
enough back of mine so that he had to break his own lanes through
this sea of orderly, quiet, desperate people.

I soon picked up a couple who turned out to be refugees from
Seoul. They had a son whom they had sent ahead of them on an
ox cart with some friends while they walked. Several times they
asked me to stop; they ran back to examine an ox cart I had passed
to make sure their boy was not aboard. After about fifteen miles
they got out with profuse thanks. We were in lonely country, but
they said they had friends nearby. I suppose there was a house I
could not see over some nearby hill. They had not found their
boy when I left them, so perhaps the "friend" was only an excuse
to stand by the side of the road until the refugee mass caught up
with them and they could resume their search for their missing son.

We drove about ten miles before the mass began to thin out, and
fifteen miles before we left the plodding refugees behind and were
able to increase our speed to twenty-five miles an hour. We sometimes went faster, but the road would not take very much more.

We passed the Marine Corps camp, and I was tempted to go in
and see General Craig, but we were late and drove on. We did not
know it then, but that was the day when the North Koreans broke
through the U.S. 24th Division and crossed the Naktong River for
a penetration of about twelve miles. In fact, the battle was raging

furiously just the other side of the mountain along which we drove, but we didn't hear any sounds of the fighting. The marines had been thrown in to plug the gap, which they did with enormous slaughter of the enemy, and they had restored the lines. I would not have found General Craig sitting in his tent that afternoon.[2]

During our brief halt outside the camp I talked Jim into coming down to Chinhae with me. I suggested he take a day off and go to Pusan the next day. We could swim, rest, and enjoy ourselves. He deserved a holiday, and besides, the next day was Sunday. Jim agreed, and we drove on looking for the southwestern turnoff which would put us on a road for Chinhae.

I was using a map of all Korea, 1:1,000,000, produced by the Army Map Service in Washington in 1945. It was the only printed map of Korea I ever saw during the war, aside from the Air Force pilotage charts, which were not much use in driving a jeep. I have the same map before me as I write. It is a bit stained and creased, marked here and there in crayon, but would be just as useful today as it was then. That would not be very much. With its small scale and the amount of information available in Washington on Korean roads in 1945, it is a wonder anyone could get anywhere using it. But you could, although sometimes in rather odd ways.

According to the map, at a place with the long name of Samnangjin about twenty-five miles equidistant from Pusan and Chinhae, the road divided. I planned to drive west from Samnangjin towards Masan and at the proper place cut off due south for Chinhae and the sea. It all seemed very clear then, and as I check my map again it still seems clear.

I drove into Samnangjin with Jim's gray jeep right behind me and stopped near the center of town. Several men with arm bands were directing traffic and questioning suspicious-looking travelers. I got my map and asked for directions to Chinhae. They told me I would have to go south almost to Pusan before I could turn west to Chinhae. But I showed them my map, which had a nice red line indicating an improved road breaking away from the Pusan road at Samnangjin and bearing west for Masan and Chinhae. They were intrigued with the map but said there was no such road. The Naktong River, wide and deep at that point, flowed near Samnangjin, and there was no vehicular crossing of the river nearer

than the outskirts of Pusan. I knew nothing of the roads in the
immediate area, but I believed my map. These emergency traffic
guards thought my map was pretty, but they knew the country and
the roads. I just could not believe that the U.S. Army Map Service
would put an arterial road on a map where none existed and
argued my point. Finally, one of the Koreans said there was a way.

I was to drive down a certain street about four miles till I came
to a railway bridge across the Naktong River. The road ascended
very steeply to the level of the railway tracks at that point, but
he thought a jeep could make it. Soldiers guarded both ends of
the bridge; if I identified myself and explained my need to get
across the river, he was sure the guards would let us drive across
on the railroad ties. I thanked him, and Jim and I started for
the railway bridge.

When we reached the bridge we understood what our guide had
meant about a steep ascent. I do not think a two-wheel drive car
could have made it up to the railway, but with several bucks and
false starts our jeeps did. I explained to the guards what we wanted
to do. They cranked their phone and called to the other side of
the river that we were friendly and not to fire on us.

Then began one of the strangest and most frightening experiences
I have ever had. I would not repeat it for anything. Still, it is fun to
remember.

At that point the Naktong is about three-quarters of a mile wide
and flows very swift and deep. The first half of the single-track
railway bridge is supported by a series of steel girders. How the
second half is engineered I do not know, but I do know that
there is nothing rising above the level of the tracks to keep even
a jeep from falling a hundred feet down into that deep, surging
blue-black river.

Although I had never driven on railroad ties before, I thought
it would be simple enough, and started gaily along. But I could not
hit the right tempo. I was driving with one set of wheels just inside
a rail and one outside. Either I went too fast and had the feeling
that the jeep was about to jump the tracks and dive into the river
before I could stop it, or in my fear I slowed down and bounced
along, up and down into the air, jiggety-jog, jiggety-jog. It was not
only uncomfortable physically, but I wondered whether one of those

slow bounces would end up with my diving, jeep and all, into the Naktong. It did not help, of course, to be able to look between the ties and see the water far below.

I had not gone a hundred jerky yards before I wished very thoroughly that I had never begun that wild ride. Any amount of driving out of my way, via Pusan or anywhere else, would have been preferable. But twenty yards behind me Jim was bouncing along in his jeep, and there was no turning around. Besides, I thought, maybe the height and the rushing river didn't bother Jim a bit. I did not want to suggest that we turn back, even if it might have been possible to back up over those ties, and show him how scared I was. Later I learned that he didn't want to let me know how frightened he was, and he found he could not back up anyway.

The worst part of the crossing was yet to come. While the high girders lasted, they gave some sense of security, a hope that if the jeep bounced to the side it might hit against a girder and be stopped from the abyss. Halfway across the girders ended, and I drove with no side rail or support of any kind to keep the jeep from going over the edge. I was very frightened. There was nothing to do but keep bouncing along. I am sure now that if I had put both wheels inside the tracks and set a steady speed of about twelve miles, I would soon have been across the bridge. But I had to learn the hard way.

Finally, I was across the bridge and riding on the tracks along the elevated right of way, with Jim right behind. The guards had said that a road would shortly lead off the railway track down to a regular road. We both kept looking for it, but there was none. There was a distant road, far, far down, but no way to reach it from the tracks. We kept going along the tracks. It was curious that the drive was just as difficult, but with no river to look at between the ties, it was only an inconvenience and not terrifying.

We drove along through the hills about a mile when suddenly we came to a tunnel. There was still no way down from the high embankment. We stopped the jeeps, and the reporter, Chang, walked through the tunnel to warn us against an oncoming train. The way was clear, and we started up again.

Once through the tunnel we were still high up on the railway embankment, between forty and fifty feet above a narrow road running along to our right, but with no way down. In the distance, perhaps five miles off, was a town with several smoking factory chimneys. With no river to cross, a five mile drive along the railway track would not be too bad if it took us to a town, except that one of Jim's tires had blown and he was rapidly buckling the rim. We had not gone very much farther when a second tire gave out.

I suppose it was fortunate that we were forced to stop, for I had noticed a very odd thing. One of the factories in that town was moving! As I watched, its smoking chimney began coming slowly towards me. A dreadful bridge, two tires gone, and now a train was coming at us on a one-track line!

The right of way had been built up with cinders, and just at the point where I stopped there was a bit of a shoulder. I ran the jeep over the rails and stopped it on the shoulder, hoping I had enough clearance. Jim did his best behind me, but he had no shoulder to run off on.

It was not long before the locomotive stopped in front of us and a lot of people, trainmen, Korean soldiers, and about three American GIs jumped off and crowded around. The locomotive inched forward, but it was obvious it could not clear my jeep. Several men lifted the jeep and moved it over to the very edge of the shoulder of the embankment. Then the train moved slowly on, the passengers laughing and cheering as they went past.

The locomotive stopped again when it reached Jim's jeep, about twenty yards behind me. Jim was right in its path. Everyone got out and there was a lot of discussion. Several Korean farmers from a nearby village joined us and added their advice on the problem of the movable locomotive against the immovable jeep. The only solution was to get Jim's jeep off the track and down to the road below. The distance was about fifty feet at an angle of fifty degrees. The farmers solved the problem.

They sent back for a lot of rope and a long pole. They tied the rope firmly around the pole and anchored it behind the rail on the far side from where the jeep was to go down the embankment. They tied the rope to the jeep and wrapped it around the pole in a windlass effect. Fifteen or twenty men were to play out the rope from the anchored pole, while someone guided the jeep down the hill.

One of the American soldiers volunteered to drive. He kicked up the engine, holding it in low-low and using his brakes, while the Koreans hung onto the rope and played it out slowly. Miraculously, the jeep reached the bottom of the embankment right side up, breaking through all the underbrush along the way, and was soon standing safely down in the road. Everyone cheered and applauded madly along the length of the train as though the home team had just scored a touchdown. The locomotive gave a series of friendly toots and soon disapppeared through the tunnel.

Despite his two bad tires and one broken rim, Jim's car at least was safely down on the road. Mine was still sitting up in the sky on the shoulder of the embankment. With everyone pushing I tried to get back on the tracks, but every time I stepped on the gas, the cinders flew viciously into the faces of the pushing farmers and they scattered. They tried digging with shovels and putting boards under the wheels. After about an hour of hard work, during which I almost gave up in despair, they had me back on the track. I do not know how they managed it, since every device had failed, and yet suddenly one of the old failures worked and the jeep was on the tracks.

I still had to get down to the road. I walked forward along the railway, considering the possibility of driving out that way. Not a hundred yards ahead was a short bridge with the spaces between the ties double the usual gap. The jeep could never have crossed it. I backed up to where Jim's car had gone down.

The farmers rigged up the rope and pole again, anchoring the pole behind the rear rail, and I climbed in to drive my jeep down. I thought that if the GI could do it, I could. When I got in and really got a look at my angle of descent, I had grave doubts I would be in one piece when the jeep hit the road.

Jim has told me I was quite a sight as the jeep went forward at that angle, the farmers hanging onto the rope behind and I driving the car in low-low, my head arched forward almost into the windshield, and my Homburg hat practically down on my nose. But the engineering concepts of those friendly Korean farmers were sound. In no time I had driven down that impossible embankment and the car was parked gently on the road.

The next problem was to change Jim's tires and his wheels. Since we both had spares, we had enough tires, although we couldn't afford any more accidents before Chinhae. When we got our tools out, we discovered some kind friend had robbed us in Taegu. We had lug wrenches all right, but neither of them fit the nuts on a jeep.

The mechanical ingenuity of those farmers was amazing. I do not suppose any one of them could drive a car, and I doubt that more than one or two had ever ridden in one. But they knew how to change a wheel without the proper tools. I tried to help at first but cut a hand in rather gory fashion and left the job to my betters. The work went slowly, but those intrepid fellows got the two wheels off and the spares on and tightened up the nuts. They had hammers, screwdrivers, and a few other odds and ends, but I don't know how they did it.

While the work was in progress, I pulled out a very precious bottle of Scotch I had been saving for some special occasion. Obviously, this was it. I could not offer the farmers money without insulting them. They were not working for pay, but to do a helpful, neighborly act.

I got their leader aside, thanked him for their kindness, and gave him the bottle of whiskey. I could tell from his expression that this was the right gift, so I suggested he have a drink now, but he refused until everyone had finished working on Jim's car.

Meanwhile, two old men with long gray beards had shown up and were sitting at the side of the road, smoking their long pipes and commenting sagely on the progress of the work. It turned out that they were the village elders. When Jim's jeep was ready, I poured a slug of whiskey into a porcelain bowl that had appeared and offered it to the leader of the working farmers. He thanked me, then promptly took it to one of the old men. I poured a second drink into a second bowl, and it was taken to the other old man. Not until the two old gentlemen had tasted the whiskey, smacked their lips, and pronounced it acceptable did any other villager touch a drop. Then they all passed the bowls around with great pleasure.

Jim gave a carton of cigarettes and a considerable sum of money to the chief farmer. At first the money was vigorously refused, but Jim explained that he was not actually giving them money. Unfortunately, he had no whiskey but he wanted to buy them a drink. Since he was unable to take them all to a drinking place, he hoped they would forgive him if he gave them the money to pay the bill for him when they went themselves. On this basis they accepted the money.

We left them, smoking American cigarettes and sipping Scotch whiskey, a group of kind and friendly farmers who had dropped their work for an afternoon to help two strangers in difficulty.

It was early evening. We knew we would never reach Chinhae before dark. In fact, darkness fell just after we got off the narrow, dirt road and reached the main road between Pusan and Masan. Because of the danger of being spotted by guerrillas or enemy infiltrators, we drove with our lights dim. Later in the night we had to turn them on full as we climbed a mountain, or we would surely have gone off the road.

My motor was in much better shape than Jim's, and I was always getting ahead, then slowing down and waiting for him. That was not too bad on the main road, but when we finally turned onto the road going directly over the mountain to Chinhae it could have been dangerous. Each time Jim fell behind I stopped and waited. In time I heard his motor chugging along and saw his lights bounce off a rock formation. I did not realize his motor was bad; I thought he was just driving slowly.

We began to climb, and after a time I lost contact with Jim, except that I could see his lights flash across the valley below. I became a little uneasy at his being so far away, because he was unarmed. I had my pistol and carbine with me and considered dropping back and giving him one. But I knew he had never fired a gun and doubted that one would do him any good. I thought it would be more to the point for me to keep both weapons and use them to cover us both rather than to give one away where it could not be used effectively.

I reached the pass and was promptly challenged by a South Korean sailor carrying a rifle. I satisfied him, explained that I was waiting for a friend to join me, and asked permission to stop in the pass until he arrived. I sat there for what seemed a very long time without hearing the sound of a car or even seeing car lights. I became really worried and told the sentry I was going back to look for my friend. I had scarcely gone three hundred yards down hill when Jim's car came crawling around a curve and finally stopped.

His engine had just given out on him; that was as far as it would go. I got behind him and pushed his jeep up to the pass and the sentry. From there we had a long, steep, winding drop straight into Chinhae. All Jim needed to get down was brakes, but as soon as the jeep began running downhill, the motor caught, and by the time he reached the foot of the mountain it was running well.

My only previous visit to Chinhae was that short stop in early July when Curt Prendergast and I were following President Rhee. But I knew that Maj. Dean Hess was now at the Chinhae airfield with his Korean unit and I was sure of a welcome and a bed.[3]

As we reached the edge of town, just before midnight, a South Korean naval officer signaled us asking for a ride. We asked him where Major Hess and his unit were located. The lieutenant wanted to go almost to the airfield, so we were in luck.

From then on it was easy. We drove up to the headquarters building, told a duty officer who we were, and asked for Hess. He was with us in no time and fixed us up with cots in a transient's room. We were thoroughly bushed. I do not sleep well, especially when other people are moving around, and we shared a room with about ten other men. But it was nine o'clock in the morning before I woke up.

CHAPTER THIRTEEN

Chinhae Idyll
and Pusan Doldrums

M Y FIRST CALL late that morning, August 19, was on President and Mrs. Rhee. The president's official residence, more a cottage than a house, stood on the top of a high bluff overlooking the blue-green bay. There was a small lawn, soon swallowed up by a heavy growth of pine. A steep path slid down the nearly sheer sides of the bluff to the sea, where a high landing jutted into the bay.

I was received by Mrs. Rhee; the president was below fishing off the pier. I climbed down the path and joined him for a few minutes to tell him I was in Chinhae as the ambassador's representative and would do anything I could to assist him. How good a fisherman Syngman Rhee was I do not know, but about half the times I visited him, he was on the wharf with a couple of guards, sitting with a line in the water. He told me he found fishing restful, that he could overcome fits of depression and think matters through more clearly fishing than any other way.

My two weeks at Chinhae were the most relaxing and pleasant period of the war. I am sure that if I had been forced to live that idyllic life forever, I would have become restive for the war. For a time, however, there was nothing so pleasant as living comfortably by myself, enjoying that beautiful scene of sea and mountains joined so sharply together. The war was only a short distance away, only a few minutes by plane; but although I could hear the guns quite clearly, it seemed far, far away. I was on my own. I was no longer restrained by the ambassador's presence, yet I never went to the actual fighting front. I was more than content to live in the large, Japanese-style house put at my disposal by the base commander. My enthusiastic curiosity of the early war days seemed to have disappeared.

I was strangely exhausted, considering the fairly comfortable life I had been living since the war began. I did not dare tell any combat soldier so, but I found my life during the Korean War, comfortable and safe as it was, more wearing and difficult than the campaigns in World War II, when numerous strange people seemed very much determined I should not live long enough to enjoy another war. Of course, this time I was older, but I think the essential difference was that in World War II I acted chiefly under orders with small latitude for erroneous personal decisions. And during that war I had no concern with other people's morale; as far as I ever knew, it was always fine. In Korea, however, I had to spend a great portion of my time and emotional energy trying to keep people from worry and despair, continuously drawing on my own emotional reserves. The Chinhae interlude was a very pleasant chance to rebuild them.

We were effectively out of the war at Chinhae. I saw President and Mrs. Rhee once or twice a day, and often I was able to help Rhee with something or other. But my major activity of note during our Chinhae interlude was liaison between President Rhee and the U.S. forces in the area in arranging several formal ceremonies. For example, President Rhee called upon Maj. William B. Kean, commanding general, 25th Division, to express Korea's appreciation for the division's heroism and sacrifices. On another occasion, President Rhee wanted to visit the marine brigade to express the same sentiments. I visited General Craig and arranged the president's meeting.

The conversation with General Craig, during which we discussed the marines' current campaign and old times in World War II, stirred an extraordinary nostalgia for the corps. I lay awake most of the following night debating whether I should ask Craig if he would want me back in uniform with his brigade. If he did, I would ask to be recalled to active duty and then tell Muccio that I was back in the service. But by morning I decided that I held a very responsible post which I should carry out. Even if the marines wanted me back, they could more easily find a suitable officer than the embassy could at that time. And I could not deny that I had grown soft and was getting a little old to be rushing around Korean rice fields under enemy fire. I suppose it was all daydreaming, but I tortured myself with this dream for several days.

Chinhae was a wonderful place to fight a war, but unfortunately I could not stay there forever. Every night I reported by telephone to Muccio in Pusan, except two nights in a row when the lines were down. Then I was happily alone, completely cut off from higher authority. But I do not think Muccio ever believed my failure to telephone those nights was due to mechanical difficulties. My undoing at Chinhae, however, was Rhee's impatience to get to work.[1]

Rhee liked the quiet and rest at Chinhae well enough, but he felt too cut off from the government at Pusan to be willing to stay there long. He made a trip by motor launch to Pusan and soon after his return decided to leave Chinhae for good. I was much saddened.

A factor in Rhee's decision was the increasing roar of guns from the Masan area which we could hear so well, especially at night. The North Koreans had also made a raid into a group of islands not far from Chinhae itself. Although the ROK Marines had repulsed the raiders with heavy losses, the president was worried. A large island lay about two miles across the bay from his house. An enemy gun placed there could blow him to pieces. One day when he was fishing a large shell or bomb fell into the water not far from his float, exploding a great geyser into the air. He was convinced the North Koreans had established themselves on the nearby island and had begun their bombardment of Chinhae.

I never discovered who fired that shot. While it was possible that the North Koreans were in any one of a dozen nearby islands, the ROK Navy and Marines could not locate them. I thought a freak trajectory from a distant gun, or perhaps a friendly plane's accidental release of a bomb, had caused the watery explosion. Dr. and Mrs. Rhee were very skeptical of my theory.

Rhee made up his mind to leave Chinhae, and I had to go back to the horrors of life in Pusan. The president and Mrs. Rhee flew over by marine corps helicopter, their suite went by motor launch, and I drove my jeep.

The embassy was located in Pusan in a three-story building occupied by USIS before the war. USIS, despite its greatly expanded functions, now had to share the space with the embassy and the consulate. There was no office for me, and I had to go through the unpleasantness of ranking someone out of space. Everyone was already crammed into inadequate quarters, and no one had thought of a place for me to sleep. I found that Ambassador Muccio had a large, beautiful Japanese-style house. In addition to the ambassador, Jim Stewart, Al Loren, and Comdr. Jack Seifert lived there. Stewart and Loren shared an extremely small room, and Seifert, who had a slightly larger room, let his chief petty officers take turns sleeping in it to get away from their crowded quarters down at the docks. In addition, there were two rather spacious guest rooms, one of which was used by Drumright when he flew down from Taegu.

Muccio welcomed me cordially, but when I asked him about office space and a place to sleep, he told me those were my problems. It was then late afternoon, so I asked Stewart and Loren whether I could sleep on the floor between their cots that night to give me time to look around. They agreed but warned me I would be very uncomfortable and would hardly have space to turn over. When we got out to that lovely house high on a hill overlooking the bay, Jack Seifert was there. He would not think of letting me sleep on the floor and offered me the other bed in his room, sending the CPOs permanently down to the docks. I had found a room in Pusan. When Muccio came out later that evening he seemed a bit surprised to find me living with him again.

There is no point in describing the activities of the American embassy in Pusan.[2] This was our most depressing period. There was something about Pusan that even infected us with doubts about victory. We had little to do, we were tired, and our tempers were short. I resumed my old routine of calling on the president once or twice a day and of visiting other high officials as circumstances dictated, including the chairman and vice-chairman of the National Assembly. I think the good offices I was able to use between the president and the National Assembly leaders, at a time when their tempers too were short and a harmful political explosion was always just about to go off, were quite helpful both to the ROK government and the joint war effort.

In 1948 I had served for about four months as an adviser on Korea to the United States delegation to the U.N. General Assembly in Paris and for about ten days in 1949 had had a similar position at Lake Success. On each occasion I did what I could to help the ROK delegation, all its members being people I had known well in Seoul. Before the war broke out I had hoped to be called back to the 1950 session, but with the war I scarcely thought about the General Assembly until one day, about the first of September, President Rhee asked me to ask Muccio to send me to Lake Success unofficially to advise the ROK delegation. I told Rhee I would be glad to go, but he would have to ask Muccio himself. Such a request could not very well come from me.

Rhee recognized that the Korea question would be the primary one before the 1950 session of the U.N. General Assembly. He planned to send the foreign minister, the ROK ambassador to the United States, and three members of the National Assembly. He believed that with my previous experience at the U.N. and my knowledge of and good will toward Korea, I could be of help to his delegation. He also very kindly said he would have more confidence in their making wise decisions if I were there, and that every member of the delegation respected me and had friendly confidence in me.

Rhee made the request to Muccio, who cabled the department suggesting that I be called to Washington to serve unofficially as adviser to the ROK delegation at the request of President Rhee, to tender such advice to the department as was desired on the Korea question, and to be in a position upon my return to keep him fully informed on a subject so closely connected with the execution of his duties.

The negative reply from Washington seemed to arrive by return telegram. It said there was no need for me at that year's session. I assume this rejection originated initially with the permanent secretariat of the U.S. mission to the United Nations. Both Muccio and I were aware that there were some men in the permanent secretariat at Lake Success, and also some others who were permanent advisers to the U.S. mission to the United Nations, who always had been antagonistic to the Republic of Korea and emotionally hostile to President Rhee since long before the war. Consequently, because of my frank championship of the Republic of Korea against the Communists, plus my knowledge of Korea, these men were unfriendly to me. None of them had ever been in Korea and very few had ever served the United States government abroad anywhere in the world, except on United Nations affairs. They seemed to believe that they could solve all international problems by memorizing the charter of the United Nations and by knowing all the precedents for U.N. activities. Their hostility toward me was not unique. They showed it in general toward all Foreign Service officers brought in from the field to advise at a U.N. session on a particular country or area. It was my observation that the U.S. delegates were quite unaware of the strong prejudice of their well-educated but often very ignorant subordinates.

Rhee did not accept the State Department's refusal. He asked me whether I would go as an official adviser of the ROK delegation, necessarily resigning from the Foreign Service to do so. He and the foreign minister had invited me several times in the past to become foreign affairs adviser to the ROK government; I was always very flattered but postponed a decision. My major objection was based on a dislike of serving under a foreign government, no matter how friendly it was to the United States. I did believe I could be of service to the Koreans, and indirectly of service to my own country, in that capacity, but I just could not bring myself to make the break. It was not that I had a future in the Foreign Service. I did not. Since I was a reserve officer, no matter how well I executed my duties I could only serve a maximum of four years.

Meanwhile a second telegram came from Washington ordering me to proceed at once for consultation, to be in Washington and New York until December. I still do not know whether the first hasty telegram originated in the U.S. mission to the United Nations and the second represented consultation among the political people responsible for Korean affairs, or whether there was a genuine mix-up. Believing the second telegram must be an error, since the first had been categorical, Muccio queried the department. The department replied that the second telegram was an error.

I had to decide promptly whether to accept Dr. Rhee's offer. I didn't know then that I would soon be back in Seoul. If I had known, I would never have considered leaving Korea. But this was a time of the greatest emotional depression for all of us in Pusan, and not least for me. Finally, on the morning of September 15 I told the president that while I greatly appreciated his offer, I could not accept it. Later that day I learned that the marines had landed at Inch'ŏn.

The embassy staff had an inkling of the landing but no precise information beforehand. In Pusan Muccio and I continued our custom of going to the daily 5th Air Force briefings in the late afternoon. Sometimes, when President Rhee went also, I escorted him. Otherwise I drove my own noisy yellow jeep out into the country to the Fisheries College where the 5th Air Force headquarters was established. On occasion I rode with Muccio, but we had reached the stage where we had seen too much of each other and had nothing more to say. It was pleasanter to drive alone. Once we got back to Seoul, however, all this changed. Good will, pleasant feelings, harmony, and avid conversation immediately replaced the irritations of the doldrums of Pusan.

A few days before September 15 we noted that two areas were blocked off on the briefing map: Seoul-Inch'ŏn and the Kunsan area in the southwest. The briefing officer informed us that 5th Air Force was forbidden to fly over those areas. Naturally, by September 15 we had learned there was to be a landing at Inch'ŏn, but the details were kept very carefully from the 5th Air Force and so from us. I have read since that the landing was an open secret in Japan, but it was not in Korea. Of course the movement of the marine brigade aboard ship and then away from Pusan meant a landing somewhere, and we did not know that other troops were building up in Japan, but the preparations and plans were mostly hidden from us. I was surprised to find afterwards that Mrs. Rhee had known more about the projected landing than I had. ROK Marines were part of the assault force, and the ROK minister of defense and the navy chief of staff had to know about the operation. That meant the president knew, which meant his wife knew.[9]

Once the landing took place, we learned more by listening to the shortwave radio from the United States than we did from the 5th Air Force briefings. The briefing officers said quite frankly they did not know anything for a fact, but they had heard this rumor or that. One day a flyer from the attack force had to land at Taegu because of engine trouble. We heard more about the Inch'ŏn landing that day than any other, and yet it was just one pilot's experience and perspective.

Yet we did not need to know the details to be exuberant. Our long retreat and exile, which seemed more like three years than three months, was nearing its end. Soon we would be going home.

A very hush-hush telegram came from MacArthur to Muccio. MacArthur hoped to capture Seoul in a few days and he planned to make a triumphal entry. He wanted Muccio to make all the arrangements for the return of the ROK government, the U.N. commission, and other diplomatic representatives to Seoul. He would supply the *Bataan* and one other large transport plane to carry them. Before the re-entry MacArthur wanted Korean police sent to Inch'ŏn by sea to .be ready to take over police duties. He also wanted essential city and provincial officials prepared to move into Inch'ŏn and Seoul as early as possible, ahead of the national government.

We began preparations at once but almost at the same time received a telegram from Washington that described tentative proposals for the treatment of the Korean question at Lake Success and asked for the embassy's judgment. Muccio, Drumright, Stewart, and I had a very long discussion to clarify our views.

The State Department was preparing its position for presentation at the U.N. General Assembly. Two basic questions were raised: (1) should the U.N. forces stop at the 38th parallel, and (2) if they crossed the parallel and conquered North Korea, what should they do about government in the north? The latter question raised a host of points. Should the jurisdiction of the Republic of Korea be extended to North Korea? Should some other government entity be established in that area? Or should the U.N. take action to unite Korea and in doing so abolish the Republic of Korea by absorbing it in a new U.N.-sponsored state? The tentative department answers were that the U.N. armies could not stop at the 38th parallel, since merely to drive the aggressor back to his point of departure would lay the groundwork for repetition of his aggression in the future, and that the U.N. should hold general elections throughout Korea as the basis for the creation of a United Republic of Korea.[4]

We entirely agreed with the department's view that our forces should not stop at the 38th parallel. When the Communists drove south across that boundary, they surrendered any claim they might have possessed to immunity from counterinvasion. For example, when Hitler's armies unleashed World War II in Europe and later Tojo's forces did the same in Asia, no one was so foolish as to insist that the Allies should just drive the Germans back to their prewar boundaries and get the Japanese out of China and the Philippines. No, we defeated their aggression and then continued on to occupy their countries. In Korea such an occupation was even more essential to unite Korea again and undo the evil which the 1945 division of the country had let loose.

Regarding the proposals for unifying Korea, however, we took sharp exception to the department's view.[5] They were talking in Lake Success and Washington, as well as in New Delhi and many other capitals around the globe, as though the Republic of Korea did not deserve any consideration as a sovereign state. They apparently did not intend to ask the ROK government whether it would assist at its own demise.

In June 1950, led by the United States, the United Nations had acted decisively to repel aggression aimed at destroying the Republic of Korea. Yet in September 1950 many members of the United Nations, including the United States, were blandly discussing a program that would destroy the Republic of Korea in the name of the United Nations. This was fantastic!

The Republic of Korea, originally created through U.N.-observed free and fair elections in 1948, had its second popular elections in 1950, less than a month before the war broke out. It had been recognized by over forty sovereign nations, one of the first being the United States. An American diplomatic mission had been in Korea since August 1948, and a Korean ambassador had been stationed in Washington since early 1949. How was it immoral for the Communists to destroy the republic by armed force but moral for the United Nations to do so by votes at Lake Success, against the will of the Republic of Korea but supported by the armed forces of the United Nations in Korea? Obviously not a single member of the United Nations, including the United States, would have considered a U.N. vote aimed at its own dissolution as anything but an unfriendly act, as well as illegal and without force. Yet many governments in September 1950, including our own, appeared willing to forget all the past, to forget Korean loyalties and sacrifices in the current war, and to act as though there never had been a sovereign Republic of Korea.

The State Department even appeared to want to prohibit anyone from South Korea going north of the parallel, or the Republic of Korea from exercising any political influence north of the parallel in the interim while a new united republic was being created and the Republic of Korea was being dissolved by the United Nations.[6] This led to a policy of prohibiting the circulation of ROK money in North Korea, continuing in office the Communist police and other functionaries, and even permitting Communists to hold public office in the new republic!

We objected to all these points. Several million citizens of the Republic of Korea were actually refugees from the Communist north, and they naturally expected to return home as soon as the fighting ended. No vote in the U.N. General Assembly could possibly stop this movement of Koreans back to their homes once the Communists were chased out. And as far as keeping the ROK from exercising influence north of the parallel, it was silly to think this could be prevented even if it were desirable. In fact, at the embassy we considered it desirable that such influence should be exerted by the Republic of Korea, a friendly state, instead of a possibly Communist-dominated, U.N.-sponsored "United Republic of Korea." But the idealistic theorists working in the United States mission to the United Nations seemed incapable of grasping the fact that an army is both a military and a political arm of a state. Half of the battle line across Korea was held by the ROK Army, and as soon as the U.N. forces advanced into the north, the ROK Army also would advance into North Korea. Regardless of any possible overt act of the ROK government, the presence of the ROK Army in North Korea would be evidence to the local populace of the republic's political existence, interest, and power.

The subsequent prohibition of the use of ROK money north of the 38th parallel assumed that the Communist money would have value once the Communists were defeated. Of course it did not, and when the North Koreans could not get ROK money, or the Americans could not pay their way in ROK money, they had serious difficulties.

To imagine that we could fight the Communists in the field and yet use their police and other civil functionaries on our behalf behind the lines was a fantastic misunderstanding of the nature and conduct of communism. Fortunately, when our armies advanced, all the Communist officials ran away. They did not dream that our benign government wanted to join with the rest of the United Nations in employing them. Nevertheless, because of this policy it usually was impossible to use the regular ROK Police who had gone north with the divisions to which they were attached, although there were no other professional police available in North Korea to keep law and order in the areas conquered by our troops.

Furthermore, to permit Communists to hold public office in a new U.N.-created republic to supersede the Republic of Korea was an ideal which could have been conceived only by men wholly divorced from contact with the real world around them. It not only ignored the causes of the current war, but showed utter ignorance of the organization and tactics of the Communist party. If this proposal were carried out, it would have enabled the Communist party to honeycomb the new republic with their agents for its early capture by the party. The U.N. would make possible what the Republic of Korea had withstood: subversion and conquest from within.

Muccio, Drumright, Stewart, and I discussed these proposals, and some lesser ones I have not mentioned, for a long time. We all agreed along the lines I have described above. When we finished, I was assigned the job of writing the telegram, basing it on our joint views.

Then a curious accident occurred. I went to my office, banged out a telegram on a portable typewriter, and took it to Muccio. He read it carefully, made some minor changes, and turned it over to his secretary to type and give to the code clerk. The telegram filled two full typewritten pages.

The next day Muccio looked through the telegram folder and was startled to find that only half of the telegram, the first page, had been sent out. The last sentence had sounded to the code man like the end of the telegram, and he had stopped there. Naturally, since this was a secret telegram, all papers and drafts related to it had been burned. The department had one-half of our answer, chiefly the affirmative part, but had not received much of our criticism.

I went back to the portable and from memory recomposed the missing second page. Muccio agreed that it was almost identical and, after prefixing some remarks of regret that an error in despatch had been made, sent it off.

The embassy continued its preparations for the return to Seoul. For a few days I was concerned that I would not make it. The ambassador amused himself by telling me there would not be space on the plane for me, and he really had me worried. I intended to go out to the airfield and hook a ride by myself if he flew off to Seoul without me. But in the end I found he was just pulling my leg.

MacArthur seems to have underestimated North Korean resistance. His original telegram indicated our return to Seoul about a week before the actual re-entry. The bitter, slow fighting through the outskirts and streets of Seoul left us in Pusan sitting by our packed bags. Not that any of us had much to carry back. During the summer I had picked up a U.S. mail bag, and I dumped everything into it that would not go into my briefbag. Various friends had brought over clothes from Tokyo, and my wife had sent warmer clothes for autumn. I was still carrying that postal sack when we fled from Seoul for the second time the following January.

A second telegram from General MacArthur informed us that he would enter Seoul on September 29, a Friday, and wanted the government and diplomatic corps to join him in a ceremony at the capitol in which he would return control of the conquered territory to the government of the Republic of Korea. In the early evening of the twenty-eighth, the *Bataan* and another C-54 arrived from Japan, and the pilots came to the ambassador for instructions. In the afternoon I had seen the president, various ministers, and the heads of the National Assembly, as well as the Chinese and British representatives, to tell them that we were going back to Seoul the next day.

That night, with the chief pilot of the *Bataan*, I worked out a seating for the list of distinguished passengers. Naturally, while I tried to balance the guests between the two planes, I gave rank priority to the *Bataan*, which was carrying President and Mrs. Rhee and, of course, the American and Chinese ambassadors. By a curious coincidence, my name also appeared on the *Bataan* list.

Muccio and I were not the first members of the embassy to return to Seoul, however. Commander Seifert had the small naval attaché's plane which he wanted to fly up. Drumright came down from Taegu and persuaded Muccio that he should go into Seoul ahead of the main party to reconnoiter. Drumright was to fly back to Pusan if he acquired any special information that Muccio might need before his arrival.

The two hard-working JAS men who had been with us on the whole trip, Carlin Wilson and Bob Smith, came to me to urge that their specialties required them to be in Seoul ahead of the main party. While I knew they chiefly suffered from the same eagerness to get back to Seoul that I shared, their arguments did make some sense. Bob Heavey, the security officer, argued with me that he should go in ahead to check on security before Muccio arrived. That too made sense. I think Heavey had asked Muccio and been turned down, but the other two had not dared to ask. I went to Muccio and suggested that Seifert fly them to Kimp'o on Thursday. I said that if the situation would not permit their entry into the city until the next day, they could wait at Kimp'o till we arrived. If they got into Seoul immediately, they could learn much of use to the main embassy contingent. Muccio agreed, and the happy men were on their way.

Seifert, Drumright, Wilson, Heavey, and Smith all reached Seoul that Thursday afternoon. They made their way through the dreadful wreckage and safely past the fighting to the ambassador's residence, which was occupied by a small force of U.S. Marines. Part of the roof had been shot off and every single piece of furniture was gone.

But the discomfort did not matter, for when these men lay down on the bare boards that night they were back home.

CHAPTER FOURTEEN

We Return

W E H A D sullenly retreated down the hot, dusty roads of South Korea for three months after being chased out of Seoul. We were often close to death, capture, or defeat. Suddenly, almost without warning, the North Koreans were in disorganized retreat and the return from our three months odyssey took only two hours.

We could see little from the plane to show that a war was still being fought below us until we approached Inch'ŏn. Then I saw the longest string of ships, stretching for twenty or thirty miles away from the harbor, that I ever expected to see off the coast of Korea. We flew low enough over Inch'ŏn to see some of the city's wounds, and we soon braked to a landing at Kimp'o airport.

The buildings were all twisted, wrecked, and gutted by fire. Here and there, off the rebuilt runway, were large bomb craters. Crisscrossed lines of machine gun bullet holes were sharply etched on the walls in the late September sun.

A very long line of jeeps, headed by a sedan for President and Mrs. Rhee, was drawn up alongside the runway as we came in, ready to carry us all to Seoul. Many correspondents had come from the city to cover the president's return, and altogether we had quite a cavalcade.

In a short time we started in single column up the road toward Seoul. I soon saw the Han River again for the first time since June 29, precisely three months before. The water flowing through the channel seemed unchanged by the suffering and bloodshed. All the bridges upriver were blown, their great spans hanging down or fallen wholly into the water. Once across the river and up the steep river bank, we were in Seoul itself. We drove from the suburb of Map'o past the Old West Gate toward the center of the city. We could hear the battle raging ahead of us in the city.

The battered streets were lined by citizens of all ages, small children and aged men and women, many holding small South Korean flags which they gaily waved at us while they cheered and cheered again as President Rhee drove past. All the adults looked gaunt and drawn from hunger or disease. There could be no question that this welcome was spontaneous. There was no one available to make them come out and cheer. They were cheering and crying because they were so happy to have Seoul free again, to see their own government returning, and to look forward to the restoration of normal life.

The sight of the broken, burned-out city was dreadful. None of the briefings or accounts we had heard at Pusan had prepared us for the terrible destruction of Seoul. The more we moved around later and examined the city in detail, the more dreadful the loss appeared. I was in Yokohama and Tokyo soon after the end of World War II, but Seoul showed far worse damage. The sight of the wreckage sickened us.

Later we found that part of the destruction was necessary to save the lives of our men. The North Koreans fought for the city, and the marines poured it on. Perhaps some destruction might have been avoided had there been less exuberance on our side, but it is hard to persuade soldiers to be gentle in the middle of a bitter, bloody battle. If the marines suspected that North Koreans were in a building, our artillery or planes destroyed the building. Most of the destruction we saw during that long ride from the river to the capitol was battle destruction.[1]

But farther on in the city, in the areas containing important buildings, very little of the destruction was from battle. The enemy had applied the torch. It was easy to see which buildings were deliberately set fire by the retreating North Koreans. The marks of fire damage were the same at the window line of every story, showing a nearly simultaneous outbreak of flames rather than the usual

upward movement of flames from floor to floor. Among the buildings burned were the General Post Office, the Bank of Korea, the
USIS center, National Police headquarters, the YMCA, and the
Christian Literature Society building. The city hall, the American
embassy, and the Chosun Hotel, which are very close together,
escaped being burned probably because the marines unexpectedly
came into that area in a circling movement instead of down the
main street.

That Friday morning we had no chance to see anything but the
dreadful battle damage as we drove along the damaged streets to the
capitol. Trolley wires were down, curling over the streets like huge
snakes. Since there was no power, the snakes had no sting. Telephone and other wires looped down into the streets, sometimes in
such profusion as to resemble weeping willows. Bits of paving were
scattered everywhere from shell holes and bomb craters. Wrecked
guns, tanks, and enemy corpses were strewn along the streets.

There were barriers of sandbags at every intersection, about
shoulder high, often with a passage through only for pedestrians.
These sandbag barriers had been knocked down along our route,
presumably by bulldozers, but we could see them on most side
streets. Later that afternoon Jim Stewart and I went on an explora-
tion of our own through the main part of Seoul and found the
barriers still standing everywhere, with just enough pulled down
to allow a jeep to pass. Sandbagged strongpoints were alongside
most sturdy buildings, usually built in a semicircle with the building
forming the rear of the little fortress. They usually were high enough
to allow for fire ports between the sandbags. Most of these sandbagged structures were built by the hungry citizens of Seoul under
Communist armed escort. The same citizens pulled them down
again in about a week's time after the recapture of Seoul.

Our long cavalcade turned onto the wide avenue leading to the
capitol. Numerous large government buildings, including the Seoul
central telephone and telegraph exchange and the Communications
Ministry, lined the avenue. Of all these concrete and brick buildings, only one small and relatively unimportant building had escaped the arsonists' fire. Everything else was gone.

The capitol, too, had gone up in flames. The great copper dome was twisted and blackened. Most of the wide windows were smashed, and irregular dark marks over the granite walls showed where the flames had climbed skyward. A few miles away, within the city toward the east gate, we could hear heavy bursts of machine gun and rifle fire and the heavier rumble of artillery, but there was no fighting near the capitol as we drove up.

Everyone quickly got out of his jeep and walked through the high, wide doors and across the marble lobby into the National Assembly room, where someone had marked the names of the guests on small handwritten cards affixed to the desks. I could smell smoke but assumed it was from an earlier fire.

We could see specks of the sky through the dome high overhead where the copper roof had been curled off by the fire. The inner glass dome had been cracked and shattered by the heat, and during the ceremony large pieces of glass broke away and crashed down to the floor a hundred feet below. All the military were wearing helmets and presumably would not have been hurt if hit on the head. But we civilians—the South Korean government officials, the representatives from the American and Chinese embassies, the British legation, and the U.N. commission—had nothing to protect us from the sharp glass. I kept my felt hat in my hands, ready at any moment to clap it on my head. I thought that I might have warning if a piece fell my way and I could at least defend myself with the Homburg. But that was not a very comforting hope. Despite the constant tinkle and crash of falling glass throughout the ceremony, as far as I know no one was hit. It was miraculous.

The ceremony has been described many times. MacArthur made a fine, restrained address restoring civil authority to the ROK government. President Rhee, deeply moved, responded by thanking the allied forces, comforting the relatives of the dead, and calling for generosity toward the enemy in time of victory. Muccio said a few words for himself and for the United States government. MacArthur closed the ceremony simply and solemnly with the Lord's Prayer The whole audience of generals, admirals, and foreign representatives joined with him. Nothing could have been more appropriate at the time of victory combined with danger and uncertainty for the morrow: "Thy will be done on earth as it is in heaven . . . as we forgive those who trespass against us . . . deliver us from evil . . . Thine is the Kingdom, and the Power, and the Glory, forever, Amen!"²

After the capitol ceremony we ate a cold but delicious army lunch and then went to Embassy Residence Area No. 2. Although a great share of the rest of the city was in ruins and every other American-owned or leased house was badly stripped and knocked about, not a house in Area No. 2 had been hurt. The North Koreans had sealed the houses almost as soon as they entered Seoul, probably with the idea of using them for their senior officials when they won the war and moved the capitol from P'yŏngyang to Seoul.

Jim Stewart and I borrowed an army jeep early in the afternoon and started a tour of the city. As we drove past the capitol we were surprised to see the large wooden building to the west of it in flames. The building was used by the U.S. military government as headquarters before the establishment of the Republic of Korea, and we were both well acquainted with it. Only a couple of hours earlier, at the time of the ceremony in the capitol, there had been no fire. The Communists arsonists were obviously still busy. Nothing could be done since the Seoul water mains had been cut. We drove on to Embassy Residence No. 1 where Ambassador Muccio, Drumright, and I had our houses. A U.S. Marine battalion was using my house as a command post, and we did not go inside. I did not want the marines to think I was pressing them for my house when they had just sacrificed so much to reach it. We looked around the compound a bit and saw the physical destruction from shell fire. A direct hit had gone down the side of our two-story servants' quarters, knocking that building to pieces and rather effectively ruining the two small residences next door, one of them quite beyond repair. Muccio's house was in about the same state as mine, and Drumright's worse.

Muccio and Drumright decided to settle down in Area No. 2 until their own houses could be repaired. Muccio was badly hurt emotionally by the loss of every lovely thing he had collected in stations all over the world throughout his mature life. It was not the monetary loss which bothered him, although his possessions were valuable, but the loss of things he had treasured for years—perhaps an early Chinese vase he had purchased with difficulty when a junior vice-consul in China, or something he especially prized from Panama. He had spent a considerable amount of his own money in having his lovely, old house redecorated the previous year so as to best display his objets d'art.

The vandalizing of his home disturbed Muccio deeply, and even after it had been repaired and furniture of a sort had been placed in it, he had great difficulty in forcing himself to return to live there. He could not forget for a long time how it had looked before, even when he had been supplied with the best furniture available to the embassy at Seoul.

Stewart and I next drove to the chancery. Perhaps for possible safety against bomb fragments, the Communists had not raised the great steel curtains that covered the front two stories of the building. But they were buckled and bent as though made of tin. One or two bombs had skipped into the side of the building at about ground level ripping a deep hole in the basement, which was filled with water in which a lone corpse floated, and thoroughly smashing that corner of the building. Unfortunately, the mechanical heart of the building was in that corner, especially the heating plant. Carlin Wilson, our engineer in charge of maintenance, made a tremendous personal effect and showed great ability in leading Korean workmen, as well as an extraordinary capacity to wangle essential materials out of the army, to get the chancery repaired. Yet he was working on the repair job until December, and until early December we sat in our cold offices without heat. Fortunately, for a Korean autumn the weather was mild. Carlin later found six dead bodies near the center of the building. The poor souls had given up politics!

Near the chancery bomb hole there was a deep ditch, perhaps dug originally as a trench but looking more like the results of an explosion. The bottom was filled with water. In the ditch, hands still bound behind them, were nearly a dozen corpses. As we were later able to reconstruct the Communist atrocities in their last days in Seoul, it became clear that these were a few of the unfortunate caught at the last minute, trussed up, and shot through the head.[3]

Bodies were so numerous, especially lying in alleys just off the main streets, that their removal and burial was a major problem. It was about three days before we could get our own special corpses removed from in front of the embassy. The blown and buckled high steel doors made entrance from the front impossible that first day. Jim and I climbed up the east side fire escape about three floors until we found an open door. Debris, rubble, and broken glass were everywhere. We climbed up an inside stairway and soon were on the fifth floor, where we both had our offices.

Considering the battle for the city, the embassy was in pretty good shape. By criteria of cleanliness and order, however, it was a shambles. Hardly a window was unbroken and thick glass was under foot everywhere. My cabinet safe, which had been left empty and unlocked when my secretary left the room, had later been locked by someone and then blown open again. Most safes in the other offices were similarly twisted by the explosions of eager searchers looking for our records. We had burned them, of course, but I suppose they did not know that, nor that their first wave of investigators had found the safes unlocked and then foolishly locked them.

The previous May, new, thick, and very pleasing rugs had arrived from the States and been put in Muccio's, Drumright's, and my rooms. The other officers still had old, nearly worn-out rugs. But when I reached my office, the new rugs were gone. The looters had shown good taste. They had not touched the worn-out rugs from the other rooms, so we were able to move them into our rooms, leaving our unfortunate juniors with bare floors.

There were no light bulbs and no telephones. We thought for a few days that the North Koreans had taken the telephones with them, until someone ran across them, along with a lot of embassy furniture, hidden in the Anglican cathedral. Apparently they had been cached away under the cross for safety from bombing for later use in a more secure time. Light bulbs were another matter. Generally we had to wait till we could bring them from Japan or the United States, but some had drifted to the various markets and could be bought back.

After we completed our tour of the embassy, Jim and I drove out to the "Gold Coast" area, about two miles to the east, where his house and many other American mission houses were located. Although the street was wide, the fallen, curling streetcar wires and the numerous sandbag barricades stretched across it forced us to go slowly. Just enough space for one jeep to pass had been broken through them. As we advanced, the sound of firing ahead grew even louder, and we didn't know what we would run into. We assumed that if we drove out of American-held territory, we would pass a sentry or military unit who would warn us. We passed a few American soldiers where we turned off to the Gold Coast, and they all looked loaded for bear. But no one called out and we just kept on driving. It was as simple as that to pass through the American lines. I suppose the soldiers did not know what to make of these two American civilians in an army jeep pushing ahead toward enemy-held territory. They probably thought we knew what we were doing, and of course we thought they would warn us of danger. Soon we saw no more soldiers.

We drove to Jim's house and found it ruined. Jim was thoroughly sickened. All his wife's clothes, his boy's toys, and the furniture were gone. So was the kitchen stove, and the floor had been ripped up. Jim had lived in the house since 1947 and become emotionally attached to it. He walked through once and then came out and said, "Let's get going!" We left and Jim never went back to see his house again. He could not bear the sight.

After we left Jim's place we drove through the rest of the Gold Coast, getting a general idea of the war damage. Everything was thoroughly stripped. Then we drove back to the center city. But only that morning the North Koreans had counterattacked U.S. 7th Division troops along the main road, just beyond the Gold Coast, and had driven them back. It was not until some days later that I discovered we had been wandering around that afternoon in no man's land. Small North Korean elements were still there while we were blithely sightseeing, but our luck held and they did not notice us.

Jim and I passed the capitol again on our way back to Area No. 2. We were startled to see a cavern of dark flames through its large open doors. The room where we sat in the morning listening to Rhee and MacArthur, accompanied by the tinkle of falling glass, was now a roaring inferno. It was fortunate for us that the arsonists had struck so late. Of course, since the whole building was built of granite and marble, only the furnishings and mouldings burned; the structure remained intact. After the roaring fire died out, the great capitol still stood, a large Korean flag waving on the flagpole in front.

At Area No. 2 Jim and I joined in sharing a gift from Mrs. Rhee. The president was back in his official residence, Kyŏngmudae. He found that many works of art had been carried away, as well as all his personal possessions. But he had found some lesser gifts in exchange, left by North Korean officers who had fled too hastily to carry them off. There were numerous bottles of vodka, Russian brandy, and Russian sparkling burgundy. The Rhees almost never drank, so they gave this "booty" away. Mrs. Rhee sent the ambassador a present of two bottles of vodka and two bottles of sparkling burgundy. Muccio was having nothing Russian and told us he would not touch the stuff. That evening before supper the rest of us first drank the sparkling burgundy, which led to a further taste for Russian adventure, and we drank up the two bottles of vodka. Muccio came in then, but he was not pleased.

I slept in Jack Seifert's house that night. My first night in Seoul I achieved my ambition of getting away from the group outside of office hours. Jack and I talked for a long time of what we had seen and what we thought might be ahead of us. Jack spoke of last seeing his wife, to whom he was deeply devoted, in this same room. She was now far away in California.

We had been on a long journey. We had faced much danger and sorrow. We didn't know what was ahead of us, but at least we were back again at our proper post in Seoul. Though the pounding of guns within the city limits only a few miles away to the east and north seemed to shake the room with increasing intensity, we were content. We were home at last.

CHAPTER FIFTEEN

Home at Last

W HEN I AWOKE that first morning in Seoul, Saturday, September 30, the roar of guns seemed a little more distant, as though the enemy were retreating before the steadily advancing marines. I learned that the North Koreans were in full retreat up the Ŭijŏngbu road, back toward the 38th parallel, on the same road they had rushed down so fiercely the previous June when their guns, tanks, and planes had been so decisive against the ROK Army. For me, it was a very pleasant turnabout. Later I had the pleasure of driving up that road past the burnt wreckage of North Korean tanks and vehicles. It was rare that I saw the white star of the United States mixed among them.

A war was still being fought around us that Saturday morning. The sounds of heavy battle came from over the northeastern ridges. Nevertheless, I thought it was time for the embassy to get back to its proper work as fast as possible. We were again at our regular post, and a thousand routine matters inevitably would press upon us for action.

Muccio and Drumright preferred to work out of the Finance House for the first few days while the embassy was being cleaned up, and they also made numerous calls at army headquarters, so that except for their very brief visits to the embassy I did not see much of them for several days. For some time I was the only political officer on duty at the embassy and so received a great variety of callers who might have preferred to see the ambassador but talked to me instead. Mostly they were people who had re-

mained in Seoul during the North Korean occupation, although
several government officials also dropped in.

That morning I dusted off my desk as well as I could, closed the
gaping drawers of my cabinet safe as much as possible, and was
back in business. The callers came in streams, some just to tell
their stories and get sympathy, some to get a glimpse into the
future, and some to ask advice or to claim protection.

One group was extraordinary for their honesty. They were three
men from the Seventh Day Adventist church—the doctor in charge
of the mission hospital, the principal clergyman, and the principal
financial officer, as I recall. Before the war, the embassy had a
contract with their hospital for our medical care, which included the
operation of the embassy dispensary.

By happy chance, Muccio and I had saved the hospital from destruction a few weeks before. Early in September, while waiting for
a briefing at 5th Air Force headquarters in Pusan, an officer had
showed us several air photos of Seoul. One was of a large building
with a huge picture of Kim Il Song hanging down. The caption on
the photo stated this was an NKPA headquarters, and the officer
who passed us the picture said it would soon be bombed.

Muccio and I both studied the picture carefully. There was
something intriguingly familiar about it, and yet it did not look like
any building we knew. Muccio finally recognized it. We were looking at an oblique air photo of the Seventh Day Adventist hospital
outside Seoul. Muccio and I both strongly urged that the building
not be bombed unless ground intelligence clearly established that
it was being used as a military headquarters. We guessed it was
still used as a hospital, possibly a military hopital for enemy
troops. The air force changed the identification of the building and
never attacked it. After we returned to Seoul we found that our
guess had been correct. The North Koreans had used it as a military
hospital, although they had failed to mark it with a red cross.

When the three gentlemen came to discuss a problem at their
hospital, they did not know, of course, how close it had come to
being destroyed and that I had had some part in saving it. They
presented me with a serious moral dilemma. The North Koreans
had used up all the hospital's supplies but in their hasty retreat
had left behind a considerable amount of ROK currency. What,

asked this Seventh Day Adventist delegation, should they do with the money? Should they spend it to replace supplies used by the enemy, or should they turn it over to us?

My personal reaction was that they should use it for the hospital, and so was Muccio's. I could not imagine a better use for the money than in the charitable work for which that hospital was famous. But we were naïve then, and Muccio advised them to turn the sack of money over to the U.S. Army civil assistance officer for determination of its proper use. For a time the money was put in our file room for safe keeping. Finally, someone on the Civil Assistance Team decided this was enemy money, therefore it should be seized by the army, and he walked off with it. I do not doubt that the money was put to some good use by Civil Assistance, but I still believe it should have been turned over to the Seventh Day Adventist hospital for their use.

Some days later the three gentlemen called on me again. This time they had a very long, itemized list of all the medicines left in their hospital by the retreating North Koreans. Most of the supplies were of American origin, obviously having been captured from our forces, probably at Taejŏn. Again, they asked me what was the right thing to do.

This time I had no doubts. The Communists had nearly cleaned the hospital out of supplies when they took over, and it seemed to me only fair that the hospital should now use the medicines the enemy had left behind. Muccio agreed with me. Neither of us was foolish enough to have the medicines turned over to the Civil Assistance people. I told the delegation to use the medicines in whatever way seemed suitable, as much as possible on charity work.

I began my report for the ambassador on our return to Seoul and conditions in the city, the first despatch to be written to the State Department by Embassy Korea since that Saturday before war had broken out. I am told it was read with much interest in Washington.

I learned that the marines had left my house and the whole compound as well. There were now no guards of any kind against possible further destruction. Jim Stewart and I wanted to get away from the embassy staff and got permission to move into my old house, partly in order to "guard" the compound.

Jim and I picked up four cartons of army "ten-in-one" rations which were stacked by the door, found some blankets and candles, and were ready to go, if we could find a jeep. None showed up for some time, but at last I found Jack Seifert, who promised to drive us over to my house if we would start before dark. Naturally, he did not like driving alone on the return trip in the darkness through the still dangerous city. We knew there were North Korean agents in plain clothes inside the city, in addition to their regulars on the outskirts. In fact, several days later a Communist unit holed up on South Mountain threw mortar fire into the city until the unit was destroyed. For reasons now forgotten, though, we could not get started on time, and it was well after dark before we left.

As Jack Seifert drove the jeep up the steep concrete drive into my yard, two figures rushed out of the house from the dark to greet me. In their excitement at our happy reunion, which they had despaired of at times, and after all their troubles and hunger, they both shed their accustomed quiet self-discipline and embraced me. One was Mr. Lee, my driver, and the other was Whaja, my maid. Through an extraordinary servants' grapevine they had heard I was coming home that night and were waiting. I was overjoyed to see these two fine people safe and well, although even in the dim beam of my flashlight I could see how tautly hunger had drawn the skin over their faces. They bore the same marks to be seen everywhere throughout Seoul on the faces of adults. It was the mark of the happy life of "liberation" which the enemy had left behind.

The other maid showed up the next day. Of all things, she had started from behind Communist lines and walked through the lines of both armies into Seoul to report for work. She had heard that the Americans had captured Seoul and just assumed I would be back at my house. Since she had spent the war on a farm, she looked plump and healthy as usual. My cook, who was busy as an auxiliary policeman chasing stragglers from their hideouts in the country, did not show up for another month. In the meantime Whaja doubled as cook.

My old house had the advantage of privacy; otherwise it was a mess. The power lines were down and the water mains were cut;

we had no light or water. Some of the tiles had been dislodged, although most of the roof was on. Every window and glass door in the house had been shattered by bombardment, bombing, or looters, and the sliding Japanese paper screens were ripped and torn. The garden side of the house consisted of two stories of sliding glass doors, Japanese fashion. Only the frames, many with jagged glass clinging to them, remained, and some of the frames sagged badly. There was not a stick of furniture of any kind in the house. Not a chair, a table, or a bed, or a single cup or drinking glass or even the smallest dish or plate. All that remained was the kitchen stove. The whole place was filthy with the refuse of soldiers from both sides, and required soap, gallons of water, and backbreaking work to clean up. After the pressures of the summer, however, I wanted to live alone, with my close friend Jim Stewart, in my own house, whatever its condition. Jim, too, preferred living in a large if battered house to comfort in what amounted to a wartime barracks.

Seifert soon drove off and left Jim and me at home. Whaja and Mr. Lee already had been working with makeshift brooms to clean up the two upstairs bedrooms. They carried two Japanese *tatami* mats, six feet by three feet, from one of the servants' rooms downstairs to the two bedrooms upstairs. Jim and I got our blankets and we were soon settled in for a comfortable night. We gave Lee and Whaja a blanket apiece for their rooms. Normally Mr. Lee slept at home, but he stayed with us that night to avoid going about in the streets after dark.

Not knowing what might happen, I kept my carbine and pistol handy. The next morning while we were having breakfast, a "partisan" was flushed from a ruined house near our front gate and shot as he ran away down the street. As far as I know, however, no one attempted to bother us.

Whaja spent part of Sunday in the markets buying plates, glasses, and cutlery. We were not set up for luxury, but we did eat adequately off some not-so-well balanced boards and slept comfortably on our hard mats. The embassy was only five minutes' walk away through the grounds of the British legation, where we were warned to be careful of booby traps and trip lines. We were even soon having guests to lunch or dinner. Among the first were Maj. Stirling

Peach and Squadron Leader Ron Rankin, who had been among my last guests in Seoul the previous June.

We had running water and electric lights again by the first of November and real beds by the first of December, a full month before we abandoned the house for the second time in our January retreat from Seoul. But when we moved in that last night of September 1950, we had had no such luxuries. However, beaten and battered though it might be, it was home.

The war was all around us, but it soon moved so far away I could not even hear the guns at night. Everything we did was touched by the war, yet our role became more like that of a normal American embassy than an embassy at war. One responsibility continued to be to uplift and maintain morale, especially following the Chinese invasion of Korea in November. With a Chinese army above us, it became increasingly difficult to carry out this self-imposed assignment, not just with the Koreans but quite as much with the American command and the foreign correspondents. I was kept busy for weeks denying that the United States intended to withdraw all its forces and abandon Korea.

We also worked hard to get our own government to take what we considered a more realistic attitude toward the occupation of North Korea and the role of the Republic of Korea. This involved numerous observation trips by embassy officers to the north. I went to P'yŏngyang three times, as well as north of P'yŏngyang almost to the Yalu River just before the MacArthur offensive failed, and once to Hamhŭng-Hŭngnam. Amusingly, I received my only wound of the war during my first trip to P'yŏngyang just after American and ROK forces captured the city in October. My misery could not be attributed to enemy action in any way, only to my own clumsiness in the dark. One night, in the pitch darkness of that cold, freezing city, I missed my footing and fell off a concrete porch two or three feet onto a concrete sidewalk, with my pistol in its shoulder holster. Something had to give way: concrete, steel, or my ribs. I wondered for several days afterward why my left side hurt so much, especially the next day when we were taken under several minutes of very lively fire by "friendly" troops and I was forced to move rather rapidly with my cocked pistol out. I continued to wonder several days later when, scarcely able to climb into a jeep in Seoul, I drove out to the Seventh Day Adventists hospital for an X-ray. Diagnosis: three nice cracked ribs.

These activities, however, are beyond the scope of this account— the earliest period of the Korean War, encompassing the American embassy's flight from and victorious return to Seoul.

My story properly closes on Sunday, October 1, when Jim and I walked to the nearby large Presbyterian church, the denomination in which both our fathers had served as clergymen and missionaries in Japan and Korea. This Sunday was a day above all for worship and the giving of thanks for safe delivery, safe return, and the defeat of a vicious invader. The church was only partly filled. Most of the congregation had not yet come out of hiding. The pastor gave an impassioned sermon of thanksgiving that freedom had returned so that churches could again be opened and citizens be free from capricious arrest and murder. I did not know him, but he recognized Jim and me, and after his sermon he told the congregation who we were in rather extravagant terms and also spoke of our fathers. He expressed great appreciation that two officers of the American embassy had come to worship in that church immediately after their return to Seoul.

After church Jim and I worked at the embassy until evening and then returned to my broken house, which was now taking on signs of life. I put one of the wicker settees from the garden on the second porch outside my bedroom and sat there looking out into the garden just as I used to do the previous June. Not exactly as in the past, however. Now my view was unimpeded by glass and the garden was gone, quite dried up and withered away. But the trees still stood to catch my eye, and the cooling breezes of early autumn blew around me.

As I sat there looking at my seared and broken garden, now mercifully sinking into the shadows of darkness, I thought back over the past three long months when a few men from the American embassy, led by Ambassador John J. Muccio, had fled down the road to Suwŏn and even farther south, and of how they had conducted themselves in their unexpected responsibilities.

Our most outstanding contribution to the war effort, a contribution which began the first day of the invasion, was to sustain both Korean and American morale. This may not sound like much, but I have attempted to make clear in earlier chapters what it meant in terms of persuading despairing men that victory was possible and that they must and could fight again. The most critical period was from June 25 to July 1, the first seven days of the war. It would be an exaggeration to suggest that the American embassy alone was responsible for the decisions of the ROK government and the ROK Army to stand and fight after their catastrophic defeat at Seoul. But I think it would be true to say that without the encouragement, the praise, and the insistence of the officers of the American embassy, the ROK government would not have found sufficient strength within itself to stand fast, nor would the ROK Army have fought for the Han River when to give up that vital line meant losing the war. The embassy profoundly affected popular attitudes and morale, among civilians and soldiers, in part because of the natural spread of confidence downward from the top leaders and in part by the superb informational program directed by Jim Stewart through the press, radio, and handbills.

The American embassy had the major role in persuading the U.S. Army to accept organized Korean combat police battalions in every American divisional area to detect infiltrators and fight as light infantry. We also were instrumental in persuading the U.S. Army to fill up its slender ranks with Korean soldiers, a program which proved to be tremendously successful.

Another of our major contributions was serving as liaison between the U.S. Army and ROK government. Initially, that government understood our army better than our army understood the Koreans, simply because the Koreans had dealt with us so much longer. Nevertheless, they had many peculiar misconceptions. Conversely, many an American officer who came over to fight for, and often gave his life for, the defense of South Korea against Communist aggression initially was hostile to the Korean government and even the Korean people. This was especially true of those officers who had served for long periods in Japan, where Koreans are held in contempt. In general, we could not particularly affect the junior officers, but we had close relations with the

United States command. It was from us that the senior American commanders drew their opinions of the ROK government and its policies. When there was friction, we tried to remove it.

There were no precedents for our work in Korea, so we made our own. I believe they were well made. Now the Department of State has patterns with which to guide any other American embassy if it should have the misfortune to suddenly find itself an embassy at war.

Why Didn't We Know?

How could we have been surprised so badly that Sunday morning?[1] In retrospect, even with all my answers I am still astonished. I, at least, had expected an attack for years and was not supposed to be caught by surprise. But I was in distant Tokyo on vacation, peacefully asleep while the guns roared and the tanks crunched southward. That is very humiliating to admit.

Communists, the Soviets, and their dupes all over the world began crying out on that bloody Sunday, and have kept up their clamor ever since, that it was the Republic of Korea which attacked, secretly supported by the U.S. government.[2] If they were planning a general invasion of North Korea that Sunday morning, the South Korean government and the American embassy were certainly casual about it. In estimating the enemy's timetable there is no question that we were poor guessers, but not even children playing at war would have launched a general invasion in our state of unpreparedness.

Consider the South Korean military! The deputy chief of staff, Chŏng Il-gwŏn and the adjutant general were both in the United States just preparing to return home. The chief of naval operations, Admiral Son Wŏn-il, was in the middle of the Pacific Ocean, a passenger on one of three patrol crafts bought in the United States and being sailed to Korea to join the small ROK Navy. I think they put into Guam just after war broke out. Fifty of the ablest officers of the ROK Army were in Japan, undergoing field training with units of the U.S. 8th Army, instead of being at their posts in Korea. Only the usual four divisions were disposed northward toward the parallel, and their main elements were well south of the border. The other four divisions could not be brought into action in less than twelve to forty-eight hours.

Two had no artillery and were short a regiment each. Imagine an army starting an invasion without a single regiment, let alone a division, disposed in force at the boundary, and two divisions not even having any artillery!

Consider the American mission. The commanding officer of KMAG, Brig. Gen. William L. Roberts, was on a ship somewhere in mid-Pacific, en route to the States for reassignment. The chief of staff and acting commander, Colonel Wright, was holidaying in Japan. The first secretary of the embassy, my humiliated self, was dreamlessly asleep in the home of a friend in far-off Tokyo. The embassy in Seoul was deserted except for the regular guards when the battle opened. The military attaché had to be aroused from bed to hear the news, over two hours after the invasion began. The naval attaché got to his office about 8:00 A.M. to work on a report and found himself in the middle of a war. The ambassador, the counselor—in fact, everyone—was asleep or doing whatever he normally did at five o'clock on a lazy Sunday morning in June. But while sleep reigned in Seoul, divisions of Communist infantry, tanks, and artillery crashed across the thinly held 38th parallel. The only Americans who knew immediately of the attack were the six unfortunate missionaries in Kaesŏng, who soon became prisoners, and the one more fortunate KMAG officer.

We must humbly accept the charge of ignorance, but not that of trickery, invasion, and bloody assault on the unsuspecting North Koreans.

During that June we were more relaxed at Embassy Seoul than we had been for many months. A pleasant spring was passing into summer, the guerrillas had been destroyed in the south, and peace and order seemed to be coming to the whole country. The national budget had just been completed for presentation to the National Assembly. The ECA program at last was under way and gave great hope for South Korea's future. The ROK Army was growing stronger steadily as training progressed and as more and more officers finished the numerous specialist schools and took their places with their units. Everyone knew of North Korea's hostile intentions, but somehow that June seemed so lovely and charming, it was hard to think of war.

I had moved to a much larger house on June 6, next door to Drumright's and very close to the ambassador's residence. What little spare time I had I spent getting settled, although I left most of that work to the servants. My younger brother Glenn arrived from the States under USIS sponsorship to teach special courses in parasitology at various colleges and universities during the summer, and naturally he moved in with me. It was fun to discuss with him all the many changes in Korea since last he had been there. Many new people arrived in town that month and some of them I had to lunch or dinner, while I went to numerous social affairs myself. Squadron Leader Rankin and Major Peach of the U.N. commission were among the newcomers who were a great pleasure to have at the table. I still continued to lunch at least once a week, and usually several other times, with Foreign Minister Ben Limb. We alternated these lunches between my house and his room at the Chosŏn Hotel. Of course we always had official matters to discuss, but we found time for much general conversation, joking, and gossip. I was very fond of Ben.

Life in my new house settled into its routine. In the long light of evening I enjoyed sitting on the veranda outside my second-story bedroom, reading a book and looking at the garden down below. Against all reason, the feeling of imminent war slipped quietly away into the peace and contentment of a busy and pleasant life.

The real answer to the question of how we were so badly caught by surprise lies in the fact that we had lived so long on the edge of a volcano, had gazed so often into its smoky, fiery depths, and had become accustomed to it. We knew it would explode some day, but as day after day, month after month, and year after year passed and it did not blow up, we could hardly believe that tomorrow would be any different.

Several times after the war began I read the claims of various distinguished gentlemen that they had called the turn on the invasion, that they had named the day.[3] These claims are nonsense. If any South Korean authority had spotted the attack, we would have been warned at Embassy Seoul. If any American authority had spotted it, he would have alerted our government, we would have been told, and we would have warned the South Koreans. The sad fact is that we were all caught without any answer to the crucial question: when?

In Seoul we knew better than almost anywhere in the world that the Communists planned to invade, and we had done what we could to prepare for that assault. That is why the embassy had an evacuation plan. But unfortunately, we did not have an agent sitting in the Russian embassy in P'yŏngyang or in the executive committee of the North Korean Labor party able to answer that question, when? Those people who now claim they saw it coming all the time are really only saying what everyone knew, that the invasion was coming sometime. But it had been coming since 1946, and at Embassy Seoul we did not need warnings that invasion was intended. We had to know when D-day and H-hour were. Unhappily for us, no one on our side guessed the answer to those essential questions before June 25. For years we had had repeated alarms of invasion. Back in the spring of 1948, when the U.S. Army still occupied South Korea, there had been many alerts with a 6:00 P.M. curfew imposed and all posts manned. Time after time we had waited for an assault that never came. Even during the first week in June 1950 the ROK Army held a weekend alert with invasion expected on Sunday. Again, nothing happened. We relaxed once more.

Throughout the American occupation there had been periodic but small-scale battles between American and Russian soldiers at the parallel, and later between American soldiers and North Korean police or soldiers. In 1949 the ROK Army took over the defense of the border against the NKPA.[4] Small-scale fire fights occurred almost every night some place along the line. Communist troops raided the south to grab prisoners for interrogation or just to test defenses. The ROK Army probably sometimes reciprocated.[5] During the summer of 1949, however, these raids changed into several large-scale battles in the Ongjin Peninsula, in the Kaesŏng area, and near Ch'unchŏn. These were not patrol actions, nor were they the undisciplined firing of trigger-happy soldiers. Large NKPA units, supported by artillery, invaded the south at least five times in the summer of 1949. The ROK Army threw sufficient strength against the threatened points to drive the enemy back north of the parallel. At the time everyone was encouraged by the defeats inflicted upon the North Koreans.

In June 1949 P'yŏngyang Radio, a dreadful propaganda station daily pouring out its venom to South Korea, announced the formation of the Democratic Front for the Attainment of the Unification of the Fatherland, commonly called the Fatherland Front. The Soviet directors of P'yŏngyang Radio were constantly thinking up new propaganda gimmicks to unsettle the south in their campaign of subversion, arson, terrorism, and guerrilla warfare. This time the Fatherland Front, allegedly composed of twenty or thirty patriotic political parties, announced a series of elections throughout all Korea during the summer months, whether the Republic of Korea approved or not, and predicted that on September 20 the flag of the Democratic People's Republic of Korea would fly over the capitol in Seoul.

All summer long the propaganda for a Korea united under the DPRK increased in volume. The attempted invasions of the south were tied to this program, perhaps as tests of the defenses of the ROK

Army. Communist guerrillas hiding in the mountains in the south coordinated their movements with these broadcasts and the border battles. The broadcasts insisted the unification of Korea would be peaceful, except for the necessary liquidation of a few "pro-American" and "pro-Japanese" traitors and the big landlords, such as "Syngman Rhee and his gang." They also said that the United Nations Commission on Korea would be driven from the country, since it was a tool of the "reactionary American imperialists."

Obviously the only way that the Communist flag could be raised over the capitol in Seoul and the only way that the president of Korea, the government, and the National Assembly could be liquidated was by military conquest of the south. Consequently, I read our translations of these daily propaganda broadcasts with very great care. Among my duties I was responsible for informing the ambassador and reporting to the department on nonmilitary activities in North Korea. That date, September 20, seemed to indicate either the start of an invasion or an estimate of the time it would take to complete the invasion and overrun the south. Naturally everyone concerned in the south watched the passing days with care and stood by for a storm on the 20th. But nothing happened. Suddenly, P'yŏngyang Radio stopped talking of the Fatherland Front, or hanging Syngman Rhee, or flying the Communist flag over the capitol. The storm of words stopped as suddenly as it had begun, with no explanation, either over the radio or in the newspapers and magazines published in P'yŏngyang.

The Communist guerrilla raids during that summer of 1949 had been so serious that the ROK Army began an all out antiguerrilla campaign even before the leaves were off the trees. The number of guerrillas was not large, but with their numerous mountain hideouts and the terror they inflicted on nearby farming villages by public murders, they were a danger to public security far out of proportion to their numbers. The South Korean government had been able to create far more security from Communist assassins, arsonists, and saboteurs in the cities than existed during the U.S. occupation, but they were determined that farmers should be just as safe as city dwellers. There is a spine of mountains running down the eastern edge of the Korean peninsula, ending in a high range known as Mount Chiri near the southern port city of Pusan. It was down this wild, barren, and uninhabited series of mountain ranges that the Communists from the north brought their guerrilla reinforcements and supplies. If the ROK Army could successfully wipe out the guerrilla units and seize their mountain bases, there would be no one for the northern-trained guerrilla units to reinforce.

From the autumn of 1949 until the late spring of 1950, a considerable portion of the ROK Army was pulled away from training and garrison duty, broken into task forces, and, despite the bitter winter, methodically thrown against the guerrillas. By April it is doubtful if there were a hundred guerrillas left alive and free in South Korea, and these were a scattered and harried lot. During the spring the North Koreans made two major attempts to reinforce these guerrilla units. The first group of two hundred guerrillas was discovered and surrounded the first day they crossed the parallel. Almost all of them were either killed or captured. I looked over their equipment after it was brought to Seoul. Much was American, such as Garand rifles, presumably supplied the North Koreans by the Chinese Communist forces in Manchuria.

The second group was not destroyed so quickly. They escaped detection longer and scattered, but eventually most of them were dead or prisoners. The ROK Army was very proud. One division, whose regiment had been chiefly involved, boastfully radioed to the north for guerrillas to be sent down immediately so they could be destroyed without the division having to inconvenience itself by taking up new positions later. The South Korean officers and men believed that man for man they were better soldiers than the Communists.

Naturally, with the constant military threat of a hostile army thirty miles away and with continuous fighting in the mountains, we at the embassy gave much thought to the security problems of the Republic of Korea. South Korean officials were sometimes impatient with us, thinking we didn't pay enough attention to these problems. But they never knew how often we sent urgent recommendations to Washington on this very subject.

United States policy regarding Korea was decided in Washington, not at the embassy. We only executed our government's policies. We were kept informed of decisions but often were not consulted in advance. Still, there was always some latitude in the interpretation of general decisions, and we always had the privilege of proposing changes.

American policy was essentially to assist the South Korean government and people for a short period of time, economically through ECA and militarily through KMAG, in developing a viable economy which eventually they could protect through their own efforts and at their own expense. ECA assistance was to end in 1952, and KMAG was strictly a training mission to assist the ROK government to develop sufficient strength to maintain domestic order and protect the border against minor attacks. Quite specifically the KMAG and arms assistance program was not aimed at assisting the Republic of Korea to defend itself against full-scale invasion from the north.

At Embassy Seoul we were not happy about this policy, and we did our best to get it changed. The leader in this attempt, naturally, was Ambassador Muccio. Like all the political officers, he believed it was not enough to help the South Koreans to maintain domestic order. They had to be given a reasonable chance to protect themselves against the one enemy likely to attack them: the northern Communist regime directed by the Soviet Union.

Not that Muccio thought strictly in military terms. Far from it. I sometimes thought his insistence that there was no point in having an independent Korea unless it was also a democratic Korea was unrealistic. I believe that with independence it was possible for the South Koreans to develop a truly democratic society, but if their independence were crushed by the Communists, all hope of a democratic Korea would disappear. Probably this was chiefly a difference of emphasis, but a difference of emphasis when put into words often sounds contradictory. Muccio saw the major problem in South Korea to be developing a society of free men, with the military problem secondary. Knowing the Communists' intention to invade and conquer, I saw the major problem to be keeping South Korea free by military means, with the question of the exact status of democracy secondary. On this question the senior staff saw the problem much as I did.

Muccio believed, however, that South Korea was very different from China. He was disgusted by the writings of so many American reporters and others who simply echoed P'yŏngyang Radio without knowing that their vilification of President Rhee and the ROK government was largely made in Moscow. Muccio had excellent personal relations with Rhee, whom he had admired from before the war for his courage, his years of determined effort for the independence of his country, and his basic belief in the democratic process. Rhee had lived in the United States most of the time since 1905. He had taken his Ph.D. degree at Princeton University under the influence of Woodrow Wilson. He wanted for Korea not just national independence but the personal freedom and independence that he himself had enjoyed during his long residence in America. Rhee was a very old man. He was arbitrary, dogmatic, and suspicious. At his age he was unlikely to change his preconceptions. Events preoccupied him with the military threat to the Republic of Korea, and consideration of this threat entered into most of his public decisions. But Muccio found that whenever he presented to the president a problem involving human rights, Rhee's response was sound and genuine. If the president were told of some specific violation of the rights of an individual citizen, of a specific case of police brutality, or of official callousness, Rhee took prompt remedial action.

When the U.S. Army withdrew from South Korea, it left part of its arms for the ROK Army. But it left no tanks, no aircraft, and no long-range guns. While such weapons were not necessary for the maintenance of internal security, they were vital for the defense of the Republic against large-scale invasion. South Korean military leaders and their KMAG advisers did a magnificent job of training a smart-looking, technically skilled, loyal "army" of about 98,000 officers and men by June 1950. It was an excellent infantry force but lacked even all the proper weapons of the modern infantry.

The KMAG commander, General Roberts, was an armored warfare man, and naturally his opinions were accepted at the embassy and elsewhere in South Korea as the last word on tanks. He had a striking combat record in France and Germany in World War II and had commanded an armored division at the Battle of the Bulge. Roberts laid down as gospel that Korea was an impossible battleground for tanks. Many a time at staff meetings I heard him expound this view. Since most of Korea is steeply sided mountains, obviously tanks would be limited to operations in the valleys. In the valleys, as Roberts pointed out, most of the area was covered by centuries-old rice fields, deep with mud. He maintained that the tanks would bog down in this mud if they ever ventured across country, and so they would be confined to moving in single file on the narrow dirt roads. What the ROK Army needed, then, was not tanks but an intelligent tank defense. We knew, of course, that the North Koreans had at least a regiment, probably a brigade, of tanks, but according to Roberts' thesis, the more Communist tanks, the more fiery death traps for Communist soldiers.

Following his advice, the ROK Army prepared tank traps along the main roads north of Seoul, arranged mine fields, and practiced with bazookas and 57mm antitank guns. They even talked of blowing in the sides of the hills at narrow passes, completely blocking the road and if possible burying the tanks as they came along.[6]

The ROK Army did not need tanks, and if the enemy brought his down so much the better, we thought. But the ROK Army did badly need long-range guns and warplanes. Just how many planes the North Koreans had was unknown; the estimate varied from one hundred to two hundred.⁷ But they did have them, whereas the ROK Air Force had only ten training planes, AT-6s, which they had armed with ground force machine guns, hand grenades, and bazookas in place of rockets. One good YAK fighter could have destroyed this whole improvised air force.

After the summer of 1949 Muccio and Roberts had tried by telegrams, despatches, and personal appeals to get 155mm guns and at least fifty serviceable airplanes allotted to the Republic of Korea. The ROK Army's biggest guns were 105mm howitzers, but the enemy had 122mm cannons. When it was learned during the spring of 1950 that MacArthur's command was scrapping its conventional fighter planes, the F-51s, President Rhee wrote General MacArthur, with Muccio's private encouragement, asking that the planes be given to the ROK Air Force instead of being junked. None of these appeals got anywhere.

Muccio was in Washington for consultations in the spring of 1950. He talked about the problems of South Korea's defense to everyone who would listen. He thought he had made progress and told me on his return that responsible officials had advised him to be patient a little longer. They expected to effect sufficient change in basic policy at least to arrange for the supply of guns and planes to the Republic of Korea. Muccio had the patience, all right, but the North Koreans did not.⁸

About the middle of June 1950 someone in Washington noticed a statement in an embassy despatch that assessed the ROK Army, as an infantry force, as better than the NKPA. Sharp telegraphic inquiry came from the Department of State: Was this true? I wrote the answering telegram.

I first wrote a draft and showed it to Colonel Wright of KMAG. Wright read it and said he agreed entirely, so I added that KMAG concurred in the estimate. I brought the draft to Drumright, who made some elaborations and additions without changing the basic estimates. Off it went. This must have been about the fifteenth of June.

I wrote that the best military estimates available to the embassy indicated that in training and spirit the ROK Army was at least the equal of the NKPA, and probably was superior, as an infantry force. But there were other elements involved than infantry, consequently it was not possible to make a solid estimate. I said that the North Koreans had an air force and tanks, and guns that could outrange any artillery in the ROK Army. Discounting the possible advantage in tanks, due to the terrain, there still remained those two unknown factors that the South Korean infantry would have to face: complete North Korean domination of the air and artillery superiority. The ROK Army was good but it was green. Before actual hostilities it was impossible to say how well it would act when hit from the air and by artillery it could not silence. Nor could we estimate how well the civilian population would stand up to strafing and bombing when there was not one South Korean combat plane to give them the slightest protection. The telegram ended by urging that these deficiencies of the ROK Army be made up as soon as possible.[9]

Just where the money was to come from to pay for these expensive necessities we did not know. Certainly not from the Military Defense Aid Program (MDAP). Congress had appropriated $10.2 million for military aid to the Republic of Korea the previous autumn, whereupon the ROK Army and KMAG had studied how best the money could be spent. In December 1949 two MDAP representatives, from the State Department and the U.S. Army, came to Korea to consult with South Korean authorities. Some South Korean officials wanted everything: a first-class air force, a navy almost second to none, full supplies for a balanced army of half a million men, and a few other incidentals. The ROK armed forces, however, were most realistic. Ten million dollars would not buy very much, especially since the Department of Defense had put the Republic of Korea in a category where it was charged with replacement costs at current rates, not at the original price. We would not have objected to this had favoritism not been shown to other countries no more under threat of attack than South Korea was. Many other countries under the MDAP program were allowed to pay for their military supplies at the original purchase price to the United States forces.

About all that could be bought for the ten million was ammunition, rifle parts, and a few other basic essentials.[10] It certainly could not supply the airplanes and the 155mm guns we were asking for. And the ROK government had almost no money to buy goods abroad. South Korea had so little foreign exchange that it was with the greatest difficulty that dollars were found to purchase ten training planes for the air force and four patrol craft for the navy. Fortunately, over 90 percent of all quartermaster items used by the ROK Army were produced in Korea and did not require foreign exchange.

In Seoul we lived always under the shadow of war, so close that paradoxically we came to accept it both as inevitable and yet as far away. We never forgot that some morning we would wake up to find the North Koreans across the parallel in great force. We never forgot this, in principle, but the precise day wholly escaped us.

We were assured at the embassy by various military figures and intelligence experts, as an absolute certainty, that the Communists could not possibly mount an invasion without first tipping their hands by large-scale troop movements to assembly points just behind the parallel and by the simultaneous establishment of huge supply dumps to support the first week of invasion. Such a movement of men and material, we were told repeatedly, would be so obvious that it would be noted by the various South Korean and American intelligence agencies interested in just that type of information. I recall being told very forcefully that we probably would have two weeks' warning, and we could be guaranteed one week's warning. Well, one week's warning was quite a cushion, and I made my personal calculations on this assumption.

Various South Korean and American intelligence agencies did gather scraps of information during June which might have been assessed as presaging early invasion. But we had lived so closely with the possibility of invasion for so long, so many other times we had learned of similar scraps of information that had turned out to mean something else, that we became careless. And we were suckers for a razzle-dazzle series of Communist deceptive maneuvers aimed at diverting everyone's attention for military matters.

The scraps of information of varying reliability did tell of a build-up of the North Korean Air Force, of additions to the tank brigade, and, most significantly of the displacement southward of several regiments and even one division. They told that supplies were steadily pouring into Wŏnsan on the east coast and to Chinanmp'o on the west, but then these ports had always been active. The intelligence reports indicated the beginning of the removal of all North Korean residents from a zone five kilometers above the 38th parallel. The reports did not, however, show the arrival of strong new forces or the construction of new supply dumps near the 38th parallel. Those were the two key questions.

Was there a significant military build-up right above the parallel of forces prepared to jump? Now we know there was, but then we had not the slightest word of it. To this day I do not know entirely how the Communists so thoroughly concealed this large build-up. It was, of course, very difficult for agents to move back and forth across the parallel, which was watched all along the line by North Korean soldiers and police. It was easier to come down to Seoul from P'yŏngyang or Wŏnsan by boat and report conditions in the far north than it was to walk a few miles from north of the 38th parallel to south of it. I knew that some people managed to do it, but of course in my job I did not know how long or who they were, nor did I want to know. It seems very likely now that during the critical last two weeks the North Koreans were able to pick up every South Korean agent near the parallel, or if not that, at least to seal the border so that none of those operating back and forth in the border region were able to come south and report in time.

Consequently, we could not properly assess the meaning of the removal of farmers from that five-kilometer zone above the parallel. This action could have indicated preparation for war and invasion, the clearing of a build-up area of all nonmilitary personnel to prevent enemy agents from detecting the preparations. We considered this interpretation, but we also recognized that there was an equally valid one which did not lead to conclusions about immediate invasion.

The Soviet Union keeps its border areas cleared of farmers and other civilians for a distance of several miles into the USSR. The main reason is to seal off Soviet citizens from contact with foreigners, since such contact so often makes them discontented with life under communism. A second reason is to make it easier for the security police to spot illegal attempts to enter the country, whether for espionage or any other reason. It appeared to us to be just as reasonable to believe that the North Koreans, who followed Russian practices in almost everything else, were now applying Soviet customs regarding border areas to the 38th parallel as it was to assume that invasion was imminent. For the latter conclusion we needed evidence of troop movements, and we never got it. As a rule such information reached Seoul from North Korea from two weeks to several months after the event. The North Korean security controls were very strict and travel was very difficult. We did not have two weeks or two months to discover that the major part of the NKPA was poised for invasion just behind the first line of hills above the 38th parallel.

Communist security measures explain our ignorance in part, but I think the greatest explanation was the superb razzle-dazzle series of deceptions that had all responsible officials in South Korea, including those in the American embassy, thinking about something else instead of studying very carefully the fragments of information leaking through from the north.

I mentioned earlier the propaganda campaign of the Democratic Front for the Attainment of the Unification of the Fatherland during the summer of 1949 and P'yŏngyang's complete silence on this subject after September 20, 1949. Suddenly, in the first week of June 1950 this propaganda program was revived with a tremendous barrage of radio broadcasts and other messages, but with such clever variations that soon everyone was thinking of nothing else.

P'yŏngyang Radio, on behalf of the Fatherland Front, appealed to all Korean patriots who wanted a united country to support a meeting between northern and southern leaders in P'yŏngyang or Seoul as seemed convenient. Almost every existing party, as well as a much larger number of nonexistent parties, were invited to participate. The appeal continued, eventually including an invitation to the ROK National Assembly to participate. Hardly anyone was to be excluded— only a few "reactionaries" like President Rhee. Universal, free elections, a united Korea, and land for everyone were the Fatherland Front's proclaimed objectives. It was alluring. Since every Korean yearns for national unity and national independence, the appeal might have had considerable effect, and even thousands of farmers who were buying their land under government land redistribution programs in South Korea might have been drawn by this promise of free land had the appeal been presented for the first time in 1950. Similar appeals had been made repeatedly in the past, however, and most citizens had come to recognize them as a façade for Communist trickery.

The agitation was so extensive and the appeals so well written, however, that even the Seoul anti-Communist newspapers carried them as news stories. At the embassy we carefully read the text of the first Fatherland Front broadcasts and pondered their meaning. We knew they were a fake, but what was the purpose behind the deception? Was it aimed only at stirring up discontent, or was there something more profound? Would the agitation be tied to large-scale border battles as in 1949? I wrote a telegram to the department describing the Fatherland Front propaganda and suggesting several possible reasons for it.[11]

After a few days, having worn out the straight propaganda value of their radio campaign, the North Koreans introduced a new device. They announced over P'yŏngyang Radio that on Saturday,

June 10, three representatives of the Fatherland Front would be at the frontier railway station of Yŏhyŏn, just north of the 38th parallel near Kaesŏng, to meet representatives of political parties to confer about unification of the country. About one hundred South Koreans also received invitations by mail.

No South Koreans, political leaders or otherwise, went to Yŏhyŏn that Sunday, but John Gaillard, acting deputy principal secretary of the U.N. commission, did. Everyone in Seoul, Korean and foreigner alike, followed his trip closely. The U.N. commission had been trying to enter North Korea or at least to transmit letters to North Korean leaders since their first arrival in January 1948 but had never succeeded in crossing the parallel or having a letter accepted. Thus the commission seized on this invitation to persons interested in the unification of Korea to send Gaillard across the parallel to meet the mysterious North Korean representatives.

Gaillard, a very fine and likeable American, was excited and delighted with the assignment. When he reached the last low hills near the parallel below Yŏhyŏn, he was stopped by South Korean soldiers. They were engaged in an intermittent fire fight with North Korean troops a few hundred yards to the north. The regimental commander told Gaillard flatly he would not permit him to cross the parallel. The South Korean colonel said he was responsible for that sector and he was not going to risk having Gaillard killed.

By chance, the two Australian military observers for the U.N. commission happened to be in the area that day and soon came along with the division commander. Rankin and Peach urged that Gaillard be allowed to go north, and finally the South Korean colonel granted permission. All firing was stopped by the South Korean soldiers, and then it died away from the north. When Gaillard stepped out beyond the protection of the hills, however, he did not know whether a trigger-happy soldier on one side or the other would plug him. Fortunately, none did.

Gaillard found the three representatives of the Fatherland Front waiting for him at a table set up on the railroad platform at Yŏhyŏn. He had literature from the U.N. commission, resolutions, communications, and credentials. The Communists refused all his materials but instead gave him a long letter for the U.N. commission, the text of which had been the original P'yŏngyang broadcast in this propaganda campaign. Gaillard tried to leave his materials on the table, but the North Koreans would have none of that. They said they were thoroughly familiar with the U.N. actions and resolutions. Gaillard had to pick up his documents and return south without exchange. He was disappointed but still pleased to be the first U.N. representative to manage to get north of the 38th parallel.

All Seoul buzzed with the Gaillard story that Saturday night and tried to comprehend the meaning. Was it possible that the Communists were ready to change their stubborn policies and were prepared to propose a realistic program for the unification of Korea? Or at least one which would enable people and goods to move back and forth? Of course, there was no reason to assume so much just because Gaillard had managed to cross the forbidden parallel, but still might there not be some meaning hidden in that near miracle? We all wondered.

The North Koreans quickly gave us something more to wonder about. P'yŏngyang Radio announced that since the "pro-Japanese imperialist Syngman Rhee regime" had not allowed South Korean political representatives to meet with the Fatherland Front representatives, the three men would go to Seoul. They would cross the parallel below Yŏhyŏn at ten o'clock Sunday morning, June 11.

To understand the significance of this announcement one must recall that the parallel had been closed to travelers for several years. By their public admission, the Communist authorities in the north were engaged in constant efforts to subvert and overthrow the Republic of Korea. Any representative of that regime walking down the railroad tracks to Kaesŏng and on to Seoul would be arrested as an enemy agent. But down the railroad walked those three men right on schedule that Sunday morning. The South Korean outpost held its fire and waited for the travelers to round the first hill. Then they were put under arrest.

I was sitting at my desk about noon when a KMAG officer telephoned Minister of Defense Sin Sŏng-mo and asked if he had heard the news. Captain Sin had not, but he was angered at the effrontery of the North Koreans and he had an immediate solution for their presence. He would send instructions to have them court-martialed and shot. I urged him not to do this, saying that aside from any question of law, shooting them would only hurt the Republic of Korea in world opinion and probably would help the Communists. I said that probably the North Korean authorities had expected them to be shot and intended to use them as martyrs in subsequent propaganda. Sin was very hard to convince. The area was under military control; they had violated basic laws; they were Communist agents; the simplest thing was to arrange a firing squad.

I urged Sin to have them sent back across the parallel immediately. I said I did not know what the Communists had in mind, but certainly they hoped to use these men to soften and confuse public opinion in the south. I said I thought the best way to handle the three "representatives" was not to harm them in any way and to get them back north as rapidly as possible. This would avoid playing into the hands of North Korea. Sin disagreed. He said that if he didn't have them shot, he would have them brought to Kaesŏng and interrogated. He might even have them brought to Seoul He would let me know later.

That night I again talked with Sin. The three prisoners had been brought to Seoul and were under military custody. They were interrogated by South Korean military intelligence officers for several days. I am convinced they were well treated and that no violence was done them. All were small-fry and it seemed odd to me that the P'yŏngyang regime would send such unknowns to overthrow the Republic of Korea. I became more certain that the North Koreans had hoped for an incident to use as propaganda. I was also impressed with the courage displayed by the three Communists in walking down that railway track into probable death by gunfire.

On Thursday Captain Sin had a happy story to tell me. After interrogating the three men and getting all the information they could, ROK Army officers drove them around Seoul and showed them the city. The prisoners professed to be astounded at what they saw. Seoul was in no way the poverty-stricken, dreadful city portrayed by Communist propaganda. In fact, it was quite an impressive place. The prisoners could not seem to get over the difference between the reality and what they had been told. By Thursday not only had all three stated their conversion from the Communist cause, on the grounds of having been deliberately deceived by the Communists, but two of them had agreed to broadcast to North Korea. They would state what they had seen and how North Korean leaders had lied to everyone in the north. On Friday night that is exactly what they did. According to Sin, the men wrote out their own stories first, minor changes were made in them by their captors, and then the men read the corrected script into microphones. The actual broadcasts were from platters.

The announcement of the broadcast was published in all the papers and given great prominence over HLKA. A good portion of the citizens of Seoul, among them my servants, were listening when the apostate ex-Communists came on the air. They did not say anything we didn't know, but the fact that they said it and who they were made it quite exciting.

What did the Fatherland Front represent? The two men testified it was only a North Korean propaganda device to unsettle the citizens of the Republic of Korea. As for military movements, both told their interrogators that they knew of none that were new or significant. A few days later the third man, who originally had refused to broadcast because of his alleged fear of reprisals against his family in P'yŏngyang, also agreed to broadcast. He told the same story.

It was a perfect performance by three iron-nerved Communist agents. In South Korea they had nearly everyone believing what we wanted to believe: that having seen the free south they had chosen freedom instead of communism. When that was believed, their testimony on military subjects also was believed. They did their job of confusing the ROK Army, government, and foreign observers, like us, magnificently. When the NKPA captured Seoul a short time later, these three men returned to their former obscurity; but if all of them have not been decorated with the Order of Stalin, that famous Georgian is without gratitude.

But this clever deception still wasn't enough. Remember, it was South Korean military intelligence which was concentrating upon questioning, studying, and guiding these three men when it should have been watching the border area. The North Koreans now used another diversion to deflect attention from military affairs.

To explain the remainder of this skillfully planned subterfuge, I must first mention the destruction of two major Communist espionage and sabotage rings in the south during the late spring of 1950. In one case South Korean intelligence did especially well. They had picked up traces of a Communist net the previous September and had taken their time unraveling it. Before they finished, the courier who carried the messages and funds between North and South Korea was actually a double-agent working for ROK intelligence. When the operation was smashed, Communist agents in the army, the police, government agencies, and among private citizens were caught in considerable numbers. Among those arrested were the chief North Korean spies in South Korea. A large quantity of radio equipment and codes, records and messages, weapons, and about ten thousand dollars in United States currency as well as a large amount of South Korean money was seized. I went to police headquarters and examined the booty. It was very impressive. Not very much later the ROK police broke up another espionage net which had been almost as productive.

The destruction of these two important nets of spies and saboteurs just before the invasion undoubtedly affected public order in and south of Seoul during our retreat. The North Korean agents were not around to stir up trouble; they were either dead or in prison.

The North Koreans cleverly used the capture of their two chief agents in South Korea for further deception.[12] When the Russians first entered North Korea they found a newly organized but powerful political party devoted to Korean independence led by one of the greatest Korean patriots, a Christian pastor named Cho Man-sik.[13] In due course the Russians placed him under house arrest. However, Cho was so popular that the Russians for a long time did not dare throw him into prison. Finally, though, he disappeared. By June 1950 no outsider really knew what had become of Cho. There were rumors: he was in prison; he was in Siberia; he had died of illness; he had been shot; some even said Cho had escaped and was hiding in the mountains.

Suddenly, without any prior indication, P'yŏngyang Radio announced that Cho Man-sik not only was alive but that North Korea was prepared to let him come south, to freedom. This announcement followed the excitement caused by the radio broadcast of the turncoat representatives of the Fatherland Front. On June 14 P'yŏngyang Radio broadcast a proposal to the authorities in Seoul. If the Republic of Korea would spare the lives of the two major North Korean spies, who had already been tried by court-martial and sentenced to death, and would permit their safe return to North Korea, Cho Man-sik would be allowed to go to Seoul.[14]

I remember talking at length about this proposal with President Rhee in the beautiful Kyŏngmudae gardens. Dr. Rhee was very definite that if Cho Man-sik could be gotten out alive, he would be glad to surrender any number of spies. However, he had doubts about the offer. He thought it might be a trick. His military and police advisers had strongly urged against releasing the two spies, but Dr. Rhee considered it far more important to save Cho Man-sik's life. He told me if Cho were well enough, he wanted to appoint him immediately to a cabinet post.

During the next few days there were several unofficial exchanges by radio between P'yŏngyang and Seoul on this proposal. Seoul did not think that Cho alone was sufficient to exchange for two high-powered spies. P'yŏngyang threw in Cho's son, who would be allowed to come out with him. P'yŏngyang said the exchange would be effected at Yŏhyŏn, just north of the parallel, but Seoul suspected trickery.

Seoul feared the Communists would get back their agents and then refuse to surrender Cho and his son. Seoul specified that the place of exchange must be at a point on the 38th parallel just outside Kaesŏng and that Cho Man-sik must come across the line and be examined by a physician before the North Koreans were delivered. Seoul wondered whether Cho Man-sik might be nearly dead and the Communists planning to pass off a near corpse in exchange for two healthy espionage agents. Captain Sin was very positive that this precaution must be taken, and Rhee agreed.

The exchange of views, all very unofficial, went back and forth over the official P'yŏngyang Radio and the semi-official ROK radio from June 14 to the 24. Absolutely everyone interested in relations between North and South Korea and in the fate of the legendary Cho Man-sik followed these exchanges with minute attention. ROK Military Intelligence, the National Police, the government, the U.N. commission, we in the American embassy all followed the negotiations with the greatest care. I thought it would be a marvelous thing if the second most popular figure in Korea, and a northerner at that, would at last be freed to take government office in the Republic of Korea. I hoped that by the time I returned from my brief visit to Tokyo, by June 27, the exchange would have been effected.

The negotiations, gossip, and newspaper stories about Cho Man-sik and the two Communist agents were still on our minds when North Korean forces attacked at dawn on June 25. No one in the south had noticed the North Koreans bringing their troops to the assembly points behind the hills that masked the border. The audience had been enthralled, watching a magician's rapid hand thrust before their eyes while the brilliant maneuver was performed by the hand they could not see.[15]

Notes

EDITOR'S INTRODUCTION

1. Robert T. Oliver, *Syngman Rhee: The Man behind the Myth* (New York: Dodd Mead, 1954), pp. 18-19.

AUTHOR'S FOREWORD

1. The Republic of Korea was established on August 15, 1948, and controlled south of the 38th parallel. The Democratic People's Republic of Korea was inaugurated on September 9, 1948, and governed north of the parallel. Both governments and their armed forces are identified by the following abbreviations: South Korea, ROK and ROK Army for the Republic of Korea; North Korea, DPRK and NKPA (North Korean People's Army) for the Democratic People's Republic of Korea.

2. The mission and activities of the United States Military Advisory Group to the Republic of Korea (KMAG), prior to the outbreak of war and during the summer of 1950, are described in Robert K. Sawyer, *Military Advisers in Korea: KMAG in Peace and War* (Washington, D.C.: U.S. Government Printing Office, 1962).

3. The United Nations Commission on Korea (UNCOK) was created by a resolution of the U.N. General Assembly on December 12, 1948. It superseded the United Nations Temporary Commission on Korea (UNTCOK), which had attempted to supervise a general election throughout the peninsula in 1948. The member states of the U.N. commission were Australia, China, El Salvador, France, India, the Philippines, and Turkey. The U.N. commission also had field observers, who were military experts, to report on armed clashes along the demarcation line .

CHAPTER ONE

1. During the period covered by this account, June-September 1950, Korean time was thirteen hours ahead of Eastern Daylight Time. All times in this narrative, Korea or Washington, D.C., are local.

2. The American Mission in Korea (AMIK) included the embassy, KMAG, the local office of the Economic Cooperation Administration (ECA), and an administrative service organization, the Joint Administrative Services (JAS). According to the *Foreign Service List* for July 1, 1950, the embassy had 108 personnel. KMAG had an authorized strength of 472 officers and men (Sawyer, *Military Advisers,* p. 50).

3. The relationship between the embassy and KMAG was described by Sawyer (*Military Advisers,* pp. 46-47) as follows:

Originally the Department of the Army had intended to place KMAG under Ambassador Muccio's administrative direction while permitting General MacArthur to exercise operational control. However, MacArthur's experience with the Joint U.S. Military Advisory Group to the Republic of the Philippines (JUSMAGPHIL) made him reluctant to accept a similar arrangement for KMAG. In the case of JUSMAGPHIL, the JCS had laid out the group's missions and MacArthur's role has been limited to minor matters having little to do with the major task of advising the Philippine forces. Unless he were granted authority to assign the objectives for KMAG, MacArthur felt that the group should be controlled by the U.S. Ambassador. To safeguard military interests, KMAG could be granted the right to communicate directly with the JCS on military matters, MacArthur continued, and he recommended that KMAG forward all military messages and reports through the Far East Command.

The KMAG's relationship to Ambassador Muccio and the American mission in Korea underwent a quick change. Since Muccio had the responsibility for carrying out U.S. policy in Korea and KMAG was an element of AMIK, he was given operational control of the group. For administrative purposes KMAG was established as an Army Administrative Area, Foreign Assignment Activity, directly under the Department of the Army. The Far East Command's responsibility was limited to the logistic support of KMAG to the water line of Korea and to the emergency evacuation of U.S. personnel from the country if the need arose. Since the Far East Command was the only U.S. military command in the area, KMAG did maintain close liaison with MacArthur's headquarters. KMAG representatives made periodic visits to Tokyo to discuss and co-ordinate evacuation plans and to keep the Far East Command informed on political and military developments in Korea.

Although the KMAG operated under the control of Ambassador Muccio, the internal direction of the group was entirely in General Robert's hands. The relationship between AMIK and KMAG centered on U.S. military assistance to Korea. All matters relating to the means, methods, and degree of such aid were of mutual interest and were carefully co-ordinated by the two agencies either at formal meetings or on a personal basis. On most other matters, particularly those involving military command or administration, the advisory group reported directly to the Pentagon.

4. For a critical portrayal of the U.S. embassy in Korea, see John C. Caldwell, *The Korea Story* (Chicago: Henry Regnery, 1952).

CHAPTER TWO

1. An official account of the initial actions at KMAG headquarters states:

Probably the first American in Seoul to learn of the invasion was the KMAG radio operator, who received a message from the Ongjin advisory detachment at about 0600 on 25 June. Soon all the KMAG officers and men in Seoul were hurrying to their posts. Initially, there was a decided air of scepticism among the KMAG staff since border raids had been common for some time. But when reports of the other attacks all along the parallel came filtering in during the next few hours, the doubt faded. The number and size of the offensives coupled with the fact that the attacks were being made along the natural invasion routes into South Korea quickly ruled out the possibility of mere raids [Sawyer, *Military Advisers*, pp. 118-19].

2. Colonel Sterling Wright went to Japan to see his family off to the United States. Wright's own return to America for reassignment had been delayed until the arrival of a new commanding general for KMAG. Ibid., p. 119.

3. Yu Chae-hŭng (1921–) graduated from the Japanese Military Academy (1940) and attained the rank of major in the Japanese army. After World War II, Yu graduated from the U.S. Military Government's English Language School in south Korea and was the first commander of the South Korean Constabulary. General Yu graduated from the U.S. Army's Command and General Staff School (1954) and served as vice-chief of staff, commander of the 1st Army, and chairman of the joint chiefs of staff, retiring in 1960 with the rank of lieutenant general. Shifting to a diplomatic career, Yu was South Korea's ambassador to Thailand, Sweden, and Italy during the 1960s. In 1971 he was appointed minister of defense.

4. After this conversation Counselor Drumright called Ambassador Muccio at his residence and informed him of the invasion reports. Both men then went to the chancery. E. F. Drumright, manuscript review, January 1971.

5. For Jack James's account of his scoop, see "U.P.'s Jack James

Was Going to a Picnic June 25," *Editor and Publisher*, July 22, 1950.
p. 10.

6. The Associated Press reporter was O. H. P. King. King described his adventures during the summer of 1950 in *Tail of the Tiger* (Caldwell, Ida.: Caxton Printers, 1961).

7. The first embassy report to Washington was drafted after this conversation. Mr. Drumright recalled the sequence of events as follows: "I got the Ambassador on the phone at his residence about 8:00 A.M., expressing the view that this was an all-out invasion. His response was, 'Let's go to the office.' We arrived shortly after eight and just before nine, after talking by phone with KMAG and the Army attaché, I drafted the urgent message that was to alert Washington to [the] North Korean invasion." E. F. Drumright, manuscript review, January 1971.

8. Counselor Drumright recalls no intentional delay because of the James cable. "Muccio and I did not know what message James filed or just when." E. F. Drumright, manuscript review, January 1971.

9. The first embassy cable to Washington on June 25 stated:

According to Korean Army reports which are partly confirmed by Korean Military Advisory Group field advisers reports, North Korean Forces invaded Republic of Korea territory at several points this morning. Action was initiated about 4 A.M. Ongjin was blasted by North Korean artillery fire. About 6 A.M. North Korean infantry commenced crossing the (38th) parallel in the Ongjin area, Kaesong area, and Chunchon area, and an amphibious landing was reportedly made south of Kangnung on the east coast. Kaesong was reportedly captured at 9 A.M., with some ten North Korean tanks participating in the operation. North Korean forces, spear-headed by tanks, are reportedly closing in on Chunchon. Details of the fighting in the Kangnung area are unclear, although it seems that North Korean forces have cut the highway. I am conferring with Korean Military Advisory Group advisers and Korean officials this morning concerning the situation.

It would appear from the nature of the attack and the manner in which it was launched, that it constitutes an all-out offensive against the Republic of Korea. MUCCIO [U.S., Department of State, *United States Policy in the Korean Crisis* (Washington, D.C.: U.S. Government Printing Office, 1950), p. 1].

10. The first embassy announcement over the mission radio was made at 1:00 P.M. It stated:

Stand by for a special announcement.
WVTP has been authorized by the Ambassador to make the following announcement.
At 4 o'clock this morning, North Korean armed forces began unprovoked attacks against defense positions of the Republic of Korea at several points

along the 38th degree parallel. Fighting is now in progress at several points along the parallel.
Korean defense forces are taking up prepared positions to resist northern aggression. Both Korean officials and the security forces are handling the situation calmly and with ability. There is no reason for alarm. As yet it cannot be determined whether the Northern Communists intend to precipitate all out warfare. New developments will be reported regularly over this station. Please keep tuned to WVTP.
Mission personnel are advised to travel about as little as necessary. The Ambassador requests that Mission personnel remain at home or at their posts, as the situation may dictate. Our next announcement will be heard at three o'clock this afternoon. [Muccio to State Department, no. 926, June 25, 1950.]

11. The U.N. commission had noted tension and "much military posturing on both sides of the parallel" in its 1949 report. To enable the commission to evaluate the military situation, the Indian representative had suggested the need for military experts in the commission. The General Assembly resolution of October 21, 1949, reflecting concern over the severe fighting of 1949, extended the life of the U.N. commission and instructed it to "observe and report any developments which might lead to or otherwise involve military conflict in Korea." Shiv Dayal, *India's Role in the Korean Question* (Delhi: S. Chand, 1959), pp. 67-68.

On March 4, 1950, Secretary-General Lie announced that "in compliance with a request from the U.N. Commission on Korea, eight observers were being sent to Korea to observe clashes along the 38th parallel." U.S., Department of State, *A Historical Summary of United States-Korean Relations* (Washington, D.C.: U.S. Government Printing Office, 1962), p. 77.

The two Australian officers were the only military experts who had actually reached Korea when the war broke out, having arrived in early June. Their report was crucial to the deliberations of the U.N. commission in Seoul on June 25 and equally important in the Security Council debate over Korea. The field observers began their trip along the border on June 9 and submitted their report to the U.N. commission on June 24. The report stated:

General situation along parallel. Principal impression left with observers after their field tour is that South Korea Army is organized entirely for defense and is in no condition to carry out attack on large scale against forces of North. Impression is based upon following main observations:
1. South Korea Army in all sectors is disposed in depth. Parallel is guarded on southern side by small bodies troops located in scattered outposts together

with roving patrol. There is no concentration of troops and no massing for attack visible at any point.

2. At several points, North Korean forces are in effective possession of salients on south side parallel, occupation in at least one case being of fairly recent date. There is no evidence that South Korean forces have taken any steps for or making any preparation to eject North Korean forces from any of these salients.

3. Proportion of South Korean forces are actively engaged in rounding up guerrilla bands that have infiltrated into the mountainous area in the eastern sectors. It was ascertained that these bands are in possession of demolition equipment and are more heavily armed than on previous occasions.

4. So far as equipment of South Korea forces concerned, in absence of armour, air support, and heavy artillery, any action with object of invasion would, by any military standards, be impossible.

5. South Korea Army does not appear to be in possession of military or other supplies that would indicate preparation for large-scale attack. In particular, there is no sign of any dumping of supplies or ammunition, petrol, oil, lubricant, in forward areas. Roads generally are little used and apart from convoy four trucks taking company from Kangnung westward to join rounding up guerrilla band, no concentration transport anywhere encountered.

6. In general, attitude South Korean commanders is one of vigilant defense. Their instructions do not go beyond retirement in case of attack upon previously prepared positions.

7. There is no indication of any extensive reconnaissance being carried out northward by South Korea Army nor of any undue excitement or activity at divisional headquarters or regimental levels to suggest preparation for offensive activity. Observers were freely admitted to all sections various headquarters including operations room.

8. Observers made special point inquiring what information was coming in regarding situation north of parallel. In some sectors it had been reported that civilians had recently been removed from areas adjoining parallel to north to depths varying from 4 to 8 kilometers. Another report received during night Thursday 22 June at regimental headquarters Ongjin was to effect that there was increased military activity in vicinity Chuyia about 4 kilometers north parallel. No reports, however, have been received of any unusual activity on part of North Korean forces that would indicate any impending change in general situation along parallel [U.N. Commission on Korea, June 29, 1950, "The Acting Chairman of the United Nations Commission on Korea to the President of the Security Council," S-1518, in State Department, *United States Policy in the Korean Crisis,* pp. 21-22].

For a critical assessment of this report, see Jon Halliday, "The United Nations and Korea," in Frank Baldwin, ed., *Without Parallel: The American-Korean Relationship since 1945* (New York: Pantheon, 1974).

12. See Appendix.

13. Harold Noble's favorable assessment of the performance of the ROK Army in the first days of the war, a theme repeated in chapters

3, 6, and 7, is significantly different from the emphasis of early KMAG reports from Korea, the evaluation made by General MacArthur on June 29, and most reports by American journalists. General Mac-Arthur's report was the most important and indelible negative appraisal of the performance and capabilities of the ROK Army.

Official U.S. observers and press accounts emphasized the failure of the South Korean forces to stop the NKPA and the confusion and "rout" aspects of their retreat from north of Seoul to south of the Han River.

The KMAG and MacArthur reports accurately concluded that by June 29-30 the ROK Army was a shattered military force incapable of defeating the NKPA without the intervention of U.S. ground forces. That part of the ROK Army had stubbornly resisted was less important, and thus overlooked, in the estimates of impending defeat.

However, Harold Noble's description of determined fighting and superior performance by certain units and commanders of the ROK Army during the first three days of the fighting, prior to the visit by General MacArthur and his staff, have been substantiated by later writers. See Sawyer, *Military Advisers,* p. 116; and Roy E. Appleman, *South to the Naktong, North to the Yalu* (Washington, D.C.: U.S. Government Printing Office, 1960), chap. 3 and pp. 262-63. The Apple-man work, the official U.S. Army history of the first six months of the war, will be referred to frequently for descriptions of military developments. The book is notably objective and fair regarding North Korean military forces and operations, an accomplishment rarely achieved by other academic studies of the Korean War or of North Korea.

Everett Drumright made the following comment on this section: "The ROK 'Army' was not an 'army' in military parlance. When the composition and arms of the ROK forces were described to General MacArthur when he came to Suwon to assess the situation, he commented, 'Why the ROK forces are nothing more than a constabulary.' So they were, and purposely so by U.S. intentional act." E. F. Drumright, manuscript review, January 1971.

14. President Syngman Rhee's cabinet in June 1950 was as follows: Acting Prime Minister and Minister of Defense Sin Sŏng-mo; Foreign Ministry, Ben Limb (Im Pyŏng-jik); Home Ministry, Paek Sŏng-uk; Finance, Ch'oe Sun-ju; Justice, Yi U-ik; Education, Dr. George Paik (Paek Nak-jun); Agriculture and Forestry, Yun Yŏng-sŏn; Commerce and Industry, Kim Hun; Transportation, Kim Sŏk-kwan; Communications, Chang Ki-yŏng.

15. The embassy might have had close and better contact with

President Rhee if Harold Noble had been in Korea on June 25. Counselor Drumright noted: "If Noble had been in Seoul that Sunday (he
was in Japan) we doubtless would have had contact with President
Rhee. But our contacts that day and Monday and Tuesday were almost exclusively with the Korean military. I do not recall any personal contact with Rhee that Sunday...." E. F. Drumright, manuscript
review, January 1971.

However, Ambassador Muccio did see President Rhee during the day
on June 25 and later in the evening for the meeting described in chap-
ter 2. Ambassador John J. Muccio, private interview, Washington,
D.C., September 30, 1971; and Walter Karig, Malcolm W. Cagle, and
Frank A. Manson, *Battle Report: The War in Korea* (New York:
Rinehart, 1952), p. 22.

Defense Minister Sin met with President Rhee and reported the battle
situation, conceding initial reverses but predicting victory in a few
days. Rhee ordered Sin to request U.S. military aid and to convene a
meeting of senior military men, including individuals not on active duty,
to consider war strategy. That meeting was held on the morning of June
26 and resulted in a controversial decision, apparently advocated by Sin
and Chief of Staff Ch'ae Pyŏng-dŏk, to launch a counterattack against
the North Korean forces. War History Compilation Committee (hereafter WHCC), *Han'guk chŏnjaeng-sa* [History of the Korean War], 2
vols. (Seoul: Ministry of National Defense, 1967-68), 2:225.

16. Clarence Ryee, director of public information in 1950, disputes
this description of President Rhee's state of mind on June 25, 1950. Rhee
writes in a letter of January 25, 1971:

> I was with President Rhee from the afternoon of June 25th to 6:00 A.M.,
> June 26th at the Kyongmudae....
> President Rhee was determined not to leave Seoul. He said he would stay
> and die with the people. It was only through the repeated advice and reason-
> ing of myself, Secretary Whang, and Mrs. Rhee, that he finally consented to
> leave. So he left Seoul in the early morning of the 27th.
> *To say that President Rhee was scared and panicky was far from the truth.*
> When Ambassador Muccio came to the Kyongmudae, the President only asked
> him his opinion concerning the situation. The President did not say he was
> leaving Seoul or ask Muccio to leave together. I know because I was with the
> President all this while. I remember he only advised Muccio to evacuate em-
> bassy officials and U.S. women and children [emphasis in original].

However, Noble's account is substantiated by Ambassador Muccio's
actions on the evening of June 25, and his later recollections of events.
See note 24, below.

17. Syngman Rhee and the former Francesca Donner were married in New York in October 1934.

18. Syngman Rhee (Yi Sŭng-man) (1875-1965) was educated at the Methodist Paejae School in Seoul. Imprisoned for more than six years for antigovernment activity, Rhee was released in 1904 and went to America. After an unsuccessful appeal to President Theodore Roosevelt to support Korea's independence, Rhee completed his education, receiving his B A. from George Washington University (1907), an M.A. from Harvard (1908), and a Ph.D. from Princeton (1910). Dr. Rhee returned to Korea in 1910 to work with the YMCA, but Japanese opposition forced him to leave for the United States again in 1912.

For thirty-three years Syngman Rhee advocated Korean independence in a vain attempt to enlist American and foreign support for Korea's cause. After World War II he returned to Korea to lead conservative political forces, first in opposition to American policies and later to victory in the 1948 American-sponsored elections that marked the division of the Korean peninsula.

Named the first president of the Republic, Rhee was subsequently re-elected in 1952, 1956, and 1960. However, the fraudulent 1960 elections led to the April student uprising, the nullification of the election, and his exile to Hawaii.

19. Paek Sŏng-uk (1896–), a Buddhist scholar and leader, was later president of Tongguk University.

20. Sin Sŏng-mo (1891-1960) graduated from the Posŏng School in Seoul. He fled to Vladivostok after the Japanese annexation of Korea in 1910 and participated in anti-Japanese activities. Sin graduated from maritime schools in Shanghai, Nanking, and London and became an officer in the British merchant marine. He returned to Korea in 1945 and entered politics, serving as home minister (1948), minister of defense (1949-51), and acting prime minister (1950).

21. Yi Pŏm-sŏk (1900-72) went to China in 1915 and graduated from the Yunnan Military Academy in 1919. He was associated with Korean troops in China and became an instructor at the Loyang Military Academy in 1933 and a leader of the Korean Restoration Army in China in the 1940s. Yi returned to Korea in 1946 and was supported by the U.S. military government as a leader of a rightist youth association, the Racial Youth Corps. He was prime minister (1948-April 1950) and defense minister (1948-February 1949) before the Korean War. Yi was a leader in the Liberal party and served as home minister briefly in 1952 before losing favor with President Rhee.

At their meeting the afternoon of June 25 President Rhee requested Yi Pŏm-sŏk's assistance with military planning. On the basis of that request, although not an active-duty military officer or a member of the cabinet, Yi participated in the military strategy session described above and took the initiative for an extraordinary cabinet meeting held early on June 27.

22. Cho Pyŏng-ok (Chough Pyŏng-ok, 1894-1960) was educated at Christian schools in Korea and studied in the United States. Cho was imprisoned twice by the Japanese for nationalist activities. After 1945 he was a co-founder of the Korean Democratic party and chief of the Police Affairs Section of the U.S. military government. Cho served as a special presidential ambassador and South Korea's representative to the United Nations before June 1950. After his term as home minister (July 1950–May 1951) Cho split with Syngman Rhee and became a leader of the opposition Democratic party and a four-term national assemblyman. Cho was the Democratic party's presidential candidate in 1960 but died of illness before the election.

Cho's actions during the first months of the war, including his meeting with President Rhee on June 25, are described in a fragmentary fashion in his memoirs. See Cho Pyŏng-ok, *Naŭi hoegorok* [My Recollections] (Seoul: Mingyosa, 1959), pp. 280-311.

23. Ambassador Muccio had taken several actions not mentioned by Mr. Noble prior to this evening meeting with President Rhee, including the following:

(1) Cabled the State Department to support a KMAG request to General MacArthur's headquarters for the immediate shipment of a ten days' supply of ammunition to Pusan. U.S., Department of State, *Chronology of Developments Following Communist Attack on the Republic of Korea, June 24-27, 1950* (hereafter cited as State Department, *Chronology*), p. 2.

(2) Met with the U.N. commission to discuss the invasion reports and possible courses of action.

(3) Warned Washington of the immediate need for U.S. air support, a familiar refrain by ROK officials and embassy officers in the following days. His cable, sent at 7:00 P.M. on June 25, stated:

Wish to inform Department that with clearing weather setting in about midday North Korean Air Force became ominously active in Seoul area. Action was initiated at 1135 this morning, when two North Korean fighters buzzed Kimpo Airport but left without bombing or strafing. Commencing this afternoon sometime after 4:00 o'clock four North Korean fighter planes strafed Kimpo Airport, making five separate runs. Airport building was slightly damaged. Standard Vacuum Oil Co. fuel truck destroyed. POL dump ignited and MATS C-54 plane which was on ground undergoing minor repairs had one engine destroyed and one wing badly damaged. Also North Korean fighters strafed Seoul airstrip, inflicting slight damage on seven T-6 aircraft. Embassy had warned C-54 this morning to leave Kimpo, and Defense Ministry was strongly advised this morning to disperse T-6's on more southerly fields. Embassy without information why steps not taken to move C-54 and T-6's earlier in day.

In view of today's air activities, it seems logical conclude North Koreans intend make full use their complete air superiority. Danger of this situation has been pointed out on several occasions to Department and defense agencies. I can only express hope that some positive and speedy action be taken at this late date to remedy this deficiency which is exceedingly serious threat and handicap to gallant ROK forces who are otherwise capable of putting up most effective opposition. As Department doubtless aware, Rhee and other Korean officials will look to U.S. for air assistance above all else. Future course of hostilities may depend largely on whether U.S. will or will not give adequate air assistance [Muccio to Acheson, no. 935, June 25, 1950].

24. Ambassador Muccio was not aware when he left the meeting with President Rhee that they had surmounted "the first of many crises," if in fact his words were the decisive influence on Rhee. Muccio was under the impression that he had failed to convince the president to stay in Seoul. The ambassador cabled Washington of President Rhee's decision to move his government to Taejŏn and his own decision to remain in Seoul. Muccio's report was received in Washington at 12:26 P.M., June 25, and increased the sense of "imminent collapse" among U.S. government leaders. State Department, *Chronology*, p. 2.

A request to examine the text of this message, no. 940, was denied with the following explanation:

In this telegram the Ambassador reported candidly on a discussion he had with the President of Korea. The telegram expresses the Ambassador's views and judgments for the guidance of the Secretary of State and reports matters imparted in confidence to the Ambassador and which became known to him only because of his official position as the representative of his Government. At the time of its dispatch, the telegram was classified "Secret."

After carefully re-examining the above-described telegram in accordance with the criteria set out in Executive Order 10501, as amended, it has been determined that its continued classification is necessary and that the document must be kept secret. Accordingly, a copy cannot be made available to you at this time [Letter, J. Edward Lyerly, deputy legal adviser for management, Department of State, November 19, 1971].

Ambassador Muccio recalled that he went to the Kyŏngmudae in response to a telephone call from President Rhee. The president informed Muccio that a cabinet meeting had been held and it had been decided that he and the government should move from Seoul. Ambassador Muccio disagreed with this decision. Muccio pointed out that South Korean troops were fighting well; not one unit had surrendered or defected to the north. That display of morale and determination was important. The ambassador said that if President Rhee fled from Seoul, his flight would soon be known and "there wouldn't be a South Korean soldier facing north." The whole ROK Army would quit fighting, Muccio argued. However, President Rhee insisted he would leave Seoul. Ambassador Muccio stated, "Well, Mr. President, you do what you want, but I am going to stay in Seoul." Ambassador John J. Muccio, private interview, Washington, D.C., September 30, 1970.

25. Ambassador Muccio reported his decision to Washington at 1:00 A.M., June 26, as follows: "In view of threat from Uijongbu area about 17 miles directly north of Seoul where North Korean tanks reportedly massed, I have reluctantly decided to carry out evacuation of dependent women and children tomorrow morning through Port of Inchon. There are three vessels in Inchon Harbor which will be used to transport these women and children to Japan. Evacuation is being coordinated with CINCFE." Muccio to Acheson, no. 941, June 26, 1950.

26. Additional details on the evacuation plan are in Sawyer, *Military Advisers*, pp. 110-12.

27. An adviser to the embassy and his wife were one of the married couples evacuated from Seoul. He wrote a detailed record of his actions and impressions during the first four days of the war on June 30, 1952, while in a rest camp in Kyoto, Japan. He was moved there after being flown from Korea to Fukuoka, Kyushu. The personal letter has been made available on the condition that the author's name not be given.

The adviser learned of the fighting about two o'clock Sunday afternoon. He went to the embassy to confirm the reports and then returned home to tell his wife the latest news.

Telephone call. Mrs. Holster asks me for a six o'clock meeting to discuss the establishment of an air-raid warden organization in E.R. 11—the US compound where we have lived for the past 15 months. At the meeting we divide the area in several blocks and assign each household space in the few available shelters. Our house has no basement. We are informed that there is no reason to be nervous. In my capacity as blockwarden I check the blackout in my district, assure everybody that these are just routine matters and finally have supper at about ten o'clock. The eleven o'clock radio repeats the old news. To go to bed is one thing; to sleep another thing. At any rate we go to bed.

11:30. Another telephone call [which said], "Come at once to the embassy. Do you have transportation?" We have our good old fur-lined jeep. A hundred times we discussed the question as to whether or not we should sell it before it is too late. There is no longer a great demand for jeeps in Korea. And all these discussions had resulted in the belief that it might be wise to keep the jeep for contingency number one. Now we are confronted with contingency number one. God bless the jeep! The jeep will stay in front of our house to be available at any moment. "May I ask for transportation?" "You will be picked up at once." I dress and leave the house. A jeep with the driver and two armed guards waits in front of our house. We rush to the Embassy. The city is completely dark. Trucks loaded with troops move in long convoys to the North.

In the Embassy building armed guards take me at once to the security officer. I am instructed to check the files of the Legal Section and to select certain documents for destruction. Here are our file cabinets. They contain the work of four years—memoranda, agreements, ordinances. I insist that my secretary assist me. She arrives in ten minutes and we work like madmen. If we throw everything on the heap of documents which is designed for destruction the work of the Legal Section will be finished. It is not so easy to liquidate in a few minutes the work of a few years. Peggy and I try to save what can be saved of our files. At 1:00 A.M. Donald Macdonald (one of the brilliant vice consuls who have become our close friends) comes to my office and informs me that the Ambassador had just issued an order to the effect that all dependents have to meet at 3:00 A.M. at certain centers in order to be evacuated. Donald tells me that the news from the front is bad. The enemy is 18 miles north of Seoul. The government decided to move to Taejon.

Telephone call home. My wife objects to being separated from me. Other women decide to stay with their husbands. The discussion becomes rather stormy and excited. "When are you coming home?" "As soon as I am through here." "I won't take any steps for my evacuation until you are back." "You are to be ready for evacuation at three o'clock." And when all my words prove futile, I fall back on the good old Prussian tradition, "evacuation is an order" and "Befehl is Befehl." (That does it.)

Female employees of the Mission have the choice between staying with the Mission and evacuation with the dependents. I try to persuade Peggy to go. She will not listen. Most of the girls decide to stay at the job. Now we are no longer so selective as far as our files are concerned. To hell with the Legal Section, ECA Mission to Korea! I find in our steel-cabinet the diplomatic passports of Stanley Earl—our Labor Adviser—and Mrs. Earl. I call him over the phone; he will be in the Embassy in ten minutes to pick up the passports. Peggy and I carry the files which are going to be destroyed to the filing room; we lock room 402—the work of the Legal Section has come to an end. It is two o'clock in the morning. Earl takes me in his car back to ER II.

At home I find my wife packing. One footlocker and one suitcase. I learn from her that each dependent is authorized to take sixty-five pounds and hand luggage. That is contrary to my information which reads that a person is permitted take with him only what he can carry by hand. I rush to the Finance House to get clear instructions on this question. We call the Embassy because there is general confusion on this point. Her information is wrong. Not more than each person can carry. There will be no porter service at Inch'on. Inch'on—that means evacuation by boat. I bring this news to my wife who realizes that she has to abandon her footlocker.

After putting his wife on one of the buses bound for Ascom City and evacuation from Inch'ŏn, he returned home.

My bed is still warm when I come home early in the morning. It is less than six hours that I was summoned to the Embassy in order to clear my files. At five o'clock Monday morning I get a big American station on my shortwave radio. Truman returned to Washington. An emergency meeting of the security council of the UN will be held tomorrow. My impression is that we here in Seoul are in the center of a global crisis. If they succeed in catching more than 2000 Americans (including almost 700 women and children) in Seoul or Inch'on, public opinion back home will insist on an immediate American intervention and an intervention may mean World War III. The success of our evacuation is a problem of world-wide significance. Another question is whether the U.S. Government shall evacuate its officials from Seoul. Can we pull out and leave the Koreans alone after all that has happened in these 4½ years? The Koreans are not responsible for the artificial division of their country into two states. . . . And this war between North and South is a Korean civil war from a superficial point of view only. It is Russia's war with the Western World. Here we are the "long-noses" as the Korean children used to call us. We were the big shots; we taught them how to run a country and how to build an army. We went from one cocktail party to another, lived a life of abundance and glamour among the misery of the Korean people. Shall we now take our cars, drive to Kimp'o and fly home? One does not sleep very well under such conditions [Adviser's manuscript, June 30, 1950].

According to an official history, "a total of 2,001 people—1,527 of them U.S. nationals—were evacuated, all of them to Japan, 923 by air and the remainder by sea transportation." James F. Schnabel, *Policy and Direction: The First Year* (Washington, D.C.: U.S. Government Printing Office, 1972), p. 71.

28. The exact number of women and children evacuated to the Ascom area and subsequently by ship from Inch'ŏn to Japan is uncertain. Estimates range from 682 to about 700.

CHAPTER THREE

1. The six Methodist missionaries were Nellie Dyer, A. Kristian Jensen, Dr. E .R. Kisch, Mary H. Rosser, Bertha A. Smith, and Lawrence A. Zellers. All were stationed in Kaesŏng except Kristian Jensen, who lived in Seoul but had accompanied Lawrence Zellers on a trip to Kaesŏng on June 24. Dr. Kisch died in North Korea in June 1951; the other five were "detained" in North Korea until repatriated in April 1953.

Their capture and confinement are described in a pamphlet by A.

Kristian Jensen, *Internment, North Korea* (New Cumberland, Pa.: By the author, 301 Market Street, 1953) ; in a biography of Dr. Kisch by T. A. Brumbaugh, *My Marks and Scars I Carry*: *The Story of Ernst Kisch* (New York: Friendship Press, 1969) ; and in an account by an Australian Catholic priest, Philip Crosbie, *Pencilling Prisoner* (Melbourne: Hawthorne Press, 1954).

The escape of KMAG Capt. Joseph R. Darrigo from Kaesŏng is described in Sawyer, *Military Advisers*, p. 115.

2. The *Reinholt* left Inch'ŏn about 4:30 P.M., June 26. Robert F. Futrell, *The U.S. Air Force in Korea* (New York: Duell, Sloan & Pearce, 1961), pp. 11-12.

3. For additional information on the evacuation, see Sawyer, *Military Advisers*, pp. 121-22; and Karig, Cagle, and Manson, *Battle Report*, pp. 25-30.

4. The battle for the Ŭijŏngbu corridor is described in Appleman, *South to the Naktong*, pp. 28-30. Appleman has concluded that General Yi Hyŏng-gŭn was justified in declining to attack. Appleman writes: "Quite obviously this attack could not have succeeded. The really fatal error had been General Ch'ae's plan of operation giving the 2nd Division responsibility for the P'och'on road sector when it was quite apparent that it could not arrive in strength to meet that responsibility by the morning of 26 June." Appleman, *South to the Naktong*, p. 30.

Yi Hyŏng-gŭn (1920–) graduated from the Japanese Military Academy in 1943 and reached the rank of captain. He was later chief of staff of the ROK Army and ambassador to England.

5. See Appleman, *South to the Naktong*, p. 24.

6. Ch'ae Pyŏng-dŏk (1916-50) graduated from the Japanese Military Academy and was commanding officer of the Inch'ŏn arsenal in 1945. Ch'ae held various positions in the South Korean constabulary in 1946-47. In 1948 he was promoted to brigadier general in the ROK Army, and in 1949 to major general and named chief of staff.

7. The ROK Ministry of Defense's official history makes no mention of an appearance by General Ch'ae before the cabinet on June 26. Noble may be referring to the meeting of senior military leaders noted above.

8. According to Clarence Ryee (letter, January 25, 1971), the ROK Army commandeered HLKA on June 25: "On Sunday morning, at 11:30 A.M., June 25th, I received a call from the Defense Minister, Sin Song-mo, saying that the war situation was very grave and that the army must take over the radio station and the information media. And he said he got approval from the President. I immediately called the President to check whether he approved. . . . I found out it was

true so I called back Minister Sin and gave him my consent."

9. The adviser to the embassy quoted above was among the embassy staff evacuated from Kimp'o on June 27. He described the events of June 26 and early June 27 as follows:

Monday is one of these beautiful Korean summer days. The week before we had a lot of rain and the roads to the North are probably a morass. The rainy season started a week ago when we attended a banquet in honor of John Foster Dulles at Chan Duk Palace. For five days it rained almost without interruption. "It Rains Rice," said our agricultural experts. Saturday the weather changed. The sky is steel blue. The weather is ideal for air attacks by day and night. The North has airplanes, but the South has neither airplanes nor anti-aircraft. Another serious handicap. It is an open secret that we failed to provide the South Korean Government with tanks and planes because we were afraid that the Rhee Government would start an offensive against North Korea at the moment at which it considered itself adequately equipped for such an attack. Those who read Rhee's public statements during the last six months will admit that such a fear was not unjustified. Today it looks almost as if the lack of tanks and airplanes may prove disastrous not only for the cause of the South Korean Government but also for the policy of the United States in the Far East. The decision of the US Government to reject Rhee's request for tanks and airplanes is indicative of a basic inconsistency in our Korean policy. Our Korean policy is characterized by three main points: we propagate the unification of the Korean peninsula, we support the Rhee Government and we are opposed to a war between the North and the South. Although the Rhee government pays lip service to the idea of a peaceful unification, it brands all those who sponsor the slightest effort to come to terms with the North as Communists and national traitors. Our friendship with the Rhee Government is a somewhat unilateral love affair. We support the Rhee Government, but the Rhee Government does not subscribe to our line of policy. There is so much talk about "puppet governments" and "satellites." We call Kim Il Song a satellite and the Russians call Syngman Rhee an American satellite. But there is a slight difference between a Russian and an American puppet government. A Russian satellite does exactly what he is ordered to do, and an American satellite does exactly the opposite of what he is supposed to do. Communist satellites are subject to the party discipline; democratic satellites can always plead that the principles of democracy exclude interference with the policy of another state. The word "democratic satellite" is self-contradictory. The Rhee Government was neither democratic nor a satellite government. When all this is over, it may be worthwhile to find out the reasons for the structural weakness of our position in backward countries. Korea is the test case; she has been the test case for almost five years. . . .

At my home I meet Mrs. Luise Kim nee Maser, who came to pay a visit to my wife. She cries when I inform her of the events of last night. Mrs. Kim is a German who married a Korean doctor in Berlin at the end of the war. After the fall of Berlin she was evacuated to Manchuria by the Russians as a "Japanese national." After the conquest of Manchuria by the Russian Army three months later she fled with her husband to Seoul. "Do you think I have to live through this a third time?" she asked me. What shall I answer? Her husband is the director of the police hospital; she has two little girls. The chances are slim that her husband will survive in case Seoul will be taken by the Northern Army. I know only too well what happened in the fall of 1948 when the Communists temporarily took over Yosu and Sunch'on. All government officials were shot. In the eyes of the North Koreans affiliation with the police is worse than anything else. No quarters are given in this cruel war. Strange—I had not thought of that during the last 24 hours. The jails in Seoul are overcrowded with political prisoners. Six weeks ago I inspected a police jail in Inch'on. The prisoners there were living under conditions which I hesitate to describe in this letter. It reminds you of a sense of the Divina Comedia. Goya could have painted what we saw there. What is going to happen to the almost 10,000 political prisoners in case the capital is to be surrendered? It is hard to imagine the acts of vengeance and hatred which the people will commit if they survive the conquest of Seoul by their "liberators." But will they survive the fall of Seoul? Modern wars are cruel; modern civil wars are extremely cruel. An inter-Korean war—to think of it is a nightmare. . . .

I ask our houseboy, Paek, to help pack the new suitcase. Paek's command of the English language is restricted to two words "who?" and "ok." "Who" stands for "I don't understand"; "ok" is self-explanatory. You can rely on his "who"; to rely on his "ok" involves a considerable risk. My wife's brown silk handbag is the first thing which I pack in the new suitcase. It is a strange experience (I had it in other emergency situations of my life). I concentrate all my attention on wholly insignificant small matters—a kind of escapism which helps me to endure the constant strain. There is enough space for a few of my wife's dresses. I have to pick three or four out of crowded footlockers and trunks. Husbands will realize what that assignment means; bachelors will never understand my problem. And there is Gregory Henderson's wooden Chinese sculpture. Gregory is another of the young Vice-consuls I mentioned before. Two weeks ago he was transferred to Pusan and he deposited his art collection with us. Extremely brilliant, interested in music and art, a most courageous fighter for freedom, justice, the rule of law and all those basic values which are at stake in the fight of western democracy against totalitarianism, Gregory became very close to us during the last year. There is a lot of talk about the deficiencies of our foreign service. My experience in Seoul has been that the selection of the young officers is excellent. Our young friends Macdonald, Prendergast and Henderson have the chance of their life these days. Donald has been attached to the Ambassador, Curt to the counselor of the Embassy, Gregory is the representative of the State Department in Pusan. Evacuation or no evacuation—they will stay in Korea. Shall I take Gregory's sculpture? It is a beautiful piece of art and I see Gregory's happy eyes when I will turn over his favored curio to him. But is it worthwhile? About a week ago, Dr. Salmony arrived from the States. . . . He is a museum expert and he is supposed to assist . . . in cataloguing the treasures of the National Museum. The Korean director of the National Museum studied in Europe for eight years and went "only twice" to the States on grants. I realized the urgent necessity of Dr. Salmony's mission to Korea and I ask myself: how many Museum experts did the Russians send to North Korea last month? Shall I consult Dr. Salmony? I am afraid that I will lose my temper. I put the sculpture in my suitcase; everything is set for the next emergency. . . .

But there are also serious discussions. Whatever the future may bring, our policy in Korea is bankrupt. It is to a large extent our fault. Korea has always been at the end of the agenda. The 38th parallel, the idea of trusteeship, the establishment of the Joint Commission and all the other basic decisions on Korea were not thought through. Nor did Korea fit into the ECA scheme. To assume that Korea would be economically self-sufficient in July 1952, was utopian. But this assumption was the basis of all ECA activities for the last 18 months. We planned the building of fertilizer, cement and glass factories. We expected to enlarge power plants and to modernize coal and tungsten mines. Korea was in a process of "industrial revolution"; we had enforced upon the Koreans a policy of austerity. All these plans were based on the theory that South Korea and North Korea would continue to be separated states. Politically minded members of the ECA Mission had repeatedly questioned whether this assumption was realistic. They pointed out that it was most likely that long before July 1, 1952 the South would have conquered North Korea or the North would have conquered South Korea. In the congressional discussions a few weeks ago the question was raised whether the building of fertilizer, glass and cement factories would not provide the Communists with installations built with money of the American taxpayer. All these warnings remained without effect. We continued to think in categories of years. We stuck to our long-term program. The Koreans had always insisted on a short-term program. The Koreans had emphasized the necessity of preparing for war. We were the ones who had operated in a political vacuum. About one week ago I discussed all these questions with Azel Hatch, the competent director of our mining and industry division. I warned against the danger that we may alienate the Korean people by insisting on our program of austerity and thus play the game of the Communists. The work of the ECA Mission to Korea was dominated and controlled by economic and technical experts. It lacked political insight. I paraphrased Clemenceau's famous words that "war is too serious a matter for generals" by stating that "ECA is too serious a matter to be entrusted to economists." Before I drive home I learn that the next night may prove crucial. If the South Korean troops are driven back again, Seoul will be lost.

On the evacuation flight to Japan, he pondered the conflicting priorities and responsibilities of the American involvement in Korea and wondered about the days ahead.

The much overstressed principle of non-intervention is a hangover from traditional diplomacy. It does not fit into the picture of a period in which we decisively determine the trend of the Korean economy. In a backward country like Korea political non-intervention is inconsistent with the granting of economic aid. Economic aid plus political non-intervention means in reality that we actively intervene in favor of the group which happens to be in power. Was it not Talleyrand who said more than 100 years ago that "non-intervention is a strange device; it is almost the same as intervention." If ECA is designed to keep Korea out of the hands of the Communists, we had to take active steps to strengthen the potentially democratic forces; we cannot remain silent if the government violates the basic principles of the democratic way of life, and we must push the Government to take progressive and popular actions. Unnecessary to say that these principles were far from being generally recognized within the mission. They reflect the opinion of a very small minority. The official view is that we are bound to support the Rhee Government and that we have to respect its decisions, subject to certain reservations in the strictly economic field. But there is more at stake in Korea than the future of the Rhee Government. The attack of the North Korean Communists is directed against democracy at large.

Will the Korean masses follow the appeal to defend democracy? Is there any democracy to defend in South Korea? Did we pave the way for democracy in Korea during the last five years? Did we insist on local self-government, trade-unions, rural cooperatives and a minimum of the rule of law? Do the Korean soldiers know what they are fighting for? And do they actually fight? [Adviser's manuscript, June 30, 1950.]

10. State Department records indicate that 92 women and 112 men were evacuated from Kimp'o on the morning of June 27. Letter, Arthur C. Kogan, Historical Office, Department of State, January 29, 1971.

11. See Chap. 5.

12. According to the ROK official military history, Yi Pŏm-sŏk took the initiative in convening this meeting, which was attended by Sin Sŏng-mo and several other cabinet ministers. WHC, *Han'guk chŏnjaeng-sa,* 2:225-26.

13. Sin Ik-hŭi (1894-1956) was educated in Korea and at Waseda University, Japan. He fled to Shanghai in 1919 and held numerous positions in the Korean provisional government. In 1948 Sin became speaker of the National Assembly and was twice re-elected to the assembly. He broke with Syngman Rhee and ran as the Democratic party's presidential candidate in 1956 but died of illness before the election.

14. The ROK Ministry of Defense study places President Rhee's departure from Seoul at 2:00 A.M., prior to the cabinet meeting. WHCC, *Han'guk chŏnjaeng-sa,* 2:226.

15. Ben C. Limb (Im Pyŏng-jik, 1893–) studied at Ohio State University and was closely associated with Syngman Rhee in activities for Korean independence from 1919. Limb was foreign minister (December 1948–April 1951) and South Korea's minister to the United Nations (1951). His diplomatic assignments included India and serving as ambassador at large (1967).

16. Ambassador Muccio's decision to remain in Seoul was made early on the morning of June 27, after the ROK government had fled from Seoul. A participant described the events as follows:

I attended a meeting between Amb. Muccio and Col. Wright at KMAG headquarters early Tuesday, June 27, 1950, where it was agreed that KMAG would also be evacuated minus 33 officers and men—communications and key staff—who would stay with Wright and move with the Korean forces. Upon returning to the Embassy, Amb. Muccio called the meeting . . . which I attended. The Ambassador stated it was his intention to remain at the Embassy claiming diplomatic immunity and he asked those of us at the meeting to remain with him on a voluntary basis. He further stated that he had cabled the State Department regarding his intention. At no time, as far as I know, was any consideration given to the entire Mission remaining in Seoul and claiming immunity. The Embassy would not have accommodated them in any event [Letter, James D. Holland, Colonel, U.S. Army (Ret.), November 19, 1970].

At 6:00 A.M., June 27, Ambassador Muccio informed the State Department of his intentions in the following cable:

North Korean forces north of Seoul have advanced slightly during the night. Best appraisal situation indicated although figures enemy strength and tanks exaggerated enemy nonetheless have numerical superiority vicinity Seoul. Embassy in some current danger owing cut off. President and most cabinet have departed south from Seoul. Acting PRIMIN and Defense Minister Sinn and Korean Army staff assert will stick it out here. I propose remain Seoul with limited volunteer staff until bitter end, sending Counselor Drumright with few FSO's south by motor vehicle to follow President. It proposed key KMAG personnel move southward via motor vehicle, timing depending upon developments, to preclude potential accusation abandonment; other KMAG personnel to be airlifted [Muccio to Acheson, no. 966, June 27, 1950].

17. The cable from Secretary of State Acheson stated: "While Department deeply appreciates willingness you and members your staff remain Seoul, it is felt inadvisable for you or any members your staff voluntarily become hostages and accordingly unless there are overriding considerations not known here Department feels you should endeavor leave Seoul to join Government before safe departure becomes impossible." Acheson to Muccio, number missing (control no. 8074), June 26, 1950.

18. Yi Si-yŏng (1868-1953) held various positions in the Korean government prior to Japanese annexation. He fled to Manchuria after 1910 and served in the provisional government in Shanghai from 1919. Yi returned to Korea in 1945 and cooperated with Syngman Rhee, becoming chairman of the Society for the Rapid Realization of Korean Independence. Yi was elected vice-president of the Republic of Korea in 1948. Yi opposed Syngman Rhee and resigned in May 1951.

19. Ambassador Muccio placed his departure at about 4:00 P.M. Glenn D. Paige, *The Korean Decision, June 24-30, 1950* (New York: Free Press, 1968), pp. 162-63.

Sawyer (*Military Advisers*, pp. 124-25) has reconstructed the events of the late morning and early afternoon of June 27 as follows (the time given for the departure of the embassy is incorrect):

Ambassador Muccio and his staff left Seoul for Suwon shortly after 0900 on 27 June, after notifying General MacArthur's headquarters that the Embassy radio station was about to be destroyed. Later in the day, without consulting or notifying KMAG, the entire headquarters of the Republic of Korea Army moved south to Sihung, half way between Seoul and Suwon. The Americans had noticed considerable excitement among the members of the Korean staff but had no real hint as to their purpose until they began leaving. When the move became known, Colonel Wright gathered his own staff and started south to try and persuade the Koreans to return to Seoul. The ROK Army headquarters' flight left the ROK units engaged north of the Capital City without communications to headquarters and alarmed the civilian populace in Seoul.

Shortly after the KMAG convoy crossed the Han River, Colonel Wright received his first definite assurance that outside help was on the way. A message from General MacArthur came over the KMAG command radio (SCR-399) located in a 2½ ton truck in the column and informed Wright that the Joint Chiefs of Staff had directed MacArthur to assume operational control of all U.S. military activities in Korea, including KMAG. Furthermore, he was sending a team—later known as the General Headquarters Advance Command and Liaison Group (short title: GHQ, ADCOM)—under Brig. Gen. John H. Church to Korea.

General MacArthur's promise to help was enough to convince the ROK Army Chief of Staff that he should return with his headquarters to Seoul.

20. Clarence Ryee, in his letter of January 25, 1971, commented on the broadcast as follows:

As the government spokesman I sent out the first news of the government moving to Suwon. Then at 10:00 A.M., without my knowledge, the army cancelled the first report. I called up [Minister of Defense] Sin to find out what happened to reverse the previous report. It was Sin's opinion that the first broadcast had had a bad effect on the morale of the army and the people. He was afraid that the soldiers would not fight if they knew the government had already given up Seoul and run away. He was also worried about the millions of people who would jam the Han River Bridge, which was the only foot bridge across the river, causing great havoc. He also said the Fifth Column Communists would try to take over the Seoul airfield. But he said he would see what he could do to correct the second report. It was the third broadcast (11:00 A.M.) which said that part of the government had moved to Suwon and part of it was still in the capital.

21. Sir Vyvyan Holt was captured in June 1950 and released in April 1953. He was knighted with the K.B.E. in 1956 and died in 1960. Captured with Holt were Vice-Consul George Blake and a clerk, Norman Philip Owen. Letters, Foreign and Commonwealth Office, July 27, 1970, and August 24, 1971.

Sydney Faithful, in a letter dated October 13, 1970, described events at the British legation as follows:

On the morning of Sunday, 25th, June 1950, Vyvyan Holt, H. M. Minister and Consul-General, on his return to our Compound in Seoul after Morning Service in the Cathedral called in at my house with some startling news. Mr. John Muccio, the United States Ambassador, had told him in strict confidence that the North Korean Army had crossed the 38th Parallel and were expected to capture Seoul in two days time. During that night and the following night in a secluded corner of the Legation Compound Holt and I burned all our confidential and secret documents.

At 6 A.M. on Tuesday, 27th, Holt and I together with our staff discussed the situation and what action we should take. Holt, a bachelor like myself, had many years experience of the Middle East but not of the Far East. I had served for 13 years in various parts of China and could claim some knowledge of Asiatics. I told Holt that there were little, if any hope of the North Koreans observing diplomatic immunity and strongly advised that we should leave Seoul immediately and proceed south by road. He insisted that he would remain and although I said that, in my opinion, we should be prisoners within 24 hours of the occupation of the city, I considered it to be my duty to stay with him. However, I made a further effort by suggesting that he should first seek advice of Mr. Muccio but Holt dismissed the idea saying that the American Ambassador would be too busy to see him. I then offered myself to seek Mr. Muccio's counsel as I was quite certain in view of our cordial relationship during the past year that he would be only too pleased to spare a few minutes of his valuable time to see me and tell me what action he was taking with his Embassy. Holt forbade me to consult Mr. Muccio and there and then he wrote a long telegraph to the Foreign Office informing them that on his own responsibility he had instructed me to leave Seoul, endeavor to reach Tokyo and despatch his telegram from the British Embassy there. I had no option but to obey. As the world now knows, Holt, Vice-Consul Blake and his clerk Owen were in captivity for about three years.

Accompanied by my clerk, I drove in a jeep to Kimp'o airfield where Mr. Stone, the American Consul, was supervising the evacuation of American male civilians, the women having already left Korea. On seeing me, Mr. Stone very kindly insisted on my boarding an aircraft about to take off with a full complement of passengers and I traveled to Japan on the floor of the plane. My clerk had to wait for a later flight that day. I arrived at Itazuke (Camp Hakata) at 7 P.M. where I was given a bed. I ascertained that owing to the large backlog of evacuees, I should have to wait 3 days for a seat in the train for the journey to Tokyo. I therefore made a long distance call to the British Embassy and explained my position. I was told that they would approach American Headquarters with a view to expediting my arrival in Tokyo. The headquarters were good enough to send an aircraft for me which arrived at Itazuke at 1:30 A.M. the following day. We left almost immediately and my clerk and I were the only two passengers in a 47-seater with a pilot and co-pilot of the United States Air Force. We spent a freezing night as the pilot apologized for the break down of the heating system. We arrived at Tokyo at 7 A.M. and the Air Force

Officers kindly drove us to the British Embassy. During the drive the pilot told me that he and his colleague had desk jobs during the day and had volunteered for this special night flight in order to continue to qualify for flying pay. He added that he had turned off the heating to avoid falling asleep during the flight. I then felt very grateful for our freezing cold night!

22. Mr. Chanteloup, in a letter dated September 2, 1970, provided the following details on his experience in Korea:

I landed at Kimp'o airport, Seoul, from Tokyo in the same plane as John Foster Dulles . . . on June 15, 1950, . . . to cover the inauguration of the new S. Korean National Assembly.

On June 18 I accompanied John Foster Dulles on his visit of South Korean army positions on the 38th Parallel. Pressmen were *not* allowed to attend the briefing given to Mr. Dulles on this occasion by Premier Sin Song-mo and the Chief of the General Staff Chae.

The North Korean invasion started on the morning of (Sunday) June 25th— at a time when I had not yet completed my special assignment in Korea.

I naturally decided to extend my stay to follow the new dramatic developments.

Tanks of the North Korean 1st Corps entered Seoul on the morning of June 28 when I rushed from the Chosun Hotel in a jeep "borrowed" from the U.S. vehicle park to seek shelter at the French Legation—5 A.M.

We left Seoul for P'yongyang by train (freight car) with a number of South Korean political deportees and a group including Britons, Americans, Turks, White Russians, etc., on July 13.

Officially (in North Korean official jargon) we were never "arrested" or taken "prisoner" but simply taken in "custody" to *protect* us from the dangers of "savage U.S. bombings."

I was released with the French group of internees one week after the British group in April 1953 [emphasis in original].

23. Bishop Patrick Byrne was born on October 26, 1888, ordained on June 23, 1915, and joined the Maryknoll Fathers a week later. He went to Korea in 1923 to begin Maryknoll work there. In 1929 he was named to the Maryknoll General Council and returned to America. In 1935 Bishop Byrne was selected to head a new mission in Kyoto, Japan. He remained in Japan until 1946, "escaping internment because of his extensive charitable activities." In 1946 he was named apostolic visitor to Korea and in April 1949 was appointed the first apostolic delegate to Korea. Bishop Byrne was consecrated in Seoul cathedral on June 14, 1949. He died in North Korea of illness on November 25, 1950. Letter, Msgr. Martino Giusti, Vatican Archives, November 28, 1970; and letter and accompanying materials, Rev. John J. McCormack, M.M., Maryknoll Fathers, January 28, 1971.

CHAPTER FOUR

1. The complete title of General MacArthur's headquarters in Japan was General Headquarters, Supreme Commander for the Allied Powers. It was abbreviated to GHQ, SCAP or simply GHQ.

2. Marguerite Higgins and Keyes Beech were among the newspaper reporters on the abortive flight. Higgins described her frantic efforts to reach Korea:

> In the first forty-eight hours after the Korean story broke, it looked as if fate, public relations' officers, and Red Yaks were all conspiring to keep us from flying to Korea to cover the biggest story in the world. At one time during those hectic hours we were actually halfway to Kimpo airfield near Seoul, aboard a big four-motored C-54. But news of Yak strafing of the field turned the plane back. In desperation we flew to Southern Japan, determined to get to Korea by fishing boat if necessary. Fortunately, we didn't have to resort to that—through a lucky fluke we had been able to hitch this ride in the evacuation plane.

Marguerite Higgins, *The War in Korea* (Garden City, N.Y.: Doubleday, 1951), p. 17.

Beech provides the names of several of the reporters and describes the mixed emotions of veteran newspapermen off to the latest war. Keyes Beech, *Tokyo and Points East* (Garden City, N.Y.: Doubleday, 1954), pp. 103-6.

3. The sections of divisional or higher staffs are: G-1, personnel; G-2, intelligence; G-3, operations and training; and G-4, supply.

CHAPTER FIVE

1. President Truman had directed General MacArthur to send a survey party to Korea to help determine the logistical needs of the ROK Army. General MacArthur formed the group from among his staff, with General Church in command. Appleman, *South to the Naktong*, pp. 42-43.

2. See Futrell, *Air Force in Korea*, p. 13.

3. Harold Noble's brother, Glenn A. Noble, had arrived in Korea in June 1950 to lecture on parasitology at Korean colleges during the summer.

4. State Department records indicate that 350 Americans were evacuated from Kimp'o on the afternoon of June 27, 1950. Futrell states, "When the air evacuation officially ended, shortly before midnight on

June 27, a total of 748 persons had been flown to safety in Japan." The higher figure includes the morning and afternoon evacuation from Kimp'o, evacuations from the Suwŏn airstrip, and foreigners. Letter, Arthur G. Kogan, Historical Office, Department of State, January 29, 1971; and Futrell, *Air Force in Korea,* p. 13.

5. While General Church's party was at Itazuke, General MacArthur received the directive from the Joint Chiefs of Staff placing him in "operational control of all U.S. military activities in Korea." Thereupon, MacArthur "redesignated the survey group as GHQ Advance Command and Liaison Group in Korea (ADCOM), and gave it an expanded mission of assuming control of KMAG and of lending all possible assistance to the ROK Army in striving to check the Red drive southward." Appleman, *South to the Naktong,* p. 43.

CHAPTER SIX

1. Additional details may be found in Sawyer, *Military Advisers,* pp. 125-27; Beech, *Tokyo and Points East,* pp. 110-22; and Higgins, *War in Korea,* pp. 19-30. Reporters Beech, Frank Gibney, and Burton Crane were in a jeep crossing the bridge when it blew up.

The Han River bridge was destroyed on the orders of General Ch'ae Pyŏng-dŏk. The premature destruction, with the loss of life and abandonment of the ROK Army units in and north of Seoul, became a political issue. With General Ch'ae dead (killed in action in July), responsibility was placed on the ROK Army engineer, Col. Ch'oe Ch'ang-sik, who supervised the demolition. Colonel Ch'oe was court-martialed and executed in September 1950. However, in September 1961 his widow started proceedings for a review of the case. In 1964 he was posthumously found not guilty because he had been following the lawful order of a superior officer in destroying the bridge. WHCC, *Han'guk chŏnjaeng-sa,* 2:250-52.

2. Kim Hong-il (1898–) graduated from the Kweichow Military Academy in 1919 and served with the Chinese Nationalist Army, attaining the rank of major general. In 1945 he was chief of staff of the Korean Restoration Army in China. When the Korean War began he was commandant of the Military Academy and was subsequently named 1st Army commander. Kim was placed on reserve status in 1951, with the rank of lieutenant general, and named ambassador to the Republic of China (1951-60). He was an adviser to the Supreme Council on National Reconstruction and foreign minister in 1961. Kim was elected

to the National Assembly in 1967 and became the chairman of the opposition Democratic party in 1971.

3. Drumright and Stewart left for this meeting about 7:35 P.M. *Activities Log,* June 27. A log of embassy activities was kept, apparently by Chief Warrant Officer Lynch, from the morning of June 27 to early on July 1. The log is among Harold Noble's private papers. Taejŏn is the capital of South Ch'ungch'ŏng Province.

4. The famous "Be of good cheer" message was sent from General MacArthur to Col. Sterling Wright, KMAG. Drumright learned of it in his telephone conversation with Colonel Wright in Seoul. See also Sawyer, *Military Advisers,* p. 125.

5. President Rhee apparently convinced Drumright that he would go back to Seoul the next day if possible. The embassy log has the following entry: "2030—Mr. Drumright returned from President Rhee's headquarters. Mr. Stewart stated that the talk with the President was very satisfactory.

"Mr. Drumright raised SECURITY (DND Telephone Exchange). Informed Col. Wright of the talk with the president. Requested that Ambassador Muccio contact him if possible. Stated to Major Sedberry (Advisor to G-3) that if the military situation stabilized that President Rhee would return to Seoul tomorrow night (28 June)." *Activities Log,* June 27, 1950.

6. This and the following sentence were provided by Mr. Drumright to clarify a garbled sequence of events in the manuscript. E. F. Drumright, manuscript review, January 1971.

7. President Truman's statement was released to the press at approximately twelve o'clock noon, Tuesday, June 27. The extraordinary declaration reversed American policy on China and increased the United States' involvement in Indochina. The full text of the announcement is as follows:

In Korea the Government forces, which were armed to prevent border raids and to preserve internal security, were attacked by invading forces from North Korea. The Security Council of the United Nations called upon the invading troops to cease hostilities and to withdraw to the 38th parallel. This they have not done but on the contrary have pressed the attack. The Security Council called upon all members of the United Nations to render every assistance to the United Nations in the execution of this resolution. In these circumstances, *I have ordered United States air and sea forces to give the Korean Government troops cover and support.*

The attack upon Korea makes it plain beyond all doubt that Communism has passed beyond the use of subversion to conquer independent nations and will now use armed invasion and war. It has defied the orders of the Security

Council of the United Nations issued to preserve international peace and security. In these circumstances the occupation of Formosa by Communist forces would be a direct threat to the security of the Pacific area and to the United States forces performing their lawful and necessary functions in that area.

Accordingly, I have ordered the Seventh Fleet to prevent any attack upon Formosa. As a corollary of this action I am calling upon the Chinese Government on Formosa to cease all air and sea operations against the mainland. The Seventh Fleet will see that this is done. The determination of the future status of Formosa must await the restoration of security in the Pacific, a peace settlement with Japan, or consideration by the United Nations.

I have also directed that United States Forces in the Philippines be strengthened and that military assistance to the Philippine Government be accelerated.

I have similarly directed acceleration in the furnishing of military assistance to the forces of France and the Associated States in Indochina and the dispatch of a military mission to provide close working relations with those forces.

I know that all members of the United Nations will consider carefully the consequences of this latest aggression in Korea in defiance of the Charter of the United Nations. A return to the rule of force in international affairs would have far-reaching effects. The United States will continue to uphold the rule of law.

I have instructed Ambassador Austin, as the Representative of the United States to the Security Council, to report these steps to the Council [State Department, *United States Policy in the Korean Crisis,* p. 18 (emphasis added)].

8. I have been unable to verify the "Act boldly'" quotation.

9. Harold Noble's description of these meetings is drawn from a three-page memorandum of the meeting and from a log kept by James L. Stewart. The memorandum is undated and unsigned, and it bears a "Secret" classification. Page one is missing from the Noble copy. They are hereafter cited as Noble Memorandum and Stewart Log. Both documents are among Harold Noble's private papers.

10. Ambassador Muccio also met with Yi Pŏm-sŏk and appealed to Yi's "patriotism to agree to have all commands to army, police and youth corps be issued through the Command Post Center." Noble Memorandum, p. 3.

11. An account of Colonel Wright and KMAG's evacuation of Seoul may be found in Sawyer, *Military Advisers,* pp. 126-28; and Higgins, *War in Korea,* pp. 25-30.

12. Everett Drumright agreed in general with this description of General Church's actions at Suwŏn. However, he noted that the situation was totally chaotic Generally Church did not know where he was or what was happening to him. He had been thrown into the middle of a losing battle and a collapsing South Korean Army. Rain, bad communications, rumors, and retreating forces caused great confusion.

Everett Drumright, private interview, Washington, D.C., September 30, 1970.

13. General MacArthur received instructions in the afternoon of June 27 to use U.S. air and naval forces to assist the South Koreans. According to Futrell (*Air Force in Korea,* p. 24), MacArthur immediately perceived the need for swift use of American air power.

> As soon as the teletypewriters which had delivered the new instructions from Washington went silent, General MacArthur turned to Partridge with a volley of oral orders. Success in Korea, said MacArthur, depended largely upon measures which would restore the spirits of the army and people. He wanted Partridge to get the Air Force into action immediately. Far-reaching results could be achieved if the air effort could be made effective that night and next day. He stressed again and again that FEAF had to hit the North Koreans with every resource at its disposal during the next thirty-six hours. He expressed a firm conviction that vigorous air action would drive the North Koreans back into their own territory in disorder.
>   Bombing missions were ordered and flown on the night of June 27-28, but bad weather and darkness prevented contact. Gen. Edward M. Almond, MacArthur's chief of staff, "was impressed with the need for air action."

> During the night Almond telephoned General Partridge and several times repeated that in order to save the South Koreans FEAF would have to display visible supporting actions. Almond stated that he "wanted bombs put on the ground in the narrow corridor between the 38th parallel and Seoul, employing any means and without any accuracy." General Partridge called Brig. Gen. Edward J. Timberlake, deputy commander of the Fifth Air Force, and General Kincaid and spurred them "on to a full-out effort" [Ibid., p. 26].

Bombing missions were flown on the morning and afternoon of June 28 in the area north of Seoul.

14. According to General Church's account, he made various suggestions to General Cha'e and "insisted that the Han River . . . be defended at all costs." Schnabel, *Policy and Direction,* pp. 72, 80.

CHAPTER SEVEN

1. President Rhee's uncertainty about United States support and Ambassador Muccio's efforts to reassure him are evident in a memorandum of a meeting that morning.

0800 June 29—JJM [John J. Muccio], JLS [James L. Stewart] called on President who is in terrible state. Mme. Rhee too is extremely nervous. During the night both have received a flock of lurid tales of the situation in Seoul. JJM delivers message and plans made. Home Minister Paek interrupts and excites the President again with what appeared to be stale news. . . . JJM does good job of outlining the situation, giving the hopeful aspects, but Rhee simply does not hear or understand. Mme. Rhee remarks that the Korean Minister to Japan has been calling on the phone continuously, again exciting the President with unfavorable news. Rhee particularly excited because Korean pilots for 10 fighter planes have not returned from Japan, hence it is obvious the Americans are doing nothing to aid Korea! After an extremely disagreeable hour and five minutes, we departed for the airfield [Stewart Log, p. 2].

2. General MacArthur testified in May 1951, following his removal from command by President Truman. U.S., Congress, Senate, Committee on Armed Services and the Committee on Foreign Relations, *Military Situation in the Far East, Hearings,* 82nd Cong., 1st sess., 1951 (hereafter cited as Senate, *Military Hearings*).

3. Harold Noble appears to be in error in this description of the actions of the 6th and 8th Divisions. According to the official U.S. Army history, the 6th Division held Ch'unch'ŏn until the morning of June 28 and then retreated south to avoid encirclement. The ROK 8th Division withdrew on June 27-28, with its weapons and equipment, to link up with the 6th Division. Appleman, *South to the Naktong,* pp. 27-28.

4. See ibid., p. 24.

5. This description of the 17th Regiment's "capture of Haeju," its evacuation of the Ongjin peninsula, and its condition on June 29 was apparently based on ROK Army announcements. While the account appears inaccurate, it has been retained because of the reference to Haeju.

North Korea claimed on June 25 that ROK forces began the war with an attack near Haeju and that the subsequent North Korean offensive was a "counterattack." The North Korean allegation was an attempt to place responsibility for the hostilities on the South. There is no mention of an attack on Haeju in the U.S. Army histories. KMAG advisers were in the Ongjin peninsula when the fighting began and have provided eyewitness accounts. The ROK Army official history of the Korean War specifically states that the "capture of Haeju" was a false report and identifies the source and circumstances of the report. The ROK Army announcement appears to have been an error due to poor communications, plus an attempt to stiffen resistance by claiming a victory. False and optimistic reports were repeatedly issued on June 25-26 to reassure the population of Seoul.

United Nations, Commission on Korea, June 25, 1950, "The United Nations Commission on Korea to the Secretary-General," S-1496, in

State Department, *United States Policy in the Korean Crisis*, p. 12;
United Nations, Commission on Korea, June 26, 1950, "The United
Nations Commission on Korea to the Secretary General," S-1505, in
ibid., pp. 18-20; Appleman, *South to the Naktong*, pp. 21-22; Sawyer,
Military Advisers, pp. 114-15; and WHCC, *Han'guk chŏnjaeng-sa*,
2:87-94, 219-23.

For recent discussions of the issue, see Karunakar Gupta, "How
Did the Korean War Begin?" *The China Quarterly*, no. 52 (October-
December 1972), pp. 699-716; Robert Simmons, Chong-Sik Lee, W. A.
Skillend, and Karunakar Gupta, "Comment," *The China Quarterly*, no.
54 (April-June 1973), pp. 354-68; and Jon Halliday, "What Happened
in Korea? Rethinking Korean History, 1945-1953," *Bulletin of Concerned Asian Scholars* 5, no. 3 (November 1973) :36-44.

6. A U.S. Army assessment of the condition of the ROK Army as of
July 1 states:

> Of 98,000 men in the ROK Army on 25 June the Army headquarters could
> account for only 22,000 south of the Han at the end of the month. When in-
> formation came in a few days later about the 6th and 8th Divisions and more
> stragglers assembled south of the river, this figure increased to 54,000. But
> even this left 44,000 completely gone in the first week of war—killed, captured,
> or missing. Of all the divisions engaged in the initial fighting, only the 6th and
> 8th escaped with their organization, weapons, equipment, and transport rela-
> tively intact. Except for them, the ROK Army came out of the initial disaster
> with little more than about 30 percent of its individual weapons [Appleman,
> *South to the Naktong*, p. 35].

Other estimates of effective ROK Army troops range from General
MacArthur's 25,000 made on June 29, to a South Korean figure of
40,000, made on July 1.

7. Ambassador Muccio and Drumright advised President Rhee prior
to General MacArthur's visit that General Ch'ae should be removed.
The premature destruction of the Han River bridge was partially responsible for the dismissal. E. F. Drumright, manuscript review, January 1971.

Chŏng Il-gwŏn landed at Suwŏn on June 30 and was immediately
named chief of staff. For a humorous account of Marguerite Higgins'
first meeting with the new chief of staff, see *Korea at War*, p. 52.

8. U.S. Navy aviators destroyed part of the bridges in August 1950,
after repeated attacks by navy and air force planes. Karig, Cagle, and
Manson, *Battle Report*, pp. 133-35.

9. General MacArthur's orders to General Stratemeyer are noted
in Courtney Whitney, *MacArthur: His Rendezvous with History* (New

York: Knopf, 1964), p. 326; and Futrell, *Air Force in Korea*, p. 30.

10. General Whitney (*MacArthur*, pp. 327-28) has written the most dramatic, and imaginative, account of the drive to the Han River:

> The briefing officer had barely put the pointer back on the rack below the map when MacArthur slapped his knee, stood up, and said: "Let's go to the front and have a look."
>
> Those who had not tried to argue MacArthur out of risks like this before and therefore did not know the futility of it, tried to explain that nothing had ever been more fluid than the "front" in South Korea at that moment. Enemy tanks and spearheads were slicing through the thinly held South Korean lines everywhere, and even this temporary headquarters was dangerously near the on-rushing North Korean forces. Furthermore, enemy airplanes were bombing and strafing almost at will along the few roads in the area. MacArthur heard them out and said quietly: "The only way to judge a fight is to see it yourself—to see the troops in action. Let's go." . . .
>
> It was a dramatic, historic, and tragic scene. In the distance across the Han, Seoul burned and smoked in its agony of destruction. On the north side of the river we could clearly hear the crump of Red mortar fire as the enemy swooped down toward the bridges. Below us and streaming by both sides of our hill were the retreating, panting columns of disorganized troops, the drab color of their weaving lines interspersed here and there with the bright red crosses of ambulances filled with broken, groaning men. The sky was resonant with shrieking missiles of death, and everywhere were the stench and utter desolation of a stricken battlefield. Clogging all the roads in a writhing, dust-shrouded mass of humanity, were the refugees.

11. General Whitney's account (ibid., pp. 330-32) is an excellent example of the hagiography produced by MacArthur's staff:

> The return trip was similar to the one we had taken north a little more than an hour before—the sedan and jeeps moving along like chips in the southward-flowing tide of a defeated nation. The vehicles were halted this time, however, by a direct enemy air attack. Once again, as in World War II, everyone dived for the ditches; and once again they looked back to see MacArthur striding slowly to the side of the road, where he stood erect and watched as the communist planes screamed down to strafe the road. One jeep was knocked out of commission, but no one was hurt. Within a few minutes we were on our way again, south to Suwŏn. . . .
>
> Indeed, even before his departure the entire Suwon area was under frequent air attack. It was well that MacArthur had ordered the *Bataan* to return to Japan instead of waiting on the airstrip, because only a few minutes before it returned to pick us up the field was bombed and strafed for the fifth time that day. Fortunately, however, the *Bataan* landed safely, and we hustled aboard and went roaring back down the runway. All of us on MacArthur's staff breathed a sigh of relief as we passed beyond the range of North Korean fighter planes.

12. General MacArthur drafted his report and recommendations on the return flight to Tokyo. He reported as follows:

The South Korean forces are in confusion, have not seriously fought, and lack leadership. Organized and equipped as a light force for maintenance of interior order, they were unprepared for attack by armor and air. Conversely they are incapable of gaining the initiative over such a force as that embodied in the North Korean Army. The South Koreans had made no preparation for defense in depth, for echelons of supply or for a supply system. No plans had been made or if made were not executed, for the destruction of supplies or materials in the event of a retrograde movement. As a result they have either lost or abandoned their supplies and heavier equipment and have absolutely no system of intercommunication. In most cases the individual soldier in his flight to the south has retained his rifle or carbine. They are gradually being gathered up by an advanced group of my officers I sent over for the purpose. Without artillery, mortars and antitank guns, they can only hope to retard the enemy through the fullest utilization of natural obstacles and under the guidance of example of leadership of high quality. . . . The civilian populace is tranquil, orderly and prosperous according to their scale of living. They have retained a high degree of national spirit and firm belief in the Americans. The roads leading south from Seoul are crowded with refugees refusing to accept the Communist rule. . . .

It is essential that the enemy advance be held or its impetus will threaten the over-running of all of Korea. The South Korean Army is entirely incapable of counteraction and there is a grave danger of a further breakthrough. If the enemy advances continue much further, it will threaten the Republic. The only assurance for holding the present line and the ability to regain the lost ground is through the introduction of United States ground combat forces into the Korean battle area. If authorized it is my intention to immediately move a United States Regimental Combat Team to the reinforcement of the vital area discussed and to provide for a possible build-up to a two division strength from the troops in Japan for an early counteroffensive. Unless provision is made for the full utilization of the Army-Navy-Air team in this shattered area, our mission will at best be needlessly costly in life, money and prestige. At worst, it might even be doomed to failure.

Ibid., pp. 332-33. Punctuation follows Paige, *The Korean Decision*, pp. 237-38. See also Paige's discussion (pp. 239-40) of the unexplained delay in General MacArthur's submission of this report to Washington.

13. Lt. Col. John McGinn's attempts to provide target information to the 5th Air Force, although not this meeting with Noble, are described in Futrell, *Air Force in Korea*, pp. 28-29.

Futrell's study substantiates various reports that air action in the first month of the war, particularly in the first ten days, was wildly inaccurate. Lacking maps and target information and encouraged to bomb for "morale" purposes, to stiffen ROK resistance, 5th Air Force attacks took a heavy toll in South Korean civilian and army casualties. Appleman (*South to the Naktong*, p. 51) has described the air action as follows: "Of immediate benefit to close ground support were the two tactical air control parties from the Fifth Air Force that arrived at

Taejon on 3 July. . . . They went into action on 5 July and thereafter there was great improvement in the effectiveness of U.N. air support and fewer mistaken strikes by friendly planes on ROK forces which, unfortunately, had characterized the air effort in the last days of June and the first days of July."

The later use of air power against South Korean civilians during the summer of 1950 is described by official historians as follows:

So, we killed civilians, friendly civilians, and bombed their homes; fired whole villages with the occupants—women and children and 10 times as many hidden Communist soldiers—under showers of napalm, and the pilots came back to their ships stinking of vomit twisted from their vitals by the shock of what they had to do. But was the fact any the worse than killing thousands of invisible civilians with the blockbusters and atomic bombs, because one could see the victims die? For the pilots, yes. For the objective, no; and the objective here was to halt and destroy an enemy whose savagery toward the people he professed to be succoring was more callous than the Nazi's campaign of terror in Poland and the Ukraine, an enemy who murdered wire-fettered prisoners of war, an enemy who if allowed to take his chances with death as a soldier in combat, would most certainly buy a hero's niche in the heaven of his barbaric choice by taking the life of at least one American soldier.

The wholly defensible, wholly abhorrent, task of warring against civilians was forced upon the Allied airmen by the Communist practice of hiding behind skirts in their stealthy approach to our all-but-beaten defenders of nonmilitary Korea—skirts literally, skirts figuratively. Of a column of a hundred refugees, half or more were more likely than not to be Communist troops whose straw covered burdens and flapping garments concealed the instruments of death designed for delivery against our men. . . .

So—we napalmed villages and strafed refugee columns, and the proof of the necessity was the gradual stalling of the advance of the westward-pressing Communists just outside Masan, last southern seaport before Pusan [Karig, Cagle, and Manson, *Battle Report*, pp. 111-12].

14. The official account of General Church's activities states:

At 1600 General Church sent a radio message to Tokyo describing the worsening situation. Three hours later, he decided to go to Osan (Osan-ni), twelve miles south of Suwon, where there was a commercial telephone relay station, and from there call Tokyo. He reached Maj. Gen. Edward M. Almond, MacArthur's Chief of Staff, who told him that the Far East Command had received authority to use American ground troops, and if the Suwon airstrip could be held the next day two battalions would be flown in to help the South Koreans. General Church agreed to try to hold the airstrip until noon the next day, 1 July [Appleman, *South to the Naktong*, p. 56].

15. Army headquarters left Suwŏn on July 4, 1950. Ibid., p. 58.

16. General Church returned from Osan about 10:00 P.M. and "met the assembled convoy. He was furious when he learned what had hap-

pened, and ordered the entire group back to Suwŏn. Arriving at his
former headquarters building General Church found it and much of the
signal equipment there had been destroyed by fire. His first impulse was
to hold Suwŏn Airfield but, on reflection, he doubted his ability to keep
the field free of enemy fire to permit the landing of troops. So, finally,
in a downpour of rain the little cavalcade drove south to Osan." Ibid.,
p. 57.

Other accounts of the hasty and unnecessary evacuation of Suwŏn
may be found in Sawyer, *Military Advisers,* p. 134; and Higgins, *War in
Korea,* pp. 37-52. Sawyer dryly notes, "This time it was the Americans
who left the ROK Army headquarters behind and decamped hastily."

17. Only General Church, at this point somewhere on the road between Osan and Taejŏn, knew of President Truman's decision to employ U.S. ground troops in Korea. Until General Church arrived, the
embassy group was aware only of a dire and distintegrating battle situation to the north. For several hours it appeared that there had been a
major breakthrough by the North Koreans and a total collapse by
the ROK forces.

18. General Church stopped in Osan to report to Tokyo the new situation at Suwŏn and his decision to move to Taejŏn. The call to Ambassador Muccio was probably made from Osan. Appleman, *South
to the Naktong,* p. 57.

General Church could have prevented President Rhee's flight
from Taejŏn and Mr. Noble's chase after the president, described in
Chapter 8, if he had informed Ambassador Muccio over the telephone
of the decision regarding American troops. However, the unreliable
and insecure telephone communications probably guided General
Church's decision to wait and tell Muccio personally in Taejŏn.

CHAPTER EIGHT

1. Chŏng Il-gwŏn (1917–) graduated from the Japanese Military
Academy in 1940 and was a captain in the Kwantung Army. After
World War II he graduated from the U.S. Military Government's English Language School and was the second chief of staff of the South
Korean Constabulary. He was promoted to lieutenant general in 1951,
to general in 1954, and was chief of staff (1954-56) and chairman of
the Joints Chief of Staff (1956). Chŏng was placed on the reserve list
in 1957 and later served as ambassador to Turkey, England, and the
United States (1960-61). He was foreign minister in 1963 and prime
minister in 1965-70. In 1971 Chŏng became a government party repre-

sentative in the National Assembly.

2. Everett Drumright reached Taejŏn from Suwŏn "about 4:30 A.M. and had urged Muccio not to leave pending verification of the rumor that caused us to flee Suwŏn." E. F. Drumright, manuscript review, January 1970.

3. The route appears to have been northwest to Kongju, then southwest to Iri, on to Chŏnju, Kwangju, and Mokp'o. See map.

4. Guerrillas were active in southwest Korea long before the war. Sawyer (*Military Advisers,* pp. 73-74) summarized the guerrilla movement as follows:

> Civil disorder and acts of sabotage had been common in South Korea since 1945, but after April 1948 such incidents gradually gave way to what appeared to be an organized guerrilla movement. Beginning with a series of uprisings on the isle of Cheju-do, off the south coast of Korea, guerrilla activity spread to the mainland in October 1948 when men who had taken part in the Yosu rebellion escaped to the Chiri-san area. Other bands formed when deserters from the ROK Army units joined with trained guerrillas from the north who infiltrated down the mountain chains into South Korea. By late 1949 these dissident elements were attacking villages and installations and becoming a serious problem.

Additional information on the guerrilla movement may be found ibid., pp. 129, 186; Appleman, *South to the Naktong;* Dean E. Hess, *Battle Hymn* (New York: McGraw-Hill, 1956); and William F. Dean, *General Dean's Story* (New York: Viking, 1954).

5. Prendergast (letter, July 31, 1970) commented:

> As for my own views, I may have been "confused" in explaining them to Harold Noble but I don't think the question of North vs. South Korea figured at all, in my thinking or that of anybody in the Embassy. The issue wasn't whether the P'yongyang regime was preferable to Seoul—nobody thought that for a moment—but rather the nature of the Syngman Rhee regime itself, and whether the United States, in return for economic aid and military support, should not pressure Rhee for reforms . . . personally he [Harold Noble] might have liked Rhee to liberalize but he saw the United States' (and his) primary role as backing Rhee's anti-communist regime against internal and external opposition to Rhee as the greater threat. The possibility of armed invasion from the North tended to be discounted.

6. The first U.S. troops from Japan, the doomed Task Force Smith of the 24th Division, were airlifted to the Pusan area on July 1 and moved by train to Taejŏn the following day. Appleman, *South to the Naktong,* pp. 60-61.

7. Mr. Gregory Henderson accompanied Harold Noble to the meeting with President Rhee. Mr. Henderson (letter, February 26, 1972)

described his experiences and impressions in Pusan from the war's start until Noble's arrival as follows.

I was assigned as Vice Consul heading the consular branch at Pusan around June 11th, 1950, replacing Mr. Robert Berry who had been reassigned and, with several other friends, left Seoul the day before the invasion began. I had a one room office in a building housing a few ECA and KMAG personnel and had bachelor quarters in a small house in the Hialeah compound—a foreign-built and foreign-occupied compound beyond Pusan. My duties were chiefly consular, especially shipping, with occasional political reporting. After two years of hectic, if entrancing, activity in Seoul, I looked forward to an easy and pleasant summer. Most of my goods—including my incipient art collection—I left in Seoul all boxed up to go out with the household goods of friends who had been assigned home to Washington. I took this step as a precaution against what we all regarded as possible invasion. The precaution failed. My things and my friends' were all caught in boxes on Inch'ŏn's piers; nothing was ever heard of them again.

On June 25th, we had a visiting ECA group in Pusan including the distinguished expert on Chinese agriculture, Dr. Owen Dawson. Governor Yang of South Kyŏngsang province gave the visitors a banquet in the handsome former residence of the Japanese shipping millionaire, Mr. Goto, at Tongnae, a building then used as a hostel. As chief diplomatic representative, I was invited. In the midst of the many leisurely courses I went out, as I often did, and talked in Korean to some inn personnel and hangers-on of the Korean official guests. From them I learned that there were rumors of an invasion over the 38th parallel. Something about the atmosphere seemed serious. It was about 7:00 P.M. I had no intimation of anything until then. Owen, at least, departed precipitously for Seoul. Another Washington ECA official, Fred Bunting, stayed with me and I eventually evacuated him.

The summer vanished. Calling Seoul, then always difficult, quickly became almost impossible. I got through once, I think, and was told to stay where I was. I did get through to the Embassy supply officer and had him put a trunk of mine on a train coming to Pusan. He did. It arrived on an almost empty train and was itself almost empty: in a time when so many wished to flee. The clouds came down over us after that. Pusan might as well have been Kamchatka, except that it had more rumors than all Siberia. We knew nothing; could find out nothing. In the place of information stood fear.

I had been told to evacuate all foreigners who would yield to my pleas that they depart (I could not force them) using therefore ships available in Pusan's harbor. I went at night to the missionary compounds (Australian Presbyterians, mostly) and contacted the few other Americans around. Soon—especially around June 28—we were inundated by scores—perhaps hundreds—(no one ever counted them) of others. Everyone south and east of Seoul came to us for evacuation. Elderly spinsters from Yŏngdong speaking only German, Embassy families like the Kinneys vacationing at Taech'ŏn beach, in South Ch'ungch'ŏng province, Marc Scherbacher caught on a trip in Kangwŏn province. By train at night, in the drizzle, bedraggled, confused, sleepy they came. I stood in the train yards with a lantern and directions to guide them on. Without pause for more than a few words, they were packed onto ships and taken to Japan. Standing under the dock's Krieg lights, I can still remember the Yŏngdong German-Swiss spinster in her old-fashioned garb sprinting up the gangway as it was being raised—too frightened even to speak German. But we were rich in ships and short in distance. It was no Seoul-Inch'ŏn evacuation in one overpacked and slow freighter with hundreds of miles to go. We offered first-class service. Our ship captains were most cooperative, their ships large, the distance to Japan brief. I stamped the shipping papers on the street taking my seal along in a closed car trunk. My memory is of evacuating hundreds. Time and excitement may have stretched the numbers a bit. But there were many. Everything they had with them could be taken. I even evacuated cars. Nothing had to be abandoned in Pusan. The abandoning for them had come when they started from their homes. Some missionaries with lifetime commitments to Korean service refused to go. The Lintons came from Kwangju, holed up in a house on the other side of the harbor where I could slip over for a bite, a welcome chat—and the company of an American woman, then the rarest treat in the Korean world. For a while, I believe she was the only American woman left free and unhidden in all of Korea. Old Ned Adams, the veteran Taegu missionary would not hear of going. I commandeered him amiably—he most willingly—to work in the USIS Information Center whose director, Gene Knez, had left just before the war and had not yet been replaced. I told him how important it was not to close the Center at this time but to make it a kind of symbol of the (then only hoped for possibility of) American will to come to Korea's aid. We turned the records up loud and rolled the music out onto Pusan's nervous and packed main street. It was my only experience with phonographic psychological warfare.

On June 29th came silence. Eerie silence. The refugees stopped coming. So did all news. We strained to hear from Tokyo what we could. We took to looking at surrounding hills, wondering when the North Koreans might burst in. There was talk of my leaving. But I had no orders to do so and, like the others, wanted to stay. I thought Ambassador Muccio would wish me to hang on. I was the only diplomat in Korea who didn't move that month. Lt. Col. Rollins S. Emmerich, senior officer present of KMAG, likewise stayed and was, informally, more or less in charge of our little group. I talked to Tokyo over the telephone once or twice and gave Doug Overton, James Pilcher, Ed Seidensticker and others in the anxious Embassy news. There were a handful of other Americans—a ship's service man, a couple of KMAG officers, one or two others. Still on June 30th, no word of U.S. intervention, nothing from the front. We felt like men who had stumbled down to some lonely beach where the tide had run out beyond their ken. Yet we sensed already the excitement of more ahead.

July 1st, a summer day of diffused light. No news filled the "headquarters" building that morning. About noon, I think it was, I "heard" a silence in Pusan's streets. Never in my life had I heard silence so obstreperous, so urgent. I looked outside. There, stretched down the main street as far as I could see, suddenly stood the Koreans, lining the boulevard in a grave, absolute and orderly silence. I asked a Korean passerby what was afoot—I, the foreign government official, with the radio and telephone. Quietly he told me to wait a moment, I would see. Five or ten minutes. Far down the boulevard, a truck rounded the bend. Then another. On they came—open dump trucks. On them, in combat dress, American soldiers. The silence rippled into applause and some cheers. It was the first platoon, God save the mark, platoon of American ground forces to enter the war. Yes, by God, a platoon of Sasebo-duty-rotten GIs. And soon there was a company. Yes, by God, even a company. And finally, when more planes could get through the Kimhae fog by evening, a battalion. History was to call it Task Force Smith. But that was much later, weeks later. Then it was only a sleepy, bedraggled, hopeful bunch of little-trained men shaken out of their Sasebo bunks. But they were American power. And this was July 1, 1950; American power was invincible. Invincible for a few more days. We thought just the way Harold Noble said he did. We no longer had a trace of fear. We no longer even had doubt. We thought we had already won the war. We were in it. And who among us recent veterans of World War II in the Pacific had ever heard of Americans being defeated—more than just a little confused? The feelings of July 1, 1950, lie eons aways from February, 1972; history hardly lets us approach let alone relive them.

But the company was there. We found one battery-operated car on the rail-road tracks. It wouldn't start. So we put most of the company in it and the ship's service man and Col. Emmerich and I and a couple of GIs pushed against this Toonerville trolley and got it started. It went gloriously ahead more than two hundred miles up the tracks right to where the action was halfway between Suwŏn and Osan. And no one ever saw a man alive of the unit again.

Writing of it now, I realize that July 1, 1950 was July 30, 1914: a little sliver of 1914, with 1914's illusions minus its God. The Europeans loved Europe and didn't want to see their Europe end. We loved the struggling Korean world of those early years and reached for anything we thought would save it: hope, armed men and illusions.

Then the tide came back in again. A full tide of men. Not companies or platoons, but regiments and divisions and medical evacuation hospitals and engineers and trucks and jeeps and tanks and even Generals like Dean. All fled before them—except the North Koreans. I spent most of my days as liaison officer to the South Kyŏngsang government, "asking" the Governor and his aides to empty schools and every conceivable building available and unavailable so the GIs could camp and occupy and latrine them. And we tried desperately to make it—did I say orderly?—so that the Koreans we were coming to save wouldn't fly out of their own buildings on the ends of GI bay-onets. How fine they were at the Governor's office—compliant and urgent and devoted and—best of all—buoyant with humor. They and I worked to-gether with true esprit de corps. I remember a U.S. officer coming in to report on a local incident. A newly-arrived GI had raped a Korean woman in broad daylight on the crowded street of a poor district. The Korean men had rushed him and cut off the offending length of his anatomy. The Governor, his secre-taries, the officer and I looked at each other with "a wild surmise." We would have had to invent the phrase if Keats hadn't. Everyone, including the U.S. officer, agreed that the Korean men had done what they ought to have done. And we proceeded with plans to evacuate the Pusan Commercial Middle School.

Then everyone else descended on us. Of diplomats, the Chinese Embassy contributed the first. So precipitous their flight that their car bogged down in a stream near Taegu, the waters rose at night and the bedraggled Chinese came in the next morning with their pants legs wet to their knees. I put the military attaché—a bright, half-Japanese Colonel named Wang—in with me and found a house for the rest to occupy. Their gratitude took the form of a permanent daily invitation to lunch at the Chinese restaurant opposite USIS's downtown information center. It was the lodge in my garden of cucumbers. And I took the measure of Chinese relaxation and humor that summer; somewhat less so of Chinese chow but it beat GI rations by many a long league and who, in those days, could resist all that nostalgic Japanese victrola music?

On the heels of my celestial friends, earthier diplomats arrived: the UN Commission, visiting Americans and hordes and hordes of correspondents; each knew less of Korea than the last. There were no hotels; none, at any rate, that anyone had ever heard of. I had one extra bed, one extra bedroom and a sofa. There was also the floor. By rough estimate I had 50 house guests in two weeks. Some were then or later quite distinguished. For some there was no later: they were killed a night or two after leaving.

Finally—it seemed a long time—into this cacophonous menagerie there moved the distant presence of the President and his lady. No one welcomed them as we had the platoon—the dear, now dead, platoon. There was no riding in open landaus as would have befitted 1914. But we heard that he was there by half-whispered rumor and knew he was occupying the Governor's brick "mansion" on the hill. In fact, the Governor told me, half proudly, but *sotto voce* as befitted military security, he had moved out to let the President move in. So I went to pay respects and tell Dr. Rhee that I would be very happy to do whatever I could. The words were pretty safe; I was very unlikely to be able to do anything. I was still almost completely out of touch with the Embassy which, obviously, had more urgent things to do than wonder about what all those rumor-laden little "cowards" were doing in Pusan. Little to nothing of our activities ever reached Embassy ears or sank in when—as through the kind offices of the Chinese Ambassador—reach them they did. With thousands dying and millions of refugees, why should it have? A war has many separate worlds; few doors open between them. There was then little room for Pusan.

My eager, infant labors at being liaison diplomat to the President were knocked quite quickly into a cocked hat by the arrival of Harold Noble perhaps as soon as the next day after the Rhees reached Pusan. Thin-beaked, beady-eyed and quick-hopping, I had the momentary impression that, in Harold Noble, a bird of prey had come wheeling in on some final moment of his quarry. He had no time of day for anything in Pusan but zeroed in at once on his Presidential victims. He was good enough to accede, however, when I asked to come along as the man who would stay when he flapped wings and was again gone. Up he went, Harold in open khaki shirt and field dress with a pistol somewhat ostentatiously belted about him. We sat in one of those exiguous and cluttered little Japanese ideas of a western reception room and the President and Mme. Rhee came in. The very first thing that happened was that Mme. Rhee asked Dr. Noble to take his pistol off in the presence of the President. I thought Harold was going to snarl; but he acceded. Dr. Rhee was gracious, nervous and worried. He had precisely that feeling of frustration which a man has who has always stalked power and finds, in the midst of great crisis, where power is needed, that he has none of it at all. Dr. Noble fully realized his plight and acted accordingly. Noble's account of what was said at the meeting would, written nearly twenty years earlier, be vastly more accurate than my memory. But the impressions of the scene in that cluttered Japanese-Western room in Pusan stand out unforgettably.

Then, almost as quickly as he had come, Harold Noble left. I met him, if ever again, only for a few minutes. With his departure I went back to tasks which, as time wore on, came to be shared by others in the Embassy who now reappeared from evacuation in Japan. With those earlier Pusan days, then, this record should end.

8. General Dean described the confused situation in Taejŏn in early July 1950 in his account of combat and captivity. Dean, *General Dean's Story*, p. 22.

CHAPTER NINE

1. President Rhee's proclamation was on July 7; the official signing was a day earlier. General MacArthur's announcement that the U.N. Command had adopted the provisions of the convention was on July 23, 1950.

2. The decision to permit President Rhee to go to Taejŏn may have been an attempt to inspire retreating ROK forces, which were moving *south* at top speed as the newly arrived American forces moved *north*. (Appleman, *South to the Naktong*, pp. 82-83.) Or the decision may have indicated a belief that U.S. troops would quickly stop the North Koreans. The performance of U.S. units in their first combat engagements on July 5-6 at Osan, P'yŏngt'aek, and Ch'ŏnan, all defeats, did not warrant confidence in an easy victory. General Dean appears to have fully understood the seriousness of his position at the time. (Ibid., pp. 65-83.)

3. General MacArthur had decided by July 6 that the 8th Army, commanded by Lt. Gen. Walton H. Walker, would "assume operational control of the campaign in Korea." General Walker officially assumed command of U.S. Army forces in Korea on July 13.

Colonel Collier was directed by General Walker on July 7 to establish an 8th Army headquarters in Korea. Collier flew to Taejŏn on the morning of July 8, found the situation too unstable for an army headquarters, and decided upon Taegu, driving there on the afternoon of July 8.

If Colonel Collier arrived in Taegu the day before this meeting with Noble and President Rhee, as Noble states, the Noble chronology is off by one day, i.e., Noble and President Rhee reached Taegu on July 9 rather than July 8. Appleman, *South to the Naktong*, pp. 109-10.

4. Colonel Collier's "courtesy call" actually had a more serious and official purpose than either Harold Noble or President Rhee understood at the time. Collier (letter, December 4, 1970) described the incident as follows:

> During mid-morning of the day in question, I received an urgent telephone message from Mr. Drumright . . . informing me that President Rhee was on a special train enroute to Taegu and Taejŏn. Because of my Eighth Army position and because Mr. Drumright knew that I was acquainted with President Rhee, the Ambassador wanted me to have the train stopped at Taegu and President Rhee notified that because of the rapidly deteriorating military situation, it was inadvisable for him to proceed farther north. In fact, Mr. Drumright made it bluntly plain—President Rhee was not to be permitted to proceed northward, past Taegu. I issued the necessary instructions to have the train stopped. (Had I not received such a telephone call, I would not have known anything about it nor would I have presumed to make a courtesy call, as Mr. Noble said.)
>
> I then drove down to the railway station. Naturally, when I entered President Rhee's car I was very diplomatic in my conversation and no doubt, Mr. Noble, who was in the President's car, might well have been under the impression that I was making a courtesy call.
>
> President Rhee was visibly upset at not being allowed to continue to the front. Meanwhile, I had alerted the Provincial Governor and he arrived on the scene. I accompanied the group to the Governor's home and then excused myself. Immediately upon my return to Eighth Army Headquarters, I notified the Embassy by phone to the effect that the mission had been accomplished and that Mr. Noble was on hand and familiar with the details.

5. By July 8-9 it was apparent that North Korean forces were not intimidated, as General MacArthur had hoped, by the presence of a few American infantry units. On the contrary, the North Koreans had little difficulty brushing the U.S. units aside. Appleman, *South to the Naktong,* Chaps. 6-7.

6. Cho Chae-chŏn (1912-70) was a legal specialist and official during the Japanese colonial period. He was elected to the National Assembly in 1954, 1958, and 1960 as an opposition party leader. Cho served as minister of justice in 1960 and briefly as home minister in 1961 during the Democratic party regime. Elected to the National Assembly again in 1963, Cho was prominent in political and legal circles.

7. This paragraph apparently refers to an incident involving General Kim Sŏk-wŏn. See Appleman, *South to the Naktong,* pp. 399-400.

8. Colonel Hess described Harold Noble's pleas for a flight over the battle area in his fascinating autobiography, *Battle Hymn.* However, the flight with a Korean pilot was omitted from the account because

of possible objections by authorities to this breach of regulations. Letter, Dean Hess, April 5, 1971; and Hess, *Battle Hymn,* p. 102.

9. Kim Chŏng-yŏl (1917–) graduated from the Japanese Military Academy in 1941 and flight training in 1943. Kim was chief of staff of the ROK Air Force (1954-56) and minister of defense (1957-60). He was ambassador to the United States (1963-64); director, Republic of Korea Chapter, Asian People's Anti-Communist League (1966); and elected a Democratic Republican party member of the National Assembly in 1967.

10. General Collier (letter, December 4, 1970) made the following comment:

> I realized that the few KMAG officers then in Taegu should have been, more properly, with the Korean units they were supposed to be advising and not back in a rear headquarters. As far as being "dispossessed," all the KMAG dependents and families had been ordered out of Korea by GHQ in Tokyo with just what belongings and hand baggage they could carry. Further, all such families were later reimbursed for whatever personal property they had left behind. As far as the "food" was concerned, I certainly had more pressing and important things to consider than what was in anyone's deep freeze or ice box. As Sherman said, "War is Hell."

11. Everett Drumright wrote a series of letters during July-September 1950, to John M. Allison, director of the Office of Northeast Asian Affairs, describing his activities and including observations on the military and political situation in Korea. The letters bore a confidential and official-informal classification and were circulated within the State Department to supplement other sources of information.

Unfortunately for the historian, Mr. Drumright concentrated upon the military situation and wrote relatively little about political affairs. This emphasis was natural at a time when United States and South Korean forces were in desperate retreat and American interests could be saved only by force of arms. However, Drumright's occasional mention of political developments provides, inter alia, a fascinating glimpse into the embassy's relations with President Syngman Rhee.

In the letter quoted below (Drumright to Allison, July 19, 1950), Drumright places the arrival of Ambassador Muccio and most of the embassy staff in Taegu on Thursday, July 13. The report describes the move from Taejŏn, the military situation in early July, and some South Korean political machinations.

> It became apparent by the middle of last week that the enemy would press hard on Taejŏn and was, in fact, within 15 miles of the city at one point. With the crossing by the north Koreans of the Kŭm River southwest of Kongju

and with the U.S. forces abandoning Choch'iwŏn and falling back to the south bank of the Kŭm, the Ambassador felt it was time to advise the ROK cabinet ministers and other civil officials to quit Taejŏn for places more remote from the fighting zone. General Dean concurred. Consequently, by last Friday virtually all ROK officials had left Taejŏn. The Ambassador flew to Taegu on Thursday with most of the staff following that day by highway. Noble, who was already in Taegu, obtained quarters in the Presbyterian compound for the Embassy group. Six of us remained in Taejŏn. I sent Floyd south Friday night with valuable USIS equipment and on Saturday afternoon I sent Donald Macdonald by jeep to Chŏnju, Kunsan, Kwangju, Mokp'o and Sunch'ŏn to advise remaining American missionaries and other foreigners to leave for safer places. I also directed that he go to Kunsan to assist in the repatriation of three US soldiers who had arrived there from the Osan area. My reason in sending Macdonald at that time was that with the seizure of Kongju, the enemy had a virtually undefended rail line and highway line by which he could quickly penetrate the Chŏlla provinces if he so desired. Neither ROK nor US has any real forces in the area, ROK having drawn its 5th Division north at the onset of the campaign and thrown it into the main battle line.

The last of the Korean civil officials left Taejŏn last Saturday—Sin Sŏngmo, Acting Prime Minister. I and my party of three remained in Taejŏn until Sunday afternoon, at which time the enemy was crossing the Kŭm northwest of Taejŏn in the face of heavy US opposition. At the time I left Gen. Dean expressed the view he could hold Taejŏn perhaps through Tuesday. He has, of course, done so—a creditable performance against a numerically superior enemy. He has been fighting a delaying action and taking a heavy toll of the enemy in doing so, pending the arrival of US reinforcements. At the same time Dean's losses have been by no means light, especially in experienced officers. Dean has had excellent support from the air force which, with the growing use of fields in Korea, is . . . increasingly effective.

I have the strong impression that the driving force of the enemy is largely spent, although it cannot be denied that, with his superior ground forces, he is still generally on the offensive. I should estimate that the great proportion of his tanks has been knocked out by air strikes. If he still has artillery, he is using it most sparingly. Perhaps his supply problems are so tremendous that he cannot get supplies to the front. I think that is especially the case on the main route south from Seoul to the Kŭm River. According to reports from refugees and aerial reconnaissance, neither the railway nor the highway are operable. Korean reports suggest that the enemy is building up some striking force in the area south of Ch'ungju with the apparent intention or driving on Sangju and Kŭmch'ŏn where the rail and highway lines from Taejŏn to Taegu lie. The enemy will have to cross some very rugged terrain to achieve this objective. I think we have sufficient forces deployed to check any such drive. We are not much worried about the enemy thrust south along the railway through Tanyang or the semi-guerrilla operations being conducted in the rugged east coast area by the enemy. We are worried, however, over the possibility that the fertile Chŏlla provinces on the southwest coast will be overrun by relatively light enemy forces. This they can do because we simply do not have the forces in there—except police and a few hundred Korean marines— to stop them. I doubt whether the enemy will commit any appreciable number of regular ground forces to the Chŏlla areas; he is more likely to send in roving guerrilla bands in much the same way he has done along the east coast. You will recall that the Communists once had some strength in the Chiri mountains. They could easily make that a base for terrorizing the Chŏllas and thus denying their manpower and rice to the ROK.

Taegu has now become the civil and military seat of the ROK. Rhee and his cabinet are still in the process of setting up. General Walker has his large 8th Army headquarters here. The U.N. Commission has a liaison team here, though its main base of operations is Pusan. Our Embassy is gathered here, as is the Chinese Embassy and the U.K. legation. Our consular office is in Pusan. [Al] Loren is the ECA representative here, while [Robert] Kinney and the rest of the ECA personnel are pretty much in Pusan. It looks as though we'll be sticking here until there is some decisive change in the military picture. Unfortunately, Taegu has the reputation of being the hottest city in the ROK. It is living up to its reputation in this respect. At the moment we are mainly striving to firm up our relations with 8th Army and with the constantly shifting ROK Government. Last weekend the Ambassador succeeded in getting Rhee to replace Home Minister Paek, who was playing politics, with Cho Pyŏng-ok. We think this is a very salutary change. Cho's appointment was followed by the designation of Kim Tae-sŏn, Chief of the Seoul Metropolitan Police, as Director of National Police. Hugh Cynn, former ROK Ambassador to Japan, has been causing much trouble by telling Rhee malicious stories; we may try to end his pernicious influence by having him sent to the U.S. on a lecture tour; he is an excellent speaker and might be of some use in that way.

CHAPTER TEN

1. General Dean's 24th Division lost the Kŭm River line on July 16 and Taejŏn on July 21. In seventeen days, July 5-22, the division had been driven back one hundred miles, suffered more than 30 percent casualties, and had 2,400 men missing in action. General Dean himself was missing after personally leading troops against North Korean tanks in the Taejŏn street fighting. Appleman, *South to the Naktong*, Chaps. 10-11.

2. It was widely believed that U.S.-ROK forces were vastly outnumbered in July-August 1950. Press accounts cited ratios of four to one, and the U.S. Army encouraged the falsehood of great North Korean numerical superiority. In reality, U.N. forces had gained an edge of approximately 92,000 men to 70,000 North Korean troops by August 4.

"Numerical superiority" became the explanation for North Korean victories and the relentless southward push of the NKPA. Rather than greater numbers, the factors involved in the North Korean successes were an effective infantry force, high morale, the momentum of a surprise attack, and the lack of preparation and performance of the U.S. and South Korean forces.

The official U.S. Army history has restored perspective to the relative disposition of forces in the following description:

Underestimation of enemy losses in the first five weeks of war led in turn to an exaggerated notion of the enemy forces facing the U.N. Command along the Pusan Perimeter. The enemy had probably no more than 70,000 men . . . as he began crossing the Naktong River on 4-5 August to assault the U.N. forces in the Pusan Perimeter. . . .

The relative U.N. strength opposed to the North Koreans at the front in early August was actually much more favorable than commonly represented. A leading American newspaper on 26 July, in a typical dispatch filed in Korea, described the attack against the 1st Cavalry Division at Yongdong as being "wave after wave." A subhead in a leading article in the same newspaper a few days later said in part, "We are still outnumbered at least four to one." Other American newspapers reported the Korean War in much the same vein. The claim that enemy forces outnumbered United Nations troops at least four to one had no basis in fact.

High U.S. Army sources repeated the statements that U.S. forces were greatly outnumbered. The North Korean forces had outnumbered those of the United Nations after the near collapse of the ROK Army at the end of June and until about 20 July, but never by more than two to one. By 22 July the U.N. forces in Korea equaled those of the North Koreans, and in the closing days of the month the United Nations gained a numerical superiority, which constantly increased until near the end of the year [Appleman, *South to the Naktong*, pp. 263-65].

3. The three major participants all used "half-trained" or untrained troops during the first three months of the war. U.S. troops from Japan, while once trained, were completely unprepared for combat in Korea due to their soft garrison and administrative duties.

The ROK Army rushed untrained conscripts and ten-day trainees into action. Many unwary Korean young men found themselves instant soldiers in July-August. Sawyer (*Military Advisers,* p. 144) describes the formation of one ROK Army regiment as follows:

The formation of the ROK 26th Regiment in August was typical of the haste and expediency surrounding KMAG's operations at the time. Early in August the KMAG G-3 Advisor called Capt. Frank W. Lukas in from the field and ordered him to activate a new regiment for the ROK 3rd Division. Lukas obtained two interpreters from ROK Army headquarters and got in touch with the appropriate ROK Army staff officers in Taegu. These, with aid of the police and other city officials, drafted youths on the streets of the town, and within a day or two they had nearly 1,000 recruits. As men were drafted, Lukas and his Korean officers formed squads, platoons, companies, and finally two battalions. The most intelligent-appearing recruits were designated NCO's and platoon leaders, while the officers who had helped to recruit them became company, battalion, and regimental commanders and staffs. When the two battalions were organized, the KMAG G-4 somehow obtained enough rifles for them. Lukas then took his regiment outside the city and allowed each man to fire nine rounds of ammunition. Shortly thereafter the regiment, clad in an assortment of civilian clothes, school uniforms, and odds and ends of U.S. Army uniforms, boarded a train at Taegu and traveled east to a sector near P'ohang-dong, where, in less than a week after its activation had been ordered, it entered combat. The ROK 26th Regiment received no formal training until April 1951.

4. The admiration of the senior embassy officers—Ambassador Muccio, Drumright, and Noble—for General Walker facilitated cordial and effective cooperation between the 8th Army and the embassy, and with ROK officials. Ambassador Muccio cited General Walker's noninvolvement in political matters, contrasting Walker's actions with those of General Ridgeway, his successor as 8th Army commander. Ambassador John J. Muccio, private interview, Washington, D.C., September 30, 1970; and letter, Drumright to Allison, August 17, 1950.

5. Cho Pyŏng-ok replaced Paek Sŏnguk on July 14. See Note 7 in Chap. 9, above.

6. Several "youth groups" flourished in south Korea after 1945 as instruments of coercion by the right or left. The most powerful organizations became part of Syngman Rhee's unofficial power structure and were used, *inter alia,* as a strongarm supplement to the police. Rhee wanted to keep the youth corps under his direct control and separate from the regular army to insure its loyalty and availability for internal political action. For a description of these groups, see Gregory Henderson, *Korea: The Politics of the Vortex* (Cambridge, Mass.: Harvard University Press, 1968), pp. 140-42, 292-94. Perhaps it was a discussion of Lexington and Concord that prompted Harold Noble to write privately that "Rhee is quite a problem. His courage is all right, but he's become a doddering old fool, and it's quite a job to keep him from doing foolish and politically dangerous things. It's a pity he isn't ten or twenty years younger." Letter, Harold Noble to his wife, Bell Noble, August 8, 1950.

7. Henry R. Sawbridge, British consul-general in Yokohama, was appointed chargé d'affaires in Korea on July 13. He remained in Korea until August 15, when he returned to Japan. Sydney Faithful returned to Korea on July 23 and, with one communications clerk, constituted the British legation. In late September Mr. Alec Adams arrived in Korea as chargé d'affaires. Letter, Foreign and Commonwealth Office, July 27, 1970; and letter, Sydney Faithful, October 13, 1970.

8. This designation occurred on July 15 and was done by an exchange of letters between President Rhee and General MacArthur. President Rhee wrote to MacArthur as follows:

In view of the joint military effort of the United Nations on behalf of the Republic in Korea, in which all military forces, land, sea and air, of all the United Nations fighting in or near Korea have been placed under your operational command, and in which you have been designated Supreme Commander of United Nations Forces, I am happy to assign to you command authority over all land, sea and air forces of the Republic of Korea during the period of the continuation of the present state of hostilities; such command to be exercised either by you personally or by such military commander or commanders to whom you may delegate the exercise of this authority within Korea or in adjacent seas.

The Korean army will be proud to serve under your command, and the Korean people and Government will be equally proud and encouraged to have the over-all direction of our combined combat effort in the hands of so famous and distinguished a soldier, who also in his person possesses the delegated military authority of all the United Nations who have joined together to resist the infamous Communist assault on the independence and integrity of our beloved land.

With continued highest and warmest of personal regard, [Syngman Rhee].

MacArthur replied to President Rhee through channels as follows: "Please express to President Rhee my thanks and deepest appreciation for the action taken in his letter of 15 July. It cannot fail to increase the coordinated power of the United Nations forces operating in Korea. I am proud indeed to have the gallant Republic of Korea forces under my command. Tell him I am grateful for his generous references to me personally and how sincerely I reciprocate his sentiments of regard. Tell him also not to lose heart, that the way may be long and hard but the ultimate result cannot fail to be victory." Mark Clark, *From the Danube to the Yalu* (New York: Harper, 1954), p. 169.

9. The officer was Maj. Gen. Hobart R. Gay, commanding general of the 1st Cavalry Division. Ambassador John J. Muccio, private interview, Washington, D.C., September 30, 1970.

10. Similar tactics, foreshadowing later U.S Army practices in Vietnam, were adopted by General Church as commanding general of the 24th Division in early August. Appleman, *South to the Naktong,* p. 291.

11. Ambassador Muccio began advocating the use of South Korean National Police with U.S. units in late July. Even after General Walker was persuaded to utilize the police, division commanders were skeptical of the proffered assistance. Drumright reported as follows:

The embassy has been preaching the desirability of using Korean manpower to the maximum extent against the North Koreans. General Walker and most of his commanders have generally opposed this policy, saying Americans would fight their own battles. However, as time has gone on, there has been some change of attitude. Practically all U.S. units are now using and cooperating well with Korean police who are useful in checking refugees and stopping infiltrators and even in using a weapon on occasion. The 1st Cavalry, for example, would have none of any Koreans when it first arrived, but after it was prevailed upon to take some police to help in warding off infiltration, it called for many more [Letter, Drumright to Allison, August 17, 1950].

South Korean national police fought as light infantry units with U.S. forces, with mixed results. See Appleman, *South to the Naktong,* pp. 351, 367, 370-71, 373, 386, 435, 466, 470.

The major accomplishment of the ROK National Police was in screening refugees and providing security against infiltration and guerrilla attacks on U.S. units. Ibid., pp. 383-84.

12. The use of ROK National Police by U.S. units led the way to acceptance by U.S. Army commanders of an expanded role for the South Korean military forces. Appleman (ibid., p. 384) has described the situation as follows:

How to use South Korean manpower to the greatest advantage became one of the most important problems early in the conduct of the war. An immediate need was for more troops to oppose and stop the advancing North Koreans. A longer range need was to build up the manpower of the allied forces to the point where they could drive the enemy back across the 38th Parallel. The program adopted was threefold: (1) fill the five ROK divisions to full strength with replacements; (2) activate new ROK divisions; and (3) attach large numbers of South Korean recruits to American units (a novel expedient).

U.S. Army commanders, at different levels, objected to points 2 and 3 (see notes 13-15 below).

13. The plan for incorporating South Koreans into American units developed from General MacArthur's visit to Korea on July 27. MacArthur told Muccio that the situation would be extremely grave for six or seven weeks. No more replacements were available in Japan, and there would be no more troops until they could be sent from the United States. Muccio informed MacArthur that there were Koreans who had some understanding of English and some quasi-military training. The ambassador was thinking of President Rhee's Youth Corps, "Rhee's goon squads," in Muccio's phrase. Muccio stated that there should be some way to put these men to use with American troops. General MacArthur didn't indicate his approval or disapproval, just nodded "as

he always did." After returning to Tokyo, MacArthur sent for General Walker's chief of staff for operations, Colonel Landrum, and discussed the question. MacArthur instructed Landrum to tell Walker to discuss the idea with Muccio and if he, Muccio, could get President Rhee to agree, 8th Army should begin to implement a plan to integrate Korean troops with U.S. units.

Muccio discussed the plan with President Rhee, who agreed with it. But Rhee never allowed the Youth Corps to be used or its personnel drafted. Ambassador Muccio became angry on one occasion and told Rhee that these able-bodied men should be sent to the front to do their share. Rhee just looked at Muccio and said, "Mr. Ambassador, you don't understand Korea." Muccio replied, "There are a lot of things I don't understand but I do understand there is a war on and those men should fight."

However, President Rhee used the Youth Corps as a semiofficial draft board. They went around the Pusan area and seized young men of draft age, often with no pretext of legality or formality. The draftees were, in a sense, "shanghaied." The Youth Corps people used the athletic grounds of several schools in Pusan. Uniforms, equipment, toothbrushes were set out in piles. The "draftees" were ordered to take off their clothes and change into the uniforms. They were given ten days of intensive training, mainly physical, and then assigned to American units. Ambassador John J. Muccio, private interview, Washington, D.C., September 30, 1970.

The implementation of the KATUSA (Korean Augmentation to the U.S. Army) program is described in the official history as follows:

Concurrent with the steps taken in August to rebuild the ROK Army, the Far East Command planned to incorporate 30,000 to 40,000 ROK recruits in the four American divisions in Korea and the one still in Japan but scheduled to go to Korea. This was admittedly a drastic expedient to meet the replacement requirement in the depleted American ground forces. As early as 10 August, Eighth Army began planning for the Korean augmentation, but it was not until 15 August that General MacArthur ordered it—General Walker was to increase the strength of each company and battery of United States troops by 100 Koreans. The Koreans legally would be part of the ROK Army and would be paid and administered by the South Korean Government. They would receive U.S. rations and special service items. The Far East Command initially expected that each ROK recruit would pair with a United States soldier. . . .

The U.S. 7th Infantry Division in Japan was far understrength, having contributed key personnel to the 24th, 25th, and 1st Cavalry Divisions in succession when they mounted out for Korea. In an effort to rebuild this division, the first Korean augmentation recruits were assigned to it rather than to the divisions in Korea. The first three platoons of 313 recruits left Pusan by ship the morning of 16 August and arrived in Japan the afternoon of the 18th. Once started, the shipments of recruits left Pusan at the rate of nearly 2,000 daily. The final shipment arrived at Yokohama on the 24th and debarked the next day, making a total of 8,625 Korean officers and men for the division. The South Korean Government at first obtained many of these recruits directly from the streets of Pusan and Taegu. In the contingents shipped to Japan, schoolboys still had their schoolbooks; one recruit who had left home to obtain medicine for his sick wife still had the medicine with him.

On 20 August, the American divisions in Korea received their first augmentation recruits—the 24th and 25th Divisions, 250 each; the 2nd and 1st Cavalry Divisions, 249 each. For the next week each of the divisions received a daily average of 250 Korean recruits. On the 29th and 30th, the 1st Cavalry Division got an average of 740, and the 24th Division, 950 recruits daily. Near the end of August the plan changed so that every fourth day each division would receive 500 men until it had a total of 8,300 Korean recruits. Except for the first groups, the recruits received five days' training at the Kup'o-ri Training Center near Pusan, which was opened 20 August [Appleman, *South to the Naktong*, pp. 385-87].

Additional information on the augmentation program may be found in Whitney, *MacArthur*, pp. 338-39. Whitney attributes the program to a plan by MacArthur; there is no mention of Ambassador Muccio's contribution. Whitney's description of the implementation of the program is wildly inaccurate and unreliable.

Schnabel states (*Policy and Direction*, p. 167), without explanation, that MacArthur conceived the "idea that South Korea might be called on to provide soldiers for American units."

14. General Walker's doubts about the limited effectiveness of the KATUSA program appear to have been borne out by experience during the late summer and early fall of 1950. Appleman (*South to the Naktong*, pp. 387-89) describes the program as follows:

Even though it initially had been the intention of the Far East Command to pair Korean augmentation recruits with American soldiers in a "buddy system," this did not work out uniformly in practice in the Eighth Army. The 1st Cavalry and the 2nd Infantry Divisions used the buddy system, with the American responsible for the training of the recruit in use of weapons, drill, personal hygiene, and personal conduct. Two regiments of the 25th Division used the system, while the third placed the recruits in separate platoons commanded by American officers and noncommissioned officers. General Church directed the 24th Division to place all its augmentation recruits in separate squads and platoons commanded by selected Korean officers and noncommissioned officers. These Korean squads and platoons were attached to American units. . . .

The buddy system of using the Korean augmentation recruits gradually broke down and was abandoned. Most American soldiers did not like the system. Most units found they could employ the recruits, organized in ROK squads and platoons with American officers and noncommissioned officers in charge, to best advantage as security guards, in scouting and patrolling, and in performing various labor details. They were particularly useful in heavy weapons companies where the hand-carrying of machine guns, mortars, and recoilless rifles and their ammunition over the rugged terrain was a grueling job. They also performed valuable work in digging and camouflaging defensive positions.

There also began in August the extensive use of Korean civilians with A-frames as cargo carriers up the mountains to the front lines. This method of transport proved cheaper and more efficient than using pack animals. American units obtained the civilian carriers through arrangements with the ROK Army. Soon the American divisions were using Korean labor for nearly all unskilled work, at an average of about 500 laborers and carriers to a division.

The U.S. divisions in Korea never received the number of Korean augmentation recruits planned for them. In September the divisions began to take steps to halt further assignments. In the middle of the month, the 24th Division requested Eighth Army not to assign to it any more such troops until the division asked for them. As one observer wrote, "The Koreans haven't had time to learn our Army technique. An American doughboy hated to have his life dependent on whether his Oriental buddy knew enough to give him covering fire at the right moment." The language barrier, the difference in loyalties, the lack of training in the recruits, and their relative combat ineffectiveness all put great strain on the attempt to integrate the Koreans. It was not strange that as fast as American units obtained American replacements they dispensed with their Korean replacements. By winter, the buddy system had been quietly dropped.

However, despite the failure of the "buddy system" under the combat conditions of 1950, the KATUSA program worked sufficiently well later, under more stable and garrison conditions, that it was still in effect in 1974.

15. Ambassador Muccio was also responsible, with General Walker, for another aspect of South Korea's military buildup: the rapid expansion of the ROK Army. Sawyer (*Military Advisers*, pp. 144-46) has described the events as follows:

General MacArthur, meanwhile, on the strength of a study made by members of his staff on 17 July 1950, concluded that the maximum ground effort of which the Republic of Korea Army was capable in the immediate future was limited to four infantry divisions, including the support required to make them effective in battle. He told the Department of the Army on 31 July that he planned to re-equip the ROK Army on this basis, though without certain heavy equipment. Some items had already been furnished the Koreans, he said, and he was screening his stocks in Japan to determine what other equipment could be spared; some items would be requisitioned from the United States.

Both Ambassador Muccio and General Walker disagreed with MacArthur's staff estimate. On 1 August Muccio offered his view to the Secretary of State, arguing that the United States should arm as many able-bodied South Koreans as possible without regard to the pre-war limitation. He and Walker, he went on, felt that the South Koreans should make the largest possible contribution of manpower to help defeat the North Koreans and to save American lives. Moreover, Muccio continued, it was probable that enemy guerrillas would continue to fight in mountain areas after the end of major operations in Korea, and ROK troops should be used to the greatest extent possible for their suppression.

How great an influence Muccio's and Walker's opinions exerted upon MacArthur's *volte-face* one week later is unknown, but he did reverse his earlier decision. On 9 August he authorized General Walker to increase "at once" the strength of the ROK Army to any level he deemed advisable and practicable. Following conferences between members of his staff and KMAG representatives, the Eighth Army commander submitted a plan for activating five new ROK Divisions along with corps and army units needed to support a ten-division Republic of Korea Army. His schedule called for activating one division by 10 September, and one additional division by the 10th of each month following until five divisions had been formed. Technical service units would be activated in phase with the divisions as the availability of equipment permitted. MacArthur concurred with this plan and asked the Department of the Army whether it could furnish the necessary equipment for such a program from zone of interior stocks. The Department of the Army replied on 2 September that minimum initial equipment (except specified items of heavy engineer, signal, and ordinance equipment) could be supplied for new ROK divisions beginning 10 November 1950 and directed MacArthur to submit requisitions for the equipment needed.

CHAPTER ELEVEN

1. According to official records, Maj. William Robert Leslie Turp was British military attaché in Korea from July 1950 to April 1951 (letter, Ministry of Defense, September 2, 1970). However, the designation military attaché appears to have been simply for convenience's sake. Major Turp's sole duty was to "endeavor to identify arms and ammunition captured from the enemy. Although he was to be attached to the British Legation, he was not, in fact, a Military Attaché and was not under the superintendence of the Head of the Legation as he reported on his one subject direct to British military authorities" (letter, Sidney Faithful, October 13, 1970).

2. North Korean forces were advancing directly toward Taegu, moving swiftly into the southwest and attacking down the east coast. In this chapter Harold Noble describes the North Korean push toward Masan, taking the action to early August. The account then shifts back to the fighting near Taegu in late July and early August. The military situation in late July and early August is described in Appleman, *South to the Naktong,* Chaps. 11-18.

3. Harold Noble was unaware, along with 8th Army intelligence, that North Korean forces had started an envelopment that almost ended the war. Appleman (ibid., pp. 210-11) describes the operations of the North Korean 6th Division as follows:

The N.K. 6th, farthest to the west of the enemy divisions, had a special mission. After the fall of Seoul, it followed the N.K. 3d and 4th Divisions across the Han as far as Ch'onan. There the N.K. Army issued new orders to it, and pursuant to them on 11 July it turned west off the main highway toward the west coast. For the next two weeks the division passed from the view of Eighth Army intelligence. Various intelligence summaries carried it as location unknown, or placed it vaguely in the northwest above the Kum River.

Actually, the 6th Division was moving rapidly south over the western coastal road net. Its shadow before long would turn into a pall of gloom and impending disaster over the entire U.N. plan to defend southern Korea. Its maneuver was one of the most successful of either Army in the Korean War. It compelled the redisposition of Eighth Army at the end of July and caused Tokyo and Washington to alter their plans for the conduct of the war.

Departing Yesan on 13 July, the N.K. 6th Division started south in two columns and crossed the lower Kum River. . . . The larger force appeared before Kunsan about the time the 3d and 4th Divisions attacked Taejon. The port town fell to the enemy without resistance. The division's two columns united in front of Chonju, thirty miles to the southwest, and quickly reduced that town, which was defended by ROK police.

The N.K. 6th Division was now poised to make an end run through southwest Korea toward Pusan, around the left flank of Eighth Army. In all Korea southwest of Taejon-Taegu-Pusan highway, at this time, there were only a few hundred survivors of the ROK 7th Division, some scattered ROK marines, and local police units.

4. See letters, Drumright to Allison, August 17, note 13 below, and August 22, 1950, Chap. 13, note 2.

5. Efforts to obtain additional information about this incident by correspondence with Yi Pŏm-sŏk in 1970-71 were unsuccessful. Noble appears to have been overly sanguine about the success of such an operation, given the activities of Communist guerrillas in the area.

6. General Craig was commanding general of the 1st Provisional Marine Brigade. Additional information about the first marine actions in Korea may be found in Lynn Montross and Capt. Nicholas A. Canzona, *U.S. Marine Operations in Korea, 1950-1953,* vol. 1: *The Pusan Perimeter* (Washington, D.C., Historical Branch, G-3, Headquarters, U.S. Marine Corps, 1954).

7. General Ch'ae Pyŏng-dŏk was killed on July 27 near Hadong. The incident is described in Appleman, *South to the Naktong,* pp. 215-

21. The U.S. unit was the 3rd Battalion, 29th Infantry, which arrived from Okinawa on July 24 and went into action the next day. Without "the six weeks of training first agreed upon, they found themselves now in a forward position, rifles not zeroed, mortars not test-fired, and new .50 caliber machine guns with cosmoline rubbed off but not cleaned." Ibid., p. 215.

8. William R. Moore was killed on July 31 near Chinju. His death and the loss of the "first three medium tanks in Korea" is described in ibid., pp. 231-33. Additional information about Moore's death may be found in King, *Tail of the Tiger*, pp. 424-28.

9. The 25th Division moved to Masan on August 2-3, completing "the 150-mile move by foot, motor and rail within a 36-hour period." The 1st Provisional Marine Brigade landed at Pusan on August 3 and was attached to the 25th Division on August 6. The Army history describes the maneuver as follows: "General Walker said that this 'history-making maneuver' saved Pusan. He said also that had the North Koreans attacked strongly on the Kumch'on front while the division was passing over the single road through Kumch'on, 'we couldn't have done it.'

"In recognizing the critical nature of the situation in the southwest and in acting with great energy and decisiveness to meet it, General Walker and his staff conceived and executed one of the most important command decisions of the Korean War." Appleman, *South to the Naktong*, p. 249.

10. The first U.S. counterattack lasted from August 7 to 12. Appleman (ibid., pp. 286-87) describes the results of the attack as follows:

On 14 August, after a week of fighting, Task Force Kean was back approximately in the positions from which it had started its attack. . . . In the week of constant fighting in the Chinju corridor, from 7 to 13 August, the units of Task Force Kean learned that the front was the four points of the compass, and that it was necessary to climb, climb, climb. The saffron-colored hills were beautiful to gaze upon at dusk, but they were brutal to the legs climbing them, and out of them at night came the enemy. . . .

At 1150, 16 August, in a radio message to General Kean, Eighth Army dissolved Task Force Kean. The task force had not accomplished what Eighth Army had believed to be easily possible—the winning and holding of the Chinju pass line. Throughout Task Force Kean's attack, well organized enemy forces controlled the Sobuk-san area and from there struck at its rear and cut its line of communications. The North Korean High Command did not move a single squad from the northern to the southern front during the action. The N.K. 6th Division took heavy losses in some of the fighting, but so did Task Force Kean. Eighth Army again had underestimated the N.K. 6th Division.

11. The 1st Provisional Marine Brigade was shifted to the defense of Taegu on August 15. The brigade fought in the first battle of the "Naktong Bulge" until relieved on August 19, when it returned to the Masan area. Ibid., pp. 308-18.

12. According to Drumright, this conference between General Walker and Ambassador Muccio occurred on July 28. Letter, Drumright to Allison, August 17, 1970 (note 13 below).

The military situation had nearly reached the breaking point by July 26. That day General Walker, extremely discouraged by the poor performance of U.S. units against the North Koreans, secretly called General Almond in Tokyo to request permission to evacuate 8th Army headquarters from Taegu to Pusan. The conference with Almond, unknown even to Walker's staff, resulted in MacArthur's trip to Korea the next day, July 27, for a dramatic meeting with Walker in Taegu.

After the meeting Walker dropped his plans to shift 8th Army headquarters and renewed his efforts to inspire resistance by U.S. units. On July 29 he issued his famous "'stand or die" order in a desperate attempt to halt American retreats. Appleman, *South to the Naktong,* pp. 205-9.

13. Everett Drumright's account of these events is as follows:

When General MacArthur was in Korea just three weeks ago today, he expressed to the Ambassador the view that there would have to be further withdrawals. Since that time General MacArthur seems to have been pressing General Walker to remove his headquarters to a more secure position and to urge the ROK government to do the same thing. On July 28th General Walker spoke to the Ambassador, but there was tacit agreement, no move would be made from Taegu unless the military situation dictated such a move. On August 16th, following Col. Landrum's return from Japan, General Walker brought up the subject once again. He said that General MacArthur was concerned, not only about the continued location of 8th Army headquarters in Taegu, but about the possibility that a sudden North Korean incursion on Taegu might result in the death or capture of President Rhee and many members of the ROK government. General Walker again stressed the commonsense desirability of the removal of the Korean Government; he also pointed out that this would relieve him of anxiety and facilitate operations in the Taegu area. The Ambassador concurred that the movement of the government would be a realistic approach. At the same time he outlined the morale and psychological problems involved. It was agreed that the Ambassador would broach the subject to Rhee and the Korean War Cabinet (composed of the Acting Prime Minister, who is concurrently Defense Minister, Home Minister, Finance Minister, Commerce Minister and Transportation Minister). Yesterday afternoon, after a discussion of the problem, the Ambassador, accompanied by Noble and me, went to see President Rhee. At the Ambassador's suggestion he called in the War Cabinet. The Ambassador then put the problem to the President and his War Cabinet. The views of the cabinet members were then solicited. All expressed the thought that it would be advisable to move the seat of government to a safer place. The Home Minister and the Prime Minister were especially emphatic in expressing themselves. But the President waxed emotional, saying Koreans could not retreat any further, that the people of Taegu could not be left in the lurch, and so on. At one point the President said that the cabinet members could leave Taegu, but that he for his part would resign the presidency and remain in Taegu to fight it out with the enemy. In the end, however, the President directed the War Cabinet to draw up a plan for the orderly evacuation of the civil government. It is understood that he later discussed the subject with the whole cabinet. At this writing (afternoon of August 17th) no final plan for removal of the seat of government has been decided upon. However, we expect such a plan to be approved and set in motion either today or tomorrow. Meantime, the President left Taegu about noon today by one of our planes for Pusan on "urgent business." He is expected to return here late this afternoon and is expected later in the evening to fly to Chinhae for a couple of days of rest, after which he will presumably go to Pusan. The Embassy and other diplomatic missions and the U.N. liaison team will presumably accompany the ROK ministers when they go to Pusan. The Ambassador will head our group, although it is his intention to shuttle if Taegu is held. I am to stay in Taegu to maintain contact with 8th Army headquarters and with the Korean ministers who remain here (Defense Minister, Home Minister and Transportation Minister, probably). Prendergast, Fatigati, Scherbacher, Col. Edwards and one or two others will probably remain here with all others going to Pusan [letter, Drumright to Allison, August 17, 1950].

CHAPTER TWELVE

1. The military situation around Taegu and the consequences of this announcement were as follows:

The enemy penetration at the middle of August in the ROK 13th Regiment sector and along the boundary in the 5th Cavalry sector at Waegwan and Hill 303, together with increasingly heavy pressure against the main force of the ROK 1st Division in the Tabu-dong area, began to jeopardize the safety of Taegu. On 16 August, 750 Korean police were stationed on the outskirts of the city as an added precaution. Refugees had swollen Taegu's normal population of 300,000 to 700,000. A crisis seemed to be developing among the people on 18 August when early in the morning seven rounds of enemy artillery shells landed in Taegu. The shells, falling near the railroad station, damaged the roundhouse, destroyed one yard engine, killed one Korean civilian, and wounded eight others. The Korean Provincial Government during the day ordered the evacuation of Taegu, and President Syngman Rhee moved his capital to Pusan.

This action by the South Korean authorities created a most dangerous situation. Swarms of panicked Koreans began to pour out on the roads leading from the city, threatening to stop all military traffic. At the same time, the evacuation of the city by the native population tended to undermine the morale of the troops defending it. Strong action by the Co-ordinator for Protection of Lines of Communication, Eighth Army, halted the evacuation. Twice more the enemy gun shelled Taegu, the third and last time on Sunday night, 20 August. At this time, six battalions of Korean police moved to important rail and highway tunnels within the Pusan Perimeter to reinforce their security [Appleman, *South to the Naktong*, p. 351].

2. For details of this marine action, see ibid., pp. 315-18; and Montross and Canzona, *Pusan Perimeter*, Chap. 10.

3. Major Hess had moved his unit to Chinhae because of the North Korean advance on Taegu and the lack of space and training facilities at other fields. Hess, *Battle Hymn*, pp. 133ff.

CHAPTER THIRTEEN

1. President Rhee's impatience and frustration at his "exile" in Chinhae were noted by Maj. Dean Hess in *Battle Hymn*, pp. 125-27.

2. Everett Drumright's letters to John Allison between August 22 and September 22 provide interesting details on the military situation, particularly on the effectiveness of the South Korean forces and the relations between the embassy and President Rhee. All but the last letter were sent from the "American Embassy, Taegu Office." Drumright described the clash with President Rhee over leaving Taegu and subsequent events in a letter of August 22.

Since I wrote you last we have had a further change of the Embassy, this time to Pusan. As we indicated in recent telegrams, the move to Pusan, on the part of the ROK Government, the diplomatic missions and the U.N. liaison group, was at the suggestion of General Walker. The matter had been under discussion for some three weeks and the move would have been made much earlier, I am certain, had not the Ambassador advised against it. But when General Walker stated on August 15 that he might not be able to hold Taegu, that in the event of a break through the enemy might be able to reach the city within six hours, et cetera, the Ambassador had no alternative but to bow to the inevitable and start negotiations with the Koreans regarding the removal of unessential war offices to Pusan. We met with Rhee and his war cabinet on the 16th. Rhee, with his typical deviousness, was the only Korean to offer opposition and his opposition seemed mainly perverse and willful. I really believe that Rhee put on his dramatics in an endeavor to cast himself in a heroic light. For my part, I am convinced that he never intended to remain in Taegu in the face of immediate danger from the enemy.

Having carried the ball in getting Rhee and his civilian ministries to depart Taegu, the Ambassador had no alternative but to go to Pusan and put in an appearance. It was decided that I should remain in Taegu, with a small supporting staff, to maintain contact with the remaining ministers (at the moment the Acting Prime Minister . . . the Home Minister, the Foreign Minister and the Finance Minister) and General Walker. This I have been doing, seeing the ministers daily and General Walker almost daily. Much of our work here these days is being taken up with refugee problems (of resettling and maintaining them and of keeping them out of the military's hair). In this field, Mark Scherbacher of USIS has been performing invaluable work. Thanks to his drive and insight many ugly refugee problems have been solved or ameliorated. There must be at least a million and a half of these unfortunates in areas still retained by ROK and their plight has certainly not been alleviated by the painful slowness with which international relief machinery is being established. Here we are almost two months after the conflict started and not a single outside relief official has shown up here, if one excludes Col. Katzin [a U.N. official]. The Korean authorities are now, with Scherbacher's advice and guidance and with the medicines made available by ECA, doing a reasonably good job with the refugees. We can only pray that some severe epidemic, such as cholera, does not break out and that the areas left us in which to settle refugees are not further constricted. In other words, should we lose Taegu and be forced to fall back on a zone around Pusan, we would be faced with some difficult problems indeed.

We are also maintaining our USIS activities here on a large scale. That is necessary because the Koreans have shown almost no ability in this field and because of need to assist 8th Army in psychological warfare and the like. We continue to get out our news bulletins, which are extensively used by the Taegu press and our Mr. Floyd actually runs the Taegu radio station, the best left to us in Korea. Jim Stewart expects to shuttle between here and Pusan so as to maintain activities at the highest level.

We have also been mighty busy acting as intermediary between 8th Army and the Korean authorities in the recruitment of Korean young men for service with the U.S. forces. A program for the recruitment of some 36,000 has been underway for the past several days. Some 8,000 of these lads are on their way to Japan or are already in Japan. They will be given some training there, outfitted and armed and sent back to Korea with American units being formed up for service here. The rest of the 36,000 are to be placed with U.S. units already in Korea. Indeed, some have already been sent to U.S. units, notably the 24th Division which has suffered severe losses since arriving in Korea. The plan is to put 100 Koreans with each American company after some very rudimentary training. To date the recruitment program has been a great success, the Koreans having lived up to their commitments to deliver quotas of men within the age limits 18-25. General Walker told us yesterday that the army authorities in Japan are most pleased with the recruits sent there. The Ambassador and I have been plugging all along for greater employment of Koreans in this conflict. Naturally, we are much pleased with this development, as well as increased use of Korean police. We need more manpower and this is the place to get it. Moreover it is manpower that is best fitted to fight the battles here and it is the manpower that should be used. Moreover,

it will give the Koreans experienced soldiers for their future army.
The Korean army for its part now has a strength of 96,000—pre-conflict
strength. The Koreans are now working on a plan to establish five new divisions
of about 10,500 men each. Already one new division is being formed and
KMAG officers are assisting in its training. The biggest hurdle in all this is
officers; the Koreans simply have not got an adequate number. The Infantry
School is being reactivated to supply this deficiency. All this is most encouraging, since I foresee a large number of Korean troops being needed to eliminate
north Korean guerrillas who will certainly be left behind to harass U.N.
forces as the latter move north. We already have that pattern in the Chinju
operations. The Koreans are good at dealing with guerrillas and I am confident they can solve that problem. By the time the present conflict is ended
the Koreans ought to have an experienced, hard-fighting force of almost
200,000 who ought to be able to guard the northern ramparts. Steps are also
underway to strengthen the Korean Air Force and Navy. Already the Korean
air force is undergoing vigorous training at Chinhae. Plans are now crystal-
izing to set up a naval training mission at Chinhae. This will probably be
under Commander Lucey, now Naval liaison officer at Pusan. It contemplates
the procurement of a few of the frigates turned back a few months ago by the
Soviets as a nucleus of the Korean Navy. I earnestly hope that the Department
will energetically support this plan if it comes to the Department for consideration. Korea will, with its long coastline, heavily indented with islands, need a
compact, fighting Navy to ward off the Chinese Communists in the period
ahead. . . .

We had a couple of Republican congressmen here the 20th and 21st. I took
them to call on the Prime Minister, General Walker, General Partridge, etc.
They had been at Ch'angnyŏng the day our forces cleaned out the Communists
with severe losses to the latter, including 13 field pieces. They had talked
with MacArthur in Japan, and Radford, and had been on carrier strikes. Here
they evinced a gratifying interest in the Korean forces and went so far as to
issue a praiseworthy statement. I found both of them intelligent and likable.
Incidentally they hold views, especially Scott, on Far Eastern policy which do
not coincide, I believe, with Far Eastern State Department policy. But in any
event, they are with us in Korea. Incidentally, both had a close look at our
USIS program here. Latham in particular made a point of saying that he had
consistently voted against the program, but that in future he intended to vote
for it. I think that is quite an accomplishment. They also had a long session
later with the Ambassador in Pusan.

The Ambassador came here yesterday by NA [naval attaché] plane to spend
the day. Rhee had arrived an hour earlier by air force plane from Chinhae.
The latter called on General Walker, had a talk with his ministers (less the
Home Minister who was in P'ohang) and had lunch with us here at the
Presbyterian compound. The Prime Minister and the Foreign Minister also
lunched with us. Rhee seemed to be in a pretty good frame of mind for a
change. Later the Ambassador told me that he had had a very unpleasant
conference with Rhee the previous day at Pusan during which he had trouble
in keeping his temper. It seems that Rhee kept declaiming at length that
Korea had 200,000 patriotic young men in the Youth Guard who needed
nothing but arms to go out and win the war (a favorite theme with him

for sometime now). The Ambassador said that he brought the President up to date on the recruitment program as well as the U.S. arms being supplied the Korean forces. He then invited the President to facilitate the entry of the Youth Guard boys either into the new Korean forces being formed or into the 36,000 being collected for admixture with the American forces. He said that Rhee had also indicated a desire to visit MacArthur in Japan to broach this subject, but that he had thrown cold water on it, pointing out that Mac-Arthur is already doing all in his power to assist ROK. Frankly, while we do not wish to report it formally, Rhee has been exceedingly difficult since he left Taejŏn, what with his exaggerated statements of Korean capabilities, his innuendo on several occasions about the lack of American capabilities, and sly references to our running out at the last moment (a feeling which I believe he has harbored all along and which I think he still entertains), and his petty requests for this and that. He has solely tried our patience on numerous occasions, but I am glad to say that the Ambassador has done a masterful job of keeping his temper.

The two Republican congressmen were Henry J. Latham, New York, and Hugh Scott, Pennsylvania. Drumright's cautionary note about differences over American Far Eastern policy alludes to an evening meeting of Latham and Scott with Ambassador Muccio and four or five embassy officers. Muccio and Scott clashed over U.S. China policy and communism in Asia. Upon his return to the United States Scott attacked Muccio twice, first in October 1950 and again during the MacArthur hearings in 1951. Secretary of State Dean Acheson defended Muccio as follows:

> He is a very fine officer who served with General MacArthur, whom General MacArthur has said very fine things about; who accompanied General MacArthur to the Wake Island conference; who was decorated by the President for his gallantry; who has stuck with the Korean Government during the most dangerous of all these campaigns, and encouraged them.
> I don't think any person, either soldier or civilian, has put his life in more hazard than Ambassador Muccio, and he performed a great service in holding the South Korean Government together in the days when they were being driven back and forth across Korea, encouraging them and putting heart in them to hold the fight against the Communist attack [Senate, *Military Hearings*, pp. 1739-40, 2156-59].

On August 30 Drumright wrote to Allison as follows:

> The last week has seen little appreciable change in the general situation. The enemy has eased his pressure on the western side of the perimeter (where U.S. forces are deployed) and has increased his pressure against ROK forces all along the northern front, with the main emphasis in the northeast area. After our forces drove the enemy from P'ohang last week, they were directed to advance northward sufficiently to straighten the line along the northern front so that it would run almost due east-west. They advanced satisfactorily

for three days, but last Sunday the enemy counterattacked, recapturing Kigye and almost enveloping P'ohang. The ROK forces put up a disappointing show, showing once again that they lack offensive qualities and a tendency to break when under severe enemy pressure. It is my impression that General Walker has lost some of his confidence in the ROK forces as a result of the P'ohang-Kigye performance. He has, in any event, sent Major General J. B. Coulter to Kyŏngju to check on the operations of the ROK 1st Corps and has thrown the 21st Infantry of the 24th Division into the fray just south of Kigye. The 24th Division had just been relieved by the 2nd Division and it had been hoped that the elements of the 24th could rest and regroup—which they sorely need. General Kim Hong-il, Commander of the ROK 1st Corps, is under fire and he will doubtless be replaced unless President Rhee interposes too strongly. General Kim has a good record for his performance at the Han River front in the last days of June, but it is clear that he is no tactician and he has the further fault of ignoring orders. Another ROK general who is slated to get the ax is General Kim Sŏk-wŏn, Commander of the 3rd Division, who would have given up P'ohang except for the strenuous objections of his U.S. advisors. Kim is the political general who was being pushed by the Yun Ch'i-yŏng-Louise Yim faction to be Chief of Staff and whose designs were frustrated only by our intervention. Kim has put up such a sorry show of late as a military commander that there should be no objection to his replacement. The Acting Prime Minister, for his part, has been hoping that Kim Sŏk-wŏn would prove a bust and will be glad to see him gone. . . .

The recruiting of Koreans for the armed forces, both American and Korean, continues apace. There was a hitch at Pusan where the President issued an asinine statement that recruitment should be voluntary. I enclose a translation of the statement. It appears that the Korean colonel in charge of recruitment was a bit rough in his rounding up of Korean recruits and this coupled with Rhee's obsession that Korean youth are burning with a desire to volunteer (which is no more true here than anywhere else), brought about the statement. Rhee's statement was pretty much ignored here in Taegu with the result that all quotas were met. In Pusan, however, recruiting came to a standstill for a couple of days, but I believe it has since been resumed on a fair scale. The integration of Koreans into the U.S. forces is continuing with good results. I talked with U.S. regimental officers at Waegwan day before yesterday who said they welcomed and were much pleased with the Korean recruits given them.

The Ambassador has had some unpleasant exchanges with Rhee over the Korean Youth Corps and Korean Youth Guard. The Ambassador's position has been that these organizations should provide the bulk of the recruits whereas the President and the leader of the Youth Corps, Kim Yun-gun, appear to want to maintain the organization intact and arm them as such. Of course, such a proposal is entirely unacceptable. In all fairness, it appears that there has been some misunderstanding. Some Youth Corps and Youth Guardsmen are in the ROK forces; but we shall insist that the number be increased and that there should be no thought of keeping these organizations intact in the face of urgent needs for manpower. Rhee has even suggested that he should go to Japan to take up this matter with General MacArthur, but we have not offered him any encouragement or facilities.

For the past few days Rhee has been sojourning at his residence in Chinhae, with occasional trips to Puṣan. While at Chinhae he has taken the opportunity to visit General Kean at his 25th Division headquarters at Masan. Harold J. Noble has been staying at Chinhae to keep contact with Rhee. Politics continues to be played to some extent despite the military crisis. Home Minister Cho Pyŏng-ok found it necessary to go to Pusan the other day to explain to Rhee the various changes he has made in ranking police officials. It seems that he had not kept the President apprised of the changes and the reasons therefor, with the result that some of Cho's enemies, and notably the former Home Minister and Yi Pŏm-sŏk (who is still hoping for a position of preferment), had insinuated to the President that the changes were political in character and designed to strengthen Cho's (and the DNP's) political fences. I understand that Cho was able to explain the changes satisfactorily to the President. Capt. Sin [Sŏng-mo], the Acting Prime Minister, is also being constantly sniped at by the politicians at Pusan, and he also had to go to defend himself before the President. Sin has been doing an extremely competent job as wartime Prime Minister, but without our active support I am certain that he would have been relieved long before this. Unfortunately, Sin's health has shown signs of breaking and it may be that he will be forced to give up some of his responsibility. Cho, by the way, has also given up drinking and so far as I know has not been to a *kisaeng* party since taking over. Cho's one fault, as I see it, is a tendency to play off one American against another in getting his aims achieved. Only yesterday he came to me about more arms for his police and uniforms. I had to tell him to stick to regular channels, namely, through the Prime Minister and the Chief, KMAG. For your private information, relations between KMAG and the Koreans are not so good as they used to be. Perhaps the tensions of the past two months have told on both sides or perhaps they have rubbed elbows too closely. General [Francis W.] Farrell, the new Chief KMAG is new to the situation and his unintentional but brusque manners have not helped. Further the KMAG G-3 (who was promoted the other day) has not endeared himself to his Korean counterparts. I am trying to do what I can to smooth out these frictions. In my view, KMAG has a big part to play here and it is essential that the best possible relationships be maintained. I feel strongly that more U.S. officers and men should be placed with the Korean units to get better performance from the latter. I believe the desirability of this is generally recognized, but the shortage of men and officers is such that it cannot be done just at present. Moreover, KMAG needs to be strengthened to assist in the training of more Korean officers (in which the Koreans are markedly deficient) and in the training of the 5 new divisions that are being formed. . . .

Samuel Floyd, our USIS radio officer, had a bizarre experience the other day. He elected, on his day off last Sunday, to take the mobile unit and tour the P'ohang area, thinking he might be able to give some performances. He arrived in P'ohang without incident, but found the town relatively deserted. He accordingly drove north, neglecting to check as to the military situation. He soon found himself driving through ROK forces who applauded and cheered him on. He immediately found himself in a deserted area. Suddenly, his mobile unit came under fire of machine guns and small arms. He tried to turn around, but his assistant who was pushing the unit was wounded. Thereupon Floyd, his assistants and the driver took to the ditch and remained there until nightfall. They found later they were in no-man's land. They were under heavy fire all afternoon. After dark they crawled to a deserted farmhouse where they spent the night. The firing, mainly from friendly forces, went on throughout the night. Finally, with the coming of dawn, they found themselves still pinned down by fire. They prevailed upon an elderly refugee who was braving the fire to inform the ROK forces nearby of the presence of Floyd and to assist in escorting him out. The refugee did so and soon three Korean soldiers came to the farmhouse and escorted Floyd and his assistant (the driver had escaped into the ROK lines during the night) to safety. The mobile unit had to be abandoned, of course. Floyd felt pretty badly about it all, so I reproved him mildly for not checking closely before going into a military area. I have asked Col. Edwards, our MA, who is going to P'ohang today, to inquire about the mobile unit, which is a pretty expensive affair, and try to recover it. Floyd's assistant's wound proved to be superficial, fortunately, and he is back on the job.

As you may know, I have received home leave orders, having been in Korea more than 26 successive months. I would like to get home for a break and a chance to see my old father, who is getting on in years, but at the same time I do not like to leave if there is a vital job to be done. Right now things appear to be very well under control and I believe there is nothing here that cannot be done just as well if not better by FSR Noble who is both able and an old hand in this country. The job is mainly one of liaison between the U.N. military command and the Korean authorities here. In a preliminary talk with the Ambassador, I expressed the view that my services could better be dispensed with now than after our return to Seoul when we will have to rebuild from the ground up. I told the Ambassador that I would be glad to return to Korea for another year or so if he wanted me. He was kind enough to say that he did want me to return. I expect to explore the matter further with the Ambassador tomorrow and, if he is agreeable, I may leave here about mid-September. . . .

Translation of Press Release, Office of Public Information, Republic of Korea, distributed August 23 and carried in Pusan newspapers August 24.

President Rhee's Statement: Decrees on Conscription or Recruiting Unnecessary: Volunteers Only Will Be Registered Upon Application.

The difficulty in carrying on our war is not so much in the lack of manpower as in shortage of arms. The members of our defense corps and Youth Corps requested us, with tears in their eyes, to arm them so that they might fight and repulse the enemy, but we were very sorry that we could not comply with their request. If they just had the weapons to fight with they would defend their homes and country even at the risk of their lives. Therefore it is not necessary to promulgate decrees for conscription or recruiting, and, furthermore, such decrees would unsettle the minds of the people. Compulsory conscription of any kind should be . . . banned immediately, so that not even one or two people might be registered compulsorily. If, after the issuance of this statement, any one should discover such an evil, it should be reported immediately to the authorities concerned, and such an act should be sternly punished. Any person who volunteers for military service should hand in an application for registration to the respective provincial governor, receiving the necessary training and obeying the orders of the respective organization. If they wait a little, they will have an opportunity to join the army as soon as arms are available for them. Weapons are coming in every day.

President Rhee took his appeal for arms directly to General MacArthur in a letter of August 12, 1950. The president requested 30,000 weapons, "even rifles," with which he believed North Korean infiltration could be stopped. Rhee also urged an attack on North Korea "instead of waiting for them to attack us." For the future, Rhee advocated that "from a practical military point of view, it would be a farsighted thing to make Korea a large warehouse of war materials." Folder, UNC-CINC, Correspondence with Syngman Rhee, MacArthur Memorial, Norfolk, Va.

Four days later, September 3, Drumright commented on the military situation and Korean recruiting as follows:

Our people are really much more worried about the northern front which is held by our Korean allies. There are reports that the enemy is building up strength south of Andong for a push either on Taegu or Yŏngch'ŏn, the loss of either of which would be a serious blow. The ROK Army has suffered serious losses, especially in good officers, and there is some doubt whether it can contain a strong enemy offensive. The next few days ought to tell. Walker has some reserves, including the UK contingent, which can be thrown in if necessary, but he would prefer to keep them intact for offensive operations. There is as yet no definite indication when we may mount an offensive or precisely how it will be mounted.

Rhee has admitted to the Ambassador that his call for volunteers and tirade against drafting was a mistake. He has now promulgated the draft law which was passed some months ago by the National Assembly. Acting Prime Minister Sin and Home Minister Cho have been finding it necessary to spend some time in Pusan lately in order to ward off attacks of political opponents. The President has agreed to the relief of General Kim Hong-il as corps commander (he will probably be replaced by General Kim Paek-il) and of General Kim Sŏk-wŏn, Commander of the 3rd Division. The Korean Officers School is getting under way near Pusan on September 4. Officers are most urgently needed. Some difference of opinion has developed between the Korean and U.S. military about activation of new Korean divisions. The Koreans want to go ahead fast while the Americans are more interested in seeing the existing five divisions maintained at full strength.

North Korean pressure and the performance of ROK units worried U.S. officials when Drumright wrote on September 8:

The last few days have been active. The enemy continues his pushing and probing on all fronts. He hasn't been able to make any progress worthy of note along the western (Naktong) front, but he has found soft spots in the ROK lines from Yŏngch'ŏn (24 miles east of Taegu) to the east coast. The Korean forces are adequate in numbers and they are better armed than ever before; but they simply will not stand fast in the face of enemy assaults. We have been trying to analyze this "let down" in the ROK forces (this applies in particular to the 1st Corps—made up of the Capitol and 3rd Divisions). The main reason seems to lie in the lack of competent and aggressive leadership. True, many Korean officers have been killed or put out of action and the ranks are depleted, but even so, many of the veteran leaders are not showing leadership. Another reason for the showing, or rather lack of it, lies in the fact that the old rank and file has been pretty well killed off and the new recruits simply will not stand. I would like to remark, however, that the 2nd Corps, ably commanded by Brigadier General Yu Chae-hŭng, is an exception. His 1st and 6th Divisions have consistently given a good account of themselves. In view of the Yŏngch'ŏn crisis, he has also been given command of the 8th Division. Consequently the 2nd Corps now consists of three divisions and the 1st Corps of two divisions. Perhaps this is repetition, but Brigadier General Kim Paek-il has been given command of the 1st Corps. The commanders of the Capitol and 3rd Divisions have also been changed in an endeavor to shake up some fighting spirit. Thus far the results have not been encouraging. Major General Coulter was sent to Kyŏngju, 1st Corps headquarters, about a week ago to try to retrieve the P'ohang-Yŏngch'ŏn situation. He found it exceedingly difficult to get any positive action out of the Korean commanders. Two regiments of the U.S. 24th Division have now been committed in the Kyŏngju area, so Major General Church has taken over in that sector and General Coulter given another assignment.

The stark truth is that unless the ROK forces reform their lines and get some aggressiveness in the Yŏngch'ŏn-P'ohang area, we shall have to abandon Taegu and fall back on a more restricted perimeter about Pusan. This has been made very clear by General Walker to the Korean authorities concerned, including the Minister of Defense and the ROK Chief of Staff. Yesterday, General Walker took advantage of Rhee's visit to Taegu to tell him bluntly that the ROK forces would have to show more fight than they have exhibited recently if Taegu is to be held. Rhee, as usual, started talking about more arms. "Give us arms to equip another hundred thousand boys; they will drive the Communists out" still is Rhee's attitude. General Walker had to tell Rhee that the ROK forces are now very well armed (as indeed they are) and that the giving of arms to untrained men is not the solution.

In one field the Koreans continue to do a bang-up job: That is in the drafting of recruits for their own and the United Nations forces. In all parts of the free area the recruitment and preliminary training of Korean youth is to be observed. The Koreans have scrupulously lived up to their commitment to supply men for the U.S. forces. I have talked with a considerable number of American officers about these Korean recruits and they have been unanimous in welcoming them and in praising their fighting spirit. In recent visits to the front, I have been struck by the appearance and attitude of these Koreans and the fine way they are being treated by the U.S. forces. Except for pay, they get about every treatment that our own troops get. I have also been struck by the great aid being given by the Korean civilian labor corps.

These men are hired by the U.S. forces to carry supplies, dig fortifications, bring out wounded, and the like. They risk their lives daily in the cause and have really been of great help in areas where there are no roads (and there are many such places).

At the request of General Walker, the Korean Army headquarters moved from Taegu to Pusan September 6th. KMAG moved along with the Korean Army Headquarters. General Walker, at the same time, activated his rear headquarters at Pusan. He now has here a very small staff of about ten officers and a few enlisted men. First Cavalry is now in charge of the defense in this area and pretty much runs things from the military side. The Korean Prime Minister keeps an office here, but it is clear he will be in Pusan most of the time. The Home Minister retains his office and staff here—as he should. The Provincial Governor is also staying here. Thus Taegu is pretty well emptied of civilian officials and even of Korean military officials. My own staff here is now down to the Military Attaché, Rolf Jacoby of USIS (the center is still going), Clerk Josef Norris and a Marine guard. The Ambassador has not visited Taegu during the past week, but may come up any day now. Rhee came here yesterday mainly at our suggestion to show himself in Taegu. He also visited the ROK 2nd Corps Headquarters east of Taegu and talked with the Commander and other officers. As indicated above, he called on General Walker. As a matter of courtesy I met him at the air field, but had no extended or formal conversation with him. He looked well and seemed to be in pretty good spirits, though I understand from the Ambassador that he had been in the dumps the previous day, in Pusan, because of the P'ohang situation and the rainy weather.

Col. Edwards and I have visited three fronts in recent days. We went to Yŏngsan, about 30 miles south of Taegu, on Labor Day. There we saw the Marines advancing west toward the Naktong and doing a very efficient and masterful job of destroying the enemy. Among other things, we must have seen a hundred dead Communists and seven knocked-out Russian tanks, as well as much other Soviet equipment. Hundreds of other dead Communists littered the hills nearby. We brought back sufficient captured equipment and war weapons that Jacoby could start an exhibition at his center. On September 5th we visited the front about ten miles northwest of Taegu where we saw elements of the 1st Cavalry Division attempting to eliminate a Communist road block which had hindered road communications with forward elements. Since that time First Cavalry has withdrawn these forward elements and has withdrawn from Waegwan (which we visited a few days ago) in order to round out the lines and make it more difficult for the enemy to carry out his infiltrating tactics. By the way, the UK unit is now in position on the Naktong in the area about 10 to 15 miles southwest of Taegu. They have seen little action so far. Yesterday, Edwards and I visited the Yŏngch'ŏn area. When we got just this side of Yŏngch'ŏn we found that the ROK forces had just withdrawn from the town in the face of a light enemy attack. While we were there ROK forces were ordered to counterattack and take the town. After some backing and filling our ROK forces deployed for the attack, let loose with artillery and machine gun fire and thus covered the advancing soldiers. They crossed the stream and advanced into town against small-arms fire of light character from the enemy. By the time we left, ROK forces had pretty much occupied

the town and the hills behind it. Altogether, it was a pretty creditable performance, though a military expert could have picked many flaws in the way it
was executed. I had a grandstand view from a hill overlooking the town and
the valley and hills beyond.

Day before yesterday a Negro engineer company which was proceeding
down the Kyŏngju highway just beyond Yŏngch'ŏn was ambushed. The
colored boys, about 120 of them, had to take to the ditches and were pinned
down by enemy fire for several hours. Eventually, a ROK engineer company
came to their rescue, driving the enemy from the vicinity of the road and
capturing six enemy trucks and ten anti-tank cannon. The colored boys came
through this experience with only six wounded and some shot-up vehicles,
all of which were salvaged. It was ascertained later, of course, that the "jigs,"
as colored boys are labeled, were on the wrong road. But that is war.

Jim Stewart is here today on USIS business. That outfit has been doing a
mighty fine job under difficult circumstances. Jim and Al Loren, of ECA,
went to Cheju last Sunday and Monday. They found matters in pretty good
shape over on the island. Five ECA consultants are now residing there. The
marines, to whom I referred in a previous letter, have now left Cheju for the
mainland. An Army recruiting center, instead, is being established on the island
and before long we should have a Cheju contingent on the fighting front. The
police have finally started taking aggressive action against the few guerrillas on
the island and a number, including one of the leaders, have been captured.

Another matter: General Partridge of 5th Air Force has been helping the
Korean Air Force in every way possible and, as a result, some of their pilots
will be flying 51s in combat within a few days. It would be desirable from the
long-range view, however, to arrange for a few of the more promising ones to
get to the United States, perhaps when the conflict is over here, for advanced
training. I believe General Partridge is sympathetic, but a decision in that
regard is out of his bailiwick. The Ambassador is all for the idea. I merely mention it in the hope that State will see fit to support the idea if and when it
comes up.

By September 11 South Korean forces were more effective and Taegu appeared secure.

The last three or four days have brought a considerable improvement in the
military situation. First, the move of all but a small skeleton of Eighth Army
to Pusan (which should have been accomplished six weeks ago), the move
of the Korean Army headquarters and of KMAG were carried out without
upsetting the Taegu population. Secondly, the situation on the north front
has shown great improvement. As I indicated in a recent letter, the Korean
troops were not fighting as well as our military felt they should be. It was at
this time that we lost P'ohang and the enemy got into Yŏngch'ŏn and cut our
highway and rail communications with Kyŏngju. It was then that General
Walker, the Ambassador and several others of us started pressing the Minister
of Defense, the ROK Chief of Staff and President Rhee to do all in their
power to infuse an offensive spark in the ROK forces. I am glad to report that
this has been done, especially in the 2nd Corps area. During the past four
days the Military Attaché and I have been in the Yŏngch'ŏn area on three occa-

sions. We saw ROK forces recapture the city on September 7; we saw ROK forces drive the enemy from the outskirts on the 8th. We went there again yesterday when we were able to drive several miles beyond the city in the direction of Kyŏngju. It was while on the road that we passed vehicles coming up from Kyŏngju. This was most welcome news and will greatly relieve Gen. Walker's anxiety. The ROK forces looked mighty good in action beyond Yŏngch'ŏn yesterday. They captured several Russian made 122mm and 76mm guns. We also saw an intact T-70 tank which ROK soldiers were driving to the rear.

We understand, although we have not had direct contact, that the ROK forces in the eastern sector are also showing offensive capabilities again. If so, we should be able to recover P'ohang and keep the enemy off the air field and our lines of communications through Kyŏngju.

The First Cavalry Division has given up about three miles of ground northwest of Taegu during the past ten days. This puts the enemy within about 8 miles of Taegu. He has the capability of shelling the city from there with his 122mm gun, but has been letting us alone for some days. The First Cavalry contained a strong enemy attack last night which had the capture of Taegu as its objective, if statements of prisoners can be believed. I am more confident than ever now we can hold Taegu.

Drumright's final letter, from Pusan on September 22, 1950, marked a turning point, albeit temporary, in US-ROK fortunes after the Inch'-ŏn landing.

I find from my files that I wrote you last on September 11th. Much has happened since that time. Between the 11th and the 15th I made visits to the ROK 7th and 8th Division fronts and to the 2nd U.S. Division front. The ROK forces looked extremely good in action north and east of Yŏngch'ŏn. Since that time the ROK forces have recaptured P'ohang and have made substantial advances toward Andong. I also visited the 1st Cavalry sector on several occasions, it being not more than a 30-minute drive from Taegu. In this area, about eight miles northwest of Taegu, the enemy has consistently put up his strongest resistance. However, in the past two days, the ROK 1st Division has got in behind the enemy north of Tabudong, with the result that he has been cut off and is threatened with annihilation. Other strong centers of enemy resistance have been in the Masan area in the south and around Ch'angnyŏng and Yŏngsan in the 2nd Division area. That division has been plagued with infiltration more than any other U.S. unit, although it has not assumed serious proportions.

Following the landing at Inch'on on the 15th, which was a well-kept secret until after it occurred, General Walker started offensive operations all along the southern perimeter, seeking soft spots through which to make breakthroughs. On the whole, the enemy, who was informed of the Inch'ŏn development by leaflets and invited to surrender, has resisted more stubbornly than had been expected. The main effort is being made in the Waegwan-Tabudong sector. Here resistance has been tenacious, particularly around Tabudong. But we have now crossed the river around Waegwan and, as I indicated above, the enemy faces annihilation at Tabudong. I feel that a breakthrough toward

Yŏngdong and Taejŏn is an imminent possibility; moreover, the ROK forces, who are advancing north along a broad front, seem to have the capability of taking the vital communications center of Andong within the near future. The enemy has been receiving little in the way of supplies and equipment recently and his losses have been heavy. His replacements are comprised largely of South Korean conscripts who are neither trained nor desirous of fighting. It is my estimate that the North Korean forces fighting on the southern front are by now more than half made up of South Koreans impressed into service. I have run across a good many of them among prisoners of war. There is much speculation now regarding the will to fight among the North Koreans once it becomes fully known that they are cut off in the north and face annihilation. It is my own opinion that the great body of replacements will surrender when the opportunity offers. But the hard-bitten North Korean veterans, including those who served with the Chinese Communists, will most likely hole up in the mountains and fight to the last. Fortunately, their number is no longer great and they should offer no insurmountable problem.

The Inch'ŏn operation has of course brought a tremendous wave of relief, both to us and to the Koreans, but more especially to the latter. It was amazing to see the way Koreans of all walks of life perked up when the news became generally known. This was particularly true at Taegu where the enemy was virtually at the gates. Now that the enemy thrust has been broken, the Koreans are not unnaturally speculating regarding the future of their country. It goes without saying that virtually all look forward to unification and the absence of anything smacking of foreign control or trusteeship (of north Korea). Rhee is getting pretty excited over the silence abroad regarding unification and solution of the 38th parallel issue. I don't know what will be our policy (though I have definite views on that subject), but you can be certain that the ROK authorities will plug their hardest for abolition of the 38th parallel and full unification under the ROK government. As I see it, this is a perfectly natural reaction on the part of Rhee and all concerned with the ROK.

We have not been kept informed of developments in the Seoul-Inch'ŏn area following the landing on the 15th. Neither has General Walker for that matter; and the 5th Air Force was forbidden to go into a restricted area about Seoul. Our reports about the operation, therefore, have come from the radio and the newspapers and probably are not equal to those available to you. However, the ROK has been alerted to have skeleton official staffs for Seoul, Inch'ŏn and Kyŏnggi Province ready to go forward at a moment's notice. I believe that the first echelons may go today or tomorrow. Moreover, the Home Minister has more than 5,000 police ready and the central government is readying a skeleton staff to return to Seoul.

Following the Inch'ŏn landing the Ambassador asked me to come to Pusan. Some of us are expecting to go to Seoul just as soon as the military give the word. Our return should occur shortly after Seoul is secured. Recent aerial photographs indicate that most of our property is intact. We do not know, of course, how much damage may have been inflicted by Navy or Marine aircraft. Also, if the enemy chooses to fight for Seoul street-by-street then we may suffer serious losses in terms of buildings.

Philippine forces landed here September 20 and have gone into Miryang in reserve. The ROK 17th regiment is being prepared for shipment to Seoul where it will serve as the palace guard. As you know, Korean Marines, who were given some training in Marine tactics in Pusan beforehand, participated in the Inch'ŏn landing.

The rice crop is about the best ever. My own feeling is that it suffered little damage from the war. If we can drive the enemy away from the present perimeter within the next two or three weeks, a good portion of our refugee problem will be largely solved (at least 60% of our refugees are from the Naktong valley areas of north and south Kyŏngsang provinces). Fortunately, we got through the hot days without epidemics. Prices are rising fast. We've got to get the ROK to collect taxes and revenues in a big way; otherwise, we are in for a serious dose of inflation.

3. If President Rhee knew in advance about the Inch'ŏn landing, a letter he wrote to General MacArthur on September 8, 1950, is exceedingly curious. Rhee urged the opening of a second front "by making an amphibious landing behind enemy lines either in Inch'on or somewhere north of Taegu." Folder, UNC-CINC, Correspondence with Syngman Rhee.

4. The decision to cross the 38th parallel and unify the Korean peninsula by a military victory over North Korea was a complete reversal of initial announced U.S. policy. On June 29 Secretary of State Acheson had stated that American policy was designed "solely for the purpose of restoring the Republic of Korea to its status prior to the invasion from the north and of re-establishing the peace broken by that aggression." However, American officials were planning for the removal of the 38th parallel as a political boundary and the destruction of North Korea from early July. Dean Acheson, *Present at the Creation* (New York: Norton, 1969), pp. 450-52.

President Syngman Rhee almost compromised secret American plans when he stated in mid-July that hostilities had dissolved the dividing line across Korea. Acheson hinted at future U.S. policy, even while American troops were in retreat, in the following cable to Muccio:

Press report June 13 [should read July 13] quotes Pres. Rhee as voicing determination ROK not to stop at 38th parallel in repelling invaders. Same report quotes US Army spokesman, presumably in Korea, as stating US forces will not only stop 38th parallel but will use force if necessary to prevent ROK troops from advancing beyond that line.

In order not prejudice US position this important and explosive question, Dept. feels every effort should be made to avoid official statements or other public discussion of course of action to be taken at such time as northern forces expelled from South Korea. This particularly true of any statements, such as that cited above, which could be taken by Koreans as prejudging US attitude toward 38th parallel.

Foregoing views being conveyed also to Defense [Acheson to Muccio, no. 3884, July 14, 1950].
United States actions at the U.N. in September and early October, culminating in the "uniting for peace" resolution of October 7, were designed to obtain U.N. sanction for U.S. military actions already decided upon.
George F. Kennan has written of his opposition to the crossing of the 38th parallel in his memoirs. His final comments on the question are worth quoting at length:

What influences were finally decisive in persuading us to go beyond the parallel and to enlist the support of the UN Assembly in this enterprise I do not know. They were, apparently, beginning to be strongly felt by mid-August; for on August 19 our representative in the Security Council Senator Warren Austin, was already talking about the impossibility of leaving Korea "half slave and half free." Mr. John Foster Dulles, too, as we shall shortly see, appears to have favored an advance beyond the parallel as early as the end of July; and this could be, I should think, taken as evidence that such a view already represented the consensus of feeling in right-wing Republican circles on the Hill. But I also suspect that the change was partly the work of our wide-eyed enthusiasts for the UN, who, like so many other idealists, often promoted with the best of motives causes which ultimately only added to, instead of subtracting from, the total volume of violence taking place in the affairs of nations.

Our advance beyond the parallel was of course based, when it came, on a UN resolution. I never approved of the involvement of the United Nations in the Korean affair, or understood the rationale of it. This was, after all, an area in which we had taken the Japanese surrender and accepted the responsibilities of occupation. There was as yet no peace treaty with Japan to define its future status. We had accepted the responsibilities of military occupation in South Korea, and the fact that we had withdrawn our own combat forces did not mean, in the continued absence of a Japanese peace treaty, that these responsibilities were terminated. We had a perfect right to intervene, on the basis of our position as occupying power, to assure the preservation of order in this territory. We needed no international mandate to make this action proper. Nor did the Charter of the United Nations require us to involve the organization in such a conflict. Article 107, while somewhat ambiguous, conveyed the general impression that problems arising immediately from the recent war were not to be considered proper subjects for the attention of the UN. This was, finally, a civil conflict not an international one; and the term "aggression" in the usual international sense was as misplaced here as it was to be later in the case of Vietnam. The involvement of the United Nations, hastily brought about by my colleagues in the State Department before I returned from my farm on that fateful Sunday, was thus in no way necessary or called for; and the later invocation of a UN resolution to justify military operations extending beyond the parallel seemed to me to represent an abuse, rather than a proper utilization, of the exceptional confidence accorded to us that time by the international community [George F. Kennan, *Memoirs, 1925-1950* (Boston: Little, Brown, 1967), pp. 489-90].

5. The State Department's policy in mid-September on the precise legal form for unifying Korea cannot be determined until the relevant documents are made public. Vague statements about "elections in Korea" may have been designed to placate some U.N. members who were uncomfortable with the idea of a United Nations endorsement of Syngman Rhee's government. On the other hand, the idea of peninsula-wide elections may have been seriously considered.

In any event, by September 30 U.S. policy explicitly limited elections under U.N. sponsorship to North Korea. On that date, Ambassador Austin made the following statement:

... The draft resolution clearly states one of the most determined objectives of the United Nations to be the Unity and Independence of Korea. At this moment, we cannot foresee the precise circumstances in which unification is to be accomplished. Even if this were not the case, we would be ill advised to try to develop here detailed blueprints for such a complex operation. Therefore, we endorse the idea of establishing in Korea a strong United Nations Commission empowered to devise practical and effective measures for achieving United Nations objectives.

The Commission would of course consult with the United Command and with the democratically selected representatives of the Korean people. At an appropriate time, elections by secret ballot, free from fraud and intimidation, under auspices of the United Nations Commission would have to be arranged. *Free Democratic Elections already have been held south of the 38th Parallel. The General Assembly has formally declared the Government of the Republic of Korea formed as a result of those elections to be lawfully constituted Government in that part of Korea in which the United Nations Commission was able to observe elections.* It is the territory and people of this Government that have been ravaged by war. It is the soldiers of this Government whose valor and patriotism have been strengthened by the United Nations Forces. The manner and procedures required to unify the country are functions for the United Nations to perform, but the Government of the Republic of Korea has unquestionably earned the right to be consulted in matters relating to the future of Korea [Secretary of State to Muccio, no. 210, October 19, 1950 (emphasis added)].

The delay in informing the embassy of Washington policy (this cable was sent nineteen days after Austin's speech, for example) must have contributed to the confusion in Korea.

President Rhee subsequently rejected *any* interference by the United Nations in the unification of Korea. He insisted that the ROK Army was unifying and liberating North Korea as it advanced. According to O. P. H. King, General MacArthur secretly agreed to allow Rhee to select the individuals whom the U.N. commission would designate as governors for the northern provinces. The arrangement was made to obtain, from the ever-suspicious Syngman Rhee, approval for a nominal role for the U.N. commission. King, *Tail of the Tiger*, p. 415.

6. American diplomatic and military authorities in Korea were initially confused about the implementation of the October 29 directive to General MacArthur for the occupation of Korea north of the 38th parallel. In a review of MacArthur's instructions for the 1951 Senate hearings Dean Acheson wrote:

> Following discussions between representatives of the Departments of State and Defense, the Joint Chiefs of Staff, on November 2, 1950, transmitted a telegram to General MacArthur which had the full concurrence of the Department of State, to the effect that it was the understanding in Washington that he was prohibiting, for all practical purposes, the utilization of South Korean personnel in civil affairs matters in North Korea. The telegram informed General MacArthur that it was not intended so to restrict him; rather it should be emphasized that he should make use of South Korean personnel in the administration of North Korea [letter, Acheson to Secretary of Defense George C. Marshall, May 21, 1951].

CHAPTER FOURTEEN

1. A description of the battle for Seoul may be found in Appleman, *South to the Naktong*, Chap. 26; and Montross and Canzona, *Pusan Perimeter*.

2. General MacArthur made the following remarks at the capitol ceremony:

> By the grace of a merciful Providence our forces fighting under the standard of that greatest hope and inspiration of mankind, the United Nations, have liberated this ancient capital city of Korea. It has been freed from the despotism of Communist rule and its citizens once more have the opportunity to live under that immutable concept of life which holds invincibly to the primacy of individual liberty and personal dignity.
>
> The ravage of war which had been visited upon your land, Mr. President, by those forces of evil which seek to subvert the spiritual qualities of modern civilization, has been viewed with universal concern and distress. And fifty-three nations of the earth rose up in righteous wrath and indignation and pledged their full effort toward your relief. Such was the spiritual revulsion against the march of imperialistic Communism seeking the conquest, exploitation, and enslavement of others. It reflects an invincible union of men and ideals against which no material weapons could long prevail, and while inevitably force must meet force, it offers hope for the ultimate peaceful triumph of that spiritual quality without which the human mind cannot produce sound

and enduring ideas. It is through the spirit that we must save the flesh.

In behalf of the United Nations Command, I am happy to restore to you, Mr. President, the seat of your government that from it you may the better fulfill your constitutional responsibilities. It is my fervent hope that a beneficient Providence will give you and all of your public officials the wisdom and strength to meet your perplexing problems in a spirit of benevolence and justice, that from the travail of the past there may emerge a new and hopeful dawn for the people of Korea.

In humble and devout manifestation of gratitude to Almighty God for bringing this decisive victory to our arms, I ask that all present rise and join me in reciting the Lord's Prayer: "Our Father which art in Heaven, hallowed be thy name. Thy kingdom come. Thy will be done, on earth as it is in Heaven. Give us this day our daily bread. And forgive us our trespasses, as we forgive those who trespass against us. And lead us not into temptation, but deliver us from evil: For thine is the kingdom, and the power, and the glory, forever and ever. Amen!"

Mr. President, my officers and I will now resume our military duties and leave you and your government to the discharge of the civil responsibility [Major Vorin E. Whan, ed., *A Soldier Speaks: Public Papers and Speeches of General of the Army Douglas MacArthur* (New York: Praeger, 1965), pp. 223-24].

3. Atrocities were committed by both sides, including the summary executions of "collaborators" by South Korean forces after the recapture of Seoul.

APPENDIX

1. This section is an adaptation of an article Harold Noble published in the *Saturday Evening Post,* August 9, 1952, entitled, "The Reds Made Suckers of Us All." The article was apparently intended as a popular refutation of I. F. Stone's *The Hidden History of the Korean War* (New York: Monthly Review Press, 1952), published in April 1952. Harold Noble's copy of the Stone book, replete with marginal notations of disagreements, indicates his sharp objections to charges that South Korea initiated hostilities. This section is neither a complete description of the events leading up to June 25 nor a comprehensive analysis of the war's origin. Rather, it is an explanation of why Noble and other U.S. officials did not anticipate hostilities in June 1950. The material is included here, despite its uneven quality, because it relates to the controversy over the war's origin and contains certain details not included in other sources, and because of the added credibility which may adhere to the account of a direct participant.

The article is reprinted with permission from *The Saturday Eve-*

ning Post, © 1952, The Curtis Publishing Company.
2. The North Korean allegation that South Korea attacked first
was made initially over P'yŏngyang Radio at 11:00 A.M., June 25. The
following is a summary translation of the broadcast.

Official announcement made by the Home Affairs Bureau of the People's
Republic of Korea. The so-called "Defense Army" of the South Korea puppet
regime started a surprise invasion of the north along the whole front of the
38th Parallel line at dawn on the 25th. The enemy, who started the surprise
operation, invaded the territory north of the 38th Parallel line 1 to 2 kilometers
at 3 points west of Haeju, Kumch'on and Chorwon. The Home Affairs Bureau
of the People's Republic of Korea has issued an order to the Security Army of
the People's Republic to repulse the enemy. At this moment, our Security Army
is putting up stiff counter operations against the enemy. The People's Republic Army succeeded in repulsing the enemy force which penetrated into
the north at Yangyang. In this connection, the People's Republic of Korea
wishes to remind the South Korea puppet regime of the fact that, unless the
puppets immediately suspend their adventurous military actions, the People's
Republic will be obliged to resort to decisive counter measures. At the same
time, the People's Republic entrusted the Home Affairs Bureau to call the attention of the South Korea puppet regime to the fact that the whole responsibility for the grave consequences arising from their reckless venture would
squarely rest on the shoulders of the South Korean puppet regime.

The following embassy comment accompanied the text: "It will be
obvious that by terms broadcast North Koreans are attempting to clothe
their naked aggression against ROK with patently absurd charges
that ROK commenced invasion. Developments during course of day
of course wholly disprove this unfounded propaganda." Muccio to
Secretary of State, no. 931, June 25, 1950.
    The DPRK and the USSR have insisted, from June 1950 to the
present, that hostilities were initiated by South Korea. Responsible
writers, to whom Harold Noble's characterization would in no sense
apply, have also raised the possibility that South Korea provoked the
North Korean attack. The distinguished journalist, I. F. Stone, was the
first to question the official explanation of the war's start in *The Hidden
History of the Korean War*.
    Stone suggested that Syngman Rhee, Chiang Kai-shek, John Foster
Dulles, and General MacArthur coordinated a strategy to reverse U.S.
Far Eastern policy by forcing a strong commitment in Asia. A provocation against North Korea by Syngman Rhee, which in turn brought a
major attack on the Republic of Korea and then U.S. intervention,
would have served the direct interests of the four principals, according
to the Stone analysis.

In an approving restatement of the Stone hypotheses D. F. Fleming
has recently written as follows:

The assumption is nearly universal in this country that Stalin pushed the
button for the North Korean attack on South Korea. After searching for
twenty years I have never found any evidence that this was true; but it is a
matter of record that early in 1949 our government laid down a defense perimeter in the Pacific that did not include Korea or Formosa and that in both
cases the ruling dictators had no future for their ambitions unless something
drastic was done. In South Korea Syngman Rhee was in dire political trouble
and had been threatening for a long time to unify Korea by marching north.
That he did so, provoking the North Korean invasion, is one of the strongest
probabilities, especially since Chiang Kai-shek on Formosa also had been left
out of the American defense perimeter and had no future unless something
happened to change Washington's policy. Both Chiang and Rhee were proteges
and close confidants of General Douglas MacArthur, our commander-in-chief
in the Far East. John Foster Dulles, Republican Adviser to the State Department and fervid anti-Communist, also had conferences with MacArthur in
Tokyo and with Syngman Rhee in South Korea shortly before the war broke
out, and on June 22 he exuberantly predicted "positive action" in the Far East.
In his carefully documented book, *The Hidden History of the Korean War,*
I. F. Stone points to many convincing indications that these four keenly interested and kindred leaders had strong reason to expect the explosion that came
on June 5, 1950, with the outbreak of the Korean War [D. F. Fleming, "Can
We Escape from Containing China?" *Western Political Quarterly* 24 (March
1971): 163].

Fleming thus maintained a view adumbrated in his earlier epic revi-
sionist work, *The Cold War and Its Origins: 1917-1960* (New York:
Doubleday, 1961). David Horowitz shared the hypothesis in *The Free
World Colossus* (New York: Hill & Wang, 1965).

Joyce and Gabriel Kolko have added new information and broadened
the debate with *The Limits of Power: The World and United States
Foreign Policy, 1945-1954* (New York: Harper & Row, 1972). William Stueck sharply disputes the Kolkos' analysis and conclusions in his
article, "Cold War Revisionism and the Origins of the Korean Conflict:
The Kolko Thesis." For a fascinating review of the basic issues posed
by conventional versus revisionist interpretations, see the Stueck-Kolkos
debate (which includes the Stueck article cited above) in "An Exchange
of Opinion," *Pacific Historical Review* 42, no. 4 (November 1973): 537-
75. Finally, for a South Korean interpretation, see Robert A. Scalapino
and Chong-Sik Lee, *Communism in Korea: Part I, The Movement*
(Berkeley: University of California Press, 1972), pp. 394-401.

While decidedly a minority position in the literature on the Korean
War, the seriousness of the allegation compels a forthright calling of the

Stone question: Is the hypothesis of a South Korean provocation supported by the available evidence?
The answer at present is no. The most interested party, North Korea,
has yet to substantiate its allegations with credible evidence. The very
term "provocation" is rendered all but meaningless by the nature of the
North Korean allegation and the known sequence of events. North
Korea did not charge a South Korean intrusion or sustained attack in
the spring of 1950, in May or early June. Such an attack might have
led to the mobilization of North Korean forces and their deployment
along the 38th parallel for an extended counteroffensive if another
incident occurred. However, according to the North Korean charge,
the South Korean attack occurred on the morning of June 25. Yet over-
whelming and indisputable evidence shows that North Korean forces
advanced across the 38th parallel at several widely separate points, including a commando landing on the east coast, early on the morning of
June 25. Eyewitness reports place the North Korean attack on Kaesŏng, for example, at 4:00-5:00 A.M., June 25. The coordinated movement of troops, preceded by artillery bombardment, could have been
accomplished only after lengthy, careful planning. That such a movement of forces could have been an instantaneous response to a South
Korean attack is patently implausible.

In contrast to the dearth of information in support of the North
Korean contention, the interrogation reports of North Korean prisoners
of war and captured NKPA documents provide a detailed account of
the shift of NKPA units to the 38th parallel in mid-June and preparations for an offensive campaign. The captured documents include a
"pre-invasion reconnaissance order from the G-2, General Staff, North
Korean Army, to the Chief of Staff, 4th Infantry Division, outlining
reconnaissance activities to be implemented both prior to and after the
initiation of hostilities." Another captured document, Field Order No.
1, is an attack plan for the NKPA 4th Division and supporting units.
These materials are included in U.S., General Headquarters, Far East
Command, *Research Supplement: Documentary Evidence of North
Korean Aggression,* October 30, 1950, folder, MacArthur Memorial.

The larger issue of responsibility for the Korean War is not affected
by this refutation of the North Korean version of events immediately
related to the outbreak of hostilities. Koreans, north or south, Communist or non-Communist, desired Korean unification. Both governments, north and south, advocated military action to achieve unification. The U.S. denied arms to the ROK precisely because President
Rhee had often stated his intention to march north and unite Korea.

When the fortunes of war changed in their favor in September 1950, the U.S. and South Korea attempted an armed unification of Korea, contrary to earlier U.S. and U.N. policy. These similarities underscore the fact that the Korean War was a civil war between two competing Korean political groups. External support from the USSR and the U.S. intervention magnified a local conflict into a major episode in the Cold War and a tragic, sanguine disaster for Koreans, north and south.

Materials now classified or otherwise not available to researchers may alter our understanding of some aspects of these events. U.S. State Department records and the personal papers of Syngman Rhee, for example, may prove particularly valuable. I am indebted to Bruce Cumings for a stimulating discussion of the possible significance of the meetings between Syngman Rhee and General MacArthur from 1945 to 1950. Unfortunately, the records of these meetings, if any exist, are not available to scholars.

3. Among the claimants was Gen. Charles A. Willoughby in *MacArthur, 1941-1951* (New York: McGraw-Hill, 1954), pp. 350-55. The "intelligence failure" is mentioned briefly in Paige, *The Korean Decision,* pp. 155-56; Schnabel, *Policy and Direction,* pp. 61-64; and in the MacArthur hearings.

4. U.S. troops were withdrawn from South Korea by June 29, 1949.

5. South Korean forces did more than "reciprocate." In some instances they precipitated the fighting by attempting to occupy positions north of the 38th parallel. See Sawyer, *Military Advisers,* p. 73.

6. However, inexplicably, there were no antitank mines in South Korea when the war began. Appleman, *South to the Naktong,* p. 72.

7. Futrell states that intelligence estimates reported the North Korean Force to have 132 combat aircraft and a total of about 2,000 men. Futrell, *Air Force in Korea,* p. 92.

8. Details of the embassy's recommendations to strengthen the ROK militarily may be found in Sawyer, *Military Advisers;* and Paige, *The Korean Decision.*

9. The full text of the cable was as follows:

Phrasing EMHDES 465, May 4, 1950 stating that "South Korean army is superior today" to North Korean army and is better equipped was intended refer to estimated superiority training, leadership, morale, marksmanship and better small arms equipment, especially M-1s, army of South Korea to that of North Korean army as distinguished from air force.

EMBTEN 683, May 11, contains good estimate strengths, equipment North Korea. North Korean power, tanks and heavier artillery, but especially air power, give preponderance strength to North despite estimated inferiority North Korean ground forces compared to South Korean ground forces.

Capacity North Korean forces conduct successful operations against south hinges primarily on capacity north overcome southern infantry superiority by undisputed command of air plus heavier artillery with consequent adverse effect both actual military operations and morale South Korean forces. Embassy believes, and KMAG concurs, should South Korean forces be strengthened by some measure air defense and heavy artillery, superiority or at least reasonable equality would rest with south vis-a-vis North Koreans (USSR or Chinese forces not considered in this estimate).

Apart from strictly military estimate, consider necessary psychological effect ROK Government and civilians constantly facing knowledge northern capacity control air at will, including capacity uninterrupted bombing Seoul, as well as general knowledge northern artillery outranges southern artillery while northern army has tanks but none here.

Invite attention fact Brigadier General W. L. Roberts, Chief KMAG, departing tomorrow by plane for Tokyo where he will board transport June 23 for San Francisco expecting arrive about July 3 en route new assignment Los Angeles. Suggest Roberts, who extremely conversant this problem, proceed Washington discuss, explain this problem [Muccio to Secretary of State, no. 857, June 14, 1950].

The estimate of South Korean infantry superiority was not borne out by events. In particular, there was a great disparity in the level of training attained by the North Korean forces. After noting the obstacles to proper training, Sawyer (*Military Advisers*, p. 78) describes the ROK Army's state of readiness as follows:

> But by 15 June 1950 only the ROK Capitol Division's 9 battalions, 6 battalions of the ROK 7th Division, and a battalion of the ROK 8th Division had completed the battalion phase of training. Thirty others were through the company phase, and 17 had not finished the platoon phase. Two battalions had 75 percent of their platoon training and 50 percent of their company training. Seventeen battalion staffs and 5 regimental staffs had participated in command post exercises; 14 battalions had taken the 8-day maneuver exercise; and 6 battalions had taken Tank Hunting Team training. All Korean troops had fired for record with the MI rifle, however, and qualification firing of other individual arms and of crew-served weapons was well along. The technical services were progressing satisfactorily despite the difficulty with which Korean Army personnel absorbed and applied technical training.

The ROK Army was not scheduled to complete battalion level training until July 31, 1950, and regimental training until October 31, 1950. Ibid.

This degree of readiness, or more correctly unreadiness, indicates that U.S. estimates of the effectiveness of the ROK Army were based on factors other than training accomplished and were, in any event, inaccurate. A corollary is that the ROK Army had not completed the minimal training required to initiate offensive military action against North Korea by June 1950.

10. On January 26, 1950, the U.S. and the ROK signed a bilateral agreement, under the Mutual Defense Assistance Act, covering the terms of the military aid arrangement. After various administrative and legislative delays, Congress approved on March 15, 1950, a $10.97 million program for Korea. The embassy had recommended a minimum of $20 million in military assistance for fiscal 1950.

By June 25 approximately $350,000 worth of spare parts and signal equipment were en route to Korea, but only about $1,000 worth had actually arrived. Ibid., pp. 96-104.

11. The embassy report and assessment of these developments was as follows:

Pyongyang Radio commenced new propaganda campaign June 7 analogous similar one 1949. "Democratic Front" deploring continued division Korea by American-Rhee police state proposes "patriotic parties" and organizations celebrate liberation day August 15 in unison, accordance following principles: (1) from August 5, for eight days, elect "unified supreme legislative organ" throughout Korea; (2) hold first session this legislature Seoul August 15; (3) hold preliminary joint north-south leaders conference Haeju or Kaesong discuss (a) measures peaceful unification; (b) create general election committee for holding elections; (4) exclude UNCOK from work for attainment peaceful unification; (5) make "north and south regimes responsible for public peace and order during period joint meeting and general election" (although "Syngman Rhee, Lee Bum Suk [Yi Pŏm-sŏk] and other criminals" not allowed participate joint meeting). Three persons to be sent south deliver copies this appeal to various parties and UNCOK.
Comment: Noteworthy first time date set for occupation Seoul, although many previous claims intention do so. Embassy estimates program purely propaganda campaign attempting off-set results recent election which portrayed by Pyongyang Radio as complete failure with popular participation only under duress. Possible some border incidents may coincide with "election campaign" but no estimate basic change military situation (unlikely this propaganda much effect South Korea since Communists all underground while "middle roaders" largely supporting ROK).
Methods of meeting this new propaganda campaign now subject informal conversation with ROK and UNCOK officials [Muccio to Secretary of State, no. 829, June 9, 1950].

12. Several espionage operations were discovered in early 1950. Noble's mention of North Korea's "two chief agents" refers to Kim Sam-yong and Yi Chu-ha, important members of the South Korean Labor party. Kim and Yi were executed on June 26, 1950.

13. Cho Man-sik (1882-?) was educated at a missionary school in P'yŏngyang and graduated from Meiji University, Japan, in 1913. Cho was active in the Korean independence movement within Korea from 1919, twice being imprisoned by the Japanese authorities, during his

career as an educator and Christian leader. In 1945 he formed an independent political party in North Korea, but in early 1946 he was prevented from engaging in political activity and later, according to reports, placed under house arrest.

14. The ROK cabinet discussed the exchange on June 16 and agreed that it would be desirable to obtain Cho's release. That evening Seoul announced that the espionage agents would be exchanged if Cho and one other prisoner were returned to the south within one week. Radio P'yŏngyang countered with a demand that the exchange take place at Yŏhyŏn station on June 20. The North Korean agents were Kim Sam-yong and Yi Chu-ha. Muccio to Secretary of State, no. 875, June 17, 1950.

15. On June 26, 1950, the U.N. commission submitted a lengthy report of the events prior to the outbreak of war. The report summarized the developments in June described by Harold Noble and reached a similar conclusion: "In the light of the evidently increasing strength of the Republic of Korea in recent months and the utterly unexpected invasion on 25 June the radio propaganda offensive calling for early unification by peaceful means seems to have been intended solely for its screening effect." United Nations, Commission on Korea, June 26, 1950, "The United Nations Commission on Korea to the Secretary-General," S/1505, in State Department, *United States Policy in the Korean Crisis*, p. 20.

Index

Acheson, Dean, 33-34, 298
Adams, Alec, 284
ADCOM. *See* General Headquarters' Advance Command and Liaison Group in Korea
Agence France Presse, 40
Allen, Curtis R., 43, 49
Allison, John M., 280
Almond, Edward M., Maj. Gen.: at Suwŏn, 85, 88; mentioned, 29, 266
American Mission in Korea (AMIK), 240
Armed Forces Radio, 46-47
Ascom City, 23
Asian nationalism: Harold Noble's views on, xi
"Asiatic-Pacific Pact," x
Associated Press, 12, 41, 242
Australia: Harold Noble's writings on, vii

Bando Hotel, 3
Bataan, 85, 91, 194, 198-99
Beech, Keyes, 262
Berry, Sam, 36, 80
Blake, George, 259
British legation: in Taegu, 137, 147, 161, 174; in Seoul ceremony, 203
Bryne, Bishop Patrick, 41, 261
Buckley, Christopher, 148-49
Bunce, Arthur C., 8, 15

Bunting, Fred, 274

Ch'ae Pyŏng-dŏk, Maj. Gen.: chief of staff of ROK Army, 27, 65, 78, 81-83, 86, 246, 268; and Han River, 39, 82-83; and Gen. Church, 79, 86, 109; briefs MacArthur, 86; death of, 167, 263, 291; biographical information on, 253; mentioned, 39
Chang Ki-yŏng, 245
Chanteloup, Maurice-Georges, 40-41, 261
Cheju Island, viii
Chiang Kai-shek, 39
Chicago Tribune, 13, 41, 102
China: Harold Noble's writings on, vii; citizens of in Seoul, 39
Chinanmp'o, 229
Chinese embassy: at Taegu, 137, 176; at Seoul, 203
Chinese Nationalists: Harold Noble's views on, vii
Chinhae: and Syngman Rhee, 118, 172, 177, 189
Chiri Mountains, 111, 223
Cho Chae-chŏn, 129, 279
Ch'oe Ch'ang-sik, 263
Ch'oe Sun-ju, 245
Chŏlla Mountains: defensive forces in, 162, 164; mentioned, 104, 106

321

STUDIES OF THE EAST ASIAN INSTITUTE

The Ladder of Success in Imperial China, by Ping-ti Ho. New York: Columbia University Press, 1962.

The Chinese Inflation, 1937-1949, by Shun-hsin Chou. New York: Columbia University Press, 1963.

Reformer in Modern China: Chang Chien, 1853-1926, by Samuel Chu. New York: Columbia University Press, 1965.

Research in Japanese Sources. A Guide, by Herschel Webb with the assistance of Marleigh Ryan. New York: Columbia University Press, 1965.

Society and Education in Japan, by Herbert Passin. New York: Bureau of Publications, Teachers College, Columbia University, 1965.

Agricultural Production and Economic Development in Japan, 1873-1922, by James I. Kakamura. Princeton: Princeton University Press, 1966.

Japan's First Modern Novel: Ukigumo of Futabatei Shimei, by Marleigh Ryan. New York: Columbia University Press, 1967.

The Korean Communist Movement, 1918-1948, by Dae-Sook Suh. Princeton: Princeton University Press, 1967.

The First Vietnam Crisis, by Melvin Curtov. New York: Columbia University Press, 1967.

Cadres, Bureaucracy, and Political Power in Communist China, by A. Doak Barnett. New York: Columbia University Press, 1967.

The Japanese Imperial Institution in the Tokugawa Period, by Herschel Webb. New York: Columbia University Press, 1968.

Higher Education and Business Recruitment in Japan, by Koya Azumi. New York: Teachers College Press, Columbia University, 1969.

The Communists and Chinese Peasant Rebellions: A Study in the Rewriting of Chinese History, by James P. Harrison, Jr. New York: Atheneum, 1969.

How the Conservatives Rule Japan, by Nathaniel B. Thayer. Princeton: Princeton University Press, 1969.

Aspects of Chinese Education, edited by C. T. Hu. New York: Teachers College Press, Columbia University, 1970.

Documents of Korean Communism, 1918-1948, by Dae-Sook Suh. Princeton: Princeton University Press, 1970.

Japanese Education: A Bibliography of Materials in the English Language, by Herbert Passin. New York: Teachers College Press, Columbia University, 1970.

Economic Development and the Labor Market in Japan, by Koji Taira. New York: Columbia University Press, 1970.

The Japanese Oligarchy and the Russo-Japanese War, by Shumpei Okamoto. New York: Columbia University Press, 1970.

Imperial Restoration in Medieval Japan, by H. Paul Varley. New York: Columbia University Press, 1971.

Japan's Postwar Defense Policy, 1947-1968, by Martin E. Weinstein. New York: Columbia University Press, 1971.

Election Campaigning, Japanese Style, by Gerald L. Curtis. New York: Columbia University Press, 1971.

China and Russia: The "Great Game," by O. Edmund Clubb. New York: Columbia University Press, 1971.

Money and Monetary Policy in Communist China, by Katherine Huang Hsiao. New York: Columbia University Press, 1971.

The District Magistrate in Late Imperial China, by John R. Watt. New York: Columbia University Press, 1972.

Law and Policy in China Foreign Relations: A Study of Attitudes and Practice, by James C. Hsiung. New York: Columbia University Press, 1972.

Pearl Harbor as History: Japanese-American Relations, 1931-1941, edited by Dorothy Borg and Shumpei Okamoto, with the assistance of Dale K. A. Finlayson. New York: Columbia University Press, 1973.

Japanese Culture: A Short History, by H. Paul Varley. New York: Praeger, 1973.

Doctors in Politics: The Political Life of the Japan Medical Association, by William E. Steslicke. New York: Praeger, 1973.

Japan's Foreign Policy, 1868-1941: A Research Guide, edited by James William Morley. New York: Columbia University Press, 1973.

The Japan Teachers Union: A Radical Interest Group in Japanese Politics, by Donald Ray Thurston. Princeton: Princeton University Press, 1973.

Palace and Politics in Prewar Japan, by David Anson Titus. New York: Columbia University Press, 1974.

The Idea of China: Essays in Geographic Myth and Theory, by Andrew March. Devon, England: David and Charles, 1974.

Shiba Kōkan, by Calvin L. French. Tokyo: John Weatherhill, Inc., 1974.